Bunty's War

Bunty's War

A young girl's diary tells a story of survival, as she grows
from schoolgirl to woman in World War Two England

Ida Greene

ISBN: 1530710618
ISBN 13: 9781530710614

Contents

Dedication

To my parents, Ida and Jack Amiss,
Without whom I would not be here to write this book,

To My husband, Al Greene,
Without whom this book could not have been written,

and
To my children and grandchildren,
Who would not be here if these events had not happened.

Preface

"I'm home, Bunty, where are you?" My husband's voice, fresh from the golf course, penetrated up the attic steps, calling my nickname to jerk me back to the present. "I'm up here, sorting stuff," I replied, slightly irritated at being interrupted now that I had begun the job I had finally forced myself to do, over which I had been procrastinating for months. Our retirement was imminent, our destination in Connecticut had been decided, and "downsizing," dirty word that it is, had now become a pressing reality.

A wandering ray of late-afternoon sunshine barely penetrated the length of the attic as I squatted awkwardly in front of a battered cardboard box I had found wedged between suitcases under the eaves. The box contained treasures too precious to discard, traveling with us through years of company transfers, each time, like us, looking a little older and more timeworn.

I had untied the string that held it together, taken off the lid and burrowed down through layered souvenirs of our lives: some kindergarten artwork saved from the children; our first wedding anniversary cards to each other; a silver and white announcement of our wedding. At the bottom of the box I had found the pile of six small, leather-bound books I had been looking for, several of them stamped with the gold inscription: *Charles Lett's School-Girl's Diary.* Time had ceased to exist as I carefully opened the maroon cover of the one stamped 1939 and began to read my daily lines of childish scrawl, smiling as I recalled how I was persuaded by my admiration of American movies to call my mother "Mom" instead of "Mum". I was once again a young schoolgirl in England, recording a glimpse of each day in that fateful year, before and after the coming of a war that would change my life forever. As I read the incredible events in my diary entries, I thought to myself: "You know, Bunty, I think this might make a good book! If I ever get around to writing it, I'll call it *Bunty's War*."

"Sorry, dinner might be a little late, dear," I shouted back down the stairs to my husband, replacing the lid on the box. Picking up the little pile of diaries, I made my way down the attic steps as the ray of sunlight disappeared from the dusty attic floor.

So here's the book. Some names of people and places have been changed, and conversations reconstructed as I remembered they would have been. "English" English will agree and/or conflict with "American English" in spelling and expressions. I hope you will enjoy reading it as much as I enjoyed writing it.

INTRODUCTION

⌘

Before it All Began

WORLD WAR TWO began for us in England on September 3, 1939. The year before, in September of 1938, British Prime Minister Neville Chamberlain had returned from Germany after signing the Munich Agreement with Adolf Hitler. Newsreels showed Chamberlain standing at the top of the flight of steps at the door of his aircraft, triumphantly waving the document which he announced would give us "peace in our time." An uneasy year followed. Although Chamberlain failed to prevent an eventual war by appeasing Hitler, he bought the British government a precious year's time to prepare for what was to come, including plans for the defence of Britain's civilian population.

Fast-forward to 1939. My home in England was in Upper Woodside, a pretty, peaceful suburb south of the city of London, its tree-lined streets bordering on the county of Surrey. We were attending church as usual one Sunday when the Vicar ended the service with a surprising announcement, greeted by a stunned silence from the congregation: "I want to announce that St. John's church hall has been designated as the neighborhood distribution point for items to be issued by the government in preparation for war. I'll let you know when there is more information."

In the following weeks the church hall became a beehive of activity, with more people streaming through its doors than it had seen in its entire history. I remember going to the church hall with my Dad and Mom to be fitted for our gas masks. They came in three sizes, Dad's (large), Mom's (medium) and mine (small). The memory of the smell of rubber and the suffocating feeling as the mask was pulled over my

head and face will always stay with me. It was a black, ugly affair with
a short, wide snout, above which was a plastic window. In addition to
the special Mickey Mouse gas masks for younger children, there was a
fascinating baglike apparatus for babies, with a small plastic window so
the baby could look out and the mother could look in. After the baby
was deposited in the bag and it was sealed shut, a handle was used to
pump air through a filtering device so the baby could breathe gas-free
air inside. When the supply of gas masks arrived, Mom, Dad and I went
to pick ours up, joining the small crowd of neighbors beating a path to
the church hall. A dour-looking representative from the A.R.P. (Air Raid
Precautions) office lectured us with lurid pictures on the horrors of the
effects of the three most likely poison gases we could expect in the
event of chemical warfare: mustard, chlorine and phosgene gas. The
reality of a coming war was beginning to sink in.

It wasn't long before classes in Civil Defence were being conducted. Volunteers were recruited from the local population for duty as
nurses, air-raid wardens, plane spotters, fire watchers, auxiliary firemen
and police, and also to join the W.V.S (Women's Voluntary Service), and
the Home Guard civilian army. In our neighboring town a huge steel
water tank joined many others erected in town centers and filled with
an emergency supply of water to help fight fires. We were told to place
a bucket full of sand on the second floor of our two-story homes, and
to keep our bathtub half-filled with water for use with a stirrup pump
to fight an incendiary bomb if one came through the roof. Luckily, this
never happened to us, but by war's end the brownish ring around our
bathtub was indelible!

On the corners of some of our suburban streets public air-raid shelters began to spring up, each a rectangular concrete block structure
with a flat roof and sandbagged entrance; these could hold upwards of

twenty people sitting facing each other on benches running the length of both sides of the shelter. Almost every London suburb had a common, a grassy stretch dating back to a bygone century when it would have been common ground for use by the locals to graze their domestic animals. Trenches were dug in these open stretches of land, to be used for emergency shelter from air raids or even (it was rumored), mass graves for the victims. Churches were required to ready their stone basement crypts as bomb shelters, and vast numbers of bulletins were issued to the public by the A.R.P. office, ranging all the way from how to recognize the "Air Raid Alert" and "All Clear" signals on air-raid sirens, to a printed list of emergency supplies for air-raid shelters in the home. Helpful suggestions as to where these shelters should be included the "cupboard under the stairs," a tiny, cramped closet with slanting head room. In most houses these were already full to overflowing with vacuum cleaners, dust mops, galoshes, umbrellas and any odds and ends that needed to be tucked away to keep the place tidy.

Mom was in despair: "How on earth are we going to manage, sitting there with just a flashlight and nothing to do while an air raid is on?" she snorted, "I wouldn't even be able to see to do my knitting. And where do they think I can keep my vacuum cleaner?"

Dad was more matter-of-fact: "Don't worry so, dear, it might never happen. We'll just go on our summer holidays as usual."

YEAR ONE--1939

☙

The Year it Began

"LIFE IS JUST a Bowl of Cherries," sang popular American crooner Bing Crosby, his mellow voice floating out of the radio on its table by the fireplace in our suburban London dining room. Among my Christmas presents had been my first diary. Beginning on New Year's Day, 1939, my schoolgirl scrawl recorded each day of a happy, carefree life. But, to tell you about "Bunty's War," I'll skip to the summer of that year, just before the bowl of cherries was about to be turned upside down. My diary begins the story...

"SUNDAY, AUGUST 13TH: SPENT NEARLY ALL DAY AT THE BEACH. WARM AND SUNNY. SUNBATHED. COOLED OFF IN THE SEA. I'M GETTING QUITE A TAN."

After my February birthday I was now a teenager, a thirteen-year-old schoolgirl, that golden summer of 1939. The entry in my diary brought back memories of the last vacation my parents and I, their only child, would spend together for many years. The three of us were staying at Bognor Regis, a resort on the south coast of England, where hotels and boarding houses advertised a sea-view. They lined the coastal road where double-decker sightseeing buses with open tops cruised by the sea front, its carefully tended flower gardens and lawns bordered by the promenade, a paved concrete walk separating the road from the beach and the lapping waves of the English Channel.

Jack Amiss, my Dad, was content with his own company, and a man who took life very seriously. He sat in his striped canvas folding chair, perched unevenly on the pebble-strewn beach, his white tee shirt tucked into a well-worn pair of Bermuda shorts. Above his sun-reddened face, the top of his balding head was covered with a large white handkerchief knotted at each corner, a makeshift hat to protect what I irreverently referred to as his "flies' skating rink" from the sun. Hunched over his open newspaper, he squinted from the sun's glare, peering through a pair of round, wire-rimmed glasses. He was engrossed in the latest news of a Europe ravaged by Nazi storm troopers as they advanced in the process of fulfilling Hitler's ambition for world domination. "Cheeky bastards!" he exploded, waking up my mother.

Stretched out in the neighboring beach chair was my Mom, Ida. Her ample figure was enveloped in a black bathing suit, a color she was convinced made her look thinner. She had been asleep, her pale face, with its hint of freckles, motionless under the wide brim of her straw hat. She was as outgoing as my father was introspective, with a warm personality that drew people to her, her gray eyes sparkling when she spoke or sang or played the piano.

Those eyes had already seen an exciting life. As a young girl she had been a pioneer in the Girl Guide movement in the chilly north of England. In her late teens in World War One she had served in a V.A.D. (Voluntary Aid Detachment) as a volunteer nurse's aide tending wounded soldiers shipped from the brutal French trenches to the port of Sunderland, where she and Dad had both been born and raised. As a newly married woman she was a different kind of pioneer, leaving home for the first time in her life to join Dad in Central East Africa, where he was sent by the British Board of Trade to be captain of a merchant ship on enormous Lake Victoria. In 1920s Uganda she suffered through pregnancy with a non-English-speaking Hindu doctor from India, then cared for a new baby daughter in frontier-like conditions in equatorial heat, long before the advent of air conditioning.

She stretched, now wide awake. With her usual resignation, she mildly rebuked Dad's outburst. "Oh, Jack," she said, "don't use such common language. It's time we start thinking of packing up, anyway."

Within sight of my parents, I lay face down on my "Li-Lo" air mattress, floating lazily near the edge of the murky waters of the English Channel, soaking up the sunshine so I could show off my tan when we returned home to London. From across the beach Mom called to me by the nickname the family had given me when we came home from Africa, after she balked when they began to refer to us as "Big Ida" and "Little Ida".

"Bunty, come on out, it's time for tea."

"O.K. I'm coming." I waded ashore through the crowd of shrieking, splashing children at the water's edge.

How could any of us have guessed that only a month later this stretch of water would be host to warships, submarines and mines, or that my seaside memories of pony rides, clowns and the "Punch and Judy" puppet show would soon be crowded out by new and frightening experiences? Even the remembered taste treat of a "Knickerbocker Glory" ice-cream sundae would fade as we were faced with rationing and food shortages, but for that one happy week we abandoned ourselves to relaxing in the sea air, stubbornly pushing aside the ominous signs of fast-approaching war.

Memories of our seaside vacation and its charms soon evaporated when we stepped out of the taxi on our return to Bishop's Hill and saw that the wrought-iron railings and gate in front of Mom's rose garden had disappeared. Only a low brick wall and a privet hedge now remained between our house and the sidewalk.

"Oh, what a shock," my mother gasped. Then she added, "But now I do remember I gave them permission to take the railings for the national scrap-iron drive being conducted in case of war. I didn't think it would be quite so soon--the house looks positively naked!"

"WEDNESDAY, AUGUST 23RD: TODAY HITLER AND STALIN SIGNED A MUTUAL NON-AGGRESSION PACT."
My diary repeated the headline on Dad's morning newspaper. Held onto the page of the little book by a rusted pin, a cartoon had been clipped from the paper. Prophetically, it showed the two dictators of

Germany and Russia from the rear, standing arm in arm, each with his free hand pointing a pistol at the other behind his back. Hitler's *Blitzkrieg*, his "lightning war," was now poised to attack its next victim: Poland.

"THURSDAY, AUGUST 24TH: MOM AND I WENT ON THE BUS TO SEE A MOVIE MATINEE. THERE'S A SHORTAGE OF BUSES. THEY SAY IT'S BECAUSE OF EVACUATION."

Mom and I had waited twice as long as usual to catch a bus to the movie matinee in our neighboring suburb. Stopping at our seat momentarily, the bus conductor took the handful of change Mom handed him to pay for our tickets. "What's causing such a delay in the bus service?" she asked him. The conductor pulled down the visor on his uniform cap, darted a furtive look around the bus passengers, then leaned over her with a conspiratorial air.

"Aw, Mum, it's bloody awful, we're so short-'anded. They've moved some of the buses orf of each of the bus rootes in London wiv their conductors and drivers, ready to collect kids to take 'em from their schools to the big train stations." Pausing for breath, he then hissed darkly: "It looks like War and Evacuation, to me." I pictured London's huge Victorian railway terminals, whose sinister black wrought-iron roofs with panes of sooty glass arched over the tracks. My stomach lurched as I visualized thousands of children pouring out of buses to be spirited away by an invisible Pied Piper from the train platforms. The evacuation trains would be bound for "undisclosed destinations" in safer areas of Britain.

"Evacuation!" I thought, "I wonder if my school, Ravenhurst, will ever go?"

Our Gang

Paul Bates and his younger sister Gwen trotted down the street as I watched from the bay window in our living room.

Seeing them turn into their driveway, I thought: "Good, now I can go and deliver their peppermint rock." As children, it was our custom to bring back from vacation for our friends these nine-inch-long cylinders of pink-coated, rock-hard peppermint candy, printed through with the name of the seaside resort. Picking up the two sticks of candy, I walked down the street.

Paul and Gwen had been my friends since shortly after my eleventh birthday, when they came to live near us in Bishop's Hill. Both had inherited blond hair and blue eyes from their Anglo-Saxon parents. Gwen, still in elementary school, was short and plump.

Fifteen-year-old Paul attended posh St. Oswald's College, a Roman Catholic boys' prep school at the top of Bishop's Hill, his school fees underwritten by a wealthy relative whose ambition was for him to go on to Seminary and become the priest in the family. Paul was talking more this year, now that his voice was no longer afflicted with adolescent squeaks. He was proud of his infectious chuckle since it had emerged in a lower key. Soon to be a very handsome man, he seemed unaware of his own good looks. When I teased him about the persistent dimple that appeared in his cheek when he smiled, he would toss his mop of floppy blond hair out of his blue eyes, shrug and say: "You can have it if you like, dimples are for girls."

There were more boys than girls my age in the neighborhood. I found their companionship more satisfying than playing with dolls, so I became a tomboy. Wearing shorts, considered "unladylike" in those days, I eagerly tagged along as they taught me to climb trees and swing on a nearby lamp-post across from the low brick wall that encircled the front of our house.

Bishop's Hill backed onto our favorite playground, Bishop's Woods, with trees and grassy clearings perfect for our outdoor games and picnics. Here we played Cowboys and Indians, whittling small branches into arrows for our home-made bows and shattering the dignity of the surrounding neighborhood with war whoops and shots from our toy cap pistols.

Many years before, the woods had been part of an estate owned by the Bishop family, who built a mansion there at the beginning of the twentieth century with the millions in profits from Mr. Bishop's chocolate factory. In the mid-1930s the Bishop family had gone on their annual summer vacation to Scotland, taking their servants with them and closing up the house for two weeks. A pair of vagrant men had broken in, made a fire to cook some food, and the family came back to find their home a burned-out shell. They moved away and the mansion was demolished.

Mr. Bishop's heirs donated the property to the local township as a small public park and bird sanctuary, along with the tennis courts, which had remained intact.

A few weeks after Paul and Gwen moved into Bishop's Hill, I began to notice a new arrival, an attractive teenage boy who took to patrolling up and down the street on an expensive racing bicycle. One day, to my amazement, he rang our doorbell. I peeked around the dining-room door when Mom went to answer the bell, and saw at close range how handsome he was, tall and slender, his straight black hair meticulously slicked down, parted, and combed to one side. His face was rather pale, with a slight hint of freckles, his green eyes fringed with long black lashes. This was the coloring my parents attributed to the "Black Irish," whose ancestors were thought to have originated from intermarriage between the native Irish, with their fair skin, green eyes and auburn hair, and the olive-skinned, black-haired, dark-eyed survivors of the Spanish Armada shipwrecked off the Irish coast in the 1500s.

"Whatever he is," I thought, suddenly shy, "he's downright handsome, but what is he doing here on our doorstep?"

"Good afternoon, Mrs. Amiss," His manner was respectful, which impressed Mom favorably "I'm Peter Donovan. We just moved here recently, and I wonder if your daughter could show me the way to Spring Glen Park?"

"How did he know our name?" I wondered. "His mother must have been talking to the neighbors!"

Spring Glen was a large, formal public park a little over a mile from Bishop's Hill, a relatively short walking distance for our young legs. I was soon showing Peter the way to the park, and by the time we returned home Peter had told me a lot about himself. His parents were divorced. A family gap of half a generation condemned him to loneliness; his four brothers and sisters were already working adults. He soon joined our little circle of friends.

Peter was obviously impressed by Spring Glen. Generations had passed since the park had been the sculptured grounds of a very large estate, turned over to the local authorities by heirs who could no longer cope with its expensive upkeep. It was now supported by the local taxpayers for their recreation; they came from all over the area to enjoy it on family outings. Children and dogs could romp on its grassy areas, and the manor house had been converted into a tea room selling cups of tea, little cakes and ice-cream bars. Next to it stood a row of Victorian greenhouses, which in their heyday had fed the aristocratic family with fruit and vegetables in the colder months. One of them still housed an enormous Victorian grapevine, tended by the park gardeners.

From atop a small rise in the park, the elegant white mansion overlooked terraced rose gardens, and formal flower beds around an ornamental fountain, to which we made pilgrimages every spring to fish for tadpoles. Across from the gardens were two velvety bowling greens where we could watch opposing teams, sleek in white uniforms, compete for their suburb or small town against our home team.

The park itself covered several acres. It was beautifully laid out with paved walks and benches between its flower borders, small waterfalls, and a round pond of water lilies circled by a weathered brick wall over which wisteria hung its floral pendants in early summer. Around the next corner Peter and I passed by flowers decorating a wishing well, pausing to drop in a couple of pennies Peter found in his pocket and stopping to make a secret wish. On our way home we made a detour to introduce Peter to Paul and Gwen. Peter had found his niche and had joined the club.

Paul Bates' kid sister, Gwen, merited membership in our club largely due to the fact that Mr. Bates had built her a playhouse in their back-yard, perfect for holding our club meetings. Peter, Paul, Gwen and I were conferring in Gwen's playhouse one day when one of Paul's school friends dropped in. William Standish had recently moved to Bishop's Hill, and immediately voted himself in as a member of our little gang. Already approaching six feet tall and filling out into early manhood, at sixteen William was the awesome "older man" who became my idol. William was not shy.

"What this club needs is a secret code, so we can communicate with each other in case of emergencies."

A born leader, William lost no time in taking charge. I was impressed by everything he did, all of it with the self-assured air of a typical prep school boy. He could draw and sketch well; he played Mom's upright piano by ear with such gusto that it shook, accompanying himself in a seemingly endless repertoire of current song hits from the radio. With my budding sense of romance, he reminded me of my favorite film star, Michael Redgrave.

Huddled together at our club meetings, the five of us held "Councils of War," deciding what to do with our spare time, and arguing about who should play the part of Robin Hood in our re-enactment of the lat-est Errol Flynn movie we had seen. In the playhouse William directed the invention of a secret code, which appeared in my diary whenever there was something too embarrassing to write in English. We also in-vented a secret language: a variation of "pig Latin," which we learned to speak so rapidly and with such enthusiasm that people within earshot gave us very strange looks.

Not willing to be eclipsed by William, Peter felt the need to assert himself by proving his own abilities, among which was an innate tal-ent for fixing things. "Oh, yes," he would say airily, looking at a frayed electrical cord or a silent radio, "I can take that apart and fix it in no time at all." And usually he could.

One day during our many conferences, William declared: "I have a great idea. Let's invite our parents to a radio broadcast. We'll write it, rehearse it and perform it for them."

Paul excitedly broke in. "Terrific, you can use our living room, I'm sure Mum and Dad will agree. We'll just move the Monopoly game over into a corner on its table."

Unlike ours, the Bates' living room was seldom used by the family, so in it we set up a bridge table on which was a perpetual game of Monopoly. We mostly played on rainy days when the weather kept us indoors, dropping the game in mid-session to dash home at tea time, and resuming our cut-throat competition again when we had the opportunity, sometimes days afterwards.

We began to plan for our radio show. Peter was in his element. His voice was full of excitement: "Hey, I have a microphone we can use upstairs in the bedroom, and a speaker we can put downstairs in the living room where our audience will be." With a note of pride, he added: "It will all be very professional."

He eventually persuaded Paul's father to drill a hole in the living-room ceiling so he could pass the electric cord for the speaker down from the bedroom above.

William, as usual, assumed the position of director, and began writing a script. It was decided we would do a skit of a B.B.C. news broadcast. William would be the news broadcaster, Peter and Paul would be reporters. Gwen and I would do any odd jobs we were told to do.

One Saturday afternoon our parents dutifully filed into the Bates' living room and sat in anticipation. There was a lot of shushing in the bedroom, then William cleared his throat and began, in his best Oxford accent. "Good afternoon, ladies and gentlemen. The Queen today is visiting the Royal Woolwich Hospital, of which she is the patron. The weather is rather threatening, but I am sure Her Majesty will make her appearance as scheduled. And now we'll switch to the hospital grounds, where the Queen is expected momentarily." A rustling of papers could be heard, then Peter's voice came through the speaker: "Good afternoon, ladies and gentlemen. This is Peter Donovan, reporting from the Royal Woolwich Hospital. The Queen is about to arrive, but unfortunately it has begun to pour with rain." He paused dramatically: "Here is Her Majesty's car now; she will be getting out of it any minute." Another rustle of paper. "Here she comes, ladies and gentlemen. The crowd is beginning to cheer." A pause ensued . . .

"But what's happening? Oh, oh, Her Majesty has slipped in a puddle; she's facing the press cameras; her legs have flown up into the air above her skirt; we can all see her bloomers . . ." With a loud click, the microphone was abruptly switched off.

A minute or two later William's embarrassed voice came through the speaker: "I'm sorry, folks, for that breach of etiquette by our reporter; he just got carried away." In those days, when it was a "no-no" to mention people's underwear--especially the Queen's--poor Peter never lived down the fact that he had mentioned the Queen's bloomers in public! Our parents were helpless with laughter, and clapped wildly.

Paul, Gwen, Peter and William floated in and out of my life, in those happy, busy prewar days. Every year my diaries followed each one of us as we grew up, our paths crossing, diverging, then crossing again, against the unwelcome backdrop of the war for years to come, and for many years afterwards.

The Showdown

"FRIDAY, AUGUST 25TH: 'AN ANGLO-POLISH ALLIANCE HAS BEEN SIGNED.'"
The terse announcement came over the radio as we ate breakfast. Britain watched with concern as Hitler absorbed Austria, then annexed Czechoslovakia. Poland could be the next on Hitler's list, and now Britain

and France had pledged to guarantee Poland's independence. My parents exchanged worried glances: a showdown with Germany was fast approaching, with the lives of millions at stake. That same day I wrote in my diary: "INTERNATIONAL SITUATION PRETTY GRIM. PACKED MY SUITCASE IN CASE WE HAVE TO GO AWAY. MUST REMEMBER TO TAKE MY IDENTITY CARD AND GAS MASK."

At the close of the school year before summer vacation, I had finished my second year at Ravenhurst, a private girls' prep school. Ravenhurst was a short bus ride away from my home in Bishop's Hill, so I was a day student rather than a boarder, for which I was eternally grateful. A faculty of stern single women, known to us appropriately as school mistresses, were captained by an equally stern headmistress, whose name rhymed with "Lizzie," so that had become her nickname. She and her staff presided over some three hundred girls. Before the summer vacation began we had been given a list of items to be packed in the event that evacuation planned for the London area schools would be carried out.

Included on my list were my gas mask and new National Identity Card. Everyone in Britain had by now received both, to be carried with us at all times; not to do so could result in arrest and a stiff fine. Ration books had been issued in anticipation of food rationing, which had not yet been introduced. A half-page newspaper clipping attached to this page in my diary announced that when rationing came, an adult could expect the following as one week's basic allowance, in ounces (oz.): Butter: 4 oz., cheese: 4 oz., cooking fat: 2 oz., margarine: 2 oz., tea: 3 oz., sugar: 4 oz., bacon: 4 oz., meat: two shillings' worth (about 4-6 oz.), milk: half a pint (Imperial measure, about 2 cups), eggs: 1. Young children would be allowed special rations of orange juice concentrate, eggs and milk, and in July, August and September, housewives would be allowed an extra pound of sugar per week to make jams and jellies while summer fruits were in season.

Mom looked as if someone had hit her between the eyes. "Oh, dear," she exclaimed, "How are we supposed to survive on *that*?" She didn't know that this would be just the tip of the iceberg.

Before classes closed for summer vacation we had several air-raid and gas-mask drills at school. When the bell rang to signal a drill, we would take our gas masks out of their flimsy cardboard boxes and put them on, then stumble down into the basement air-raid shelter to sit on long benches facing each other in the dim, damp air. I can still remember that sickening smell of my clammy rubber mask. On our first drill we all burst into laughter when we put on our masks and saw each other as grotesque creatures from outer space, pointing with muffled cries of "Oh, look at *you*" as we recognized our friends. Even funnier to us were the strange whiffling sounds made by the suction as we inhaled and exhaled. We called these noises "rubber raspberries," and a contest developed to see who could make the loudest ones.

"All right, girls, enough of the merriment," came the muffled voice of Pie Face, our Latin teacher, as she attempted to restore order. "It's time to test our masks."

We each put a piece of paper on our lap, bent over it and inhaled, producing a chorus of rubber raspberries. If the paper leaped up and stuck to the snout of the gas mask, this proved it was airtight and, hopefully, gas-proof. At first this produced a wave of giggles, but we soon found that laughing in a gas mask used up the air inside and steamed up the window so we couldn't see out. After our first dose of semi-blindness and near-suffocation, gas-mask drills became a serious business.

"SUNDAY, AUGUST 27TH: THERE'S A BARRAGE BALLOON IN SPRING GLEN PARK!"
During those last weeks before the war, barrage balloons had arrived in the Greater London area, each one anchored to an Army flatbed truck by a steel cable. Once inflated, over five hundred of them would rise over London like a school of huge silver fish, to protect the city from attack by low-flying enemy bombers. Dad was skeptical of their defensive powers. Frowning, he growled: "What a damn waste of taxpayers' money! Any fool can see that they'll be sitting ducks for a Nazi fighter's

machine guns." Mom and I were silent. We didn't dare dispute Dad when he was in this kind of a mood.

Our doorbell rang. On the front doorstep stood Paul, Peter and Gwen, disheveled and breathless, their faces flushed from running.

"Come on in," I said, as usual. "What's up?"

"No time to come in, Bunty." Paul's voice cracked with excitement as he impatiently puffed a strand of blond hair out of his eyes. "Just tell your Mom we're off to the Glen. We've heard there's a barrage balloon there! William and George have already gone to see it."

We alternately walked and ran to the park, stopping abruptly in front of a grassy clearing where a flatbed truck was parked; on it was a semi-inflated barrage balloon about sixty-five feet long and twenty-five in diameter. Made out of thick, silver-coated fabric with three inflated tail fins at one end, it looked like a huge, fat Walt Disney invention as it flopped gently on its truck. Nearby were two tents providing living quarters for the crew tending it.

Evidently the news had flown around the neighborhood. An assortment of onlookers was already assembled, among them William and George. Curiosity drove us closer until a khaki-clad figure shouted hoarsely: "Stand back there, you kids; that's close enough!" We retreated, realizing that we would have to accept what was now an exciting novelty as part of the strange new life to which we were rapidly being introduced.

Sir John's Air Raid Shelter

"MONDAY, AUGUST 28th: SCHOOLS STILL OUT ON SUMMER VACATION. HAD A VISIT FROM WILLIAM STANDISH, THEN GEORGE WATTS ARRIVED. BEGAN TO DIG A HOLE FOR THE AIR-RAID SHELTER."

Our house was a favorite visiting place for my neighborhood friends. Mom nearly always had newly-baked scones and cookies on hand, and her welcome was open and genuine. William was almost a daily visitor, but George lived at the other end of the neighborhood; we usually only saw him once a week when he picked me up to go to the ice rink. George was my ice-skating partner. We had met when we were both in elementary school and had discovered there was a large indoor ice-skating rink in a neighboring suburb. By the time we were old enough to travel by ourselves on the commercial bus route, we had begun attendance at Ravenhurst Boys and Girls Schools respectively. By no stretch of the imagination could George be called robust, but his tall, slender body was wiry and surprisingly strong, topped by a pale oval face with serious hazel eyes and unruly brown hair, which was usually squashed under his school uniform cap. He was accident-prone and riddled with allergies; my diaries frequently noted that he was in bed with some ailment or minor mishap.

A non-candidate for rough contact sports, George had caught my passion for ice-skating. Our weekly allowances were spent on bus fare and entry fees for the ice rink, skating boots and blades, and an occasional cup of tea or bottle of soda at the ice-rink tea room.

We faithfully attended the ice rink on Wednesdays when both of the Ravenhurst schools were closed for the afternoon. Together we had learned the basics of figure skating and had now graduated to learning ice dancing. Today, tanned from his vacation, George looked as fit as a fiddle.

The comings and goings of my friends never fazed Mom. She bustled to the front door when William arrived. "Come in," William, I've just made some lemonade," she said. Then, a few minutes later: "Oh, George, what are you doing in our neighborhood? How nice! Come on in."

Within minutes we were all sitting with glasses of lemonade, munching on Mom's latest baked treats. I thought it strange that Mom didn't offer refills, but the boys were too busy talking to notice. Mom had other plans for them.

Early in 1939, the government made Anderson outdoor air-raid shelters available to people living in areas likely to be bombed in the event of a war. Dad had ordered one, at a cost of seven English pounds. The shelters were cost-free to lower-income families. Named for the British government's Home Secretary and Director of Air Raid Precautions, Sir John Anderson, they were designed to accommodate six people. One day, two husky men with a truck had deposited in our front hall a large carton containing six panels of galvanized corrugated steel, each curved at the top, and two straight ones, accompanied by a small burlap bag of nuts and bolts with a sheet of explicit instructions on how to construct the shelter. The carton had been sitting there for weeks, waiting for its contents to be unpacked and assembled if or when we might need them. Today Dad was miles away on a job, but the latest radio news bulletins, plus the timely visit of two able-bodied teenage boys, convinced Mom that in his absence there was no time like the present to make an executive decision.

"I've been thinking," she said, after we had finished the lemonade and cookies. "Mr. Amiss is away on a job, but now would be a good time to start putting the air-raid shelter together."

William heaved his burly frame out of his chair, glad of the opportunity to assert himself in front of George.

"Oh, yes, I agree, but first we need to dig a hole to put it in."

That was all Mom needed. Pickaxes, gardening forks and shovels were plucked from the shed, and William took charge. Poring over the instruction sheet, he declared: "The hole will have to be in the back lawn, far enough away from the house so that if it collapses during and air raid it won't fall on the shelter"

As much as Mom loved gardening, Dad hated it, but he felt it his duty when he was home to care for the back lawn. He would toil over it, pushing the rather blunt hand mower and muttering nautical epithets to the world at large. He would never admit it, but the lawn was secretly his pride and joy.

"This should be far enough away," declared William, and proceeded to mark out a rectangle on the lawn, four and a half feet wide and six and a half feet long. Next he marked off squares on the turf inside its perimeter. "O.K., it's time to start," he ordered. The two boys and I took up our shovels and began to peel off square pieces of turf inside the marked-off area. By supper time a neat stack of turf was piled on the lawn, and we were ready to start digging the following day in the hard, sunbaked clay soil.

"TUESDAY, AUGUST 29TH: GOT ON WELL WITH THE HOLE. WILLIAM, PAUL AND GWEN ALL HELPED TO DIG. SPENT ALL DAY IN THE HOLE EXCEPT FOR MEALS AND AN OCCASIONAL PAUSE FOR REST. MY HANDS HURT."

Paul and Gwen cheerfully offered to help William and me. George, probably wary of being recruited again, didn't put in an appearance. Mom kept us well supplied with her lemonade as we sweated over our digging. The boys used pickaxes to loosen the soil, which the girls shoveled out into a nearby pile to be used later to put on top of the assembled shelter.

Some time that afternoon, Paul, who had been measuring our progress with a yardstick, tossed back a damp lock of blond hair from his forehead and shouted: "Hooray! It's four feet deep!" The rest of us managed a weary cheer and threw down our shovels. After another round of lemonade and cookies, the two boys dragged the heavy steel panels into an upright position in the hole and bolted them together, three with curved tops on each side and a straight one on the back. The remaining straight panel with a pre-cut opening for the door stood at the opposite end, resulting in a structure with a rounded roof standing partially in the ground. Exhausted, we left the next step for the following day.

"THURSDAY, AUGUST 31ST: A HEDGEHOG FELL INTO THE SHELTER LAST NIGHT. NAMED IT 'BOMB.' WE FINISHED THE SHELTER AND PUT SOIL FROM THE HOLE, AND TURF FROM THE LAWN, ON TOP. MOM TREATED US ALL TO A MOVIE."

"Bomb" rolled into a prickly ball, but was duly removed by William with a pair of borrowed gardening gloves.

"It looks lovely," said Gwen, dusting off her shorts and gazing with pride at the completed shelter. The boys set up folding canvas chairs on the remains of the lawn, and we flung ourselves into them. Mom appeared with lunch sandwiches and more lemonade.

"Won't Dad be surprised?" she said. "Now all of you just tuck in to a nice lunch, and then I'll treat you all to the movies as a 'Thank You.'"

I privately thought, "I wonder what Dad will think when he sees his precious lawn dug up? Bet he'll have a few choice words about that!"

Dad was never at a loss for a few choice words. Mom said it was due to the enlargement of his vocabulary when he was in the Royal Navy.

Lunch over, William, Paul, Gwen and I had a quick wash, changed into clean clothes and headed out to catch the bus to the Astoria movie theater in our neighboring suburb. Trips to the movies took up a lot of our leisure time in those days; in fact, each visit could take up almost a whole day. There was at least one movie theater in every suburban town, several of which were within a short bus ride. The theaters had grandiose names: "Astoria," "Regal," "Palace," "Rex," "Majestic," "Empire," "Rialto," "Hippodrome," and "Odeon," living up to them with upholstered red plush folding seats and Art Deco vestibules. The Astoria was the Cadillac of our local movie theaters. There was a mezzanine with snacks and cups of tea, and in addition to the main film ("Grade A"), the program included a second, usually inferior one ("Grade B"), a cartoon, a newsreel and a series of previews of coming attractions. About halfway through this crowded program, heavy red velvet curtains were drawn across the stage in front of the movie screen, and the lights went up to herald an intermission, allowing patrons to stretch their legs, ease their bladders, or just go for a cup of tea. Those who remained in their seats were treated to a recital by the large theater organ. Glowing with lights, and with the organist already playing on its multi-level curved keyboard, it rose dramatically from below the stage to stop in front of the curtains, while mini-skirted girls strolled down the aisles of the theater with trays suspended from around their necks, selling cigarettes, ice-cream bars and small boxes of candy (at that time smoking was still allowed in movie theaters). After its recital, the organ descended again into the nether regions; the lights were dimmed; curtains, organ and cigarette girls disappeared, and the program then resumed or began all over again. I can't remember ever hearing of a local movie theater burning down, but there was a well-remembered blue haze in the theater and a smell of cigarette smoke that lingered in our hair and clothes on the way home.

On this occasion the newsreel was foreboding, with martial music playing in the background. The commentator intoned: "French forces and those of Britain and her Empire are training at their bases." The pictures showed masses of soldiers doing pushups in France, England, Canada, India, Australia and South Africa. Even the Grade B Western didn't cheer us up.

Evacuation!

"FRIDAY, SEPTEMBER 1ST: GERMANY INVADED POLAND. BLACKOUT BECAME OFFICIAL. EVACUATION OF CHILDREN FROM GREATER LONDON AREA AND OTHER LARGE CITIES HAS BEGUN. FINISHED THE AIR RAID SHELTER."

Contemptuous of the Anglo-Polish alliance, Hitler had invaded Poland. England retorted with an ultimatum for Nazi withdrawal from Poland. Would Hitler call England's bluff?

Two days before war was declared, London braced as her inner-city children began their evacuation to safer areas. I wondered if and when Ravenhurst would be evacuated, too. I wouldn't have long to wait to find out.

The assembled Anderson shelter stood in its hole in the backyard lawn, with a pile of excavated soil sitting nearby waiting to be shoveled on top of it. Tossing heavy soil upwards to cover the top and sides of the shelter was even more exhausting than digging the hole had been. Our arms and shoulders were aching by the time we had arranged the dried-out turf squares on top of the soil to add the finishing touch.

William stood in front of the shelter, critically viewing the result of our labors. "We ought to get the hose out and water that turf, or it won't grow," he said, in his best foreman's voice.

Paul, Gwen and I glowered at him from the lawn chairs into which we had collapsed after the last piece of turf had been put in place. We couldn't have moved if we had tried.

William got the message. "Oh, I know what you're thinking: 'It's *his* idea, let *him* get on with it.' So O.K., *I'll do it!*" And he stomped off to get the hose. With a martyred air he watered the turf, which by next morning had obligingly turned from brown to green again.

Mom had a worried look on her face. "Let's not bother telling Dad the shelter is finished--he'll see it soon enough next time he comes home," she said, in an attempt to put off the inevitable explosion when Dad would see what had happened to his beloved lawn. I could hardly wait!

"SATURDAY, SEPTEMBER 2ND: COMPLETE BALLOON BARRAGE IS UP OVER LONDON, FLYING AT ABOUT SIX THOUSAND FEET-- INCREDIBLE! WAR SEEMS INEVITABLE. WENT TO MY PIANO LESSON. OUR SCHOOL IS TO BE EVACUATED ON MONDAY! DAD CAME HOME FOR THE WEEKEND."

"Quick, Bunty, come out and see!" Mom's voice oozed excitement. I came down the stairs two at a time and joined her in the backyard. My diary recorded the event, and what a sight it was! I remember feeling the thrill of pride when I looked up to see, in the sunny blue canopy of the sky, almost five hundred helium-filled barrage balloons which had risen over London. They stretched as far as the eye could see toward the city, spaced four hundred and fifty yards apart, each one tethered atop its steel cable to form a shield of glinting silver above our heads.

"That floppy balloon we saw in Spring Glen Park is somewhere among them on duty, standing up at attention," I thought, marveling that I actually had known one of the silver monsters that made me feel so much safer.

It was to be a banner day for me in another way. I didn't know it at the time, but after today I would have no more piano lessons for the rest of my life! Impatient at having to sit so long on a piano stool, I had decided that learning to read music was something my brain didn't want to accept, and I hated my piano lessons with a passion. My only comfort was in the fact that if I played the week's homework assignment well enough, Miss Gibbs, my long-suffering teacher, would reward me after each lesson with a rebate of half of my sixpence in tuition money. I had figured out a way to achieve this without reading the music: memorize the homework assignment and play it by ear without any errors! This nearly drove poor Miss Gibbs up the wall, but she knew I had won.

"Good for you, Bunty," she said between gritted teeth, and gave me back three pence almost every week. I never did learn to read music, but to me it was worth the effort of memorizing each stanza of "Strauss Waltzes for Beginners" because saving up those rebates would eventually amount to a free ticket to the ice rink and extra pocket money for bus fare to the movie theater!

We were expecting Dad home for the weekend. He caught the first train home this morning after he heard the news that Ravenhurst was going to be evacuated. After the usual round of homecoming hugs and kisses, he went off upstairs to change out of his business suit. On coming home, his first concern was always to check the lawn to see if it needed cutting. As soon as he had headed out the back door I heard him roar: "Bloody Hell--how did *that* get there? And what's happened to my lawn?"

Mom and I peeked out the back door. Dad stood, hands on hips, staring at the Anderson shelter cowering in the displaced lawn whose remnants were now neatly piled on top of it. However, after checking to make sure all the nuts and bolts were in the correct places and had been tightened to his satisfaction, he mellowed.

"Well, it looks a hell of a lot better out there than it did cluttering up our front hall, anyway. Let's go out to dinner."

"SUNDAY, SEPTEMBER 3RD: WENT TO SCHOOL FOR EVACUATION REHEARSAL. ENGLAND DECLARED WAR ON GERMANY. ROTTEN OLD HITLER! AIR-RAID SIRENS SOUNDED, BUT NO AIR RAID. SIRENS GOT US UP AGAIN AT 3 A.M."

"Come on, Bunty, time to get up. We're due at Ravenhurst by nine o'clock". Mom's voice sounded urgent, jolting me awake at 6 a.m. Munching my breakfast toast, I could hardly believe that only two weeks ago we had been enjoying a carefree vacation at the seaside. By eight o'clock on this cloudy Sunday morning, Mom and I were on the bus to Ravenhurst. In the suitcases we carried were packed the items on the list we had been given a few weeks before.

"I feel like a human package," I grumbled, when Mom had handed me a large label marked with my name and school to pin on my coat lapel.

Mom also was wearing a label. Ever resourceful, she had found a way to get herself evacuated with Ravenhurst, having successfully con-vinced Lizzie, our headmistress, that a volunteer "Evacuation Assistant" would be needed to act as liaison between the girls and the school authorities, should any problems occur. At first I had felt embarrassed to be the only girl in the school with a mother tagging along, but I had long since resigned myself to it. I knew Mom too well to argue.

"Over here, Bunty." Molly, one of my classmates, yelled to me over the heads of dozens of girls gathering in pre-assigned squads in Ravenhurst's auditorium, the Great Hall.

"We're to wait here for an 'Important Announcement,'" she added, with the air of one who was a step ahead of everyone in knowing what was going on. Mom and I sat down near our squad number, marked in white chalk on the elegant parquet floor of the large assembly hall, after dumping our luggage on the small pile already there. An assortment of tennis racquets and field hockey sticks were roped onto suitcases; backpacks bulged with the necessities we thought would sustain us for as long as the war would last. Most of us were sure it would all be over in a few weeks--Christmas at the latest--and that Britain would return, victorious, to life as we knew it. The buzz of chatter subsided as Lizzie climbed up the steps to the stage and blew a whistle.

"Girls," she said, "you are to leave your luggage by your squad numbers and assemble in the same place at nine o'clock tomorrow. I'll see you all then." There was nothing more for us to do.

"Let's go home, Bunty," said Mom, and we went back to the bus stop. By eleven o'clock that morning Mom, Dad and I were sitting in the dining room by the radio waiting for a scheduled speech by Neville Chamberlain, the Prime Minister. Dad's normally florid face was strangely pale. Mom fidgeted with her hair, pushing it back from her face with nervous hands. At eleven fifteen the B.B.C. radio announcer intoned in a funereal voice: "This is London. You will now hear a statement from the Prime Minister."

I imagined a hush over Britain, its population glued to radios in country cottages, suburban houses, city apartments, pubs, and wherever else they happened to be. Then came the quiet but firm voice of the Prime Minister, telling us that Hitler had ignored the British ultimatum demanding that Germany withdraw from Poland by eleven o'clock that morning. " ... I have to tell you that no such undertaking has been received, and that, as a result, this country is at war with Germany." Neville Chamberlain sounded so tired.

We sat for a moment and looked at each other without a word, then Dad cleared his throat: "Well, that's it, then," he said. The skittish little schoolgirl in me felt as if she had swallowed a large lead balloon, and for once I couldn't think of anything to say. Mom got up and silently padded into the kitchen, where there would be privacy for her tears. We heard running water as she filled the electric kettle to make some tea.

Suddenly the air-raid sirens began to wail. Our "London Air Raid Instructions" pamphlet told us to take cover as soon as we heard an air-raid warning. London was sixty miles inland from the English Channel, merely minutes for enemy bombers. Knowing that poison gas might be used, we hastily put on our gas masks and dashed down the backyard to the shelter. Stopping on the way to snatch three folding lawn chairs from the garden shed, Dad jumped down with them into the shelter, landing with a sickening "squish" on the clay floor spattered by a rain shower coming in through the gaping door.

We sat in the damp gloom, whiffling quietly in our gas masks. I tried not to giggle as I thought of rubber raspberries. Minutes went by.

"Oh, I forgot to turn the tea kettle off!" Mom heaved herself out of the shelter before we could stop her. With relief we saw her reappear in a few minutes, steaming kettle in one hand and teapot in the other. She handed them carefully down to Dad in the shelter.

"Oh, the water had boiled, and it would have been a shame to waste it," she croaked through her gas mask. "Nothing's happening out there, not even the sound of a plane. If we're quick we can go back for some cups, tea, sugar, milk and that tin of cookies in the kitchen."

The remembered image of the three of us in gasmasks carrying cups, tea, milk, sugar and a tin of cookies to the shelter still makes me laugh. We spent the next uneventful hour sitting in the shelter on our lawn chairs, having taken off our oppressive gas masks to reinforce ourselves with the welcome tea and cookies.

A steady blast on the sirens sounded the "All Clear." We trudged back up to the house, to be awakened at three o'clock next morning by the undulating "Alert." After another uneventful hour in the pitch blackness of the cold, damp shelter, the "All Clear" saw us grope our way back up the yard, guided inadequately by the faint light from our hooded flashlight.

"MONDAY, SEPTEMBER 4TH: GERMAN PLANES DRIVEN BACK AT COAST LAST NIGHT. MOM AND I ARRIVED AT HOVE ABOUT 4:45 P.M. WE ARE BILLETED WITH NICE PEOPLE, MR. & MRS. KEMP."
Goodbyes had been said last evening to the neighbors; Peter, Paul and William were all on hand for sad farewells. St. Oswald's College had opted not to evacuate, so Paul and William were left to what was so far an uninterrupted prep school routine. Never a willing academic

student, but quite gifted at woodworking and fixing things around the house for his mother, Peter had chosen to leave school and take a job, having registered for evening courses at a local technical college. All of us promised to write regularly to keep in touch.

Six-thirty next morning found Mom, Dad and me up and dressed. We gobbled an almost un-tasted breakfast.

Dad sounded anxious: "Write as soon as you get to your 'unknown destination' so I'll know where you are and that you're alright."

He tried to make light of our departure, but his voice was gruff with emotion, and I could see his eyes brimming as he gave us both a hug and a kiss. He turned and hurried from the room and we heard the front door slam as he left to catch his train for work. Tears were running down Mom's cheeks, and I felt wetness on mine, too.

I went from room to room, wondering if I would ever see the house again. At eight o'clock Mom locked the door, and we were off to begin an odyssey which was to last for the next several years.

On the sidewalk outside Ravenhurst's protective wrought-iron gates, small clusters of parents and girls were saying tearful farewells. Mom and I sat down by our luggage to wait for the signal for departure. The day dragged on. Mid-morning apples were eaten, followed by the lunch sandwiches we had been told to bring. We talked, sang, dozed and stretched. By three o'clock I wondered if we would be sent home again.

"Girls, our train has left the London terminus on its way to pick us up. Form up into your squads, choose a partner, and walk *slowly*, following your assigned mistress to the Ravenhurst station platform. Make sure you have your stamped postcard addressed to your parents with you, so you can send it as soon as we have arrived to let them know your new address." Lizzie's voice percolated from the stage through the chatter in the Great Hall. It struck me how confident she was in her new role as caretaker for three hundred girls and all our faculty members.

On the station platform the lads from Ravenhurst Boys' School were already excitedly milling around, much to their schoolmasters' distress. I saw what I thought was George's school uniform cap in the distance.

The train, packed with city children from London, screeched to a halt at the station. In my imagination it was one of a stream of giant Pied Pipers, spiriting children away by the thousands, to leave London without the sound of young voices and the sight of children playing. The thought vanished like a punctured soap bubble as we piled on board, chattering excitedly, carrying luggage on our backs and in our hands, gas masks in their cardboard boxes slung over our shoulders.

Excitement battled with uneasiness as the train lurched away from everything that was familiar and sped through the peaceful countryside past mysterious stations whose names had been removed. Prior precautions had been taken to prevent identification of the evacuation routes and their destinations; if the information had reached Nazi spies, it was feared that most of London's children could have been annihilated by sabotaged tracks or by German planes alerted to bomb the trains.

It had only been two weeks since Mom, Dad and I had traveled home by train from our vacation on the south coast. Mom and I began to recognize landmarks we had passed. Sure enough, at last through the dust-streaked train window we caught a glimpse of the English Channel. We pulled into the station at Hove, only a few miles from where we had been on vacation!

I shall never forget how grateful we were to ladies from the Women's Voluntary Service who were on the platform to give us cups of cool water as we crowded, hot, tired and dirty, off the train. Buses took us to our new prep school home, Hove County School for Girls. After a much-needed wash we were given a cup of tea and a cookie.

We then sat cross-legged on the floor of the school gym in weary rows like so many puppies in a dog pound, wearing our pinned-on identification labels, waiting to be claimed and taken to our billets by residents who had volunteered to take in evacuees. One after another, girls were picked up. Didn't anyone want a girl and her mother?

"My name is Bob Kemp. I've come to take you home. My wife Emily is making us some supper." The man's voice sounded friendly and welcoming. In his early thirties and slightly built, he gathered up our suitcases and put them in the trunk of his small car. I could see a tear roll down Mom's cheek, as Mr. Kemp drove us to a pleasant two-story house in a suburb of Hove, where we met Emily, his young wife. This was their first home. Emily showed us to their attractive guest bedroom with great pride, then served us a light supper. We were almost too tired to eat it before we rolled gratefully into warm, comfortable beds.

The Phony War

There was a holiday-like atmosphere about those first few weeks of evacuation.

My school friend Molly bubbled over as we walked back to our billets from the matinee at one of Hove's movie theaters. "Wow, Bunty, I didn't know evacuation would be such a lark! Only half a day in school, and just think, we can do almost everything we want to when we want to do it! This is the first time my parents haven't been breathing down my neck; it's the most fun I've ever had! Hope it lasts forever. Let's go down to the beach and see what's going on. We still have time before supper."

I hardly saw Mom; she was busy with her duties, making the rounds of the Ravenhurst girls to check for any problems. Without any home influence there was a sense of freedom most of us hadn't known existed.

We lost no time exploring our new surroundings, finding to our surprise that a brisk walk brought us to the open grassy hills of the South Downs. It was only a short walk in the opposite direction to Hove's broad beach, and a brief bus ride to the neighboring town of Brighton with another beach, shopping, and even more important, a large, indoor ice rink! I thought wistfully of the figure skates and skating outfits I had left behind in Upper Woodside.

"SUNDAY, SEPTEMBER 10TH: 'BRITISH EXPEDITIONARY FORCES HAVE LANDED IN FRANCE. AMERICA HAS ANNOUNCED HER NEUTRALITY,'" declared the B.B.C. news announcer in a matter-of-fact tone. With no mention of these historic events, my diary recorded: "DAD CAME TO VISIT US. HE'S BEEN BACK TO BISHOP'S HILL TO CHECK ON THE HOUSE. HE BROUGHT ME A BOX OF CHOCOLATES. TOOK HIM FOR A WALK ON THE DOWNS."

Government contracts were taking Dad to many destinations around Britain to supervise the installation of water-purification plants at airfields, military camps and factories. He was away for weeks at a time, but had recently returned to Upper Woodside for an inspection tour of our deserted house. I could hardly wait for news of the old neighborhood.

"Hello, Dad, how are things back at Bishop's Hill?"

Dad tried to look well-informed, although he was good at inserting his own editorial remarks into most of what he said. "Well, the neighborhood is very quiet, as a matter of fact, with most of the children gone. Colmans' and Paddingtons' houses are deserted since they went off to safety in the country near their relatives. They will be back again before the children are ready for school, I'll bet. I saw the Standishes. You'd never recognize their backyard! Now that the government is urging civilians to produce their own food to help out with the rations, Mr. Standish had their lawn and flower beds dug up and he's planted vegetables. William has been building a chicken coop. Remember, I always said he had two left feet--well, I think he's got two left hands, too."

Dad had been critical of William's clumsiness, as the boy grew into a man's body. Now I bristled with indignation as he made fun of William's workmanship.

"Oh, Dad, I don't expect it will matter to the hens," I snapped. Dad was so surprised by my tone of voice that he said no more. I quickly changed the subject. "Dad, by the way, next time you go to see if the house is O.K., could you bring my skating stuff back with you?"

Dad nodded. He seldom forgot anything; my spirits soared.

"SATURDAY, SEPTEMBER 16TH: BRUCE FERGUSON IS BILLETED ACROSS THE STREET FROM ME. HOW LOVELY--I GET ALL THE LUCK! FOURTEENTH DAY OF THE WAR AGAINST HITLER. DOWN WITH THE NAZIS! VIVE LA FRANCE! CONFUSION TO GOEBBELS, HESS, VON RIBBENTROP AND THE GESTAPO!"

My diary sounded surprised that the war had already lasted two weeks. In my childish mind I had expected a lightning victory, once the British had gone to help the French bring it to an end! We all knew the names of Hitler's closest henchmen, but the magic name of Bruce Ferguson obviously took top billing. Along with William, Paul, Peter and George, Bruce would also float in and out of my life for the next few years.

I didn't yet know the whereabouts of George, but there were several Ravenhurst boys billeted in the cul-de-sac where the Kemps lived. The close proximity of Bruce was more than I could ever have hoped for. I can still remember the first time I heard the haunting music of the popular song "Deep Purple" from across the street, and realized how beautifully Bruce played the piano. I had had a tremendous crush on him for two years, watching from our living room bay window as he roller-skated past our house in Bishop's Hill, never pausing to look my way. Now, at fifteen, tall and slender, with dark good looks, he was painfully shy; to me he came across as an aloof fellow who seemed unattainable, which made him all the more attractive to this already blossoming teenager, as she entered the "boy-crazy" period of her life. Mom viewed this hero-worship of mine with humor.

"Oh, Mom, he waved his handkerchief at me today," I gushed.

"You sure he wasn't just blowing his nose?" she retorted.

"WEDNESDAY, SEPTEMBER 27TH: 'WARSAW SURRENDERS'" was in large letters on the board in front of the newspaper stand. My diary recorded: "MOM WENT BACK TO UPPER WOODSIDE FOR A FEW DAYS. WENT FOR A WALK IN HOVE PARK THIS MORNING WITH SOME OF THE GIRLS. SCHOOL YEAR STARTED THIS AFTERNOON. MY THIRD YEAR AT RAVENHURST. BEGAN LEARNING LATIN."

Poland didn't stand a chance against the onslaught of the Nazis; Hitler had overrun yet another country in a shrinking free Europe. Meantime, I was beginning my third year at prep school. French was mandatory at Ravenhurst in our first year, for eleven-and twelve-year-olds. Now that I was entering my third year, a second foreign language was added to the curriculum. We could choose between German or Latin. I chose Latin, which was taught by a virginal schoolmistress on her first assignment out of University. She was tall and angular, with faded blue eyes darting nervously behind round, metal-rimmed glasses in a pale, moon-like face. Ravenhurst's schoolmistresses all had nicknames, a tradition carried on from one generation of students to the next, but being new, our Latin mistress didn't have one for us to inherit, so we dubbed her, somewhat cruelly, "Pie Face." Poor Pie Face was the butt of our school-girl humor and scorn. Cartoon drawings of her would mysteriously appear on the Latin class blackboard, and we plotted during lunch hour in the safety of the school lavatory how to make her life miserable. We probably succeeded.

Backyard Chickens

In the midst of our evacuated bliss came increasing reminders that there really was a war on. A sobering illustration occurred at a special school assembly when Lizzie introduced a Mr. Cartwright from the Ministry of Information. A mousy-looking man, sixtyish, with a pinched face, he took the podium with a sudden burst of fervor.

"Girls, you must now realize the peril we face as a nation. Be warned of the presence of enemy spies in Britain! You are not under any circumstances to talk about military affairs to anyone, or be overheard in public places discussing information that might be of use to the enemy.

THINK BEFORE YOU SPEAK!" His tone convinced us that this was no trivial matter, but he lost the attention of his audience as he droned on and on, endlessly belaboring the point and often repeating himself.

Warnings began appearing on posters and billboards all over Britain. One of them showed a group of people gossiping in a pub. On the wall behind them was a shadowy picture of a sinking ship, with the words: "Careless Talk Costs Lives." I forgot most of what Mr. Cartwright said with his thousands of words, but I never forgot the picture on that poster.

"SUNDAY, OCTOBER 1ST: MR. KEMP BEGAN TO BUILD A CHICKEN COOP, WITH ME 'HELPING' AND MR. KEMP DOING ALL THE WORK." Fresh eggs were in short supply, in fact shorter than the ration of one per person per week. To make for easy storage and transportation, especially for the armed forces, most of Britain's eggs were being processed into a nasty-smelling yellow powder. This could be reconstituted with water and cooked to resemble scrambled eggs or to make dry, musty-tasting cakes and cookies, which Mom said in disgust were "hardly fit to eat."

The government was urging civilians to keep hens and other edible livestock to supplement the food rations, so chicken coops and rabbit hutches began appearing in backyards all over Britain. Mr. Kemp and his neighbor Mr. Dearborne decided to buy a few chickens each.

"I say, Bob," Mr. Dearborne's voice floated over the garden fence. "What kind of fowl are you going to get?"

"Oh, I thought Rhode Island Reds. Emily likes brown eggs."

"But I've heard that White Leghorns lay better. I think I'll try them." Mr. Dearborne sounded as if he had done his homework.

Both men were soon sawing and hammering, and I was given the dirty job of applying creosote to the chicken coop made by our wheezing host, who seemed to have an asthma attack at the drop of a hat. Having recently read *The Adventures of Tom Sawyer*, I appealed to the chivalrous nature of the Ravenhurst boys billeted around us, resulting in a sweaty, creosote-spattered work crew, from which eventually emerged a creosote-covered chicken coop.

At last the hens arrived: six large, shiny, rust-colored Rhode Island Reds. This was my first encounter with such creatures, but they somehow brought out the mothering instinct in me. I promptly named "the girls" Vera, Ermintrude, Cecily, Winifred, Gertrude and Pamela, and appointed myself their custodian, feeding them daily with military precision, and waiting impatiently for their first brown egg. I waited and waited.

By October 4th the Nazis had crushed Poland. After a massive victory parade in Warsaw, they were now free to turn their attention to the Western Front. In Hove we began to see increasing numbers of searchlight drills--long, crisscrossing shafts of light piercing the night sky for hours on end. Then came the stunning proof that Hitler had not forgotten to strike at Britain.

"THURSDAY, OCTOBER 12TH: The B.B.C. radio news announcer voiced the same shock and outrage felt by all who heard him, when he reported: 'A NAZI U-BOAT HAS SUNK H.M.S. *ROYAL OAK* IN SCAPA FLOW.'"
This was the first Nazi attack on British soil, with its tragic result; the loss of one of Britain's proud battleships, sunk in one of Scotland's so-called "impenetrable harbors" with the loss of eight hundred and thirty-three of its crew.

Ignoring the real news of the day, my diary observed only: "HENS GETTING ON O.K. NO EGGS YET. MR. KEMP HAD TO GO TO BED WITH ASTHMA."

Having expected an instant bout of egg-laying from "the girls," I decided there must be something lacking in their diet, so I went next door to consult Mr. Dearborne.

"Mr. Dearborne, I hear your White Leghorns are laying beautiful white eggs like clockwork, and I wonder if I can have the recipe for the mash you're using?"

"Why, certainly, Bunty. It's nice of you to be so concerned, especially with Bob under the weather and not able to take much interest in his hens." He wrote out the recipe and handed it to me. "Lots of luck, and if you need any help, remember I'm always here."

After a week "the girls" were eating out of my hand but still hadn't produced an egg, which I took personally as a betrayal of my devotion to them.

"SATURDAY, OCTOBER 14TH: MOM AND I ATTENDED THE OPENING OF THE NEW BISHOP HANNINGTON MEMORIAL CHURCH IN HOVE." Now that we had settled into our evacuated life, Mom and I realized how much we missed our church-going back in Upper Woodside at St. John's. Mom said to me: "You know, Bunty, this is the year you would normally have had your confirmation at St. John's. I think we should join the local parish church here in Hove."

"O.K.," I replied, "let's see if we can find it."

"I can't believe it, Bunty," said Mom, as we attended the dedication ceremony at the brand-new, brick Anglican church within walking distance of our billet.

"Wait 'til we tell Dad the name of this church, Mom, what a story this will make!" And here's the story.

James Hannington was born near Hove in 1847, and as a young man he studied for the ministry. He went to Uganda as an Anglican missionary and was ordained Bishop of Eastern Equatorial Africa in 1884. The following year, at thirty-eight years of age, he was murdered by the natives. On a hilltop overlooking Kampala, capital city of Uganda, Namirembe Cathedral was built to honor his memory. Rebuilt several times, the present cathedral has a seating capacity of more than three thousand people.

I was born in Kampala, Uganda, and baptized as an infant by the Anglican Bishop of Uganda in Namirembe Cathedral! Incredibly, a world war had brought me to Hove, England, to the church where I would confirm my baptismal promises, on the other side of the world from the one where I was baptized in a church dedicated to the memory of the same martyred Christian bishop, James Hannington!

At the Bishop Hannington Memorial Church in Hove, the following Sunday, I attended the first special ten o'clock service set aside for Ravenhurst's boys and girls, after which I signed up for confirmation classes. Mom was convinced it was the hand of God.

"WEDNESDAY, OCTOBER 18TH: HENS MOVED TO MR. DEARBORNE'S. AT SCHOOL I WAS ELECTED PREFECT OF MY CLASS!"
It seemed that every time Mr. Kemp went near the chicken coop it triggered an attack of asthma, so he dismantled it and sold all six Rhode Island Reds to Mr. Dearborne, who comforted me by saying I would be allowed visiting privileges whenever I wished. Slow learners that they were, even with their new association with real winners, it wasn't until November 17th that my diary reported: "ONE OF 'THE GIRLS' HAS LAID AN EGG. THE EIGHTH WONDER OF THE WORLD!"

My election to Prefect of my class was little short of a miracle, in view of my irreverent attitude toward not only my teachers but also toward education in general. This was my first brush with the burden of leadership.

I looked up from my dictionary. "Hey, Mom, I've just read what the word 'prefect' means. In Roman times I'd have been a commander in the Pretorian Guard! Wow! But at Ravenhurst it will only mean delivering announcements from Lizzie to the class and being sure the classroom is left tidy at the end of our school's half-day, ready for Hove County School's turn in it."

"Never mind, dear, it's the honor that counts." Mom's attention was focused once more on the thick khaki sock she was knitting for the W.V.S., destined for a British soldier somewhere in France.

I shrugged and went on with my homework.

"SATURDAY, NOVEMBER 4TH: MOM AND I TOOK THE TRAIN TO HAMPTON TO STAY WITH THE HORNES FOR THE WEEKEND. WENT

SHOPPING IN KINGSTON AND BOUGHT A FIELD HOCKEY STICK, SHOES AND PADS. DAD BROUGHT MY SKATING OUTFITS FROM HOME. HE SHOWED US OVER HIS FAMOUS 'JOB.'"

Before the war, Dad's company was awarded the contract for a huge new waterworks at Hampton, on the River Thames just north of London, which would supply additional purified drinking water for the city. Dad was designated Chief Construction Engineer for what he called "The Job." He had hired a Mr. Horne as his foreman, who generously provided a room in his house where Dad could stay while the work was in progress.

Mrs. Horne had written to Mom: "We'd love to have you and Bunty come for the weekend; it must be miserable not to be together with this wretched war on." It was our first reprieve since evacuation. The November weather was unseasonably mild and sunny, so Mom, Dad and I sat on the grass of the river bank to eat a picnic lunch.

"Isn't it lovely here, Jack?" said Mom. "It makes you forget all about the war." The Thames was fringed with weeping willows in its upper reaches and its waters were usually crowded with small family pleasure boats on weekends. The families waving to us from the river could never have guessed that their boats would be needed the following year for a much more challenging task than carrying their fishing rods and picnic baskets.

The next day, with characteristic gusto, my father proudly showed Mom and me around "The Job," the newly built waterworks which, back in those days, was among the largest in the world. We marveled at the size of the pumping equipment and filter beds still under construction, and the finished powerhouse, all green tile and chrome, housing the row of turbines which would eventually throb with energy. As we left through a gate in the fence topped with barbed wire, the armed soldiers guarding it brought us abruptly back to the present: we were at war, and the "The Job" was a military target!

Returning to Hove with my beloved ice skates and skating dresses brought by Dad from Upper Woodside, I could hardly wait to take the bus to Brighton Ice Rink the next Saturday morning. The music of "The Skaters' Waltz" greeted my ears as I stepped onto the ice for the first time in more than two months. Tentatively I tried all the twirls and jumps that I had learned before the war, and wondered if I could remember the ice-dancing steps I had begun to learn with George. I missed him. With the exception of his periodic bouts in bed, he had been a reliable skating partner. Together we had mastered the steps of the waltz on ice, and ice dancing had become my obsession. There was a short interval in each skating session for dancing. The loudspeaker blared: "All beginners off the ice," and the peripheral mob of sweaty, giggling skaters stumbled off to get a cup of tea or rest their protesting muscles. Behind me I felt a tap on my shoulder.

I turned to look with astonishment into the amused brown eyes of a perfect stranger. "Hello, my name is Larry," he said politely. "I've been watching you on the ice. Would you care to dance with me?" Stocky and muscular, he looked to be several years older than the schoolboys from Ravenhurst. Not only intrigued, I was flattered. I managed to nod my head.

"Yes, thank you," I stammered, semi-frozen with surprise. I was on the ice with him before I knew what had happened, submerged in the exhilaration of sweeping across the open ice to trace on its surface the steps of the waltz as he led me through them.

"The waltz is the only dance I know, Larry," I gasped, out of breath and astonished at his professionalism.

"Oh, don't worry. I'll soon teach you the other dances, if you'll let me." He was as good as his word. I don't remember ever knowing his last name, but Larry showed up every Saturday morning. In the next few weeks he taught me the other ice dances I had longed to learn: the dreamy slow foxtrot, dramatic tango and breathtaking ten-step. I was thrilled. Out of the corner of my eye I could often see Bruce Ferguson watching incredulously. My diary said: "HEAVEN SIMPLY MUST HAVE AN ICE RINK IN IT."

"SATURDAY, NOVEMBER 18TH: TIME TO PUT THE CLOCKS BACK AN HOUR."
We had now returned to G.M.T. (Greenwich Mean Time), from the hour ahead on British Summer Time. Next year would see some tinkering with the clocks again, with something new added.

The Blackout

"THURSDAY, NOVEMBER 30TH: RUSSIA INVADED FINLAND. WE BEGAN KNITTING SQUARES TO MAKE INTO WARM BLANKETS FOR FINNISH REFUGEES. GALE FORCE WINDS OFF THE ENGLISH CHANNEL."
While the world still watched and waited for war to reach the Western Front, the Russian onslaught on Finland generated newspaper photos of its pathetic civilian victims. Before the war, Ravenhurst girls had sewed and knitted for local hospitals and orphanages. Now we rallied to a new cause, the plight of the people of Finland. It was decided to pitch in and make them some warm blankets. Colorful scraps of woolen kitting yarn were donated at our billets by our hostesses, and the W.V.S. provided us with whole skeins of it. Hundreds of knitted squares would be needed to be sewn together to make the blankets. Winter was coming and we had no time to waste, so we brought our knitting to school. During morning break, lunch hour and between classes, knitting needles could be heard clicking away. "Blanket Bees" kept groups of girls busy sewing the finished squares together; as each blanket was ready it was rushed to the W.V.S. for dispatch to Finland.

This was my first involvement with such a project, and I was very touched. I thought to myself, "Even if the blankets never reach those poor people, I hope they will know somehow that we're really trying to do something to show them someone cares." I was growing up.

The mild, golden days of autumn were over. We could smell the cold sea fog as it rolled in from the English Channel; winter was on its way. The B.B.C. weather forecaster announced: "Channel gales are expected to batter the south coast in the next few days."

This afternoon at the end of November, Molly and I went for our usual walk on the concrete promenade overlooking the beach. We were taken completely by surprise when a gigantic gust of wind suddenly blew us almost off our feet.

"Hang on, Molly," I gasped. The wind began to howl and sting our faces. Turning our backs on the next gust, we held on to each other on the exposed promenade, struggling to stand upright. As the wind increased to a terrifyingly loud scream, the surf fell with a roar on the stony beach, sucking pebbles with raging force into the sea, only to dash them back on the beach again minutes later.

We glimpsed the little fishing boats, now pulled up the beach to rest lopsidedly against the sea wall, a safe distance from the fury of the waves. Using all the energy we could muster, we managed to fight our way back across the street to the shelter of the houses on the sea front, and after what felt like hours we reached our billets, exhausted and thankful.

Mom didn't scold me, as I had expected; she hugged me instead. "I was so worried, Bunty, but thank God you're home safe and sound. Take off that hat and coat and have this nice hot cup of tea."

I caught sight of myself in the mirror in the Kemps' front hall, bedraggled and shaking from Molly's and my scary experience. Sipping a hot cup of tea, I tried to think of something witty to say, something clever and positive, but I just said weakly: "Well, Mom, Molly and I have learned our lesson: never ignore gale warnings on the radio weather forecast. You can't fight the English Channel!"

"SATURDAY, DECEMBER 2ND: THE TOWNS OF BRIGHTON AND HOVE HAD A FULL AIR-RAID DRILL. EVERYONE HAD TO PUT ON GAS

MASKS AND GO TO THE NEAREST AIR-RAID SHELTER FOR HALF AN HOUR. AFTERWARDS, I WENT SHOPPING WITH MRS. DEARBORNE AND BOUGHT CHRISTMAS CARDS."

Entire towns and cities across Britain periodically tested their preparedness for air-raids. Offices, stores, schools and streets emptied during these drills, which ultimately saved panic and untold numbers of lives. But December was here, and Christmas cards had to be bought, so that we could still cling to life's comforting traditions.

At the beginning of December, Ravenhurst exchanged school hours with Hove County girls. They would now attend for the first half of the day, leaving us to the afternoons. Darkness arrived earlier each day; by now the blackout was upon us before we could walk home. "This time last year it was peacetime, and the lights were on," I thought. Only last year? It seemed so much longer.

After classes we formed groups according to the location of our billets. Walking two-by-two, we held hands for support in the enveloping blackness, stumbling along on the sidewalk behind the schoolmistress with her hooded flashlight, careful to keep the couple in front of us always in view. Our long, winding line was dubbed "the crocodile." Cars and buses, headlights shrouded with black hoods, slid eerily past us on the road. Girls dropped away as their billets were reached, until we were all safely home.

The crocodile brought something new into our lives. Never had we felt so connected with the heavens as we did on our way home in the blackout. On clear nights, waiting to cross a street gave us time to look up and see the majestic constellations in the black sky above, so near that it felt as if a brilliant garment of stars could drop at any minute like a cloak around our shoulders. Some nights, when the moon was full, the landscape was as brightly lit as the street-lights we remembered, and we felt exposed and vulnerable.

Searchlight beams crisscrossed the sky every night, practicing to look for what was so far a non-existent enemy. They wouldn't have long to wait, but we were too tired to speculate, as we trudged wearily back to our billets.

Changing Billets

The elderly minister at the Bishop Hannington Memorial Church was a Reverend Mortimer Guinness. His required series of confirmation classes in which I was enrolled were, to my delight, coed. True to existing schoolgirl and schoolboy tradition, we had to find a nickname for our instructor, so we huddled over this one day before class. The self-appointed leader of the boys made the decision.

"Well, the only Guinness I know about is the brew served in pubs, so let's call him "Old Beery." So he was. If the reverend was aware of this, we never knew he had found out, but if he did, Old Beery suffered his nickname and our occasional disrespect in class with Christian good humor.

For me, life at Hove flowed serenely along, a continuing lark, with time to enjoy a variety of activities other than schoolwork. As December crept onto the calendar I began rehearsing with the Ravenhurst Girls' choir and also with the much more exciting coed one at church, as we prepared for traditional Christmas concerts.

My diary reported countless teen flirtations, at which I was getting plenty of practice. Then came an upheaval: Mom and I moved our billet.

"SATURDAY, DECEMBER 9TH: MOVED OUR BILLET TO THE DEARBORNES."

Moving billets was quite common. Our departure might have been accelerated when, on my way one evening to the Kemps' lavatory, I found the door to the bathroom ajar and peeked in to surprise a nude Mr. and Mrs. Kemp sharing a bathtub full of hot water together.

"What are we going to do now?" wailed Mom, upon being told by a somewhat embarrassed Mr. Kemp that they had decided it was time for us to change our billet. After several months of evacuation, hosts understandably grew weary of sacrificing the privacy of their homes to effervescent schoolchildren, but others always seemed to pop up to take their place. When I came home from school two days later, Mom was all smiles. "Guess what, Bunty, the Dearbornes have offered to take us in," she exulted.

I was thrilled. I had always liked the Dearbornes more than the Kemps anyway, and I would once again be close to my beloved six Rhode Island Reds. "Aren't we lucky, Mom?" I said. "Moving in with the Dearbornes will be lovely, but I'm surprised they want us, now that the baby is due so soon."

Mom's eyebrows wiggled as they always did when she was figuring something out. "You know, Bunty, I was just thinking. Maybe Mrs. Dearborne wants to have me in the house when the baby comes. Since the war, you know, hospital beds are needed by the military, and in cases where the doctor doesn't anticipate any problems, women are having their babies at home. A midwife will deliver the baby, but I'm sure there will be things I can do to help. Remember, I was a practical nurse volunteer in the last war."

I must have temporarily abandoned knitting for the Finnish refugees. My diary records: "BEGAN TO KNIT A BABY COAT FOR THE 'GREAT EVENT.'"

"FRIDAY, DECEMBER 15TH: ROYAL NAVY SHIPS CORNER GERMANY'S POCKET BATTLESHIP *ADMIRAL GRAF SPEE.*"
The headline on our newsstands made us realize that somewhere Britain was fighting a war. The crack Nazi warship *Graf Spee* had been sinking record numbers of British merchant ships, but now the British had an opportunity for a showdown with her at the Battle of the River Plate in South America. The damaged *Graf Spee* was cornered and took refuge in Montevideo harbor in neutral Uruguay. The British Royal Navy had effectively blockaded her escape, hoping that when she tried to run would offer a perfect opportunity to sink her. However,

this was not to be. Her captain scuttled the *Graf Spee* in Montevideo harbor, and then committed suicide. The Royal Navy's victory was a hollow one.

"THURSDAY, DECEMBER 21ST: DAY OF 'THE EVENT.' IT'S A GIRL! SCHOOL HAS CLOSED FOR CHRISTMAS HOLIDAYS. I WAS SENT NEXT DOOR TO SHEILA'S HOUSE TO HAVE LUNCH, GO TO THE MOVIES, THEN STAY OVERNIGHT."

When I arrived home from school there was a state of uproar at the Dearbornes. The baby was on its way. Mom didn't talk to me about such things so I was deplorably ignorant about the details of sex or childbirth. My only knowledge about childbirth came from the snippets of conversation I overheard when Mom had her friends in to tea, back at Upper Woodside. My general impression was of a horrific happening. I remember saying to myself: "You won't catch *me* ever going through *that* gruesome stuff!"

Mom and the midwife were too busy to say more than "hello," before I was hustled out to a neighbor's house to stay overnight. Hours later, with the help of the midwife and Mom, the Dearbornes' baby girl was brought safely into the world. Next morning I was allowed to inspect the small feminine bundle, pink and puckered in her cradle, nestling in the soft white folds of the baby coat I had knitted. She would soon need a bedroom. It was decided that by Easter Mom and I would have to move again. But in the meantime there would be Christmas--our first in exile.

"FRIDAY, DECEMBER 22ND: WENT TO STAY AT HAMPTON FOR CHRISTMAS. WE SHOPPED IN KINGSTON FOR CHRISTMAS GIFTS FOR THE HORNES."

The Hornes again opened their home to my parents and me, this time to share their family Christmas with three "displaced persons." On Christmas morning there was a knock on my bedroom door. I opened one eye--and it was still dark outside. I staggered to the door and opened it, to be greeted by the Hornes' two small boys, Jimmy and

Jerry, who were almost too excited to speak. Their voices rose in a squeaky crescendo: "Come on, Bunty, let's see what Santa brought."

As I stumbled down the stairs with them, little Jerry shyly took my hand. "Bunty, don't you think Santa will be awfully dirty after coming down so many sooty chimneys?"

I said the first thing that came into my sleep-soaked brain: "Oh, don't worry, Jerry - his reindeer probably lick him clean between stops."

In no time everyone was downstairs by the Christmas tree with hot cups of tea. We exchanged small gifts, and as if they anticipated my need to make a record of the next year of my life, the Hornes gave me a "Charles Lett's School-Girl's Diary" for 1940.

Mom decided that when we left Hampton we would take the train back to Upper Woodside to check on the condition of our home before we both returned to Hove.

Where is Home?

"WEDNESDAY, DECEMBER 27TH: MOM AND I TOOK THE TRAIN TO UPPER WOODSIDE FOR A COUPLE OF DAYS. COULDN'T STAY IN THE HOUSE, THE ELECTRICITY AND WATER ARE TURNED OFF. STAYED WITH MRS. WHITE. WENT TO THE ICE RINK WITH GEORGE."

Mrs. White lived in our neighborhood in Upper Woodside. Almost as round as she was tall, she, like Mom, had been raised in the north of England; this bond had made them close friends. Her main topic of conversation was her family, to whom she was totally dedicated: "Our Arthur" (her husband, absent more than present), "our Roger" (her son, now serving in the R.A.F.), and "our Betty" (her live-at-home married daughter) were her life's breath and her reason for being. Her cooking was heavy on dumplings and Yorkshire pudding. We spent our two-day stay with her feeling delightfully full.

I had brought my ice skates with me from Hove for a date at the local ice rink arranged in one of my letters to George. I announced proudly: "Hey, George, I met a fellow at the Brighton rink who showed me some new dance steps." I had forgotten his reluctance to try anything new. George floundered with me through the new waltz steps learned from Larry. He looked relieved when the dance session was over and the mob of skaters resumed their never-ending cycle around and around the rink.

George had moved back to London from Hove, as had a growing number of Ravenhurst boys and girls. He had transferred to St. Oswald's College, which had opted not to be evacuated, and was happy to find Paul Bates in some of his classes.

On a back page in my diary was a list of the names of my classmates, and opposite more than half of them I had written "Gone Home." Along with their parents, many of Ravenhurst's students were tired of evacuation and the toll it took: separation from family, living with strangers, lack of education, inconvenience, and the uncertainty of not having the same roof over their heads for more than a few months, while London remained as peaceful as before the war. With mixed emotions, I wondered what was ahead for me.

Before leaving Upper Woodside, Mom and I made a final check on the house. With its electricity turned off, it stood, forlorn and cold, amid its weed-filled flower borders. Standing in my deserted bedroom, I felt a surge of nostalgia and homesickness. I had to leave quickly before the tears came, snatching up a few odds and ends to take back to Hove on my way out.

"FRIDAY, DECEMBER 29TH: WENT BACK TO HORNES FOR NEW YEAR'S EVE. DAD WAS FIRST FOOT, TO BRING THEM GOOD LUCK FOR NEXT YEAR."

According to Scottish and North-of-England tradition, a year of good luck for a home is guaranteed if the first foot in the new year to cross the threshold belongs to a dark-haired man. At my grandmother's house in Sunderland, the First Foot knocked on the front door at the stroke of midnight on New Year's Eve, bringing with him a piece of coal, some salt and a bottle of wine, to symbolize plenty of warmth, food and drink for the year ahead.

Our house in Bishop's Hill had no First Foot that year, but even though there wasn't much dark hair left on his balding head, Dad carried on the First-Footing tradition at Hampton by sharing it with our Christmas hosts.

"KING GEORGE V1 VISITS TROOPS IN FRANCE AND INSPECTS FACILITIES AND EQUIPMENT ON THE MAGINOT LINE," declared the newspaper headlines. The "Phony War" continued. Newspapers showed photos of King George visiting British troops at the Maginot Line in France in December, 1939, and on New Year's Eve newspaper photographers took pictures of British and French soldiers raising glasses of wine together, without any sign of an enemy to interrupt their toast to the New Year.

So ended 1939, filled for me with a kaleidoscope of happenings and emotions. The war we had expected to have won by Christmas didn't seem to be progressing as we had anticipated. It was just as well, on this New Year's Eve, that we were unable to see into the year ahead.

Mom and Dad

Our Gang

William the Genius: Siphoning out the Anderson Shelter

Percival and Me

Spitfires and Hurricanes win the Battle of Britain

∞

End of the Lark

UP TO NOW, evacuation had been fun, or as my schoolgirl pals and I would have put it, "a real lark." The next few months would cause the war to invade our lives in ways we could never have imagined.

"MONDAY, JANUARY 8TH: FOOD RATIONING OFFICIALLY BEGINS TODAY. AT LEAST NOW WE WILL GET OUR SHARE. GAVE MY RATION BOOK TO MRS. DEARBORNE. MOM AND I TOOK THE BUS TO SHOP IN BRIGHTON. BOUGHT MY FIRST PAIR OF SHOES WITH A HEEL! I FEEL VERY GROWN UP."

Coupon books for food rationing had been issued months ago, but now the rules were put into action. Housewives had to register with a grocery store and butcher of their choice, who would collect the coupons and sell them corresponding rations. According to the number of coupons collected for each rationed food, the storekeeper would be entitled to order refills for his next supply. As evacuees, we had to turn over our ration books to our hostesses.

I was almost fourteen years old, and, whether I liked it or not, on the threshold of womanhood. The signs were all there, including the embarrassment of having to go with Mom to shop for a bra, which I wore with alternating feelings of grudge and pride. However, the tomboy in me was finally beginning to give way to feminine vanity, especially when I thought of the unconquerable Bruce Ferguson. Shoes had not yet been rationed, so a variety of sizes, colors and styles was still available. I kicked off my flat-heeled school shoes and tried on for the first time a pair with a higher, modestly shaped heel. I couldn't suppress a giggle as I wiggled my feet, reflected in the mirror which stood on the floor of the shoe department.

"They look O.K, but how on earth do people walk in them?" I asked Mom. Balancing carefully, I took a few wobbly steps and realized that vanity could not be appeased without sacrifice. "Oh well," I said, with resignation, "when I wear these I'll just have to try to remember to walk, not run."

The winter of 1939 set record-breaking low temperatures throughout the whole of Europe. In the north of England, tracks were blocked by snowdrifts higher than the roofs of the trains. All over Britain businesses came to a near-standstill; telephone and telegraph lines were down, disrupting communications. In Hove, ice and snowstorms often sent us home early from school before the blackout could make the homeward walk too dangerous. We wore all the clothes we had brought with us in layers, waddling to and from school like a flock of overstuffed penguins. The savage cold snap continued for the entire month of January, almost paralyzing the south coast.

Snow removal in Hove was normally so unnecessary it was almost unheard of, so the fallen snow had frozen untouched on roads and sidewalks, covering them with a sheet of ice in the sub-freezing temperatures. Unable to navigate, all road traffic disappeared. In those days, most individual homes were not centrally heated, but burned small coal fires in each room. In their frigid houses people used up the month's coal ration in their fireplaces too quickly for it to last until the following month's allowance. Drugstores experienced an unprecedented boom in sales of rubber hot water bottles. Getting around outdoors was a challenge to everyone's ingenuity. Some of us resorted to putting on a pair of knee socks over our high rubber boots to get a little traction for walking. Commuters who had skis could be seen skidding along on the icy streets and sidewalks trying to get to work. It was a winter I would never forget.

"FRIDAY, FEBRUARY 9TH: A LIVE MINE HAS BEEN WASHED UP ON THE BEACH!"

At last winter was releasing its grip, but now something new had happened. The news had spread like wildfire from billet to billet. Sitting next to me as we gathered for our daily assembly at school, Molly was almost bursting with excitement. Turning to me, she said in a hoarse whisper: "Hey, Bunty, let's go down to the beach as soon as we can and have a look."

Before I could whisper back that this wouldn't be such a good idea, Lizzie hurried up the steps of the stage to the podium in the Assembly Hall. With worried urgency she addressed the rows of girls in front of her.

"Girls, I know you have had freedom up to now to go on the beach whenever you pleased, but I must tell you that it is strictly 'off limits' until further notice. That mine is still unexploded, and it would be foolhardy of any of you to attempt to go near the sea front until it has been dealt with."

With some relief I watched Molly's face fall as her mind absorbed the implications. The English Channel, at the edge of which I had been happily cavorting on vacation only six months ago, had been sown with mines. Each black steel spiky sphere, some measuring as much as ten feet across, contained enough explosive to blow up any enemy ship or submarine that rammed its lethal horns.

As the Channel gales raged that winter, one of the mines had broken loose from its mooring cable, washed ashore, and had chosen Hove beach for its resting place. Hove's Civil Defence teams immediately sprang into action. We heard reports that the sea front hotels and houses had been evacuated and barbed-wire barriers had been put up several streets away from the beach to keep would-be onlookers from harm if the mine detonated.

The mine was eventually defused by a Royal Navy bomb disposal squad and Lizzie's edict was relaxed. Molly and I could hardly wait.

Taking our turn with dozens of other children, we gleefully climbed all over the mine, now harmless and leaning like a huge, drunken, black hedgehog on the pebbled beach waiting to be carted away, then re-armed and sent back to its watery duty.

"FRIDAY, FEBRUARY 16TH: FOURTEEN YEARS OLD! EIGHT BIRTHDAY CARDS, SOME CHECKS FROM THE RELATIVES IN SUNDERLAND, HANDKERCHIEFS, BATH CRYSTALS, CHOCOLATES, AND MY FIRST BOTTLE OF PERFUME (PREWAR, FROM DAD). MR. DEARBORNE GAVE ME A BEAUTIFUL WHITE, NEW-LAID EGG FOR MY BREAKFAST."

My fourteenth birthday was just another school day, but with it came the last snowfall of the winter, and small gifts from caring friends and family that touch and warm the heart. Topping it off was the breakfast treat of the egg from one of Mr. Dearborne's White Leghorns and a wonderful chicken dinner produced by Mom.

The six unproductive Rhode Island Red "girls" were gradually dis-appearing, one by one, martyred for the war effort to grace meals that we shared with the Dearbornes. Before taking a bite at dinner that eve-ning I must have wondered briefly if this was Pamela or Gertrude, but in those days of skimpy meat rations, hunger won out over sentiment.

Bishop Hannington's Ghost

"SATURDAY, FEBRUARY 24TH: SET THE CLOCKS AHEAD ONE HOUR. BRITISH SUMMER TIME! DAYLIGHT SAVING--IN FEBRUARY! THEY SAY IT WILL SAVE ENERGY AND INCREASE PRODUCTIVITY FOR THE WAR EFFORT. AT LEAST WE HAVE THE WEEKEND TO GET USED TO IT."

Daylight Saving Time at this time of year proved a mixed blessing. Children and office workers groped their way through the blackout to school and work in the dark mornings, but the extra hour of daylight in the afternoons was welcome to them and to the farmers, although there were probably still many confused cows. *Double* British Summer Time was yet to come!

"WEDNESDAY, MARCH 13TH: FINNS SURRENDERED TO RUSSIANS. BRUCE MOVED HIS BILLET. ROTTEN LUCK."

There was depressing news on the war fronts, but especially for me on the home front.

"Oh dear," I moaned to my poor, long-suffering mother, "now I'll never have Bruce for a friend!" Then with a sigh I rationalized: "But we'll be moving our billet ourselves soon, too, so I might have never seen him again anyway. I'll just have to blame it on the war."

Exhausted after a gallant three months' fight with antiquated war equipment, the outnumbered Finns had been overwhelmed and forced to surrender to the Russians. Although the League of Nations had expelled Russia in December 1939 for failing to halt its invasion of Finland, the onslaught had continued to its tragic end.

"Attention, girls!" One of the buxom sixth-form girls stood in front of the "lower classes" at assembly, appealing to us for our chattering to stop so she could be heard. "How many say we should still go on knitting squares to send blankets to Finland?" The vote was a unanimous "Yes."

"SUNDAY, MARCH 17TH: PALM SUNDAY. I WAS CONFIRMED AT THE BISHOP HANNINGTON CHURCH THIS AFTERNOON BY THE BISHOP OF CHICHESTER. GOODY! NO MORE CONFIRMATION CLASSES!"

Confirmation class was as boring as the Sunday School classes I remembered at St. John's back at Upper Woodside, and poor "Old Beery" had probably ended up with a new crop of gray hairs after being bombarded every week at each session with tough questions from fifteen rambunctious Ravenhurst boys and girls. To our delight he became rattled very easily, and we took full advantage.

It wasn't until the day of the confirmation service that I began to feel the full impact of the occasion, as Mom carefully draped the large square of soft white material over my head, centering the tiny cross she had embroidered on it above my forehead and securing it with bobby pins.

As I joined the procession of confirmands from other Anglican churches in the area, I suddenly felt very close to my parents. I fingered the gifts they had given me: the little gold cross on its slender chain around my neck, and in my hands the small, leather-bound prayer book stamped in gold with my name. I have treasured them all of my life. The length of the church aisle seemed endless as I approached the Bishop of Chichester, resplendent in his clerical regalia and flanked by members of the local clergy whose churches formed his diocese. As I repeated the words to him confirming the promises made by my parents at my baptism, I thought: "Old Beery looks *so* happy!" Then, caught by a flight of fancy, I imagined that the ghost of Bishop Hannington would be pleased, too, if he could see me all the way from Namirembe Cathedral in Uganda, being confirmed at his memorial church in Hove!

"THURSDAY, MARCH 21st: "WE SAID SAD FAREWELLS TO DEARBORNES AND THE NEIGHBORS. WE'LL HAVE MOVED TO OUR NEW BILLET WHEN WE GET BACK FROM EASTER BREAK. ARRIVED HOME AT UPPER WOODSIDE AT 2:30 P.M. IT'S GOOD TO BE HOME." "Goodbye, dear. We'll miss you. Don't forget to stay in touch." Mrs. Dearborne gave me a hug. They needed their extra bedroom now that the baby was old enough to be moved into it. Tears came as Mom and I said our goodbyes to the Dearbornes and the neighborhood which had been our home for the past six months, another uprooting from people who had been friendly and kind. Suitcases in hand, Mom and I took the bus across town to our new billet at the home of a Mr. and Mrs. Charles Coker. We gazed in awe at the handsome two-story Georgian brick house near Hove's sea front. Mom rang the front doorbell.

A small boy answered the door. His shrill accent was typical of London's East End. "Aw, yew must be the new hevacuees. There haint nobody 'ome at the moment. They tole me to tell yer to put yer bags in the front 'all. They'll be sife there until yer comes back arfter Heaster." Without another word he turned and went back up the stairs.

Mom looked puzzled. "Well, Bunty, what a welcome! Anyway, our suitcases are both locked so they will be O.K. I wonder who he was? And where on earth could the family be? Oh well, we'll find out when we get back after Easter."

Closing the ornately carved front door behind us, we took the bus to Hove railway station and boarded the train for London.

A little over an hour later, Mom was opening our own front door. Her nose wrinkled with displeasure as she stepped into the front hall. "Phew! Smell that awful mildew! Doesn't smell much like home, does it? But I suppose we should expect it, after so many months of emptiness."

Dad had made arrangements for the water and electricity to be reconnected for our visit. Mom and I went through the rooms, opening windows and doors to the spring breeze and sunshine; the house once again began to smell more like home.

Tearing out handfuls of weeds from the wilderness of overgrown flower borders, I found a few spring blossoms which I arranged in a vase in the front hall. I spent another hour weeding, while Mom bustled about, airing beds and mattresses and bringing blankets out of storage chests. Before the shops closed, we took the bus to our old shopping center and stocked the larder with some rations. By black-out time, Mom had magically produced a cooked meal, served at the dining-room table on the blue-and-white Willow Pattern plates I had missed so much.

Still on my mind was the outdoor Anderson air-raid shelter. To our dismay it had filled with two feet of water while we were gone. The only solution I could think of was that our one remaining aluminum saucepan would have to be pressed into service the next day to bail the water out. But Dad was coming home for the weekend; he would know what to do. Having shed my mind of this weight of responsibility, I drifted off into a contented sleep in my own bed.

"FRIDAY, MARCH 22ND: DAD CAME HOME FOR THE WEEKEND. HAD A VISIT FROM GEORGE AND ALSO PETER. THEY MADE A LOVELY

BONFIRE FROM GARDEN WASTE FROM THE FLOWER BORDERS. LATER, WILLIAM CAME TO VISIT."

My letters to the boys had prepared them for our homecoming. They lost no time in coming to see us; our house felt like itself again.

George and Peter took one look at my pile of uprooted weeds and obligingly raked them up, took them outside the backyard fence and made a bonfire. In those days we weren't as aware of air pollution as we are now, so the boys enjoyed their bonfire without one twinge of conscience.

It seemed like ages since I had seen William. He had now graduated from prep school and had volunteered for service with the Royal Air Force, taking a part-time job in his father's engineering office while he was waiting to be called up. When he appeared at our front door that evening, my heart skipped a beat. William's blue eyes, well-controlled brown hair and infectious sense of humor reminded me even more of film star Michael Redgrave. At seventeen he was well built, six feet tall and still very self-assured. In my estimation (and probably his), there was nothing he couldn't do.

William's self-assurance was about to be tested. The Anderson shelter was still full of water. When Dad had come home for the weekend he just shook his head and went on mowing what was left of the lawn. But William couldn't resist the challenge.

William the Genius

"SATURDAY, MARCH 30TH: SPENT ALL DAY HELPING (OR HINDERING) WILLIAM TO SIPHON THE WATER OUT OF THE AIR-RAID SHELTER."

I was almost in tears as William and I looked down into the flooded Anderson shelter. Feeling useless, I uttered the obvious. "What we really need is a stirrup pump."

"Well, we don't have one, so we'll have to improvise." There was a trace of irritation in William's voice.

Among his many attributes, William was resourceful. Within a couple of hours, a comic-strip contraption stood on the shelter. Perched half-way up its side and wedged in place with large rocks from Mom's rock garden was an ancient metal washtub with a handle on each side. Draped over each handle was a piece of garden hose, a long one hooked up to the water supply from the house, and a shorter one with an end dangling into the water inside the shelter. Its other end went up and over the washtub handle, then downward into a bucket that sat on the lawn alongside the shelter.

William turned the faucet on at the house, then came back to the shelter, squatting to use the long hose to fill the shorter one, while keeping his thumb over the end below the surface of the water in the shelter. When the short hose was full, he told me to put my thumb over the other end of it to keep the water in it.

"Now, whatever you do, don't take your thumb off until I've counted to three," he ordered." William was again in complete charge. "One-two-three," he bellowed. At "three," we both released our thumbs. Miraculously, the water began to siphon from the shelter through the hose, up over the washtub handle, and down into the bucket. My job was to empty the bucket once it was full, and replace it with a spare one before too much water spilled onto the already soggy lawn. I'll never understand how or why, but eventually we could look down into the shelter and see its muddy floor, which was already beginning to dry out. Once again it was ready and waiting for an air raid.

My admiration knew no bounds. William was a genius! Wisely, Mom had been staying out of our way, but now she charged out of the house with a camera, immortalizing our moment of triumph with a photo of the two of us at the side of the shelter, covered with mud and surrounded by the maze of equipment. I still treasure that picture, labeled: "Genius and Helper, 1940." William kept his copy too, and showed it to me on one of my visits to England forty years later!

"MONDAY, APRIL 1ST: MOM AND I LOCKED UP THE HOUSE AND TOOK THE TRAIN TO HOVE. ARRIVED AT NOON. WENT TO OUR NEW BILLET. MET THE COKERS."

The Coker family were a far cry from the Kemps and the Dearbornes. While the latter were "middle class," the Cokers were "lower middle class" except for the fact that they owned a lucrative sea front restaurant, and could afford to live in a good middle-class neighborhood. Elsie Coker welcomed us at the front door, her plump little figure enveloped in a shocking pink, flowered housedress.

"'Ello, ducks, sorry there weren't none of us 'ome when you came before, we wuz all down at the caff." She panted up the stairs ahead of us and showed us to our room. "'Ow about a cuppa tea? Now you jest come down when you're ready."

On our arrival downstairs for the welcoming tea, we were met by "Auntie Gert" Gump, Elsie's sister, who doubled as the restaurant's "hostess" when she wasn't doing the housekeeping at home. She thrust out a hand to each of us: "Glad ter meecha," she wheezed, "I 'ope you'll soon feel at 'ome 'ere." Also there to greet us were the Cokers' two daughters, Betty and Bonnie, ages ten and twelve. Sitting shyly in the corner was Tommy, the thin, nervous nine-year-old who had appeared to show us where to put our suitcases. Lowering her voice to a hoarse whisper, Gert explained to us that he was an evacuee from the poor East End of London to whom the Cokers had opened their home at the beginning of evacuation.

Our host, Charlie Coker, was at work cooking in his thriving restaurant business at the beach. Appropriately painted in bright orange letters was its name: "The Orange Cafe." The paved concrete promenade below which it was built gave it a reinforced ceiling, qualifying it for another large sign above the front door, which read: "Air Raid Shelter."

Eating out was popular in Britain in World War Two. Special rations were granted to restaurants by the government, and the servings on their plates were often closer to prewar quantities than our ration coupons could supply. On Sundays the Cokers treated the whole family (now including Mom and me) to a full-course noon dinner. I can still almost smell the aroma of roast beef and Yorkshire pudding that wafted from the restaurant kitchen into our eager noses as we sat around one of the tables with its orange-and-white checkered tablecloth.

"TUESDAY, APRIL 2ND: WENT TO HYGIENE CENTER THIS MORNING WITH MOM. THERE WERE SIX 'CLIENTS' ALL WAITING TO BE DECONTAMINATED. THIS AFTERNOON BOUGHT A NEW PAIR OF WHITE SKATING BOOTS."

We were still on Easter break from school, and today seemed to me like a good time to replace my old, outgrown skating boots with new ones. "Mom, could we go into Brighton today and get me a new pair of skating boots? These old ones are getting so small they make my feet hurt."

Mom held the purse strings. She thought for a minute. "Yes, I know, Bunty, but I'll make a bargain with you. Lizzie has loaned me out to work at the Hygiene Center this morning. If you come with me, we'll have some lunch, and then I'll go with you to get your skating boots this afternoon."

Mom had kept herself busy during evacuation with her volunteer work. Although she was attached to Ravenhurst, Lizzie didn't always have liaison work for her to do for the school, so she volunteered wherever she was needed in the community. One of her duties was helping at an outpatient clinic where evacuees were sent if they had a hygiene problem. Some of the younger children from the East End slums of London had come from (and, unfortunately, to) homes where they became hosts to unwelcome parasites.

I had never seen hair with "nits" in it before, nor had I ever seen such pathetically thin, smelly, frightened children. The little oval cases full of lice eggs adhered so tightly to hair that the entire strand with them on it had to be cut off and burned. Small children were frightened to see a nurse coming at them with a pair of scissors and had to be held still so she could snip the hair off. Some of the children had ringworm, and their heads had to be shaved. Both must have been terrifying procedures for a small child to undergo without its mother's reassurance. I sat in the waiting room and held one small, sticky hand after another, vainly offering words of comfort until a child's turn came in the examining room, where Mom was helping the nurse with the delousing. The combined smell of disinfectant and stale urine in that place is one I have never forgotten.

That afternoon, new white skating boots in hand, I realized once again how many blessings I had to count.

Hitler's Lightning War

"TUESDAY, APRIL 9TH: 'GERMANY INVADES NORWAY AND DENMARK'" screamed the newspaper headlines. Seemingly unconcerned, my diary was matter-of-fact: "BACK TO SCHOOL AFTER EASTER RECESS. WENT FOR A WALK BY THE SEA."

"How about a walk along the sea front, Bunty?" Molly's tone reflected the fact that she had been incarcerated in her billet too long. I had just heard the latest news broadcast, and was once more overcome by the feeling of having swallowed something heavy and indigestible. Hitler's armies were getting closer.

"I'll be there in half a tick, just let me get my windbreaker jacket on; some fresh air is what I need," I shouted from the row of pegs in the Cokers' front hall, where it was always a challenge to find my own clothes.

As we caught sight of the English Channel that bright, windy April day, we were suddenly acutely aware that this stretch of water was all that separated us from a war that was coming closer. Hitler unleashed an onslaught upon the ill-prepared Norwegians with vastly superior naval, land and air forces. The struggle was over in two months. Thirty-five thousand British and Allied troops were rescued by ships of the Royal Navy, escaping to England along with King Haakon of Norway. As German armies swept into Denmark, the Danes collapsed in twelve hours, helpless to defy the momentum of the Nazi steamroller. But we were still sure the Nazis would get no further.

"WEDNESDAY, MAY 1ST: WENT TO MORNING CHOIR PRACTICE AT SCHOOL. HAD AN AIR-RAID PRACTICE IN AFTERNOON, LED BY 'PIE FACE.' OUR GEOGRAPHY TEACHER, 'OLD POSSIE,' BROUGHT UP THE REAR WITH ANOTHER LANTERN."

Back at Ravenhurst our air-raid drills took place in the school basement; at Hove there was a large, concrete dugout at the edge of the playing field, dark and damp, with earth from the excavation piled on top of the structure. It could hold several hundred people. Lining the walls inside were wooden benches. The objective of each drill was to empty the school building in as few minutes as possible. I remember long lines of Ravenhurst girls trotting through the sandbagged entrance of the shelter to sit by the light of the two sputtering oil lanterns for half an hour, singing songs and telling jokes in the semi-darkness. Then we would trail back to our classrooms and be given our lessons to do for homework.

For the next few weeks air-raid drills were held almost daily, and one day Lizzie triumphantly mounted the stairs to the podium at assembly and announced: "Congratulations, girls, you've done it! Yesterday you made it out of your classrooms and into the dugout in three minutes, mistresses, oil lamps and all!"

"FRIDAY, MAY 10TH: GERMANY INVADED HOLLAND AND BELGIUM! BRITAIN OCCUPIED ICELAND. CHURCHILL BECAME PRIME MINISTER. NO CLASSES AT SCHOOL, JUST A SPECIAL ASSEMBLY TO TELL US WE COULDN'T GO BACK TO LONDON FOR THE WHITSUN HOLIDAY. MOM AND I WENT BY TRAIN TO HAMPTON."

The handwriting was on the wall and Churchill knew it. In his first speech to Parliament as Prime Minister, he spoke the words which over the years have become familiar to people all over the world: "I have nothing to offer but blood, toil, tears and sweat".

All too soon we were to know what he meant.

In view of the impending fall of all the Western European countries to the Nazis, Lizzie and other heads of schools on the south coast must have had orders from the London authorities not to allow evacuated children to disperse to their homes in the London area for the upcoming national holiday. Today, when Lizzie mounted the stage at assembly, her face was grave. "Girls," she said, "I know that many of you were planning to join your families for the Whitsun holiday, but the situation in Europe is looking very bad. We must be prepared for whatever happens and we need to be all together if we have to re-evacuate. None of you may return to the Greater London area." A murmur rippled through the rows of girls. "Re-evacuate!" I thought. "Where on earth can we re-evacuate *to*? There are still close to two hundred of us!"

Dad had arranged for Mom and me to spend the holiday with him at the Hornes', so once more we took the train from Hove to Hampton, which was too far away from London to be off-limits.

German Panzer divisions hurtled through Holland and Belgium toward the English Channel coast. Queen Wilhelmina of Holland and her government followed King Haakon of Norway to seek sanctuary in England. They would soon be followed by General Charles de Gaulle of France.

"FRIDAY, MAY 17TH: AT SCHOOL WE HEARD THAT HEINZ HAS BEEN PUT IN AN INTERNMENT CAMP BECAUSE HIS FAMILY IS GERMAN."
"Not Heinz, that's impossible," I thought. Shocked whispers spread through the rows of girls at school assembly. Heinz was our beloved school janitor at Ravenhurst, back in London. His family had escaped from the Nazi pogroms in Germany when he was very young. He had been educated in England, and in our eyes he was as English as Yorkshire Pudding. We had never thought of him as German, but, wary of enemy informers, the authorities did.

"SUNDAY, MAY 19TH: BELGIUM HAS CAPITULATED: NOW THERE'S ONLY FRANCE STANDING BETWEEN US AND THE GERMANS. AFTER CHURCH WENT FOR A LONG WALK AND HEARD THE CUCKOO FOR THE FIRST TIME THIS YEAR."

Even with the Nazi sword of Damocles hanging closer and closer to our heads, after Ravenhurst's special Sunday morning church service my friends and I could still change our clothes and escape to the beauty of the countryside. We were adept at collecting empty birds' nests, shinning up trees to find them.

Every year I strained my ears to be the first to hear the call of the European cuckoo arriving back from migration, believed to be Nature's official announcement of the arrival of summer. To me, the female cuckoo was the most despicable of birds, sneaking into another bird's nest to lay her egg, then abdicating from any further nurture of her offspring by leaving it in the care of the incumbent parents. Sometimes we found the tiny, naked corpses of the baby cuckoo's nest-mates lying on the ground, ousted by the growing intruder to make more room for itself. Indignantly, I thought: "Those stupid birds; they feed the little brute and teach it how to fly, even after it has murdered their own babies." Sometimes Mother Nature made no sense to me at all!

"SATURDAY, MAY 25TH: THE GERMANS ARE AT CALAIS! SPENT THE MORNING AT BRIGHTON ICE RINK. HAD A LOVELY TIME."

In retrospect, this must have been one of the most bizarre entries in my diaries. It was as if nobody had listened to the news; today Brighton was alive, as always, with Saturday activity! People shopped, went to the movies, crowded the buses. The ice rink teemed with skaters. Happily skating, I must have either been unaware or unconcerned that the Nazis were at Calais on the French coast, within shelling distance of the south coast of England. Since 1939 there had been war posters all over Britain which said: "Keep Calm and Carry On," and the Saturday morning crowds in Brighton showed every sign of "carrying on" with neither fear nor panic. I was probably equally convinced that there could be no problem. After all, Dad had said: "We have nothing to worry about. Hitler will surely be stopped by the Maginot Line."

The Miracle of Dunkirk

"SUNDAY, MAY 26TH: NATIONAL DAY OF PRAYER. WENT TO CHURCH THIS MORNING. POURING RAIN; GOT SOAKED. WENT TO COKERS' RESTAURANT FOR LUNCH. THE SEA FRONT HAS BEEN EQUIPPED WITH GUNS."

One of the British monarch's titles is "Defender of the Faith." The hesitant voice of King George VI came over the radio calling the nation to pray for the British and Allied troops in France, and also all civilians there and in Britain. That morning churches were full to overflowing. What we didn't know was that we were praying for a miracle. History books now call it "the Miracle of Dunkirk."

For the next week my diary rattled on about daily activities at school and at home. The frequent letters between myself and William, Paul and Peter were as flippant and witty as ever, never indicating a sign of anxiety, foreboding or despair.

Peter's letters were few and far between. He sketched brief outlines of his assembly-line job in a small factory, followed several nights a week by courses at the local technical college. Still two years away from being eligible for the R.A.F., on weekends he put on his Home Guard uniform for training and an occasional overnight camping trip, which he referred to as a "bivouac." "Would you believe it?" he gurgled in one of his letters, "we've got two women in my regiment. They aren't bad to look at, but they are such old hags--twenty if they're a day, and they're hopeless at putting up a tent!"

The bivouacs were at the mercy of the notorious caprices of the English weather; he described pitching his tent on ground that was a "muddy mess." I had a suspicion that he had substituted "muddy" for "bloody," a favorite expletive among men and boys, but considered in those days to be inappropriate to use in the presence of women and girls.

We were unaware that a news blackout had been imposed upon Britain from May 26 to June 4, while more than three hundred thousand desperate men were rescued from a wide strip of sandy beach a hundred miles across the Channel from Hove, at the French seaside town of Dunkirk.

During those few days, Molly and I made several trips to the sea front. "Look," she said in disbelief, "they're putting huge guns in all the gun emplacements." Prevented by a fence of coiled barbed wire from getting any closer than across the street, we could just make out the sandbagged gun emplacements on the sea front, swarming with sweating men in army uniforms hastily installing the large guns, their barrels all pointing toward the beach.

"Look at the beach, Bunty, not a blessed thing on it." Molly's round face looked perplexed. The stretch of pebbles usually dotted with small, beached fishing boats was strangely empty, nor were they to be seen anywhere offshore.

"That's odd, Molly." I looked up and down the length of the beach. "Where could they have gone to, and all at one time?"

Little did we know that they had been called out on a life-or-death mission.

As the days went by, stories began to circulate about the Dunkirk evacuation. It was rumored that every available boat within miles of the south coast of England had gone to help in the rescue of the British Expeditionary Force and other Allied soldiers trapped under fire on the beaches between the Germans and the sea. We didn't hear the full story until years after the war.

Owners of fishing boats and rowboats from south coastal towns, family motorboats and sailboats from far up the rivers, even the paddle steamers that took holidaymakers to the Isle of Wight in peacetime rushed to volunteer the use of their boats and crews. With their shallow draft, the little boats were able to reach the long lines of men wading out toward them, under German attack from the shore and from the air, and ferry them to larger ships offshore. Some sailed directly back to the nearest points on the English coast with as many men as they could carry crammed into their small cabins and on their decks. Time was crucial; they refueled their boats and returned again and again, day after day. The exhausted, dirt-encrusted rescuers took little or no time to eat, sleep, wash or get a change of clothing.

The more fortunate of the little boats survived to be repaired later; the wreckage of those whose luck ran out was washed ashore by the tide.

"TUESDAY, JUNE 4TH: 'THE PRIME MINISTER, THE RIGHT HONORABLE WINSTON CHURCHILL,'" announced the B.B.C. newscaster.
Mom called to me up the stairs: "Bunty, come down quickly, and hear Winnie." No smiles greeted me as I dropped my evening's load of homework on my bed and ran down the stairs, already hearing the dramatic tones of the familiar voice booming out from the radio as the recording of Churchill's historic speech to Parliament was broadcast.

"Winnie's" tone was sombre as he addressed the British House of Commons, but it gradually took on a courageous defiance that lifted and squared Britain's sagging shoulders. In part, he said: "... we shall defend our Island, whatever the cost may be, we shall fight on the beaches, we shall fight on the landing grounds, we shall fight in the fields and in the streets, we shall fight in the hills, we shall never surrender ... "

The world listened, and took notice. Mom and I listened with the four Cokers, Auntie Gert and Tommy. Naked fear was on Charlie Coker's face. The miracle of Dunkirk was over. Now the British people stood alone against the Nazi war machine.

War on Our Doorstep

"FRIDAY, JUNE 7TH: HAD AN AIR-RAID WARNING AT 1:45 THIS MORNING WHICH LASTED AN HOUR. SPENT A CRAMPED HOUR IN THE CLOSET UNDER THE STAIRWELL (COKERS' AIR-RAID SHELTER). CLEANED IT OUT READY FOR NEXT TIME. AFTER SCHOOL MICHAEL CROWLEY CAME TO ASK ME OUT FOR A WALK!"

The Air Raid Precautions manual advised that if no reinforced shelter was available, a refuge should be found in the house near an inside wall, away from the danger of flying glass. The only place the Cokers had that came anywhere near this was the cleaning closet under the stairwell.

"Well, we ain't got nothin' better, so that'll 'ave to be our air-raid shelter," Charlie had declared at supper one night. "Not that we'll ever need it," he added. He was wrong. The following night the entire household was awakened from a sound sleep by the whining of air-raid warning sirens. Clutching our gas masks, all eight of us squeezed into the closet among mops, brushes, scouring powder and an old vacuum cleaner. I suppressed a giggle, remembering the game "Sardines" we used to play at my Grandmother's house, squashed in the same kind of closet at our family New Year's Eve parties. An hour passed quickly as we sang and told stories by the dim rays of a flashlight. When the "All Clear" sounded we were all wide awake, so we cleaned out the closet before going back to bed. We endured many more "Alerts" and "All Clears" in that closet, but at least now we could all sit down.

A beautiful Victorian house stood on the next street with its back to my new temporary home. One of its upstairs windows faced my bed-room, just far enough away for me to make out the color of its blackout curtains. Cokers' backyard was separated from its spacious grounds by a sturdy wooden fence. Daydreaming at the open window of my bedroom after school one day, I was startled to see, studying me intently from the open window of the house opposite, the face of a boy who looked a little older than myself. With a quick smile, the face disappeared.

That summer evening, with hair newly shampooed and still wet, I answered the front doorbell ready to tell whichever of the girls it was that I couldn't go out with wet hair. (The only electric hair dryers back then were in beauty parlors.) I opened the door and found myself staring at an incredibly handsome young man. He had velvet brown eyes, fringed with black lashes that any girl would envy, in a tanned face topped with a mop of dark wavy hair. Tall and athletic, he was a dazzling sight in white cricket pants and a royal blue prep school blazer. There was an unfamiliar quiver inside me that I had never felt before as I stood there with my wet hair, wanting to sink into the Cokers' doorstep.

The apparition spoke in a velvety voice to match his eyes: "I'm Michael Crowley, and I live in the house in back of yours. I've seen you at your window and I was wondering if you would like to come out for a walk." I thought to myself: "Bunty, you've really blown it this time; why did you have to wash your hair this evening?" Dry-mouthed, I managed: "I'm sorry, but I can't go out with wet hair, Michael." Despondently, I thought: "This is it, Bunty, you'll never see *him* again!" But with a grin, he said: "See you tomorrow, then."

The war all but vanished from my diary as superlatives about Michael filled its pages. He was a genius to rival William when he rigged a small box dangling precariously from heavy twine and a pulley, which he strung across the intervening space between his window and mine above our backyards. This was used to exchange a prodigious flow of notes after school, when we should have been doing our homework. His next invention was a private telephone line: another long piece of twine, tautly strung from his window to mine, with an empty tin can attached to each end, through which we could actually talk to each other. I had left one genius behind at Bishop's Hill; here was another, and right on my doorstep! But Michael made the mistake one day of introducing me to his best friend, Charles de Vere, an evacuee from the posh Mayfair district of London.

Charles de Vere was an aristocrat. His family had a luxurious summer home in Hove, next door to the Crowleys, to which they evacuated from London, enrolling Charles at Michael's prep school. The two had become good friends. In contrast to Michael, Charles had thin blond hair and was slightly built, pale and pimply. The only possibly attractive thing about him was his occasional, funny little one-sided smile, but in spite of his mild appearance, he had the overbearing manner of one who was used to getting his own way and ordering servants about.

Charles was sweetness itself toward me, as if he were sharing Michael's friendship with me as a condescending kindness. At first he accompanied Michael and me on our walks, but it wasn't long before he appeared alone on the Cokers' doorstep.

"I say, Bunty, I'd like you to come with me and watch the tennis finals over at Hove Park. Michael has to study for a test, so I thought I'd ask you to go instead."

Curious, I went with him. He chatted harmlessly on the way, but suddenly pulled out a penknife from his pocket and opened it as we neared a deserted corner of the park. He smiled, and I thought: "Oh Lord, that crooked smile reminds me of one of the bad guys in the mystery movie I saw with Mom the other day!" I began to look for an escape route.

Charles meandered over to a large tree and stood behind it. As time went by and he didn't emerge from behind the tree, I thought: "What on earth is he doing? Maybe he's had a sudden urge to go to the bathroom or something! I'd better not go and look, just wait where I am."

I kept my distance. In awhile I heard him say sweetly: "Come over here, Bunty, I have something to show you. It's a surprise."

"Oh dear!" I was imagining all kinds of lurid possibilities.

"Should I go or not?" Then, common sense overriding my nervousness, I scolded myself: "Don't be so silly, you can trust him." There were plenty of people in the park within hearing distance, so I decided that if I needed to scream they would surely come to my rescue. Gingerly I stepped over to where Charles was standing with the penknife. I sighed with relief when I noticed he had retracted the blade, then looked with curiosity where he was pointing. There on the smooth bark of the tree he had carved his initials and my own, enclosed in a wobbly heart with an arrow through it. Envisioning an unwanted entanglement, I decided there and then never to see Charles alone again.

I have often wondered if people speculated whose initials those were, on the tree which by now must be a giant in the park.

"MONDAY, JUNE 10TH: ITALY CAME INTO THE WAR ON THE NASTIES' SIDE."
We often nicknamed the Nazis the "Nasties." Winston Churchill pronounced it "Naarzies," and referred to Italy's dictator, Mussolini, as "the Italian Jackal". I remembered hearing my parents talk about the jackals in Africa slinking in for the leftovers after a stronger animal had already made a kill. Now the whole of Western Europe was the Nazis' kill; would England be the leftovers?

"THURSDAY, JUNE 13TH: 'IT HAS BEEN ANNOUNCED BY THE HOME OFFICE THAT UNTIL FURTHER NOTICE THERE WILL BE A BAN ON RINGING CHURCH BELLS,'" said the B.B.C. newscaster.
Mom and I joined the Cokers to listen to the radio news while we ate breakfast. I could hardly believe my ears! Four days ago I had gone early to church, and to my surprise, "Old Beery" had let me ring the church bell. Now there was suddenly a radio announcement banning the ringing of church bells! The temptation for a bit of whimsy was irresistible.

"Wow," I exclaimed, "but I couldn't have sounded *that* bad!"

Mom burst out laughing: "You really must have made a mess out of ringing that bell, Bunty," she gasped, "but I'm surprised they heard it all the way up at the Home Office in London".

She stopped laughing as we listened to the reason for the ban. Until further notice, church bells all across Britain would be rung only by order of the military as a signal that enemy paratroopers had been dropped in the area. With the war almost at our shores, a future German invasion had now emerged as a real possibility.

"MONDAY, JUNE 17TH: FRANCE OFFICIALLY SURRENDERED! DRIZZLY DAY, BUT IT CLEARED UP IN THE EVENING, SO WENT FOR A WALK ON THE DOWNS WITH MICHAEL."
We heard the news when we returned from our walk. The Germans had simply bypassed the Maginot Line by invading France through Belgium; the French were ordered out of the fortifications with nothing left to defend. On a clear day the white cliffs of Dover could now be seen by the Nazis, about twenty-five miles across the English Channel from Calais. And all along that coast were thousands of London's evacuated schoolchildren! I thought: "Another move? *You bet*! But where to this time?"

"TUESDAY, JUNE 18TH: LISTENED TO BROADCAST OF CHURCHILL'S SPEECH TO HOUSE OF COMMONS ON THE NATIONAL SITUATION."
Winston Churchill's voice again crackled through the room as his address to the House of Commons was broadcast on the radio that evening. He made it clear that Britain would stand firm against Hitler. We listened, enthralled, to his speech, and the words which would go down in history: "The battle of France is over, and I expect that the battle of Britain is about to begin. Let us therefore brace ourselves to our duties, and so bear ourselves that if the British Empire and its Commonwealth last for a thousand years, men will say: 'This was their finest hour.'"

We braced for invasion.

France Falls

"FRIDAY, JUNE 21ST: WENT TO SCHOOL THIS MORNING FOR GYM. WALKING BACK TO MY BILLET, I WAS NEARLY RUN OVER BY A TANK!"

"I don't believe it. It's coming straight at me!" I had started across the street, but now the shock went right to my legs, and I ran in panic back to the safety of the curb. This was the first time I had actually seen a full-sized tank at close quarters as it rumbled by. When my heart stopped pounding I was indignant. "At least you'd think he would have slowed down for a pedestrian," I muttered to myself. It took me a few minutes to realize that the tank driver probably couldn't even see me beneath him from his perch high above the street!

The town of Hove had taken on the appearance of an armed camp. Squads of soldiers jogged and exercised along the promenade-, now strung with barbed-wire barricades and off-limits to the public. The number of sandbagged gun emplacements had multiplied. Army trucks and cars joined the buses and bicycles which already clogged down-town streets, constantly causing traffic jams in Hove and its twin town of Brighton, while dozens of "half-tracks" with mounted machine guns rattled along the roads leading to the beaches.

"SATURDAY, JUNE 22ND: FRANCE SIGNED AN ARMISTICE WITH GERMANY."
The "Armistice" was France's official surrender document and Hitler de-manded a vicious revenge for the ceremony. Determined that France should be as thoroughly humiliated as Germany had been at her own surrender after World War One, he had ordered the same railway coach that had been used when the Germans signed the 1918 Armistice to be brought from a Paris museum for the purpose. To make his vengeance complete, Hitler then had the railway coach exhibited to the German public in the Lustgarten, Berlin. We all knew his next step would prob-ably be to invade England.

One by one the countries of Western Europe had fallen, and were now under the brutal heel of their Nazi occupiers. But they were not forgotten by Britain. I am still touched when I remember how the B.B.C. played the national anthem of each occupied country before a nightly news broadcast until they were liberated five years later.

"THURSDAY, JUNE 27TH: "WENT TO THE TOWN HALL THIS MORNING. PASSED A MEDICAL EXAM FOR EVACUATION TO CANADA."

Some time ago, when Hitler's *Blitzkrieg*, or "lightning war" in Europe began to look unstoppable, Dad had come on one of his visits to Hove. He took me aside, his face serious, expressing the concern he was feeling. "Bunty, dear, Mom and I need to talk to you. Let's all go in the living room and sit down."

Dad's voice was gentle, so different from his usual gruff manner. I knew something was very wrong. There was a sick feeling in the pit of my stomach.

Mom and Dad sat on each side of me on the couch. Mom held my hand. Dad put his arm around my shoulders. "Bunty, your Mom and I have been talking over the terrible repercussions of this war that are still to come. The Nazis will probably invade Britain after they have taken Western Europe. You know we're hearing reports from the European underground in the newly occupied countries about the atrocities being carried out on young girls by Nazi soldiers, and although it will break our hearts to let you go, we think it would be safer for you to be away from England until the war ends. We've been exploring the possibilities."

Mom and Dad had joined thousands of British parents wrestling with the agonizing problem of how to protect their children in the event of a German invasion. One of the girls in my class said that her father had bought a pistol and was prepared to shoot his family and then himself, rather than be tied up and forced to watch Nazi soldiers rape his daughter and torture his wife, as the European underground stated had been happening.

Meantime, in Britain, a voluntary overseas evacuation program for children, the Children's Overseas Reception Board (CORB), had been proposed, and after the fall of France it was approved by Parliament. The cost of the sea voyage was prorated according to the financial means of the parents; also the children had to have a destination and an overseas sponsor to guarantee their custody. Postwar statistics report that 2,664 CORB children were evacuated, some to the United States but most to the British Dominions: Canada, Australia, New Zealand and South Africa.

Dad continued: "We've written to Uncle Arthur and Auntie Belle in Sunderland. We've heard that Mrs. Howland, their housekeeper, has a brother, George Duffy, living in Winnipeg, Canada. She's sure he and his family would be willing to take you into their home as an evacuee. Arthur has just sent me their address; they are probably down-to-earth, decent people like Mrs. Howland. But before we go any further, Bunty, if they are willing to have you, would you be willing to go?"

I gulped, trying to digest all Dad was saying. "Well, it would feel a bit strange, going to live so far away with people I've never met," I said, trying to convince Mom and Dad, but mostly myself, that I could accept the idea. "But when you come to think of it, I didn't know any of the folks I've lived with in Hove, either, and we can get to know the Duffys through their letters before I go."

In the letter from the Duffys sent in reply to ours they readily agreed to sponsor me. Their photos and letters that followed in response to ours revealed a caring and pleasant middle-class family with a comfortable home and a daughter about my age. A born optimist, I reassured myself. "Well, Bunty, by now you must feel you already know the Duffys through their letters, and you know what the family all look like from their photos, just as they will recognize you from yours. And after all, think what a great adventure it will be crossing the Atlantic."

My medical exam had now been passed and here I was, on the waiting list, one step closer to boarding a passenger ship bound for the New World. Mom and Dad bought me a new suitcase, tennis racquet, white tennis dress and shoes. Mom bought some Donegal tweed and had her tailor make a warm winter coat for me. Dad took a photo of me wearing the coat and sent copies to all the family in Sunderland. All that remained now was to await my turn for a sailing date.

On one hand, I looked forward to the adventure, but lately the B.B.C. news had admitted that "wolf packs" of Nazi U-boats were ravaging Allied shipping in the North Atlantic Ocean, Britain's lifeline for food and war supplies from North America. It would not be known until history later revealed that more than a million tons (144 ships) were sunk in the North Atlantic in the month of June 1940 alone.

Dad knew this ocean well. He had crossed it many times early in World War One, while serving as an engineer on oil tankers in the Merchant Marine, ferrying crucial supplies to Britain. Later in the war he was called up from the Royal Naval Volunteer Reserve and served as a second lieutenant engineer in the Royal Navy. Three of the ships he served on were torpedoed in the Atlantic. I remembered that day long before the war, when he showed me his old World War One photo album. "Yes, we were torpedoed three times. I was never a strong swimmer, you know, Bunty. I thought each time I was a goner, but blow me down, luck was on me side and I was rescued each time by the skin of me teeth. Here's a photo taken by one of the men on board our rescue ship, showing the *San Zeferino* going down."

CORB was implemented, using some of the scarce space on various passenger liners for evacuees, and no problems had been reported. The Duffys were excited about my forthcoming journey; they had made plans for me to travel by train to Winnipeg from wherever my port of arrival would be, probably Halifax, Nova Scotia. I began to wait for my sailing date to come up and tried not to remember that photo of Dad's ship sinking that I had seen so many years ago.

"SUNDAY, JUNE 30TH: GERMANS HAVE OCCUPIED THE CHANNEL ISLANDS.FIRST BRITISH TERRITORY TO BE INVADED."
The British Channel Islands are nearer to France than to England, but news of their occupation brought with it an aura of gloom: it seemed like a preview of things to come. The British Government gave the islanders the option to evacuate, but most decided to stay. For the first time in history, the British flag was taken down and the Nazi swastika flew in its place. The Channel Islanders were to suffer Nazi domination for the next five years.

Evacuated Again!

"WEDNESDAY, JULY 10TH: WENT TO SCHOOL THIS MORNING. CHOIR PRACTICE. RAVENHURST IS GOING TO BE RE-EVACUATED. DON'T KNOW WHERE!"

At least choir practice gave us some reassurance of normalcy, but otherwise another upset was looming in the shape of a re-evacuation. Once more there would be a physical and emotional upheaval, beyond my control. I had the helpless feeling of a puppet on strings manipulated by a malevolent puppeteer. And I was also learning that in life nothing lasts forever. Now I would have to leave the friends in Hove I had grown to love in the ten months we had been there. My Dad's favorite saying, that the people in our lives are like "ships that pass in the night," at last made sense. I despaired of ever feeling secure again.

Three days later, the *Luftwaffe* attacked its first British target. The Scottish port of Aberdeen was bombed, with sixty civilian casualties resulting. Next came the English port of Falmouth and the Welsh port of Swansea, with thirty dead.

Some history books record this was the beginning of the "Battle of Britain," the first phase of Hitler's plan to conquer Britain, which I was soon to see and experience at firsthand in its full fury. But for now, Ravenhurst was on the move again. Dad took the train from Hampton to see Mom and me off on our next journey.

"SUNDAY, JULY 14TH: AT 9 A.M., DAD AND MICHAEL CAME TO SEE MOM AND ME OFF AT BRIGHTON TRAIN STATION, BOUND FOR AN UNKNOWN DESTINATION. ARRIVED AT EGHAM, SURREY, AT 2:30 P.M. AND FROM THERE WENT BY BUS TO THORPE VILLAGE HALL, WHERE WE WERE GIVEN A SMALL BOTTLE OF MILK AND A COOKIE. OUR BILLET IS A HOUSE AT THE END OF A COUNTRY LANE. GREAT PLACE TO SPEND SUMMER HOLIDAYS!"

Michael was visibly upset as he made me promise to write. I was sad to leave this budding romance, but excited and curious about the next chapter in our evacuation adventures. This new evacuation, we were told, was temporary. An hour on the train took us inland, north and west, away from the vulnerable south coast. Here we would be safe until another host school could be found to accommodate us when our new school year began in September. In a little over an hour we reached the country town of Egham, and buses took us to Thorpe Village Hall, where we waited for our hosts to pick us up. Ravenhurst girls were billeted all around the surrounding countryside in ancient farmhouses and in the modern homes of London commuters. We discovered to our surprise that we were only an hour's drive away from Upper Woodside!

Mom and I were billeted in a large, modern brick house at the end of a country lane in Thorpe Village. Mom had her own bedroom and there were twin beds in mine. Mom parked her suitcase in her room and went off on the train to Hampton to spend the weekend with Dad. I was unpacking my few belongings when I heard a familiar voice downstairs.

Molly came up the stairs two at a time. "Oh, Bunty, how lovely to be together again--and this time in the same billet!"

The other twin bed was soon covered with Molly's unpacking. I couldn't have wished for a better roommate. For the next two weeks Molly and I were inseparable, exploring our new neighborhood and making friends with local girls and boys our own age, who were also celebrating their summer vacation.

"SATURDAY, JULY 20TH: WHAT A WEEK THIS HAS BEEN! RAVENHURST HAS CERTAINLY LEFT ITS MARK ON THORPE VILLAGE!"
At ten o'clock each morning those of us who were billeted in and around Thorpe Village dutifully reported to the church hall for roll call. Two of our weary school mistresses checked us off on their list to be sure nobody was missing, then the rest of the day was ours. There was no attempt by Lizzie to keep track of or to organize our activities; she was probably too busy arranging to relocate her remaining evacuated girls to an area where another prep school could accommodate all of us--no easy task in competition with so many other schools re-evacuated from the south coast.

Living in the country was a novelty for us. Food here was plentiful; we wolfed down the generous portions of home-cooked meals provided by our hostess, Mrs. Leary, whose husband was away serving with the British Army in India. Their two young sons, Christopher and Clyde, were delighted to have our help tending the dozen or so chickens in their backyard chicken coop.

"Hey, Chris, I have a great recipe for mash." I dictated to him Mr. Dearborne's recipe, scribbled in the back pages of my diary, and he wrote it down on the back of an envelope. We didn't stay in Thorpe long enough for me to decide whether or not it had any beneficial effect, but the hens would probably have been just as happy without it, delivering our breakfast eggs on time each day. On our first morning, Molly and I lingered over a breakfast like the ones we remembered from before the war: new-laid eggs, bacon, freshly baked bread and creamy butter.

"Whee!" I whooped. "What shall we do today, Molly?"

"Well, I think after roll call we should take a walk around the village and get oriented first." Molly was always methodical.

Chris interrupted: "Oh, I'll take you fishing if you like!"

"Well, neither of us has ever used a fishing rod. I can just imagine how awful I'd feel to be tangled up in fish line while a huge fish darts away from under my nose in some lake or river."

Chris laughed: "Not to worry; you won't be able to brag about the one that got away where we're going. It's just a stream about a block away from here, and all we'll need will be a couple of nets and some jam jars."

Molly and I knew how to fish for tadpoles!

The following days passed all too quickly as Ravenhurst girls reveled in the freedom of living in the country with no classes or supervision. I often wonder if Thorpe Village ever recovered from what must have gone down in its oral history as "the Legend of the Ravenhurst Invasion." We swarmed over the countryside on long hikes and filled to overflowing the local bus that took us to the movies in the next town.

Barefoot, we raced and rolled on the grass with unrestrained joy, fished for newts and tadpoles in little streams, climbed trees on the village green, and terrorized local residents by racing around on borrowed bicycles. For a short time, evacuation was again "a lark."

Although by now about a hundred girls had already returned home to attend the reopened branch of Ravenhurst in London, two hundred were still evacuated, and the country villages could offer no school building large enough to accommodate all of us. The end of summer vacation was approaching and we knew that soon there would have to be another move.

"WEDNESDAY, JULY 31ST. GOODBYE THORPE, HELLO GUILDFORD! OUR TRAIN ARRIVED AT 4:30 P.M. NO BILLET FOUND FOR MOM AND ME, SO WE SPENT THE NIGHT AT A CHILDREN'S ORPHANAGE--UGH!" "Now I know what Oliver Twist must have gone through," I groaned, "this is really gruesome!" A forbidding pile of granite, the brooding gray hulk of the orphanage reminded me of *Wuthering Heights* and Frankenstein's castle rolled into one. After a very uncomfortable night, Mom and I sat on a backless bench at a long wooden table with the orphans. Breakfast was a bowl of watery porridge (now I knew what Dickens meant by 'gruel,') accompanied by burned toast and weak tea.

A billet was found for me but not for poor Mom, who had to spend another night at the orphanage. This proved to be the proverbial straw that broke the camel's back. Next day she said in disgust: "Well, Bunty, I've had enough; I think I'll give up life as an evacuee," and she took the train to Hampton to join Dad at the Hornes'. In a few days Mom and Dad opened up the house in Bishop's Hill and Mom moved back into it.

Ravenhurst had adjusted to sharing a building with a host school at Hove; at Guildford we found ourselves sharing one with a second evacuated school as well. The girls from each of the three schools barely had time for three classes per day, colliding with each other in the halls, as one group changed places with the next. Chaos prevailed.

Guildford was not only brimming over with re-evacuated schools rescued in the nick of time before the *Luftwaffe* began bombing the south coast, but it was also full of wounded men from Dunkirk. Guildford's hospital bulged with the more seriously injured, and the streets swarmed with "walking wounded." When the first tales were heard of local girls being molested by lusty soldiers, Lizzie imposed a curfew on Ravenhurst; all of us had to be in our billets by 6 p.m.!

I wrote in a letter to Mom and Dad: "I feel *so* miserable; the school's overcrowded, the town's overcrowded and, with four girls sharing a bedroom, my billet's overcrowded, too."

I hoped they would hear my S.O.S.

Hitler Warns England

"FRIDAY, AUGUST 2ND: 'LEAFLETS WERE DROPPED ON BRITAIN YESTERDAY,'" reported the B.B.C. announcer uneasily, on the news at breakfast time.

Low-flying Nazi planes had released a blanket of paper over Britain. On each leaflet, a copy of a speech by Adolf Hitler warned the British of the futility of any further resistance. Written in English, it was entitled: "A Last Appeal to Reason, by Adolf Hitler." The reaction of the British people was summed up in a newspaper photo showing an air-raid warden and two housewives reading one of the leaflets and laughing their heads off!

In response to Hitler's leaflets, a new spirit of defiance was born in Britain and a new "war cry" emerged on the home front. It began with a famous comic on the B.B.C., who yelled at the studio audience: *"Are we downhearted?"* and the roaring reply was *"No!"* The catchphrase caught on. It could be heard all over; housewives waiting in line for rations called it out, and bus conductors would sometimes stand among their passengers to shout the question. Everyone on the bus would roar: "No!" followed by a morale-boosting cheer loud enough to raise the eyebrows of people on the street as they watched the cheering busload of passengers go by.

"THURSDAY, AUGUST 8TH: HITLER BEGINS PLANS TO LAUNCH 'OPERATION SEA LION': THE INVASION OF BRITAIN."
This would have made a sensational, terrifying newspaper headline, if it had existed! It wasn't until long after World War Two, however, that the full story was released about Hitler's plan, which was to culminate in his invasion of British soil. This was labeled "Operation Sea Lion." Mercifully, civilians in England were unaware of Hitler's plan, but we would soon be experiencing its beginnings.

Immediately following Dunkirk, Hitler ordered his chiefs of staff to organize the invasion of Britain. Within a few weeks, an armada of boats was assembled in German, French and Belgian harbors, including two thousand landing barges to carry one hundred and sixty thousand German troops to towns along a forty-mile stretch of the south coast of England. Flushed with the success of the *Blitzkrieg*-style warfare by means of which he had conquered the countries of Western Europe, Hitler was now determined to finish off Britain without slowing his momentum. But unlike his conquests by land, this project was complicated by the barrier of the English Channel, a notoriously stormy stretch of water 350 miles long, 21 miles wide at its narrowest and 150 miles at its widest.

Hitler's plan looked simple in theory. Convinced that he was a military genius, in his mind the successful conquest of Britain was a foregone conclusion following her huge losses of men and materiel before and at Dunkirk. When carried out as planned, he reckoned that German armies would occupy London by August 15th. He was determined to get on with this project quickly in order to follow it up with his plan to conquer Russia, "Operation Barbarossa."

However, the German admirals were not optimistic about a successful confrontation with the Royal Navy. Also, Hitler's generals warned him about the capability of the R.A.F. to inflict incredible damage on the venture, so he reluctantly agreed to postpone the invasion until he had destroyed the R.A.F.

The completion of Operation Sea Lion would be postponed again and again, and finally abandoned, but its first phases would soon be felt in Britain, including Ravenhurst and Upper Woodside.

Meantime I was miserable and homesick in Guildford, only twenty-one miles from home.

"FRIDAY, AUGUST 9TH: WHOOPEE! HAD A LETTER FROM MOM SAYING I AM TO COME HOME TOMORROW. PACKED ALL EXCEPT OVERNIGHT NECESSITIES."
"Gosh," I had complained to my friend Jess the day before, "our class is down to fourteen of us from the thirty we started out with a few months ago. I wish I could go home, too."

As if by magic, next day a letter telling me to pack arrived from Mom and Dad, who also had had enough of my evacuation.

"SATURDAY, AUGUST 10TH: THIS AFTERNOON WILLIAM'S DAD DROVE DOWN TO GUILDFORD TO PICK ME UP AND BRING ME HOME. MOM AND MRS. STANDISH ALSO IN CAR. HAD A VISIT FROM WILLIAM THIS EVENING."
Mr. Standish, William's Dad, whose government job entitled him to an extra gasoline ration, drove over to Guildford. Picking up my suitcase, I ran out to meet the car as he pulled into the driveway of my billet. He hugged me and stowed my baggage in the trunk.

William's Mom had come along for the ride. She leaned out the window by the front seat: "This was a good excuse to come out for a ride through the lovely Surrey countryside, Bunty, and it wouldn't take any more petrol, so I thought I'd join the welcoming committee." She glanced over to the back seat: "And we've brought a surprise for you."

Mom's head popped up over the back seat. "Come on, Bunty, hop in here with me. We'd have had you out of that mess sooner, but it's taken me awhile to get the house back into shipshape condition and straighten up the garden. You'll be happy to see your own bedroom again, I bet."

The house looked sparkling. Fresh flowers were in vases in the front hall, the table was set for dinner with my beloved Willow Pattern dishes. William landed on our doorstep shortly after dinner, ready with a bear hug when I went to the door.

"Welcome back, Bunty. Missed you, and I'm so glad you're home. No air raids, so we can have some fun together until I get called up for the R.A.F. I'm going to apply for pilot's training. Just think, I might get to fly one of those Spitfires yet!"

He stayed until almost midnight, catching me up on local gossip. By the time he left, weariness overcame me; it had been a long day. Feeling rescued from bondage at last, I fell happily asleep in my own bed that night.

"SUNDAY, AUGUST 11TH: HAPPINESS! BACK HOME AGAIN. PETER CAME TO VISIT. CAN'T QUITE BELIEVE I'M HOME AGAIN TO STAY. SCHOOL TOMORROW."

While I was evacuated, Peter had become old enough to join William in applying for enlistment in the R.A.F. when he turned eighteen. William's eighteenth birthday had just passed; he was ecstatic. Now he was just waiting for his call-up papers to arrive, but Peter would have to wait another year for his eighteenth birthday. While he was waiting he had joined the Home Guard. Begun before the war with civilian volunteers between the ages of seventeen and sixty-five, this home-based army of "Weekend Warriors" had swelled to a million strong by 1940. Gradually, "hand-me-down" uniforms and obsolete rifles had been replaced, and now the Home Guard had become well-equipped and trained, ready to help in the defence of Britain.

Handsome in his khaki uniform, Peter kept us entertained with accounts of his Home Guard training, especially his well-embroidered tales of the overnight bivouac camping trips. Sounding slightly man-of-the-world, he said, with a twinkle in his eye: "You should have seen the girl recruits at last weekend's bivouac getting all tangled up trying to put up their tents, then slipping and sliding all over the place in the mud and falling 'plop' on their bottoms. I don't know how they will ever manage on maneuvers when they get into the A.T.S." (Auxiliary Territorial Service, the equivalent of American WACs.) He added innocently, "Of course, some of them will probably have different kinds of maneuvers in mind!"

"MONDAY, AUGUST 12TH: TOOK BUS TO GO BACK TO SCHOOL AT RAVENHURST. IT'S SO GOOD TO SEE SO MANY OF MY FRIENDS BACK FROM EVACUATION, BUT UGH, ALL THOSE RULES!"

My first day back in the familiar building brought a lump to my throat; the day was punctuated with reunions, hugs and squeals of recognition as old friends greeted me. With a full day of school, my education was back on track, but in the laxity and freedom of evacuation the school's traditional rules had almost been forgotten. My diary reported how miffed I was that first day when Pie Face had stopped me in the hallway on my way to my locker to hang up my school blazer and change my Oxfords to the required indoor shoes.

"It's nice to see you back, Bunty, but where are your white gloves? Remember, they must always be worn with your school uniform. You're not evacuated now, you know."

I muttered uncomplimentary things under my breath at her retreating back.

Arriving home after school, I burst into the house. "Mom, school is super! More than half of my old classmates are back from evacuation, and the boys' school is jumping, too!"

Life was once more a bowl of cherries, but not for long.

The Battle of Britain

"TUESDAY, AUGUST 13TH: WENT TO SCHOOL ON BUS. WILLIAM CAME TO VISIT AND STAYED FOR DINNER."

Not a word about the war in my diary, but if we had only known, August 13th was the day Nazi *Luftwaffe* chief, Field Marshal Goering, had ordered his bomber pilots to begin the "softening up" of Britain in preparation for invasion. This was the date designated as the beginning of an all-out air offensive to achieve Goering's goal. To the Nazis it was "Eagle Day"; we knew it as the date of the beginning of the Battle of Britain.

In the ensuing days, Nazi bombers attacked British ports, also shipping in the English Channel, but the defending R.A.F. fighters exacted from the *Luftwaffe* high losses in aircraft. Goering changed his tactics; his goal now was to cripple the R.A.F. by wiping out its airfields. He boasted to Hitler that his *Luftwaffe* could annihilate the R.A.F. in four days, but the R.A.F. thought otherwise.

The Battle of Britain was destined to rage on, day after day in the skies over southern England, for a hundred and fourteen days. Outnumbered and exhausted, the young R.A.F. pilots pitted their dwindling squadrons of Spitfire and Hurricane fighter planes against hundreds of attacking enemy bombers and fighters, coming in to land, then taking off again after only enough time to refuel.

"THURSDAY, AUGUST 15TH: SCHOOL ALL DAY. PLAYED TENNIS IN MY LUNCH HOUR. AFTER I CAME HOME, NAZI PLANES DROPPED BOMBS ON CROYDON AIRPORT. WE WATCHED FROM BACK BEDROOM WINDOW. NO DAMAGE DONE. IN AIR RAIDS OVER SOUTH OF ENGLAND R.A.F. DESTROYED 144 NAZI PLANES."
British government censorship avoided giving to the Nazis any confirmation of their successes in the air war by downplaying reports to the media and exaggerating claims of planes destroyed by the R.A.F., so 144 was probably a wrong number!

In Upper Woodside it was another glorious summer day, with a clear blue sky and warm sunshine. William had kindly mowed the lawn for Mom. Returning from school, I found them both relaxing on the newly mown grass in lawn chairs, with cups of tea. I had just poured a cup for

myself when we heard some air-raid sirens wailing in the distance, followed almost immediately by the throb of aircraft engines and a sound
we had never heard before: an eerie, high-pitched scream, then several
moments later a thud, and the roar of a plane's engine as it banked
steeply away. Mom said: "Hurry up, you two, let's go upstairs. We
should be able to see better from there what's happening."

Hastily setting down our cups on our way through the kitchen,
the three of us raced up the stairs to the back bedroom and threw
open the window that looked towards Croydon, a few miles away.
Taking turns using Dad's binoculars, we watched one plane after another dive almost vertically on some distant target with that same
screaming noise. Mom passed the binoculars to me: "Look, Bunty,
the R.A.F. must be practicing maneuvers down at Croydon Airport.
Maybe they're going to be putting on one of those air shows like the
ones we used to watch at Croydon before the war, remember? Aren't
they good? Look at them diving and then zooming up into the sky
again. But I don't ever remember hearing that funny noise at the air
shows, do you?"

I watched, spellbound, as the planes performed what looked like a
timed ritual. "William, what are those little black specks they seem to
be dropping after they dive? They must be practicing something new
before they race back up into the sky and away."

Almost roughly, William said: "Give me the binoculars, Bunty, quick.
Oh, my God, those little black specks, as you call them, must be bombs!
Can't you hear the 'woof' after they drop them? And I can see puffs of
smoke rising from the ground; this isn't a practice, it's an air raid!"

We learned later that the German Junkers-88 Stuka dive bombers'
engines had special sirens installed, designed to make the sound of
their attack more terrifying. The Stukas had come and gone in a matter of minutes, leaving behind a rising cloud of smoke. The three of us
stood looking out of the window in disbelief. Belatedly, air-raid sirens
howled in Upper Woodside. Wardens' whistles could be heard, clearing
the streets of pedestrians. My stomach sickened; we had just witnessed

our first real air raid. We headed for the Anderson shelter and sat there, bracing for another attack, but none came.

Declassified information released after the war told the full story of the bombing of Croydon Airport. Hitler had given specific orders that Croydon (in those days London's major civilian airport) should *not* be bombed. He wanted it kept intact because he envisioned himself landing there in triumph as the master of his new kingdom once the Nazis had conquered Britain.

The raid had been carried out by mistake by twenty-three Junkers-88 dive bombers, which, due to a navigational error, got lost on their way to their real target, the R.A.F. fighter base at Kenley airfield in Surrey. It was reported on our news that there had been no damage to Croydon Airport, but in reality the raid killed sixty-two civilians and injured one hundred and fifty-four, leaving the airport's runways and buildings badly damaged. Hitler was furious; his plans for a "grand entrance" had been ruined.

Britain Survives

"SUNDAY, AUGUST 18TH: AIR RAIDS HAVE BEGUN ON LONDON. HAD TWO ALERTS TODAY, ONLY AN HOUR LONG EACH, NO BOMBS, BUT LOTS OF NOISE. HAD TEA IN THE SHELTER."

"There goes 'Moaning Minnie' again," sighed Mom, as the neighborhood air-raid siren began to wail loudly in our ears. We ran for the shelter with cups of tea. This time we realized how close we were to the *Luftwaffe*'s main target, the city of London, and that the German bombers would have to fly over our suburb to get there.

We learned to identify the German aircraft by the peculiar, uneven pulsing of their engines. Next came the ear-splitting sound of antiaircraft or "ack-ack" fire, which continued until the enemy planes had passed over Upper Woodside on their way to London, to be repeated again when they came back over Upper Woodside on their way to their home bases in Europe. Conversation became impossible.

"I didn't realize how noisy it would be," I shouted, "the racket is deafening. Next time I'll wear ear plugs!"

After the "All Clear" sounded, small boys would rush out to gather pieces of shrapnel from ack-ack gun shells that had rained down on the neighborhood during the alert. These pieces of jagged metal were shown off, swapped and admired by little boys throughout the war.

British factories were working day and night to replace the armaments lost at Dunkirk, but ack-ack guns were in short supply, especially in our suburb. Listening in our Anderson shelter, we were puzzled at first when we heard rounds of gunfire at our end of Bishop's Hill, then more rounds a few minutes later, further up the street. Could there be two new guns in our neighborhood? When we were sure the bombers had gone on their way to London, we crept back into the house and looked through the big bay window in our living room. We were just in time to see a large gun hauled by an army truck roll quickly down the road, where it stopped and fired off a few rounds. It passed by our window again on its way back up the street, apparently to repeat the performance. We learned that this was going on all over London to deceive the Nazis into thinking we had twice as many ack-ack guns as we really did.

"MONDAY, AUGUST 19TH: BROUGHT THE BEDS DOWNSTAIRS."
London's first air raids were short and sporadic, and Mom complained: "Bunty, I don't know about you, but I'm sick and tired of being jolted awake by air-raid sirens, leaping out of bed and stumbling down the stairs half asleep to go out to the Anderson shelter several times in the middle of the night. Don't you think it would better to sleep downstairs?"

"Yes, Mom, I do, but how will we move the furniture? "Not to worry, dear, we have two healthy helpers I can call on. They both owe me for all those cookies over the years!"

There followed a great deal of heavy breathing and muttering by Peter and William. They moved the sofa in the living room over against the wall and two lounge chairs were relocated into the dining room. Twin beds and bedding were brought from the front bedroom and installed in the living room next to the piano, shattering the elegance of the decor. But by now we weren't thinking of appearances!

"TUESDAY, AUGUST 20TH: 'IN PARLIAMENT TODAY, WINSTON CHURCHILL PAID TRIBUTE TO THE R.A.F.,'" said the B.B.C. newscaster. We gathered around our radio to hear the recording of the great orator's speech, commending the bravery of the young pilots who had won this phase of the Battle of Britain in the skies. It ended with the words which were to become immortal: "Never, in the field of human conflict, has so much been owed by so many, to so few." Deeply moved, we wept.

Goering had given up his boast that he would destroy the R.A.F. in a few days. He decided that the losses incurred by the *Luftwaffe* were too high to continue, and that a change in tactics was going to be necessary.

For four days there was no mention of air raids in my diary. The skies were gray and deserted in the rain. Bone-tired pilots and ground crews of the battered remains of Britain's fighter squadrons enjoyed a respite at their bomb-pocked airfields.

The cost of the Battle of Britain to both sides had been enormous. Postwar estimates are that a total of three thousand aircraft were lost and thirty thousand civilians killed. And Goering still hadn't cracked the Brits!

The Battle of Britain had so far averted invasion, but it would phase into a new ordeal to be experienced by us in Upper Woodside. This would be called "the Battle of London," or "the London Blitz."

"'LORD HAW-HAW' URGES BRITISH TO GIVE UP; THREATENS AERIAL BLITZ."
This headline dominated the front page of the morning papers. William Joyce was born in Brooklyn, New York, of an immigrant Irish father and an English mother. Joyce was three years old when the family moved to

Ireland, then to England, when he was fifteen. At seventeen, an admirer of Hitler, he became an active Fascist. In 1939 he fled from England to Germany to avoid arrest and internment, and became a willing tool of the Nazis. Captured by the British military in 1945, he was executed for treason on January 3, 1946.

Throughout all of World War Two, Joyce, alias "Lord Haw-Haw," broadcast Nazi propaganda regularly to the British people from Hamburg, Germany. In his cultured English accent, the words "Germany Calling" prefaced what would be a torrent of vicious, vitriolic half-truths and outright lies, aimed at lowering the morale of the British and undermining their faith in the British government.

Amazingly, Haw-Haw had a fascinated audience; one estimate is that thirty-three percent of the British population listened regularly to him, and fifty percent, periodically. For the most part, he became a national joke. Dad listened to him occasionally for amusement, but this time his face grew crimson as he yelled: "Oh, shut up, you cheeky sod," seized the knob on the radio and almost broke it as he turned it off. Little did he realize how serious Lord Haw Haw's threat of *Blitzkrieg* from the air would prove to be.

Blitzkrieg From the Skies

"FRIDAY, AUGUST 23RD: AWAKENED AT 2:24 A.M. PLANES OVERHEAD, AT 3 A.M ACK-ACK FIRE BEGAN. WENT DOWN INTO SHELTER. ALERT SIREN SOUNDED AT 3:20 A.M. AIR RAID LASTED THE REST OF THE NIGHT. AT SCHOOL TODAY. EVERYONE HALF ASLEEP."

The Battle of Britain continued, but the *Luftwaffe's* daylight raids on ports and airfields had lessened. The Germans were losing too many of their bombers to R.A.F. fighter planes. After the war it was revealed that Hitler had ordered Field Marshal Goering, *Luftwaffe* chief, to switch to night bombing; the targets would now be major cities including London.

The unrelenting noise of last night's air raid had made sleep impossible. On the bus to school next morning the usual hum of conversation was missing; most of the commuters were asleep in their seats. At Ravenhurst, tired girls and teachers tried to concentrate on lessons while coveting a nap, instead. Girls began to skip their morning classes and turned up just for the afternoons, others missed afternoon classes as well, simply too tired to walk to the bus stop.

"MONDAY, AUGUST 26th: 'LAST NIGHT BERLIN WAS BOMBED BY THE R.A.F.'"
The B.B.C. news announcer had a hint of triumph in his voice. In spite of German air superiority, the R.A.F. carried out orders to bomb Berlin, to demonstrate Churchill's defiance in retaliation for *Luftwaffe* attacks on civilian populations in Britain's cities, and to flaunt in Goering's face his promise to Hitler that Berlin would never be bombed.

Hitler's vindictive reaction was that of an infuriated madman; he ordered the *Luftwaffe* to prepare for an aerial *Blitzkrieg* on the city of London and its inhabitants. And so the "London Blitz" was born and arrived, unwanted, on our doorstep. We would feel its fury as it grew.

"THURSDAY, AUGUST 29TH: THE LUFTWAFFE BOMBED LONDON, LIVERPOOL, BIRMINGHAM, COVENTRY AND PLYMOUTH. THE R.A.F. AGAIN BOMBED BERLIN! "
Newspaper headlines reported the latest *Luftwaffe* assaults on British cities and praised the courage of the R.A.F. bomber pilots who followed up their first air raid on Berlin with another on each of the two following nights.

I wrote in my diary: "AIR-RAID ALERT LAST NIGHT LASTED FROM 9 P.M. TO 4 A.M. OUR ENTIRE CLASS TURNED UP FOR LESSONS TODAY! SPENT EVENING HELPING WILLIAM TO FILL SANDBAGS FOR THE SHELTER."

The three consecutive R.A.F. raids on Berlin were cause for great celebration in Britain, bringing a much-needed boost to our sagging morale, after the terrible losses at Dunkirk. Instead of bemoaning our defeat, Winston Churchill had given a challenge to civilians on the home front to do our part in the fight for our island by carrying on with life as normally as we could. I think it must have been the inspiration of his words that brought our entire class to school that day after being up all night.

William greeted me when I arrived home. "Bunty, hurry up and get your clothes changed. We have a job to do: that Anderson shelter needs some sandbags around the door and I've got the ingredients."

Normally I was delighted to see William, but I could feel a sour expression creeping across my face. "You've got to be kidding; I've been up all night and sweating over a school desk all day, and now all I want to do is get some sleep."

"Not until we've filled these sandbags; then you'll be tired enough to sleep through the noisiest air raid!"

I thought to myself: "How did I ever get involved with a heartless tyrant like him?" Then, as I changed out of my school uniform, I reasoned, "but he has Mom's and my safety at heart, so I won't be mad at him, at any rate, not this time."

I walked down the yard to the pile of sand William had put in front of the shelter, and held out an empty bag for him to fill. He was right: I slept like a log that night in the shelter!

"FRIDAY, AUGUST 30TH: THIS IS NOT JOLLY! THREE SHORT RAIDS TODAY AND ALL NIGHT FROM DUSK TO DAWN; 9 P.M. TO 4 A.M. I'M SO TIRED!"

Now that we had all-night air raids Mom and I had given up trying to sleep in our beds and simply went out in our pajamas to the Anderson shelter at bedtime to spend the night there. The shelter was too damp and too small for us to lie down, but snatching catnaps sitting up in a lawn chair was better than leaping in and out of bed at intervals all night long.

"I wonder what we'll do when it gets cold outside?" Mom had been a good Girl Guide; she believed in always being prepared.

I was too tired to think of a good answer.

Although it was not made public for several days, on this date the Dutch ocean liner *Volendam* carrying among its passengers CORB evacuees bound for Canada, was attacked by a Nazi wolf pack in the North Atlantic. The *Volendam* was torpedoed and damaged, but all on board were safely transferred to other ships in the convoy. I was glad I hadn't been given a sailing date yet, but just for now my mind was on trying to sleep so I could stay awake!

"TUESDAY, SEPTEMBER 3RD: ANNIVERSARY OF THE WAR! SHORT AIR-RAID ALERTS ON LAST FEW NIGHTS. STAYED HOME FROM SCHOOL. MOM GAVE A TEA PARTY. MOLLY IS HOME FROM EVACUATION."

Could it have been only a year? It felt like a lifetime. I thought of all the people who had passed through my life in those months since war was declared and wondered where they were now. They had passed out of my life, probably forever. Dad's words once again ran through my mind: they had all been "ships that passed in the night." I was glad to see Molly at school; at least I still had a few friends left.

"'Winnie' has told us to 'Keep Calm and Carry On,' so I'm going to give a tea party and Hitler's not going to stop me," announced Mom, "and be damned to him and his air raids." I joined her friends in the dining room. Mom had set the table with her best tea set and fancy tablecloth. All six invitees, including William's mother and Mrs. White, were decked out in their best dresses and jewelry as if to thumb their noses at the constant danger from the skies. Luckily the siren was silent while cups of tea were poured and Mom passed a plate with a modest assortment of hoarded chocolate-covered cookies, carefully spaced on their large paper doily, where they looked a bit lonesome. Mom set down the plate, lifted her teacup and said: "Let's have a toast: 'Down with

Hitler!'" Chuckling, we all lifted our cups and yelled in unison: "Down with Hitler, bottoms up!"

On the days that followed, air raids continued day and night. My diary reported: "WENT TO SCHOOL. BUS WAS LATE. TWO ONE-HOUR RAIDS, 9:30 A.M. AND 1:30 P.M." And the next day: "OVERNIGHT RAID. WENT TO SCHOOL. WAS LATE; HARDLY ANY BUSES RUNNING. RAID AT 10:30 A.M. AND ANOTHER AT 3:10 P.M. EACH LASTED ONLY ABOUT AN HOUR."

It was becoming more and more difficult to get to school, but I was determined to "Keep Calm and Carry On," as exhorted by the large billboard on the bus route to school. My diary reported the air-raid alerts that punctuated our lessons with trips to the basement shelter during classes, followed by the others we had to live with at home, which lasted all night. Then I had a brilliant idea.

"Mom, it's getting almost impossible for me to get to school on time by bus these days. How would it be if I had a bike to ride? Then I wouldn't have to depend on buses any more?" It worked!

"FRIDAY, SEPTEMBER 6TH: "SLEPT THROUGH MOST OF OVERNIGHT RAID. HEAVY GUNFIRE AT 2:15 A.M. AND A NOISY RAID JUST AS I WAS ABOUT TO GO TO SCHOOL. NO BOMBS DROPPED NEAR US, THANK GOODNESS. CAME HOME FROM SCHOOL AFTER LUNCH. HOT DAY. MOM, WILLIAM AND I WENT SHOPPING AND BOUGHT ME A BIKE."

Since the daylight air raids became a regular occurrence, the bus services had become unreliable; buses were rerouted where bomb craters or wreckage blocked the roads, and some routes were closed altogether. Mom agreed that I needed a bicycle to get to school on time.

When William heard the news, he again took charge. "Yes, I believe I know quite a bit about bikes. I'll go with you." This was right up his alley, and he wasn't about to be left out.

The day had dawned like one left over from July, with hot sun and not a cloud in the blue sky. The *Luftwaffe* seemed to be taking the day off, so that afternoon the three of us took the bus to our neighboring suburb where there was a shopping center with a hardware store that sold bicycles. Mom and I watched while William spent an hour scrutinizing all the bicycles, finally finding one that met with our unanimous approval.

"I'll bring it home for you, Bunty," volunteered my hero, with the air of a Knight of the Round Table. So William rode the bike home several miles in the sweltering heat, while Mom and I rode home in comfort on the bus. He and the bicycle arrived home after we did. Red-faced and sweating, a strand of damp brown hair sticking to his forehead while a little channel of wetness dripped down it into one eye, William looked as if he had reached the point of no return. He never let me forget his sacrifice that day; he reminded me of it again on one of my visits to England forty years later!

Not wanting to embarrass William, I named my bicycle Percival, after my favorite Knight of the Round Table.

The London Blitz

"SATURDAY, SEPTEMBER 7TH: HOT, SUNNY DAY. STAYED INDOORS ALL MORNING EXPECTING MOANING MINNIE BUT NO SIRENS SOUNDED. AT 4:45 P.M. CAME A TERRIBLE AIR RAID ON THE CITY. HUNDREDS OF NAZI PLANES STARTED A TERRIFIC FIRE AT THE EAST LONDON DOCKS. FIRES STILL BURNING WHEN NIGHT RAID BEGAN."

Mom and I had wondered why there had been no air raids so far that day, but in late afternoon Moaning Minnie began to wail. After the noise of the sirens died down, we heard what sounded like a swarm of angry bees approaching. Headed for the shelter, halfway down the backyard we stopped and looked up. A terrifying sight in the sky above our heads temporarily immobilized us with shock. As far as the eye could see, like a plague of black locusts, were hundreds of Nazi bombers flying wingtip to wingtip in tight rectangles, formation after formation, surrounded by their escorting fighter planes, heading for the City of London. History has since recorded that on this raid there were almost four hundred bombers and more than six hundred fighters, a Nazi armada covering eight hundred square miles of air.

As we watched, glinting silver in the late afternoon sun against the blue canopy of sky, a handful of tiny R.A.F. fighter planes began to weave their way through the Nazi formations to challenge the advancing mass of metal. I felt a lump in my throat and tears soon followed. Mom and I stood on our back lawn with tears running down our cheeks, watching those little Davids as they dared to confront such a mighty Goliath. We couldn't move, but it was almost unbearable to watch; our hearts ached for the young men battling against such enormous odds to protect us and the city. Planes spiraled down in flames before our eyes. Suddenly realizing our danger, we ran to the shelter until the horrible spectacle had eventually passed over Upper Woodside and the All Clear sounded for us at last.

Moaning Minnie wailed again as darkness fell. On our way to the shelter for the night, we looked toward the city and saw a savage red glow lighting up the entire horizon. The city of London was burning! White searchlight beams probed the sky, crisscrossing to focus on enemy planes for the pitifully few anti-aircraft tracer shells to find their mark.

All night long, waves of *Luftwaffe* bombers fed the fires started that afternoon, raining more death and destruction on London's crowded East End and the docks. We heard later that the fires were so widespread and intense that London fire companies gave up trying to battle them, having to watch vainly as they burned themselves out.

We sat, afraid, frustrated and helpless, in the shelter. We were beyond words, and we were too tired to talk anyway. Fear was replaced by rage and hatred, but exhaustion finally claimed us and we slept.

Some time later we were jolted awake by a bomb screaming down to explode with a giant crash nearby. When we climbed out of the shelter next morning, we heard it had fallen in front of St. John's Church, only a few blocks away.

The Battle of Britain, its conquest by air, planned by the Germans, entered into its next terrible phase. The R.A.F. had won the first phase by the skin of their teeth; postwar estimates state that, when it ended, only two hundred and eighty-eight fighter planes were still in service--an eleven-day supply, according to their average losses during this period.

But now the Battle of London had begun. The London Blitz had started in earnest, and in Bishop's Hill we knew with trepidation that this time we were part of the target. Tight security prevented us from knowing the tiny number of fighter planes defending us against the Nazi hordes; it was just as well!

The spectre of invasion lurked in the back of our minds; rumors had multiplied about enemy landings on the south coast, but no invasion fleet had appeared. What we didn't know was that Hitler had postponed "Operation Sea Lion" landings from their new date of September 11th to allow the German navy to sow mines in the English Channel, to protect the flanks of a full-scale German invasion now planned for September 24th.

"SUNDAY, SEPTEMBER 8TH: PETER AND WILLIAM CAME TO SEE IF WE WERE O.K. HAD A VISIT FROM PAUL BATES, HOME FROM SEMINARY. TOOK HIM TO SEE THE CRATER AT ST. JOHN'S. THE AIR IS FULL OF SMOKE FROM THE FIRES IN THE CITY."

Throughout the day, a pall of black smoke drifted south from the city, shrouding Upper Woodside in an eerie half-light as the sun struggled to penetrate it. Its acrid fumes were in our eyes, throats and nostrils. It saturated the air around us for days to come, as the city's fires burned themselves out.

That morning William was first to arrive, and was soon sitting with a cup of tea on one of the comfortable living-room chairs now in the dining room. He had just said: "I came over to check and make sure you two girls were O.K. after last night's raid," when the doorbell rang and Peter erupted into the front hall. Without pausing to take off his coat, he flopped down in a comfortable chair.

Mom quickly poured him a cup of tea. After a few gulps, he was obviously bursting to tell us something. He peeled off his coat as he began his story.

"Listen to this. I was walking home from the bus stop at the top of Bishop's Hill last night when that incendiary raid began again on London. All of a sudden an incendiary bomb whistled down and landed almost at my feet. It lay there sputtering and, for a few seconds, I was so surprised I just stood there looking at it. "

"Whatever did you do?" Mom broke in breathlessly.

"Well, I didn't want it to explode," Peter continued, waving his hands in the air, "and I was so scared that I suddenly had to pee, so I just peed on it. It stopped spluttering, but I didn't hang around to see if I'd put it out; I ran like hell." The room rocked with our laughter.

"That's one for the books, Peter," said Mom, wiping the tears from her eyes with her apron after she had stopped laughing, "and just think what a great war story it will be to tell your grandchildren!"

The doorbell rang again, and in came Paul Bates. "Hello, everyone. Glad to see you, Pete and Willy. I've been visiting the family for the weekend. Just thought I would stop by before I go back to seminary and see if you were O.K. after that raid yesterday." His face looked strained.

Mom hugged him. "Thanks, Paul, so thoughtful of you. How are your family, and how do you like your new home?"

The Bates family had moved to a suburb on the other side of London while we were evacuated to Hove at the beginning of the war, and we hadn't seen Paul for almost a year. He had grown taller and filled out. His blue eyes still twinkled as I remembered them beneath his thatch of blond hair, but the barber had done a lot of clipping on the floppy mop I once knew.

"The family are fine," he replied "Gwen likes her school. Mom is settled, but lonely now that Dad is stationed in Iceland. Big brother Steve has joined the R.A.F. I'm really not home very often these days; they work us pretty hard at the seminary."

From then on, William, Peter and I nicknamed Paul "the Cardinal," so he would keep in mind our great expectations from his chosen career.

Mom brought the teapot from the kitchen. "Well, Paul, you're just in time. Have a cup of tea, then go down with all of them and see what damage was done by the bomb that narrowly missed St. John's Church last night."

St. John's Church was off-limits. There was a police barricade across the road outside the church grounds. A yawning hole had been blown by the bomb as it had buried itself in the middle of the road, closing it to traffic. The barricade forced us to stand well back from the crater. The bomb must have severed a water main: water was spurting into the street. Several houses across the street seemed to have been damaged, but were still standing. The police wouldn't allow anyone near. St. John's appeared not to have been damaged. Reassured, we trudged back to Bishop's Hill. I thought to myself: "No buses to school tomorrow; thank goodness I can ride Percival and detour around that crater to pick up the road to school on the other side."

When I got home, Mom was looking at a picture in the newspaper. She said: "Look at this photo of the King and Queen, Bunty. Here they are walking through the rubble in the East End of London right after an air raid, to comfort those poor souls who have lost their homes, and the Queen in her high-heeled shoes, too!"

King George VI and Queen Elizabeth did much to boost morale and endear themselves to the hearts of citizens during the London Blitz. History records that Queen Elizabeth wrote to her sister: "Sometimes it makes me feel almost ill. I can't tell you how I loathe going around these bombed places; it breaks one's heart to see such misery and sadness." Later in the Blitz, when a five-hundred-pound bomb exploded on Buckingham Palace, she said she was glad that she could now "look the East End in the face".

Bombed Out

"TUESDAY, SEPTEMBER 10TH: RODE MY BIKE TO SCHOOL IN THE MORNING, BUT WAS TURNED BACK BY POLICE. UNEXPLODED INCENDIARY BOMB ON OUR BASKETBALL COURT AND A DELAYED ACTION BOMB BURIED IN THE FOOTBALL FIELD AT THE BOYS' SCHOOL."

I had been riding to school on my new bike, Percival, without any problems, but today I was stopped at a police barrier across the street at Ravenhurst by an English "Bobby" and an air-raid warden.

"Sorry, Miss, you'll 'ave to turn back, I'm afraid." The burly policeman sounded apologetic. "There's a hunexploded incendiary on yer netball court out back there,' he continued, "and over there at the boys' school a hunexploded bomb arf buried in their football field. The schools will bofe 'ave to be closed until such time as the disposal squad 'as time to defuse 'em."

With no other option, I pedaled back to Bishop's Hill to tell Mom the news. "They told me that both schools will be closed indefinitely, until the bombs have been dealt with, and heaven knows when that will be," I said, trying not to look too unhappy about it.

"Wait 'til I tell Dad once more that all he's getting for his tuition bills is an uneducated daughter," Mom wailed.

Although I didn't know it at the time, I had had my last class at Ravenhurst, and I would never see Lizzie, Pie Face, Molly, Jessie, or any of my Ravenhurst friends again.

"WEDNESDAY, SEPTEMBER 11TH: WENT TO THE ICE RINK THIS MORNING WITH WILLIAM, BUT IT IS CLOSED. HAD THREE AIR RAIDS TODAY."

Rationalizing that the obvious alternative to school was to have fun, William and I optimistically took a bus to the ice rink. A large sign on the locked doors said: "CLOSED INDEFINITELY DUE TO WAR CONDITIONS."

William said in disgust: "Well, so much for 'Keeping Calm and Carrying On.' Let's go home."

As we boarded the bus we heard the air-raid sirens, convincing us that closing the ice rink sounded like a sensible decision. Air raids continued day and night; some days there were three, some four, then came the long overnight raid we grew to expect as blackout time arrived.

"SUNDAY, SEPTEMBER 15TH: HAD A RELATIVELY PEACEFUL NIGHT, FOLLOWED BY A HORRIBLE RAID THIS MORNING AND AGAIN THIS AFTERNOON. BOMBS DROPPED IN NEXT TWO STREETS TO OURS. BLAST LIFTED TILES OFF OUR ROOF. ALL UPSTAIRS CEILINGS HAVE FALLEN DOWN. ONE OF MOM'S FRIENDS WAS KILLED."

Dad was home for the weekend from his latest job near Wrexham in North Wales. Mom and I sat at the breakfast table, looking out through the French doors of the dining room into the back garden, which was beginning to show signs of fall. Mom's pink, purple and white asters flooded the flower borders with color as if to brighten the view of the ugly Anderson shelter standing in its hole, and the last roses of summer were gallantly showing off on the trellis arching over Dad's homemade concrete birdbath. All at once the air-raid sirens sounded.

"Oh damn Hitler, can't a feller even have his breakfast in peace?" Dad was indignant, but not too perturbed. Working away from home, he had so far missed what it felt like to be included in the *Luftwaffe's* worst efforts as they concentrated on the city of London itself.

"I suppose we'd better take the rest of our breakfast into the shelter, just in case," he conceded.

Snatching up cups of tea and remnants of toast, we dashed down the yard. My knitting was already there from the last time--a pair of gloves for Peter's mother. I had just taken it out of its protective bag when we heard the now familiar, uneven throbbing of German planes and responding fire from the ack-ack barrage. But this time there were also sounds of explosions getting closer to us, and after the "All Clear" we heard that another bomb had fallen near the church.

Things got worse during the afternoon raid. A bomb screamed down toward us, directly over our heads. Holding our breath in terror, we experienced that split second of silence before the explosion, wondering if the next moment would end in oblivion. We felt the suction of the bomb almost drawing us up toward it as it fell. The shelter seemed to sway with the force of the blast. Our eardrums felt as if they would burst. We sat in stunned silence for an instant, then Mom shouted: "The house, the house--is it still there?"

She lunged toward the shelter doorway, ignoring the fact that bombs were still dropping, but Dad grabbed her arm and hauled her back into the shelter. Mom sat on her lawn chair sobbing, until the noise outside had subsided. We all clambered out of the shelter and looked down the backyard toward the house. To our relief, it was still there. Tears rolled down our faces and we just stood there and held each other. Smashed terra cotta tiles from the roof littered the flower beds.

The bomb had fallen in the "Dig for Victory" gardens behind our back fence, just a few yards from the shelter. Still in shock, Mom said shakily: "Well, as long as we're still here, I'll make us all a cup of tea."

Not long after the "All Clear" our elderly volunteer air-raid warden, Mr. Brown, knocked on our door.

"There were several direct hits on the next street, and I'm just checking to see if you're O.K.," he said in a wobbly voice, "but I have bad news about Mr. and Mrs. Greenaway." Mrs. Greenaway was a friend of Mom's.

"Oh, please tell us what happened." Her voice was filled with anxiety.

The warden struggled to continue: "Well, they had just come home in their car when the sirens went off, and they sat in the car for awhile before getting out to take cover. Their house received a direct hit." His voice quavered as if squeezing out each word. "When they were found, they were still sitting in their car seats. Both were dead; the blast from the bomb was so great that it blew the glass windshield into the car and their heads were severed from their bodies."

Dad and I recoiled in horror; Mom began to cry softly. The war had literally struck close to home for the first time, killing people who were our friends. Our lives would never be the same again and for the first time we felt fully the capacity for pure hatred.

From this day on, the residential southern suburbs of London were to receive showers of random bombs the *Luftwaffe* decided to drop on us. We were convinced that as well as the bombs they deliberately jettisoned on residential areas on their way to their main targets in the city, the Nazis also dumped on us any leftovers on their flight path back to their bases in Europe.

Dad exploded: "Well, Bunty, that's the last straw! I have to go back to Wrexham tomorrow, but before I go I'll see if I can get someone to come and patch the roof temporarily, then as soon as I arrive in Wrexham I'll make arrangements with my landlady to let you and Mom come to Wales, away from the bombing. There's no education here for you now, and none in the foreseeable future. We might as well make up our minds to leave the house to good luck, and hope it will be left standing."

September 15, 1940 is now officially recognized as the climax of the Battle of Britain. We couldn't have known at the time, but history tells us that with Britain still stubbornly refusing to sue for an armistice, two days later Hitler decided to postpone the invasion, "Operation Sea Lion," indefinitely. Instead, he planned to crush the spirit out of the British from the air while turning his attention to a full onslaught on Russia, his "Operation Barbarossa." But the spectre of invasion would continue to haunt us for the coming years, and the *Luftwaffe* wasn't yet through with London, or with Bishop's Hill.

"MONDAY, SEPTEMBER 16TH: B.B.C. REPORTS THAT DURING SEPTEMBER THE R.A.F. BROUGHT DOWN 185 NAZI PLANES! IT RAINED ALL DAY WITHOUT STOPPING. SPENT ALL DAY TRYING TO CLEAN UP BEDROOMS. WILLIAM AND HIS PARENTS CAME TO SHARE OUR SHELTER FOR THE NIGHT."

"Oh, Bunty, just look at my beautiful rugs, they're ruined!" Although the number of enemy planes reported as destroyed was impressive, Mom was more concerned about her beautiful, thick Mairzapur bedroom carpets from India, encrusted with ceiling plaster which had fallen from the bomb blast during yesterday's raid. A steady rain coming through holes in the roof left by the missing tiles turned it into a cement-like substance, almost impossible to scrape off. We did our best, then, soaking wet ourselves, abandoned it in disgust.

William and his Dad were still a few days away from completing their Anderson shelter, so for the next two nights they shared ours. Outside, the London Blitz raged. Inside, the six of us sat propped up on our lawn chairs with pillows wedged between our heads and the shelter's metal sides. Our parents fell asleep almost immediately. William and I struggled to muffle our giggles every time their pillows slipped and fell with a "plop" on the dirt floor, waking them up with a start.

Throughout that first night the noise of the air raid outside the shelter was almost drowned out by the chorus of assorted snores inside. Periodically, everyone woke up when a bomb fell close by, or when one of us climbed out of the shelter to use the bathroom (or a convenient bush), or when someone else began shuffling around, groping in the dark for an escaped pillow.

"TUESDAY, SEPTEMBER 17TH: THREE RAIDS TODAY. DIDN'T ATTEMPT TO GO TO SCHOOL. STANDISHES AGAIN CAME TO SHARE OUR SHELTER FOR THE NIGHT."

The next night was equally uncomfortable in the sardine-like conditions in the shelter, but outside it was cloudless, with a full moon. In wartime it was called a "bomber's moon," but to William and me, looking at it from the door of the shelter through Dad's binoculars, it was a thing of beauty, as was the star-studded arch of the sky around it. I remembered walking back to my billet from school at Hove in the winter blackout, and the wonder I felt.

I said in a whisper to William: "You know, I can't help thinking that in spite of all this destruction there's something more powerful above it all, keeping life in proportion; the beauty of nature, the coming and going of the seasons, the permanence of the moon and stars up there. It gives me comfort and hope. How about you?"

William said nothing, just squeezed my hand.

Refugees!

"WEDNESDAY, SEPTEMBER 18TH: STANDISHES FINISHED THEIR OWN SHELTER. NO MORE FEELING LIKE A CAN OF SARDINES! WE ARE LEAVING LONDON! DAD HAS A PLACE FOR US IN NORTH WALES, WHERE THERE IS A GOOD GIRLS' PREP SCHOOL. BUT FIRST WE'RE GOING TO SEE UNCLE BRYAN AT LEICESTER ON OUR WAY TO WALES." However comforting it had been to have William with me, I had to admit that, without the Standishes, our shelter was actually roomy!

The London Blitz showed no signs of lessening in intensity and it was obvious that we were caught up in an endless and impossible struggle to carry on our normal lives. Dad had made the necessary arrangements for us to be with him in the safety of North Wales, two hundred miles away from the bombing.

Mom said quietly: "Bunty, I know how hard it's going to be for us, closing up our home and going to live again with strangers, and a new school for you, but at least we'll all be together and you'll have a chance to finish your education. And just imagine what the neighbors will say when we come home again speaking Welsh!"

Once more I had to get my mind around the idea of moving to a strange place and a new life, leaving William, Peter and Paul behind again in the south of England. For how long this time? Would I ever see them again? I threw myself across my bed and cried.

As fate would have it, a few days later it was reported that on this day in the North Atlantic a Nazi U-boat had torpedoed the liner *City of Benares*, carrying among its passengers ninety CORB evacuees. The ship sank in thirty minutes, and only thirteen of the ninety children aboard survived. That clinched it for Mom and Dad: my name was withdrawn from the waiting list for Canada. They need not have bothered; the tragedy also marked the closing of the CORB program by the British Government.

"Well, Bunty," I said to myself, "your evacuation to Canada isn't going to happen after all; goodbye, Duffys. But although in some ways it's a bit of a let-down, I must confess I'm mostly feeling relieved. Most important, the three of us are still together and safe."

I slept well that night, as I'm sure did Mom and Dad.

"SUNDAY, SEPTEMBER 22ND: SPENT ALL MORNING PACKING. WENT TO SAY GOODBYE TO WILLIAM AND PETER'S MOMS, AND SOME OF THE NEIGHBORS."

Peter stopped in that afternoon to wish us a safe journey. "You know what a rotten writer I am, Bunty, but I'll do my best." His voice was unusually serious. In a near-whisper, he added: "I'll miss you." Blinking hard to hide my tears, I gave him a quick kiss.

William came to see us after supper. He looked miserable, but didn't say very much. He stayed with us all evening until the night raid began, then reluctantly bade us farewell before going off to join his parents for the night in their newly finished air-raid shelter.

"Be sure to write, love." His voice sounded strangely gruff.

"You too, and God bless," I whispered. The words were oddly squeaky. After he left the tears came again, and that same old feeling of being a helpless puppet on a string.

"MONDAY, SEPTEMBER 23RD: MR. STANDISH DROVE US TO THE STATION IN LONDON. DAMAGE ALL OVER THE PLACE. RAILWAY STATION PRETTY MUCH BASHED-UP." MOM AND I LEFT WHAT REMAINS OF ST. PANCRAS STATION AT 12 NOON AND ARRIVED AT UNCLE BRYAN'S IN LEICESTER ABOUT 4:15 P.M. HAD A WONDERFUL NIGHT'S SLEEP."

One more time we had packed the few personal belongings we could carry and prepared to leave the house. The holes in its roof had been given temporary patches, and we had cleaned up the bedrooms as best we could. As I had done many times before, I went from room to room, wondering if the house would still be there the next time we came back to Upper Woodside.

A horn tooted outside. It was time to leave. Mom locked the front door. Not trusting ourselves with a backward glance, we got into the car with our suitcases. On the drive into London to the big railway terminal, we were appalled at the scenes of devastation. Everywhere buildings were crumpled into piles of rubble. In some of them searchlights shone through the morning mist on weary Civil Defence crews digging for survivors, while ambulances waited.

At the big Victorian station, the once-elegant arched roof of wrought iron and glass was now twisted and gaped open to the sky. We picked our way past piles of broken glass swept up after the air raids until we reached the platform, where the black hulk of our train was standing, its steam engine making hissing noises and puffing out clouds of smelly vapor, as if impatient to begin tugging at the long string of passenger cars behind it.

We had always had reserved seats on the train before the war, but now they were a thing of the past. Mom was anxious.

"We'll have to keep our eyes open, Bunty." Her voice rose to a shout: "Oh, quick, nip into to that compartment, I can see two empty seats!"

Mom and I scrambled aboard; a whistle blew, and in minutes we were lurching out of the station. In addition to civilians, the train was crowded with uniformed servicemen and women. Those who couldn't find seats in the compartments sat in the long corridors of the train on their suitcases or duffel bags, making it almost impossible to squeeze past them to the bathrooms. I can't ever remember saying "Excuse me, please" so many times in succession.

The air reverberated with the sounds of humanity, as people shouted to be heard above the noise of hundreds of conversations. British uniforms and accents mingled with those of other European countries, the battered remains of whose forces had fled to Britain in the hope of returning some day to their homelands.

The train gathered speed, chugging north through countryside from which alternately sprouted stacks of smoking factory chimneys and fields of golden grain. After about five hours we pulled into another station blackened with soot, and Mom shouted: "Time to get out, I can see Uncle Bryan standing on the platform to meet us."

According to plan, when we reached the Midlands we interrupted our train journey to North Wales at Leicester, which had been spared from the intense bombing raids we had just left behind, to spend a few days of rest and relaxation.

One of the passengers helped us take our bulky suitcases down from the luggage rack above our seats. We stepped off the train with cramped legs and feet into the waiting arms of Mom's younger brother, Bryan Ditchfield, a big, six-foot-plus bear of a man, built just like my grandfather and with the same genial disposition. Picking up our suitcases as if they were light as two feathers, he boomed: "Marnie and Maureen are waiting at home; let's go."

We followed Uncle Bryan to his front door. The front hall was crowded with people all talking at once: Uncle Bryan's wife, Marnie, my little cousin Maureen, and behind them, to our surprise, Gram and Grandpa Ditchfield from Sunderland. They had also come to Leicester for R&R, respite from the intensive bombing in Sunderland whose seaport, shipbuilding and coal-mining industries were a prime target for the *Luftwaffe*.

What an unexpected and wonderful family reunion! Ten years my junior, my four-year-old cousin Maureen didn't impress me as much of

a companion on this visit, but after many y
again and have remained close friends eve

No wonder my diary records a "wonder
first entire night we had slept through in mor
dured thirty-one consecutive days and night:
ordeal would continue. By the time the Battle
Blitz were over, the Nazi bombing had gone o__ days and
nights. Mom and I counted our blessings to have escaped to safety.

The next few days at Leicester did wonders to restore our spirits
and energy. We enjoyed such luxuries as long walks, clothes shopping
and movie-going without hearing an air-raid warning. We felt strength
returning to our tired bodies, and renewed hope to our bomb-scarred
minds.

But soon it was time for us to resume our journey.

A Foreign Land

"MONDAY, SEPTEMBER 30TH: ARRIVED AT WREXHAM ABOUT
3:30 P.M. DAD MET US AT WREXHAM TRAIN STATION. MET OUR
LANDLORD, MR. LLEWELLYN, HIS WIFE, AND DAUGHTER MEGAN."
We were greeted at the door by Dad's Welsh landlord, Mr. Llewellyn,
a small, slightly built man with a cigarette dangling from one corner of
his mouth. His pinched face almost suggested that malnutrition was a
fixture in his life.

"Follow me, thank you." Mr. Llewellyn spoke in the lilting accent
typical of the Welsh people.

I was shown to my tiny bedroom, while Mrs. Llewellyn, a large apron
over her flowered housedress, bustled about making a pot of tea. She
and her ten-year-old daughter Megan were thin; both looked as under-
nourished as our landlord, and our landlady was obviously pregnant.
It was also obvious that they could use the rent money for our rooms.
The small brick house was clean, but rather unattractive and sparsely
furnished, with well-worn furniture.

only a few minutes to unpack my small collection of posses-
Then, putting on a smile for my parents to hide my homesickness,
went downstairs to tea.

"TUESDAY, OCTOBER 1ST: WENT INTO TOWN THIS MORNING
WITH MOM AND MRS. LLEWELLYN TO HAVE OUR RATION BOOKS
TRANSFERRED, THEN TO THE EDUCATION OFFICE TO SEE ABOUT A
SCHOOL FOR ME. ENROLLED AT WREXHAM PARK GIRLS' SCHOOL."
I soon realized we had moved to a different country; a place where
people spoke the guttural Welsh language on every street corner, and
whose musical English sounded like a long, strangely accented song.

Once the largest town in Wales, Wrexham was quite unlike anywhere I had ever been before. Trading in sheep, cattle and other animals since medieval days, its "beast market" was famous, as was its
leather industry. In the Industrial Revolution of the nineteenth century
Wrexham's industries expanded to include coal mining, beer-brewing
and brickmaking. Fortunately for us, Wrexham's current industries
didn't interest the *Luftwaffe* pilots, who had a prime target at the port
of Liverpool, thirty miles away.

Mrs. Llewellyn left us at the old market square where the beast market had been. It was surrounded by restored, half-timbered buildings.
In two of them Mom found a butcher's and a grocery store where she
could shop for our rations.

We explored the town center with its quaint Victorian glass-roofed
arcades and small shops. As we walked past a newsstand, a large poster on the sidewalk proclaimed: "LONDON BLITZ CONTINUES: SINCE
SEPTEMBER, SIX THOUSAND KILLED, TEN THOUSAND INJURED." I
said a quick prayer for the safety of the friends we had left behind.

After visiting two offices, one to transfer our ration books and the
other to enroll me at Wrexham Park School for Girls, Mom said: "It's
such a lovely day, let's walk over to see this famous St. Giles's church
I've heard so much about."

On a hilltop overlooking Wrexham, we found St. Giles's Parish Episcopal Church, with its old stone walls and windows glowing golden in the morning sun. Its richly carved 135-foot tower dating from the sixteenth century is known as one of the Seven Wonders of Wales. I noticed a large stone tomb standing near it in the churchyard. Letters carved into the stone spelled out a name: ELIYU YALE, ESQ.

"Look, Mom, there's a poem carved on one side of it." I leaned closer to read the inscription.

The poem eulogized a man I had never heard of before, who had been Lord High Sheriff of Denbighshire County. Wrexham is the county seat, which is why "Eli" is buried at the Parish Church of St. Giles. How could I ever have guessed that sixty years later, in my new American homeland, I would be living in Connecticut, in a town just a few miles away from the great New Haven university named after its benefactor, Elihu Yale? And how could I guess that on its campus is the Wrexham Tower, a scaled-down replica of the one on St. Giles' Church? Another strange coincidence in my life's journey. My life seemed to be filling up with coincidences--or were they part of a special destiny designed for me? I began to wonder!

"THURSDAY, OCTOBER 3RD: WENT TO WREXHAM PARK GIRLS' SCHOOL FOR THE FIRST TIME. CAME HOME WITH MARGARET THOMAS AND BESSIE JONES."

I tried on my new Wrexham Park school uniform; it was distinctly more old-fashioned than Ravenhurst's. Reluctantly, I had put away my rather stylish Ravenhurst "A-line" school tunic, beige blouse and beige stockings, substituting Wrexham Park's shapeless, box-pleated garment and black stockings, and replacing the cheerful coat-of-arms badge on my Ravenhurst blazer pocket with one showing a black lion on a red background. I never did find out how that originated, but under it was a Latin inscription. Loosely translated it said: "Modesty, At All Costs." My rebellious nature asked: "Am I going to like this school?"

It was an easy walk from Llewellyns' house to my new school, a dull, red brick building, but with an aura of elegance about it.

"Let me introduce a new student from London," intoned Miss Davies, my new home room mistress. I cringed, with memories of my early elementary school days when I had to stand up to greet a sea of strange faces at school after school, as Mom and I followed Dad and his work around England.

After classes were over, two of my new schoolmates walked over to me. They were an odd couple, to say the least. Maggie was tall and thin, with straight, light brown hair resting on her shoulders. It was parted to one side and rescued from flopping into her eyes by a lone bobby pin. Her round-rimmed glasses slid down whenever she moved her head, triggering a reflex action to push them back to the bridge of her nose. Bessie matched my short height and was slightly pudgy. With fair skin, blue eyes and blonde braids, she could have boasted Anglo-Saxon ancestry, in contrast to the stocky Welsh girls in the class with their Celtic heritage of darker skin, brown hair and eyes.

"I'm Margaret Thomas, but call me Maggie, and this is Bessie Jones," said the tall girl rather breathlessly.

"And I'm Elizabeth Jones, but everyone calls me Bessie," said the blonde female Anglo-Saxon, holding out a tentative hand. As I shook it, Maggie peered at me through the round frames of her glasses, which immediately slid down her nose a fraction of an inch. Shoving them up in place, she said: "We were hoping you'd like us to walk home with you, as it's your first day."

Wondering how they had singled me out for their friendship, I stammered: "Of course, I'd love it."

They were as good as their word, and remained my best friends for the next two years, the three of us sharing laughter, tears and schoolgirl confidences as if we had known each other all our lives.

"FRIDAY, OCTOBER 4TH: THIS SCHOOL'S NOT SO BAD. SEVERAL OTHER ENGLISH EVACUEES HERE. I'M WAY BEHIND IN MY STUDIES,

THOUGH, ESPECIALLY IN LATIN. THEY HAVE ASSEMBLY ON FRIDAYS ENTIRELY IN WELSH; DIDN'T UNDERSTAND ONE WORD!"

As if my life hadn't already been full of challenges, next came a new unwelcome one. Wrexham Park girls were now more than a month into the new school year. Their education was uninterrupted by the war, and I soon realized how far behind I was.

I complained to Mom: "Oh, I'll never catch up. Worst of all, I'm two years behind in Latin!"

It was a shock to discover that the school's Latin curriculum had been started two years before Ravenhurst's. Two foreign languages were required for graduation, so since I had opted to add Latin to French at Ravenhurst, it seemed logical to try to continue with it. Miss Lloyd, my new Latin mistress, was a pleasant improvement over Ravenhurst's Pie Face. After my first Latin lesson, she asked me to stay behind after class.

"Bunty, I can help you to catch up if you would like me to, but it will mean you'll have to stay behind after school. If you are willing to do that, check with your parents to see if they agree, and we'll work at it together."

Week after week she stayed after school with me to study. I never did quite recapture the lost years of vocabulary, but eventually I was able to translate Caesar's *Gallic Wars*, Book VIII and Ovid's *Metamorphoses*, although rather painfully, along with the class. A little jingle in my diary says it all: "Latin is a language; at least it used to be; It killed off all the Romans, and now it's killing me!"

"SATURDAY, OCTOBER 5TH: HAD A LETTER FROM WILLIAM. SIX PAGES!"

William's letter told of the ongoing London Blitz, continuing fragmented sleep, and the struggle to keep up the daily routine of living. Our worlds were two hundred miles apart; it seemed like two thousand. Missing him terribly, I put down his letter and tears of homesickness again took over.

In retrospect, there was a very good thing about my separation from William; now I had time to concentrate on schoolwork!

"SUNDAY, OCTOBER 6TH: TOOK A BATH IN A TIN WASHTUB IN THE KITCHEN."

Not far from its town center, Wrexham fanned out into streets of nineteenth-century houses, most of which looked like dark red brick boxes, row after row, each crowned with a dark gray slate roof. The Llewellyns lived in one of these. It was unheated and drafty, and there was no bathroom, only an indoor toilet and washstand. Coming down with a cold I felt chilled, but I really did need a bath! I wondered how I could take one in a washbasin!

Mom sounded apologetic. "Mrs. Llewellyn says you can take a bath in front of the coal fire in the kitchen, dear."

While I was thinking: "How on earth can I do that?" Mom and Mrs. Llewellyn appeared, carrying by its handles a large, empty metal washtub between them. It reminded me of the one William and I had used to drain the Anderson shelter! They set it down in front of the open kitchen fireplace.

"Aha, Bunty," I thought, "remember when you read that book *How Green Was My Valley*, where the Welsh miners had nowhere to wash the coal dust off themselves at the mine, so they sat in a tin washtub of hot water in the kitchen and took a bath? This must be it, but that was back in the last century!"

Sure enough, Mrs. Llewellyn took two kettles full of boiling water off the kitchen fire and poured them into the tub.

"Now, look you, we'll cool it off with some cold water, and you'll have enough for a nice warm bath, Bunty."

I just nodded my head, peeled off my clothes and got into the warm water. Armed only with soap and a washcloth in the confines of a half-filled washtub, with my knees up around my neck, I knew just how those Welsh miners must have felt.

Before going to bed I wrote in my diary: "OH WELL, I DO FEEL LOTS LIGHTER WITHOUT ALL THT DIRT; AND AT LEAST I'M CLEANER AND WARMER NOW!"

"MONDAY, OCTOBER 7th: HAVE A COLD BUT CAN'T AFFORD TO MISS SCHOOL, I'M SO FAR BEHIND. I'M BORED STIFF HERE! I HATE WREXHAM. I HATE SCHOOL!"
Compared to Upper Woodside, Hove, Thorpe Village and Guildford, Wrexham was boring. Although there were two movie theaters, there was no ice rink, no beach to enjoy, no gardening to do, no William or Peter bursting into the house with chatter and laughter to share, no irreverent, fun-loving schoolmates.

I worried and wondered if each letter from William and Peter would be their last. Again, I flung myself across my bed and cried. But strangely, as the weeks went by, I began to experience a surprising change; my boredom was gradually replaced with the true joy of learning. I was becoming a good student!

Bad News

"THURSDAY, OCTOBER 24TH: LETTER FROM MRS. BALDWIN. BOMBS DROPPED ON BISHOP'S HILL HAVE DEMOLISHED TEN HOUSES. OUR HOUSE LOST ITS ROOF, WINDOWS AND OUTSIDE DOORS."
Mrs. Baldwin was another friend of Mom's who lived across the street from our home, near the end of Bishop's Hill. Telephone service was gone, she explained, and she had decided to send a letter because then she could write more than a telegram would permit. The contents of her letter were grim. Dad took the next train to London. When he arrived back in Wrexham two days later, he had a sad story to tell.

"Our house is in a terrible mess," he began, not knowing how to hide his distress from us. "Blast from the bombs has lifted off the roof, the ceilings upstairs have all collapsed, outside doors are blown out, and shattered glass from the windows is all over the inside of the house." He put his arms around Mom, protectively. "And I hate to have to tell you this, dear, but some looters must have walked right in through the open doorway after the raid. The filthy bastards cleaned out our good clothes from the bedroom closet, as well as the silverware from the dining-room buffet. They also took our clocks and my short-wave radio, and Lord knows what else!

"Before I came back to Wrexham I went to the War Damage Commission office to apply for an inspection. We have to see if the foundation is still sound; if not, the house will have to be demolished. We'll just have to hope for the best. In the meantime I've hired a contractor to cover the roof, rehang the front and back doors, and nail plywood over the window frames."

At least the house would be made safe from the rain coming in and from further looting, until it appeared on the War Damage Commission's priority list for inspection. I expected Mom to cry, but she was obviously in a state of shock, and it would be awhile before the news would take effect. In the following weeks we worried and waited for the report on the house's foundation. Good news finally came: "Foundation sound. House unfit to live in, but not damaged beyond repair." We still had a home to go back to! But when?

The next day brought letters from William and Peter. I shed tears of relief that they were safe after the bombing, although they repeated the bad news our neighbor had already given us about our house and said that fortunately their homes had escaped being damaged in the air raid. We expected to hear the worst about casualties, but again good fortune had smiled. Our neighbors were safe in their air-raid shelters; miraculously, there were no deaths and only a few cuts and bruises.

"MONDAY, OCTOBER 28TH: ITALY HAS INVADED GREECE. ANOTHER DOWNED GERMAN PLANE IS ON VIEW NEAR OUR SCHOOL--A DORNIER 'FLYING PENCIL.'"

With the devastating news from Bishop's Hill on my mind, my attention was certainly not on a new war front in the far-off Mediterranean, where Italian dictator and Hitler's Axis ally, *Il Duce* Mussolini, had invaded Greece. My mind was on things closer to home: worry over the continuation of the London Blitz and my struggle to keep up with my studies in Wrexham.

Although Wrexham was a lot safer than London, we were still experiencing reminders of the war. Nazi planes were being shot down in increasing numbers by Wrexham's ack-ack guns as they flew over its airspace to bomb the docks at the key transatlantic port of Liverpool. Many planes survived their damage and force-landed, usually in fields around town.

Pinned to this page of my diary was a yellowing newspaper cartoon. In the background of the picture is a field, out of which sticks the tail of a wrecked enemy plane with a Nazi swastika painted on it. In the foreground, a farmer is giving directions to a tourist at the edge of the field. He points down the road and says: "If you want to find the village, go down the lane, past the Messerschmitt, bear left at the Dornier, then turn sharp right at the two Heinkels. You can't miss it!"

I was surprised to see Dad had arrived back early when I came home from school. Ever the opportunist, I pleaded: "Oh, Dad, please can we take a walk while it's still daylight to see one of the German bombers that's been shot down?"

"Go on, the two of you, while I get dinner ready." Mom sounded relieved to have us out from underfoot while she tackled the rations in the Llewellyns' tiny kitchen. Dad and I walked past my school to the edge of town. In a field ahead of us was the downed German bomber. Its narrow fuselage was intact, as if the pilot had been careful about landing it, and little boys were climbing all over its black hulk. I stopped one of them and asked him what kind of plane it was.

"Well, look you, me Dad says it's called a Dornier Flying Pencil because it is so narrow-looking, you know. There's a Heinkel over there in the next field. It's sure I am that the crews must have been taken prisoner." The boy smiled and dashed back to join his friends in the Dornier's cockpit."

Enthusiastically, I said: "Oh, Dad, let's go and look at the Heinkel." Dad pretended not to hear. He merely glared at the Dornier and growled: "Well, at least this is one less of the bastards. Let's go home for dinner."

"THURSDAY, NOVEMBER 7TH: ROOSEVELT IS PRESIDENT OF THE U.S.A. FOR A THIRD TERM. HOORAY! SOMETHING HAS HAPPENED TO THE LONDON BLITZ."
President Roosevelt's personal friendship with Churchill had drawn the British people close to the United States. We were glad to hear we still had a friend as President across the Atlantic.

Once again, Hitler had ordered a change of tactics for the German *Luftwaffe*. The intensity of the Blitz on the docks and the centers of trade and commerce in the city of London lessened, but Nazi targets were now designed for the purpose of demoralizing the civilian population, both in the city and in the suburbs, in a new effort to break their spirit. Hitler still dreamed of leading a conqueror's parade into a surrendered Britain.

"FRIDAY, NOVEMBER 15TH: NAZIS BOMBED TWO LONDON HOSPITALS; COVENTRY WAS BLITZED, DESTROYING THE CATHEDRAL."
The London Blitz as we knew it was over. November 4th was the last of fifty-seven consecutive days and nights of intensive bombing. Many devastating raids would follow, but the London Blitz had failed to crush the spirit of the civilians in that battered city, or that of the British people. Goering considered that the price his *Luftwaffe* had paid in loss of aircraft and their crews during the onslaught was too great to be worth continuing.

"I wonder what that Nazi devil has up his sleeve for us next?" Mom asked, as we listened to the radio news that morning. We would soon find out. Hitler's next strategy to crush Britain would show his growing vindictiveness in attacking civilian and non-military targets. The evening newspapers had photos of the carnage at two of London's hospitals, reeling from the *Luftwaffe*'s bombs. The sight of the victims and of war damage turned our stomachs.

"Lord Haw-Haw," Germany's nauseating English-speaking radio propagandist, delivered a new message aimed at intimidating his British listeners. The Germans, he said, would use their air superiority to demoralize the British by attacking targets chosen from the famous German Baedeker guidebook. He warned that every historic landmark listed in the guidebook would be bombed until none was left standing.

Although the "Baedeker Raids" didn't officially go into effect for another two years, the news of the bombing of beautiful and priceless Coventry Cathedral, which had been a place of worship for over nine hundred years, was a foretaste of what was to come. History tells us that five hundred Nazi bombers took part in the raid. But the indignation aroused by this deliberate act of vengeance, and the vicious Baedecker raids later, served not to break Britons' spirits, but only to enrage them.

"MONDAY, NOVEMBER 25TH: IT'S COLD HERE. HAD THE DAY OFF FROM SCHOOL TO WATCH THE PARADE FOR WREXHAM'S 'WAR WEAPONS WEEK.'"
Mom and I had arrived in Wrexham in our summer clothes when the weather was still warm, but we now needed our winter clothing. Before we left London, Mom had given William's mother a front-door key to our house, then she had packed away our winter clothes in a cabin trunk, out of sight of possible looters. A few weeks ago she had sent William's mother a list of the warm clothes we would need, which Mrs. Standish had offered to pack and mail. After two weeks of wandering around the British Post Office, the large box finally turned up. Mom said: "Am I glad to see my winter coat again! It must be about ten degrees colder here than it is in London. And am I glad I hid our warm clothes from those wretched looters!"

I hung up my new Donegal tweed coat, which I was to have worn to travel to Winnipeg. "I wonder what I would have been doing today, Mom, if I had been evacuated to Canada instead of ending up here in Wrexham?"

Mom was very quiet, and it dawned on me she must have been thinking I could have been at the bottom of the Atlantic Ocean! Wrexham wasn't so bad, after all.

"Hey, Bunty, let's meet down at the market square on Monday and go to the parade." My new friends Maggie and Bessie were anxious to introduce me to some of the local goings-on.

"War Weapons Week" parades were held in towns all over Britain during the war to boost morale. The parade route through Wrexham was lined with cheering townspeople, eager to show appreciation for the efforts of the armed forces and volunteer war organizations. Schoolchildren were given the day off to attend; elementary school students were already jumping around on the curbs, waving the small Union Jack flags supplied for the occasion. We heard cheering in the distance, then swinging round the corner came a uniformed brass band, followed by units borrowed from the nearby Army, Navy and Air Force bases with their marching bands and anything on wheels: tanks, anti-aircraft gun carriers, trucks, and whatever other equipment they could spare. Men and women in the uniforms of volunteer services: Auxiliary Fire Service, Air Raid Wardens, Home Guard, Women's Voluntary Service and British Red Cross made up large contingents. Bringing up the rear of the parade, the local Boy Scouts and Girl Guides were given a rousing cheer as loud as those for the brass bands and polished marching of the uniformed men and women.

Mrs. Llewellyn went to watch the parade with Mom. After she had been standing for half an hour, she felt faint, and Mom caught her frail body as she fell to the sidewalk. An A.R.P. warden ran to help, but she revived after a few minutes. Mom confided to me later: "If that woman doesn't start eating for two, she'll lose that baby!"

Christmas in Exile

"FRIDAY, NOVEMBER 29TH: CHESTER GOT HIT LAST NIGHT. WENT TO BED AT 1:45 A.M. GUNS AND BOMBS STILL BANGING AWAY IN THE DISTANCE."

Chester was about ten miles away, just across the Welsh border in England. It would have qualified well for Lord Haw-Haw's Baedeker list. No British town was richer in archeological and architectural treasures; Baedeker undoubtedly described it as one of the most visited towns in England, with encircling city walls dating back to the Romans, an exquisite cathedral and perfectly preserved medieval buildings. Happily, today's tourists see Chester with its war damage repaired, and once more it is one of the most picturesque towns in their pocket guidebooks.

"MONDAY, DECEMBER 9TH: GOT "A" IN MY FRENCH EXAM AND "A" IN BIOLOGY. WHOOPEE!" I BEAT ETHEL WATKINS! THINGS ARE LOOKING UP ALL OVER! WE HAVE CAPTURED 4,000 ITALIANS IN NORTH AFRICA."

"A"s and "B"s started showing up on my test and exam papers, despite the much stricter atmosphere at Wrexham Park, and mistresses who were intolerant of anything short of excellence. Not only was I becoming a reformed student, I was also actually relishing my competition with a luscious blonde in my French and biology classes. Ethel was not only beautifully sexy, with her blonde hair, blue eyes and curves in all the right places, but she was very smart, too. I envied and hated her when we first met; she made me very aware of my boyish short haircut and lack of interest in girly clothes, but by the end of my exile in Wales, we were not only able to play off each other as competitors but were also the best of friends.

I thought: "I wonder what Lizzie and Pie Face would say if they could see their problem student now?" Just "wondering" was a source of great satisfaction!

Meantime, there was still a war on. The North African desert campaign against Mussolini's troops was going well at this point for the Allied Eighth Army, led by the flamboyant General Montgomery, known to all as "Monty"; in fact, it was astonishing how the Italians were surrendering in overwhelming numbers. A cartoon appeared in the newspapers showing two British "Tommies" lying propped up against a palm tree at an oasis. One was saying to the other: "I don't have any trouble getting to sleep these nights; all I need to do is start counting Italian prisoners instead of sheep!"

"THURSDAY, DECEMBER 12TH: "WE HAVE CAPTURED SIDI BARRANI AND MORE THAN 40,000 ITALIANS THIS TIME!"
North Africa was half a world away, but it was a morale booster to read about the Allied successes. However, the Italians, who continued to surrender by the tens of thousands, were by now putting a strain on the Allies who had to house and feed them!

"I can hardly blame the poor bastards," commented Dad, glancing at Mom and me over his newspaper. "If I were them, I'd be looking for a square meal, too!"

Another cartoon found its way into my diary from Dad's newspaper. It showed a British private standing outside a desert headquarters, with lines of Italian prisoners, their hands on their heads, behind him, stretching to the horizon. The officer in charge is saying to the private: "How on earth did you get so many prisoners?" The private replies: "Sorry, sir, I just happened to mention that we sometimes have beef stew for dinner!"

"FRIDAY, DECEMBER 20TH: SCHOOL CLOSED FOR CHRISTMAS VACATION. TOOK A BAGFUL OF MR. LLEWELLYN'S EMPTY CIGARETTE BOXES BACK TO THE TOBACCONIST FOR THE WAR EFFORT."
"Mom, I'm so bored!" I complained. Living in someone else's house, especially with six people in one as small as the Llewellyns', I always

seemed to be colliding with someone else in a hallway or on the way to the front door, so I spent most of my time in the privacy of my tiny bedroom, taking refuge from the noisy activity in the house to do my school work and write letters, propped up with pillows on my bed; the only place in the room where I could sit down.

As the winter weather closed in and daylight became shorter, the long walks that I had looked forward to earlier in the year had all but vanished. Maggie's and Bessie's company couldn't compare with William's and Peter's visits. I found some compensation in William's and Paul's frequent, lively letters, as well as much less frequent ones from Peter, but my diary bemoaned my boredom with life by mentioning that I had already knitted two baby sweaters for Mrs. Llewellyn, and had just finished a large-man-sized Royal Air Force blue one to send to William for Christmas.

Mr. Llewellyn must have sensed my boredom; he was always thinking of an errand or two for me to run. Sometimes it was to return a library book, and on Fridays he often handed me a battered shopping bag full of small white boxes, and said: "Bunty, love, is it something you would do for me? Will you return these to the tobacconist next time you go past?" Paper was in short supply; every scrap was needed for recycling. Although cigarettes were rationed, enormous quantities were smoked. Their only useful residue was the paper boxes they came in, which were collected and taken back to the tobacconist shops to be recycled, with a few pennies' reward for returning each one. Mr. L. was always ready to accept the change I brought back, but never shared any of the reward with me! He must have thought *he* was doing *me* a favor!

"WEDNESDAY, DECEMBER 25TH: DEAR OLD SANTA SLITHERED DOWN THE CHIMNEY TO LEAVE ME MONEY FROM SUNDERLAND RELATIVES, NEW SLIPPERS, A NEW DIARY, A BOX OF CHOCOLATES, A TURQUOISE NECKLACE, AND MISCELLANEOUS CANDY, ORANGES AND NUTS."

The Llewellyns shared their Christmas with us. Mom had helped with the food shopping, finding some "under the counter" goodies such as an orange or two which had escaped onto the black market, an institution which flourished in every city, town and village, during these years of scarcity.

Mom's initiation into Wrexham's black market had been at the butcher's; she heard that he sometimes sold "under the counter" unrationed meat such as chickens and also rabbits provided by the local poachers. She waited in line for over an hour to ask the butcher if he had any, but he shook his head. Before Mom left, the woman behind her in the line spoke to the butcher in Welsh. He replied, also in Welsh, then went into the back room, brought out something wrapped in newspaper, and handed it to the woman. Mom almost exploded when she glimpsed, hanging out from between the newspaper pages, a pair of chickens' feet! Privately, I was glad she hadn't found a rabbit for dinner, but I would have loved that chicken! As for Mom, she lost no time in asking Mrs. Llewellyn to give her a crash course in conversational Welsh, ready for her next trip to the butcher's.

This time last year we had been with the Hornes in the south of England; now we were sharing Christmas with a family in North Wales. "Where would we be next Christmas?" I wondered.

"MONDAY, DECEMBER 30TH: THE CITY OF LONDON HAS BEEN SET ON FIRE AGAIN BY INCENDIARY RAIDS. BLAST THESE HUNS! BLAST THEM TO HELL! SEVERAL OF SIR CHRISTOPHER WREN'S MOST BEAUTIFUL CHURCHES WERE BURNED OUT. HEAVY CIVILIAN CASUALTIES."

My diary entry was a howl of rage and frustration. Hitler had targeted central London again with incendiary bombs, burning out the area around St. Paul's Cathedral. Miraculously, Wren's eighteenth-century masterpiece survived the conflagration once more, but the thought of the reduction of some of his exquisite little churches to charred skeletons sickened me with hatred for the Nazis. I thought of the Londoners in that ravaged city, and as I said a prayer for them, I murmured thanks for our own escape from the holocaust of the London Blitz and its aftermath.

That New Year's Eve, "First-Footing" didn't seem so important. I could only hope that our good luck and safety would continue in the year ahead.

ஃ

A Little Life Lost

"FRIDAY, JANUARY 3RD: R.A.F. BASHED BREMEN. WALKED TO TOWN TO GET OUR WEEKEND FOOD RATIONS, ALSO UNRATIONED MEAT PIES AND TEA CAKES. IN THE PARK THE CHILDREN ARE SLEDDING." Rallying from the Battle of Britain, the R.A.F. began to strike at Hitler's supply lines, Bremen and other German ports. Although Britain still stood alone against the Nazis, there was a new glimmer of light on the horizon. A lifeline of planes and volunteer air crews from the U.S. had begun to filter across the Atlantic, and Lend-Lease was being debated in the halls of Congress.

"Bunty, I've got my shopping list ready for you." I was on Christmas vacation from school, and Mom was beginning to send me on more errands these days. There was no bus for her to ride, and her feet were getting worse with arthritis, so I walked into town to collect our week's rations to spare her the painful trip there, and then back again, carrying heavy groceries.

Unlike our hostesses during evacuation, Mrs. Llewellyn didn't have our ration books; Mom did her own cooking. To avoid a melee in the tiny, cold kitchen, she resorted to buying as many ready-made meals as possible. Fish and chips and cooked meat pies were not rationed, although there was a long wait in line for them. On Fridays, for a special treat at teatime, we ate a round, flat, sweet raisin bread called a tea-cake. Toasted and spread, while it was hot, with some of the butter ration, it was delicious. All that starch and fat didn't make for a healthy diet, but at least it kept us feeling full!

On my walk into town I watched children playing in the park. Memories returned of last winter in Hove, ice skating and sledding with laughing, rosy-cheeked friends. I thought: "Here in Wales I'm just a spectator, on the outside, looking in." And also, uneasily, I realized I wasn't a child any more.

"SUNDAY, JANUARY 12TH: LONDON HAD ANOTHER FIRE RAID. MOM, DAD AND I ATTENDED AN A.R.P. DEMONSTRATION ON 'HOW TO DEAL WITH AN INCENDIARY BOMB.' WENT TO ST. GILES'S PARISH CHURCH FOR EVENING SERVICE. BEGAN KNITTING SOCKS FOR THE ARMY WITH KHAKI YARN FROM THE W.V.S."

The city of London was still enduring Hitler's aerial *Blitzkrieg* with which he hoped to win the war. The worst incendiary raid of all was considered to be in December 1940, on the 114th night of the London Blitz. A newspaper photographer captured an iconic photo of St. Paul's Cathedral in the light of the searchlights, with the silhouettes of fire-gutted skeletons of buildings all around it. The huge gold cross still shone atop its dome as the great church emerged through surrounding clouds of dense black smoke. It was saved largely due to the efforts of a special group of firefighters who were determined not to let it be destroyed. The photograph became a symbol of British resilience and courage.

I closed my eyes and visualized again that unforgettable first day of the London Blitz last summer, when hundreds of Nazi bombers set fire to London. I could almost smell the curtains of smoke that drifted over Upper Woodside afterwards, leaving an indelible reminder in my memory.

Today, in the middle of the A.R.P. demonstration, I suppressed a giggle as I thought: "I wish we had Peter here to tell them how *he* dealt with an incendiary bomb!"

Although we missed attending services at St. John's, Mom, Dad and I found new comfort in the beautiful old church of St. Giles at Wrexham.

At Evensong there was always a special feeling of peace and hope with which to end the day.

I must have done nonstop knitting at Wrexham. At least using khaki yarn was a change from R.A.F. blue. But I had to laugh at my diary entry. Surely I didn't mean knitting socks for the *whole* Army?

"WEDNESDAY, JANUARY 15TH: GERMANY IS GOING TO THE AID OF THE ITALIANS IN THE MEDITERRANEAN. OUR EIGHTH ARMY HAS CAPTURED BARDIA IN NORTH AFRICA, ALONG WITH 30,000 MORE ITALIAN PRISONERS! BITTERLY COLD DAY. SLID ALL THE WAY TO SCHOOL ON FROZEN SNOW. ONLY TEN OF US SHOWED UP IN MY CLASS. SAW A SQUAD OF SOLDIERS TRYING TO MARCH. ONE OF THEM LOST HIS BALANCE AND SAT DOWN UNEXPECTEDLY ON THE ICE."

In order to protect his source of Balkan oil, Hitler could not put off much longer rescuing Mussolini's troops from the advancing Greeks. Soon the Germans would intervene in North Africa to rescue the Italians there, too.

Dad gave his little wry grin. "The Germans had better hurry up and get to North Africa, or at the rate we're taking Italian prisoners, our side will have the whole Italian Army to feed!"

Wrexham was in winter's grip. Snow clearance equipment and expertise then wasn't what it became in later years. The local authorities did a fair job of keeping the sidewalks free of snow, although they glazed over again overnight. Maggie, Bessie and I skidded all the way to school on the icy pavement. We held onto each other to stay upright, occasionally crashing to the ground as our feet slipped and we landed in a giggling pile, with our arms still linked.

This morning as we floundered along, we were surprised to hear a hoarse voice behind us bawl: "Move it, lads, pick 'em up, 'eft right, 'eft right." A squad of soldiers out for exercise from the neighboring Army base came abreast of us, marching with military precision along the side of the road where snow had been compacted into several inches of ice. They overtook us, arms swinging rhythmically up and down as they marched. Just then, one of them in the last row slipped and sat down suddenly on the ice. With difficulty he staggered to his feet and then slithered off in embarrassed haste to catch up with his comrades, none of whom missed a beat in their marching or broke ranks to help him. Helpless with laughter, the three of us ended up once more in a tangled heap on the sidewalk.

"SUNDAY, JANUARY 19TH: SNOWED ALL NIGHT AGAIN, BUT AT LEAST IT MAKES THE DIRTY STUFF LOOK CLEAN. IT NOW MEASURES THIRTY INCHES IN MOST PLACES. BUSES AND TRUCKS BEING DUG OUT. MRS. LLEWELLYN LOST THE BABY."

It snowed and snowed. The roads were a disaster; everywhere there were stranded buses and trucks surrounded by men trying to dig them out. After some of the girls were injured from falls on the ice struggling on their way to and from school, "the Welsh Dragon" (our nickname for our bad-tempered headmistress) at last relented and closed Wrexham Park's doors for a week, after which we were able to wade to school safely through the melting slush.

In the middle of this bitterly cold night I was awakened by a woman's screams. Lights came on in the house; I heard hurrying feet and the murmur of lowered, urgent voices. On my way to the lavatory I met Mom, fully dressed. As she rushed by me, she said: "Go back to bed, Bunty; everything's all right." Next morning I was told that Mrs. Llewellyn had had a miscarriage. Mom and the midwife had stayed up with her all night. I thought of the Dearbornes' beautiful baby girl back in Hove, and my heart ached for Mrs. Llewellyn, but although she had lost her baby, she was safe; in her run-down condition, she could have died, too.

"FRIDAY, JANUARY 24th: GOOD OLD 'MONTY.' OUR EIGHTH ARMY CAPTURED TOBRUK IN NORTH AFRICA AND 25,000 MORE ITALIAN PRISONERS! WHATEVER WILL WE DO WITH THEM ALL?"

In contrast to the frozen wastes of Wrexham were the blazing sands of the North African desert. Attached to many pages of my diary with rusty paperclips were fragile newspaper clippings, war news headlines and maps of the battlefronts as the Allies swept westward from Egypt to take over Mediterranean coastal towns from the Italians.

Hitler was furious with his Italian partners for their poor performance in the North African arena, where Mussolini's armies were currently fleeing from the Allied advance. The brilliant Nazi general Erwin Rommel was sent with his "Afrika Korps" to begin a new offensive. Rommel's cunning and skill soon earned him the title "the Desert Fox" and proved to be a costly challenge for British General Montgomery.

"SUNDAY, FEBRUARY 16TH: THIS IS MY FIFTEENTH BIRTHDAY! SOME MONEY FROM SUNDERLAND, BUT OTHERWISE JUST ANOTHER DAY. STAYED IN ALL DAY DOING HOMEWORK. WENT TO EVENSONG AT ST. GILES CHURCH IN EVENING. IN THE NEAR EAST, TURKEY IS GETTING READY FOR WAR."

There were no extra rations for birthday parties. I complained to Mom: "Our homework load is terrible on weekends. They must think all we have to do in our spare time is read textbooks and write reports! What a way to spend a birthday!"

Mom tried to comfort me: "The war can't last forever, dear. Just wait, Bunty, when it's all over we'll have the biggest birthday party ever."

All day long on my fifteenth birthday I had sat up in bed to study, with a textbook on my lap, the only fairly flat surface in my bedroom for writing reports and essays. After hours of writing, concentration and memorization, the tranquility of the evening service at St. Giles's was a welcome respite to put my life back into perspective again.

Turkey eventually came into World War Two on the side of the Allies, but never actually participated in the conflict which had already flung our family members and friends to the corners of the earth. Two cousins were in the Far East in Singapore, another in Egypt, an uncle was on the North Atlantic, threatened by Nazi U-boats, and another had survived the trauma of Dunkirk, but with permanent emotional damage. Paul's father was serving in Iceland. William wrote to say he was hoping to be sent to Canada for pilot training as soon as his papers came through for him to join the R.A.F.

As my fifteenth year began, my diary again reflected my feelings of isolation and boredom. I missed William, Peter and Paul more with every letter, and even grudgingly I missed George, though he hardly ever wrote. There was plenty of activity at school, but I thought petulantly to myself: "I believe that living in an all-female society like this must be what it's like to be in a nunnery! But from what I've seen of the boys here, I don't mind!"

Letters from the boys back in Upper Woodside told about the lessening of the air raids in and around our suburb, and how they were making new friendships. Their world and mine no longer had much in common; I had the feeling that I was gradually losing them.

"SATURDAY, MARCH 1ST: BULGARIA JOINED THE AXIS. YELLOW SWINE! SPENT MOST OF DAY IN BED, FEELING ROTTEN AND DOING NOTHING BUT STILL FEELING TIRED. MOM THINKS I HAVE THE 'FLU'."
My immature view of the Balkan countries entering the war on the side of Germany was one of sheer contempt. But they really had no choice, and the overwhelming power of the Nazis' need for oil crushed them one by one.

Meantime, unknown to me at the time, this was not just another cold; I had the 'flu. My health had not been good since we had arrived in Wales. Diary entries tell of loss of weight, colds, coughs, and days in bed feeling "rotten". Periodically, I noted in my diary: "HAD PANCAKES FOR DINNER." Month after month of a skimpy, poorly balanced diet on rations was taking its toll on my teenage body's need for good nutrition. Several times my diary reported: "HAD RABBIT FOR DINNER." Mom must have mastered enough "conversational Welsh" to get an occasional one from the butcher. I wished she hadn't!

"TUESDAY, MARCH 11TH: I'M FEELING A BIT BETTER. MOM LET MAGGIE COME FOR A VISIT THIS AFTERNOON. THE 'LEND LEASE' BILL HAS BEEN SIGNED INTO LAW BY PRESIDENT ROOSEVELT."

The 'flu had kept me in bed for almost two weeks, with no energy to talk, read or even get dressed. I was probably sick enough to go to the hospital, but in wartime hospitals were needed for sick servicemen and women and other priority patients, so the rest of us had to just go to bed and hope for the best.

As I began to feel better, Maggie came to visit. Bounding up the stairs into my bedroom, she saw me propped up in bed. Turning to her with a welcoming smile, I said: "Oh, Maggie it's great to see you!" Maggie promptly passed out on the floor. I was horrified. Surely I didn't look *that* bad! But at fainting Maggie was an expert. She suddenly revived, and said with a smile: "Oh, I did it again." She "did it again" often during our stay in Wrexham but never seemed the worse for wear, just scared us all half to death.

Thanks to Maggie, I shall always remember that this was the day President Roosevelt signed the Lend-Lease Act, to lend Britain an influx of food, weapons and equipment in return for ninety-nine-year leases on nine British bases on the eastern coast of Central and North America, stretching from British Guiana to Newfoundland.

Dad was actually bubbling with enthusiasm as we listened to the news on the radio. He said, gleefully: "This is what Churchill meant when he said to Roosevelt: 'Give us the tools and we will finish the job.' Good for Roosevelt for getting the bill through Congress!"

Lend-Lease was the lifeline Churchill had been hoping for, and it can be credited with bringing Britain back into the World War Two conflict with the boost she so badly needed.

Dad only had one negative comment that I remember: "Too bad they send us all those terrible Grade B movies with Lend-Lease, though," he grumbled; "they must want us to think all Americans are cowboys and gangsters!"

Hitler's Deputy Arrives

"SUNDAY, MARCH 16TH: WENT TO STAY WITH THE GRIFFITHS."

Mr. Llewellyn was due to report to the Draft Board in a few weeks; Mrs. Llewellyn announced that she would close up the house and go to live with her mother for the duration of the war. We were going to have to move again. The week after, it seemed that all our problems were solved.

"Dad, I was talking to Doreen Griffith at school, and she says her Mom and Dad are willing to rent us rooms in their big house." I had come home from school feeling important that I had found us a potential new home.

"Wonderful," said Dad, after he and Mom met with Mr. Griffith. "They have a lovely home, and I've arranged for the rent and the date we can move in. It's a bit far out of town, but there will be a bus to get me to work and to get you to school."

"Oh, Dad, please can I have Percival sent up from London so I could ride my bike to school? We've been lucky so far that nobody has stolen him. I've missed him terribly, and I wouldn't have to use the bus when the weather is good."

"That's not a bad idea, Bunty," Dad agreed. "I'll telephone William and have him put your bike on the train as soon as possible."

Three days later I was at the Wrexham train station to collect Percival and ride him home.

The Griffiths lived in an upscale house in a suburb a few miles outside of Wrexham. The house was beautiful, but the housing arrangement proved to be a disaster. This was an unhappy home. The Griffiths bickered at each other over everything including Doreen, whose life was that of a spoiled only child who manipulated both of them to her own advantage. Worse, they treated us as interlopers rather than tenants. After a month, we were looking for somewhere else to live.

"FRIDAY, APRIL 4TH: WE LOST BENGHAZI IN NORTH AFRICA TO GERMAN TROOPS."

"The Desert Fox," Nazi General Rommel, and his crack Nazi troops, the Afrika Korps, were on a roll in Libya, North Africa, re-taking from the Allies the towns they had captured from the Italians. In defeat our spirits fell as quickly as they had risen in victory.

"SUNDAY, APRIL 27TH: WE ARE MOVING AGAIN! I SHALL BE GLAD TO GET OUT OF THIS MISERABLE HOUSE WITH ITS MISERABLE OCCUPANTS."
Life had become intolerable at the Griffiths'. The only thing they seemed happy about was the rent check. But, thanks to Dad and a good real estate agent, coming up would be my "World War Two Move Number Nine!"

"TUESDAY, APRIL 29TH: THINGS ARE LOOKING UP! MOVED BACK TO WREXHAM TO NEW LODGINGS."
"Come in, and welcome to you." Bronwyn Evans and her father were at the front door of the modern, two-story brick house in a much better neighborhood than the Llewellyns', but still within easy walking distance of town and school. In his late fifties, Mr. Evans, a slightly built man with thinning hair and a sadness about him, had recently become a widower. In contrast, his plump, nineteen-year-old daughter Bronwyn sparkled with life and good humor. She had taken over the household routine after her mother died, and showed us through the house before ushering us upstairs to our rooms. Bouncing up the stairs at her heels was their exuberant Welsh Corgi, "Davey," named whimsically after the patron saint of Wales, Saint David. I bent down to pat him, and he wagged his little stub of a tail so hard I thought he might wag it off altogether.

"There's no hurry for you, my dears," Bronwyn sang out in her lilting Welsh voice. "When you're settled in, just come down and I'll have tea ready for you."

On our guided tour of the house we saw a large billiard table in a corner of the parlor, also a thick cork dartboard on the wall. This house was obviously lived in and enjoyed! The thought of my mother whiling away the hours playing billiards and darts while I was in school for the day sent me into a fit of the giggles. I buried my face in the pillow on my new bed and shook with relief and laughter. When I recovered enough to come down for tea, this time my smile was a real one. Already we felt comfortable in our new "digs." The house was light and airy; somewhere we could hear dance music playing and Bronwyn singing. We would live here happily until we left Wales.

"SUNDAY, MAY 4TH: "DOUBLE BRITISH SUMMER TIME BEGAN (2 HOURS AHEAD). LIVERPOOL HIT BADLY LAST NIGHT. R.A.F SHOT DOWN 18 NAZIS. HEARD THE CUCKOO FOR THE FIRST TIME THIS YEAR. SUMMER IS HERE."

Double British Summer Time was enforced from 1940 to 1945, to save energy and to enhance the war effort by giving more daylight hours to agricultural and factory workers. In addition, according to postwar statistics, it saved for the season the equivalent of seven million dollars in fuel costs and also reduced the crime rate and the number of road casualties. There was a downside, however. We were going to school every morning in the dark, and couldn't get to sleep at night because all summer the sun was still shining at ten o'clock! The farmers complained loudly that their cows were coming to the barns to be milked at the wrong times, and in the northern reaches of Britain, the Scots protested that they were spending the first half of every day in the blackout

Dad looked up from reading his newspaper: "Those damned U-boat wolf packs are still making mincemeat out of the North Atlantic shipping," he snarled, "and the blasted *Luftwaffe* seem to be able to bomb Liverpool at will, to destroy the docks and ships trying to unload their cargoes. They still have the upper hand there, I'm afraid. It's all very depressing. To hell with Hitler."

Nazi U-boat "wolf packs" continued with their stranglehold on Britain's North American lifeline for food and military supplies. The

Luftwaffe continued to blitz the port of Liverpool to destroy ships and cargoes that had escaped the submarines. For seven nights, air-raid sirens wailed in Wrexham. We lay awake listening to the familiar sounds of attack and defence--Nazi bombers droning overhead in the dark and bombs and anti-aircraft shells exploding in the distance.

It was good to see something on a brighter note in my diary. Once again the return of the cuckoos was celebrated with as much front-page news as the American groundhog awaking from its winter nap to see its shadow. My diaries always reported when I heard the cheerful sound of the cuckoo for the first time. On the same date last year I had heard it on the South Downs at Hove! I thought of how close we had come to death in the months between, and said a heartfelt prayer of thanks for our survival.

"SUNDAY, MAY 11TH: LONDON HAD A BAD RAID LAST NIGHT. WE BROUGHT DOWN 33 NAZI BOMBERS. WENT FOR A WALK IN AFTERNOON WITH MOM AND DAD. PICKED SOME BLUEBELLS FOR BRONWYN."

While we were enjoying a walk in the beautiful countryside around Wrexham picking fragrant wild hyacinths to put in a vase, the people of London were reeling from its last major air raid. History calls it the worst raid of the London Blitz. Fires and high-explosive bomb damage were widespread not only to targets like bridges, warehouses, factories and railroad lines, but also some of the beautiful historic buildings through-out Westminster, including several medieval churches and the Gothic grandeur of the Houses of Parliament and Westminster Abbey. Records show that one and a half thousand Londoners were killed and over two thousand seriously injured in this raid.

"TUESDAY, MAY 13TH: HITLER'S DEPUTY RUDOLPH HESS LANDED IN SCOTLAND AND GAVE HIMSELF UP!"

My version of one of the most bizarre stories of World War Two, the ar-rival of Hitler's Deputy on British soil (based on the first sketchy reports), filled two entire pages in the space in my diary labeled "Memoranda." In my fifteen-year-old scrawl I wrote: "On the night of Monday, May 12th, German radio announced that Deputy Fuehrer Rudolph Hess had disappeared in an airplane and failed to return. The report said Hitler had given orders that Hess was not to fly at any time, and speculated that either Hess was insane and committed suicide or that he had had an accident." My diary continued:

"In the early hours of Tuesday, May 13th, several miles away from the estate of the Duke of Hamilton in Scotland, a farmer saw an airplane flying low over one of his fields. He saw a parachute coming down, so he grabbed a pitchfork and waited for it to land. The man on the parachute hit the ground and injured his ankle. When he saw the farmer standing over him with a pitchfork, he smiled and tried to get up. Satisfied that the man was not dangerous, the farmer dropped his pitchfork and helped him to the farmhouse.

"The man refused a cup of tea, but took a glass of water. He chatted with the farmer's family in good English, and showed them a photo of his little boy. The farmer called in the local Home Guard. When they arrived, the man told them his name was Alfred Horn. Later, he revealed that he was Rudolph Hess, Hitler's Deputy, and showed photographs to prove it. His ankle was broken, so he was taken to Glasgow Hospital, where he was given psychiatric tests. These showed that he was quite sane and in good health, refuting the German news statement that Hess had lost his mind. He was then taken to an undisclosed destination."

The details and purpose of Hess's incredible mission to Britain are still contradictory and shrouded in mystery; the whole true story may never be known. Officially it was reported as the unauthorized, bizarre act of a self-motivated, slightly unbalanced individual. Another version is that Hess undertook a mission to fly to Scotland and parachute onto the estate of the Duke of Hamilton at the direction of Hitler to persuade the duke, a member of the now discredited Anglo-German Fellowship Association, that Britain could not win the war and should surrender.

Whatever the true facts were concerning his arrival in Scotland, Hess was detained by the British for the remainder of the war, found guilty of war crimes at the Nuremberg Trials in 1946, and sentenced to life imprisonment. He died at ninety-three, in Spandau prison in West Germany, his grandiose "coup" having been a total failure.

Turning Points

"MONDAY MAY 26TH: TODAY'S BAD NEWS: H.M.S. *HOOD* HAS BEEN SUNK BY THE *BISMARCK*! BETTER NEWS AT SCHOOL: ENGLISH CLASS INTERRUPTED WITH A SUMMONS FOR MAGGIE AND ME TO PLANT POTATOES, WHICH TOOK ALL MORNING AND MOST OF THE AFTERNOON."

The battle cruiser H.M.S. *Hood*, commissioned in 1920, had had an illustrious career with the Royal Navy. In 1941 the battle that sank her was fought with the German battleship *Bismarck*, then the largest and fastest in the world in her class. The *Bismarck* had been decimating tons of Allied shipping on Britain's supply lines, and had so far effortlessly escaped the Royal Navy. On May 24th, she was pounced upon by the aging H.M.S. *Hood* and other Royal Navy ships in the Denmark Strait.

The *Bismarck* sank the *Hood* in minutes, blowing her apart with a direct hit before withdrawing to safety. Of the 1,419 officers and men on board the *Hood*, only three survived. The nation mourned their loss.

I shall never forget the stricken look on Dad's face when he heard the news. His identification with the fate of the *Hood's* lost crew was personal; he had barely survived the sinking of three ships he had served on as a Royal Navy lieutenant in World War One. This was one of the few times I had ever seen him moved to tears. "Those poor lads, they didn't have a chance," he said bitterly. Then he raged at the *Bismarck*, pounding his fist on the table: "I hope our boys can get the bastard and send her to the bottom!" He wouldn't have long to wait.

Meantime, on the home front, Britain's "Dig for Victory" campaign had been brought to the schools. A representative from the Ministry of Food came to Wrexham Park to give a lecture at a school assembly one morning.

He began: "Good morning, girls. As you know, all over Britain civilians are being encouraged to produce as much of their own food as possible; fruit bushes are being squeezed into flower beds and lawns are being dug up to grow vegetables." His graying moustache quivered as he warmed to his subject: "Now girls, *you* can help the war effort by growing vegetables too, right here at school. One of our experts will come to your school and instruct you in how to plant and grow them. I know you will enjoy taking vegetables home to your parents and sharing them with your neighbors."

To our amazement the "Welsh Dragon" agreed! She allowed him to ask for volunteer gardeners, and he quickly started to take down names; Maggie and I were at the head of the line. The flower borders around the school were soon dug up and ready for National Service.

By now we had already been shown how to plant lettuces; Maggie and I each had a row of them doing nicely. Today it was time to learn how to plant potatoes.

It felt quite important to be called out of class. For me, it was a relief to be rescued from a particularly sarcastic attack on one of my essays by a hard-to-please English mistress, nicknamed "Old Smutty." I thought: "Wow, what a break; I could really get used to this!" I closed my English book in triumph, ignoring the dirty look "Old Smutty" turned in my direction as I made a hasty exit into the exhilarating freedom of the outdoors.

"TUESDAY, MAY 27TH: THE ROYAL NAVY SANK THE NAZI BATTLESHIP *BISMARCK*. HOORAY FOR THE ROYAL NAVY! HORRIBLE LESSONS THIS AFTERNOON. I'M FEELING PRETTY ROTTEN ABOUT LIFE IN GENERAL, TODAY."

When the *Hood* was sunk, Churchill issued his famous command to the Royal Navy: "SINK THE *BISMARCK*." An avenging fleet was assembled to hunt her down. That story in books and movies has now become a classic. The *Bismarck* was finally sunk!

Dad reacted with a whoop of satisfaction. "Serves the bastards right," he exulted, "three cheers for the Royal Navy." To him, the men lost on the *Hood* had been avenged, and Britain's honor saved.

History calls this victory one of the early turning points in the war, but I thought: "My whole generation is growing up on hatred, justified by vengeance. Will we ever be able to change, after the war is over?"

"WEDNESDAY, JUNE 4TH: WATERED LETTUCES IN MY LUNCH HOUR. HAD A GREAT CHEMISTRY LESSON THIS AFTERNOON. MADE HYDROGEN SULPHIDE GAS - NEARLY EXPIRED! SCHOOL HAD TO BE EVACUATED UNTIL LAB WAS AIRED OUT!"

In an ex-flower bed Maggie and I lavished tender, loving care on our lettuces, which were growing well. A week ago the school's advisor from the Ministry of Food had lined up the volunteers and yelled at us in his gruff Welsh voice like a top sergeant addressing his new recruits: "Girls, you're doing a fine job, but I want you to watch me now, and I'll show you a little trick about how to get your lettuces to grow a heart." Intrigued, we gave him our full attention. Producing a ball of thin twine from his pocket, he continued: "You take a length of thin string like this, and tie it round the whole lettuce like I'm doing".

Feeling a bit sorry for my little plants, I obediently trussed the poor things up and hoped for the best. I thought: "If I were a lettuce I don't think this would encourage *me* to grow a heart!" But now, a week later, I noticed that each one had formed a plump little "heart" of edible leaves; it had worked!

Our chemistry course was commonly known as "Stinks," and on this occasion it earned its name. Our young Chemistry mistress broke school tradition by allowing us to call her "Nella" instead of Miss Robinson. She was my favorite teacher. Nella treated us like adults, trusting us to follow textbook instructions and obey safety rules while performing experiments. Today we were working with our lab partners using concentrated acids, heating them with other chemicals in glass retorts to transform them into new substances. Somehow our class experiment backfired and a cloud of acrid smoke emerged from the lab. Fire alarms went off and girls came running out of classrooms from all directions, coughing and with eyes streaming, to empty the school until the fresh Wrexham air had blown away the offending fumes. We could only imagine the tongue-lashing poor Nella must have had from the Welsh Dragon!

"SUNDAY, JUNE 22ND: GERMANY HAS INVADED RUSSIA! DRIZZLY DAY. AWFUL, BUT IT CORRESPONDS TO THE TOWN, I SUPPOSE. DID SOME HOMEWORK. THERE'S NOTHING ELSE TO DO. THE BOYS HERE ARE WORSE THAN NOTHING."

In my mind's eye I saw again the old 1939 newspaper cartoon of Hitler and Stalin having signed a nonaggression pact, arms on each other's shoulders in seeming friendship, while each points a pistol at the other behind his back with his free hand. The treaty was smashed as Hitler flung his Panzer divisions without warning across the Russian borders. The *Luftwaffe* pounded every town and city in their path. Another *Blitzkrieg* had begun--the two pistols in the old cartoon had been fired.

Churchill's reaction was immediate, broadcasting Britain's pledge to support Russia against his favorite name for Hitler, "that bloodthirsty guttersnipe."

Hitler fancied himself as a military genius, reasoning that with a Nazi victory over Russia, Britain would capitulate without his bothering with an invasion to finish her off. He was impatient to begin his "Operation Barbarossa," the invasion of Russia, in order to complete his grand plan for the Nazi conquest of the whole of Europe by his unstoppable war machine as soon as possible. Some history books tell us that his goal was victory by the end of October, before the European winter set in. Another turning point in the war had been reached.

News of Hitler's decision to turn away from Britain and attack in the other direction came to us as a welcome reprieve. The greatest surprise was the realization that the Russians were no longer our enemies; they had inadvertently become our allies! Strange bedfellows, indeed!

On the home front, Mom was sounding impatient: "Bunty, you can't keep complaining about being in Wrexham all the time; you'll just have to make up your mind to make the best of being here and not being at home, and be thankful we're all alive."

Even this noble thought didn't cheer me up; my social life was nil. I had grown up surrounded by the friendship of boys. I was peeved that here none of them had so much as noticed that I existed. I thought: "Either they are altogether clueless or they simply hate the English! I'll probably wither away and die before any of them will make a move in my direction!"

Bessie's and Maggie's company was my only source of social activity in my own age group; we took in an occasional movie, went for long walks and picked wildflowers in the beautiful countryside, rode our bicycles to nearby villages and had long talks together. I thought: "There's got to be something more to life than knitting socks, gardening for the war effort, reading, walking and homework. Bess and Maggie must be sick and tired of hearing me complain, but they can't identify with my life back in London; their lives are completely devoid of boys so they don't know what I'm missing - or what *they* are, for that matter!"

William's letters only made things worse; he seemed to be enjoying life!

"FRIDAY, JULY 18TH: I WAS PICKED TO READ A GOVERNMENT PAMPHLET TO EVERY CLASS IN THE SCHOOL, ON 'HOW TO COLLECT WILD HERBS, AND WHAT TO COLLECT!'"
The Government had begun to realize what a valuable national resource it had in the millions of schoolchildren throughout Britain, even those at elementary school age. Now that it had them digging for victory, it came up with a new job for them: to collect medicinal herbs to supplement the dwindling supply of Britain's chemical medicines.

At morning assembly, the Welsh Dragon announced that a student had been selected to keep classes informed about this new opportunity for Wrexham Park girls to help the war effort. Then she dropped a bombshell. I couldn't believe what I was hearing. "Girls, I hope you will respond generously with your time and effort. Bunty Amiss will visit each class to read the Government instructions." After I recovered from the shock, I threw myself into this new cause with as much enthusiasm as I had for "Digging for Victory" or "Knitting Blankets for the Finns."

Clutching my government pamphlet, I trotted to each class, urging them to jot down the names of herbs to be collected from the hedgerows, woods and meadows in the neighboring countryside, with descriptions of the plants, where to find them, and the months of the year in which collect them.

On the list were rose hips, rich in vitamin C, a native substitute for the citrus fruits imported from America and the Mediterranean before the war. Wild English roses grew in profusion, their bright pink flowers filling the country air with heady perfume in summer. After blooming, their ripe red seed pods, or hips, could be processed into a thick syrup, then bottled and dispensed to babies and young children as a vitamin C substitute. I remembered seeing it in rows of bottles on the shelves in St. John's church hall on baby clinic day, before we left Upper Woodside.

Among other items on the list were foxglove leaves, a source of digitalis, and sphagnum moss, with antibiotic properties for dressing battlefront wounds, found in wooded areas.

Wrexham Park girls could be seen scouring the countryside on Saturday mornings, carrying small sacks and clutching slips of paper, then uttering shrieks of triumph when something on the list was found. Back at school, the contents of the sacks were sorted, dried and packed, ready for collection. I am sure that Britain's schoolchildren must have grown in self-esteem, knowing they were included in a nationwide pool of willing labor, proud of the fact that even kids on their days off from school could help out in the war effort.

"V" for Victory"

"SUNDAY, JULY 20TH: SOMETHING NEW: THE 'V FOR VICTORY' CAMPAIGN BEGAN. WENT WITH MAGGIE TO THE PARK TO COLLECT LIME FLOWERS."

A new morale booster had been added to "Are We Downhearted?" This novelty was the "'V' for Victory" campaign. As a nation, from Churchill on down, we all began to raise a salute with two fingers spread into a "V" shape. It became irresistible as a gesture when saying "goodbye" to each other, accompanied by a wide grin; it was used by bus conductors as a greeting to boarding and departing passengers. Just to see it made everyone smile, lifting our spirits and hopes as no other symbolic gesture had since the beginning of this weary war. The "V" sign stuck, and eventually spread worldwide.

Our government's herb list included flowers from the lime (linden) trees to be collected in July, adding that the flowers had properties that were needed to make pills to cure an incredible range of ailments: cystitis, tonsillitis, bronchitis, earache and nausea among them, and Maggie's favorite, nervous disorders.

Maggie and I took our sacks through the open gate in the iron railings encircling the local park, where we found a lime tree whose fragrant flowers were hanging in small, pale green bunches on branches above our heads, just out of reach. After a few futile efforts to snatch bunches of flowers by jumping up to catch them, Maggie said: "You know, Bunty, we're not going to get anywhere by standing here on the ground and trying to reach them by jumping up and down this way. Why can't we climb the tree instead?"

Tree-climbing was right up my alley; I had been well trained by Peter and William back in Upper Woodside, and had gained invaluable experience during our evacuation to Thorpe Village. Excited, I said: "Why didn't I think of that, Maggie? Here I go!"

I was happily perched on one of the lower branches, picking bunches of lime flowers and tossing them down for Maggie to put into her sack, when two uniformed park attendants appeared. Their faces flushed when they saw us, first with astonishment, then with rage. One of them looked up and bellowed at me in his Welsh accent: "Now look you, girl, what do you think you are doing climbing one of the trees in this park? Did you not read the notice forbidding it when you came in the gate? You can be prosecuted for this, you know!"

Terrified, Maggie didn't have the presence of mind to faint; instead she was poised for flight. I managed to slide out of the tree onto the ground and grab her by the sleeve to stop her, just in the nick of time. As coolly as we could, we showed the park attendants our credentials, Maggie's sack and the government list of herbs to be gathered. Mollified, the two men told us where we could find some lime trees outside the park.

As Maggie and I beat a hasty retreat before they changed their minds, she commented: "Too bad we didn't have a lime pill or two handy, for them and for us, too. The pamphlet says lime flowers are used to make medicine to calm the nerves!"

"FRIDAY, JULY 25TH: LAST DAY OF SCHOOL UNTIL SEPTEMBER! I PLACED FIRST IN MY CLASS AFTER EXAMS! WILL WONDERS NEVER CEASE?"

I raced home from school that afternoon with the exam results. For once, Mom was speechless. Dad had arrived home from work, and his reaction showed me a new side to his normally undemonstrative character. Throwing what he called "manly restraint" to the winds, he gave me a crushing bear hug that almost took my breath away. I could almost hear him thinking: "At long last my money hasn't been wasted on those monumental school fees!"

"Well, Bunty," Mom found words when she had recovered from the shock. "Dad and I were beginning to wonder if you would ever settle down to serious school work, but leaving London has turned out to be the best thing we could have done for your education."

I was remembering my days at Ravenhurst. Lizzie and Pie Face had probably despaired of my ever becoming a serious student. If they could have heard about my exam results, they would have received the news with sheer disbelief!

All innocence, Mom looked at me with a straight face. "I guess all that hard studying should have a reward of some kind. What do you think?" I shrugged, puzzled, visualizing a pound or two to put into my savings account for college. Unable to tease me any longer, she laughed and said: "How about a trip back to London?"

Dad broke in: "We wanted it to be a surprise. It will take about three weeks, but I've arranged for the water and electricity to be turned on at the house, so you can be comfortable for the time you'll be spending there. We've written to the boys and some of the neighbors and told them not to breathe a word to you until we could tell you ourselves."

My world was rosy again; I could hardly wait to start packing. But in the meantime, another milestone was about to appear in World War Two.

"SUNDAY, AUGUST 10TH: WENT WITH MOM AND DAD TO RHYL FOR THE DAY. GREAT DAY FOR SWIMMING, BUT NO LUCK--BEACH IS FULL OF TANK TRAPS!"

Since we had moved to Wrexham, Mom and I hadn't been away from its confines to see much of the surrounding area. Mom asked Bronwyn what would make a pleasant day's trip for us while Dad was off from work for the weekend.

"Oh, you really should go to see Rhyl. The people around here and from Liverpool go there for their holidays, at least they did in peace-time. It's not that far, and you will see the sea! There's a bus that goes there from town, too."

So on this beautiful warm day in August, we were off on a bus trip to spend the day at the seaside. It was relaxing to see the beautiful old Victorian houses that lined the road opposite the promenade with its traditional Victorian bandstand. Mom headed for a vacant bench and we sat down to admire the view of the golden sand and blue water that we had anticipated. There was nobody on the beach or in the water.

Instead, between us and the waves of the Irish Sea marched a long line of concrete gun emplacements. The rest of the beach was studded with tank traps resembling rows of huge concrete teeth, and other obstacles stretching from the gun emplacements down into the water.

Dad took out his binoculars. "Well, there's a nasty welcome waiting for any of those Nazi bastards who attempt to invade Wales from this direction! I'll bet there are plenty of Nazi sympathizers across that stretch of water in Eire who would let them, even though they are supposed to be neutral."

"Oh, Jack, don't be such a grouch. You'll spoil our lovely day by just thinking of such a thing. Hitler's too busy now with Russia, anyway." Mom's optimism usually shone through, especially when she heard Dad say something negative. Dad put his hands in his pockets and said no more.

My diary added: "LOVELY SCENERY. WALKED ON SEA FRONT, LISTENED TO THE BRASS BAND, HAD AN ICE CREAM, HAD TEA, HAD A DOUGHNUT, TOOK SOME PHOTOS, CAME BACK TO WREXHAM, UGH. BUT IT WAS A NICE DAY OUT."

"TUESDAY, AUGUST 12TH: 'SIGNING OF ATLANTIC CHARTER ANNOUNCED,'" sang out the newspaper boys.
Ailing President Roosevelt had sailed out on the U.S. cruiser *Augusta* to meet Churchill on the new British battleship *Prince of Wales*, off the coast of Newfoundland. Here they signed the Atlantic Charter, which set into words the postwar aims of both countries.

The event flickered on movie screens all over Britain, and our handkerchiefs came out when Roosevelt, Churchill and their staffs, along with the crews of both ships, stood bareheaded on the open deck of the *Prince of Wales* to share a church service. Raising their voices together they sang three hymns they all knew: "O God Our Help in Ages Past," "Eternal Father Strong to Save" and "Onward Christian Soldiers."

Churchill said later: "When I looked upon that densely packed congregation of fighting men of the same language, of the same faith, of the same fundamental laws; of the same ideals, and now, to a large extent, of the same interests, and certainly, in different degrees, facing the same danger, it swept across me that here was the only hope, but also the sure hope, of saving the world from measureless degradation."

Another milestone had been reached in World War Two.

"THURSDAY, AUGUST 14TH: MAGGIE ON VACATION AT SEASHORE, SO BESSIE CAME WITH ME TO SCHOOL GARDEN. MAGGIE AND I ARE GROWING LOTS OF DIFFERENT KINDS OF VEGGIES NOW. HARVESTED SOME PEAS, BEANS AND PARSLEY, CARROTS, BEETS AND TURNIPS, BEFORE I LEAVE FOR A WEEK IN LONDON. BESSIE SAYS HER BACK HURTS. SHE'S REALLY OUT OF SHAPE!"

"Oh dear, my back hurts." Bessie straightened up slowly with a handful of green beans.

Compassion wasn't on my mind. "Oh, Bessie, just be thankful you're harvesting all this good stuff without having had to plant and water it all these weeks." I silently added: "She should have volunteered with us, then she wouldn't be so pudgy now!"

Maggie and I took satisfaction in our good health and stamina since we had begun to dig for victory. She hadn't fainted once--and I had noticed with surprise I had developed some pretty nice curves the last time I looked in the mirror! I wondered if William and Peter would notice.

In our careers as gardeners, we had learned how to plant and cultivate many vegetables we had never attempted to grow before. The garden was a communal one, shared with other "Dig for Victory" volunteers, so we all took only our fair share of what was ready for harvest. Maggie and her family were away on vacation, so Bessie and I shared the veggies between Bessie's family, Bronwyn and Mom.

"SUNDAY, AUGUST 17TH: STAYED INDOORS ALL MORNING PACKING. I CAN HARDLY WAIT FOR TOMORROW! BUT I'M WONDERING WHAT THE HOUSE WILL LOOK LIKE. WILL IT REALLY BE HOME? AND HOW ABOUT THE BOYS?"

It had been almost a year since I had set foot in Bishop's Hill. So much had happened since then, both in my life and in those of William, Peter and Paul. I wondered if it would all be different this time we met. One thing was for sure: we were all growing up! But would we ever be the same people again?

Upper Woodside Revisited

"MONDAY, AUGUST 18TH: COLD, DAMP DAY. LEFT ON THE 9:30 A.M. TRAIN FROM WREXHAM. ARRIVED IN LONDON AT 3 P.M. WILLIAM AND HIS MOM WERE HOUSEWARMING WHEN WE CAME HOME. SO MUCH TALKING TO DO. STAYED UP 'TIL MIDNIGHT."

"Mom, I'm almost afraid to look, in case it's not all there!" But I forced myself to keep my eyes open as the taxi rounded the corner into Bishop's Hill. At first glance, everything looked the same, but as we approached the house we saw stretching beyond it the empty spaces where ten houses had been. We had been spared the sight our neighbors must have seen directly after the bombing when the skeletons of the houses had stood, one wall here and another there, tattered wallpaper and maybe a fireplace still attached to them. The War Damage Commission had demolished the wreckage; all that was left was a sea of rubble.

We walked through the space in the front hedge where our wrought-iron gate had been, and up the front path. On the outside, the house looked better than we had expected. Doors were back on their hinges; windows, still without glass, were neatly boarded up. We looked up at the roof, now replaced and watertight, with patches of new terra cotta tiles. Mom muffled an "Oh!" of distress. The new tiles were a visibly different shade of red from the few originals, creating quite an eyesore.

"Oh dear," Mom complained, "I do wish they had paid more attention to getting them all to match." Then, with a shrug of resignation, she added, "I suppose it's too late now. At least we won't need buckets to catch the rain in the bedrooms any more!"

She turned the key in our front door, and William and his Mom rushed to greet us with "Welcome home, travelers" and affectionate hugs. Mrs. Standish had even put some flowers in the front-hall vase, gathered from the weed-choked flower beds, and William had a cheery fire burning in the dining-room fireplace to dispel the dampness of almost a year of vacancy. Mom and I were both touched by their thoughtfulness, sniffling into our handkerchiefs a little as we realized how much the common experience of wartime strengthened the precious bonds of friendship.

Dad had arranged for the utilities to be turned back on for our visit. The electric kettle could be heard in the kitchen, whistling and spluttering in readiness to make us all a celebratory cup of tea, to be served with a cookie or two from the biscuit barrel Mrs. Standish had brought with her.

Daylight lingered late on these evenings of Double British Summer Time, but we had learned to be practical. We knew we had to call a halt to our torrent of catch-up conversation to get ready for the approaching blackout.

Mrs. Standish shrugged her ample figure into her coat, saying: "Oh, my goodness, where did the time go? I'd better get home and make some supper. Jim will soon be home from work and wondering where on earth I am!"

"Don't wait supper for me, Mum. I'll stay awhile longer." William was back to normal!

Mom heaved herself out of the overstuffed chair which had migrated into the dining room along with the other living-room furniture when we brought the beds downstairs in the London Blitz.

"Well, it seems our blackout curtains must have been lost when the windows were blown out by that bomb. I'll go and see what I can find to put over the windows temporarily." She tossed the words over her shoulder as she started up the stairs. Minutes later, William and I heard her rummaging in the storage trunks in our upstairs "box room."

Taking advantage of our privacy, William and I found time for a little hand-holding and a quick kiss or two before Mom reappeared with an armload of old blankets. "You're tall enough to drape these over the plywood", she said to William, who sprang willingly into action. Worried that this makeshift wasn't "blackout-proof" enough to trust the electric light, we lit candles and sat in the firelight's glow, catching up on events of the past months, until we were too tired to talk any longer. Mom and I headed for bed, and William departed across the street with his hooded flashlight.

"WEDNESDAY, AUGUST 20TH: SPENT ALL MORNING CLEANING UP BEDROOMS. TOOK OUT EIGHT BUCKETS FULL OF CEILING PLASTER! WENT SHOPPING FOR A FEW BASICS. WILLIAM SKIPPED WORK, AND PETER CAME OVER ABOUT 6:30."

The windows at the back of the house had been sucked outwards into the yard. At least this made it easier to clear the fallen ceiling plaster off the rug in the back bedroom. The blast had blown the windows at the front of the house into the rooms, so the front bedrooms were a different story. When we had left Upper Woodside last year, Mom's lovely Indian bedroom rugs had been a sorry sight, but nothing compared with now: they were full of shards of glass from the windows, embedded in them, along with the plaster. They were beyond repair. Filling buckets with this kind of debris was a slow business; even wearing gloves, I soon had to put band-aids on my fingers from the tiny slivers of glass. Shattered glass must have shot across the guest bedroom--a stream of missiles, scratching and gouging the walnut panels on the furniture as they went. When Mom surveyed the scene she said nothing, just wept.

I worked for several hours carting buckets of bedroom ceiling plaster out to the garbage while Mom aired out bedding on the backyard clothesline, and checked drawers and closets to see what else might have been stolen when the house was open to looters.

"Let's relax and have a cup of tea, Bunty. Then we'd better go to the shops and get a few things in the house to eat." Mom was ready for a break.

"Good idea, I'll be glad of a change while I still have the energy. I don't want to see another bucket for awhile!"

When we arrived back from grocery shopping, Mom and I found a note attached to the front door: "SURPRISE PACKAGE WAITING IN AIR-RAID SHELTER." I dashed down the garden path and peered into the gloom inside the Anderson shelter, to see William sitting grinning on a lawn chair. He and Peter had both taken temporary jobs to occupy their time while waiting to be called into the R.A.F. Their hours seemed suspiciously flexible, but we didn't ask questions! To my great relief, the boys hadn't changed, except maybe to become taller and even more handsome than when I had last seen them.

"THURSDAY, AUGUST 21ST: MOM AND I TOOK THE BUS INTO CROYDON. HAD LUNCH AT HEMMINGS. WHAT A MESS CROYDON IS!" After our struggle to blackout-proof the dining room, Mom had said: "I think that, as long as we're home, we'd better go into Croydon and buy some more blackout curtain material. I may not have time to make up the curtains, but at least it will be ready next time we come home for a visit so I can work on them then."

I could hardly remember the last time we had shopped in Croydon, the next large town south of Upper Woodside. It was a fascinating place, with historic remains of a settlement mentioned in the Domesday Book in 1086, becoming an important medieval market town. Croydon's crowning glory had been its open market, but over the years the outdoor stands had been displaced by indoor shops. I remembered when the entire narrow length of Market Street was lined on both sides with market barrows, open stands on wheels which in peacetime had been piled high with all kinds of vegetables, fruit, flowers, secondhand knick-knacks, china, clothing, toys and cheap jewelry. It had all changed drastically. Today there were fewer barrows and the lettuces and apples had been spread out to look like more than there were, but the vendors still shouted, "Cum an' git yer termartoes 'ere, 'arf a crown. Git yer letticies 'ere, fresh terday," to attract customers passing by.

Croydon also had several large, modern department stores and dozens of small shops. They had changed since the war, their windows now crisscrossed with wide bands of tape to prevent them from shattering in air raids. There were empty spaces everywhere, where bombed-out buildings had been torn down. Shoppers crowded along the sidewalks in the High Street and in and out of the shops despite their pathetically depleted stocks. In one of the department stores we found enough blackout material to replace the dining-room curtains.

While we were in the store, Mom treated us to lunch in its once-elegant restaurant. She tried not to look disappointed as we were each served an almost transparent piece of ham lurking between two slender slices of the "National Loaf," a far cry from the prewar menu. We looked at our plates in dismay and both burst into laughter after the waitress had gone, so as not to hurt her feelings. Only the tea tasted the same, renewing our spirits as well as our tired bodies; we seemed to have been walking for miles. Energy restored, we took to the town sidewalks again.

Exhausted, we caught the bus home. I strained to see through the bomb-blast netting on the bus windows when we passed the Ravenhurst schools on our way back to Upper Woodside, and glimpsed them still standing serenely in their tree-shaded grounds. I thought: "I wonder where my old schoolmates could be now, and if they ever think of me?" But by then it was time to get off the bus and walk home to Bishop's Hill.

"FRIDAY, AUGUST 22ND: PETER TOOK THE AFTERNOON OFF FROM WORK. WENT TO TEA AT HIS HOUSE. MOM AND I VISITED WILLIAM'S PARENTS IN THE EVENING--STAYED UNTIL MIDNIGHT."
Mom had missed her friends, too, and Mrs. Donovan had some war stories of her own to share. She carefully avoided Peter's encounter with

the incendiary bomb, probably knowing that he had told the tale better than she could have.

Peter said innocently: "Mom, Bunty and I will do the dishes to give you two a chance to talk." He washed and I dried; we were alone at last to catch up on our own age group: "Guess what happened to so-and-so … " Having been out of the mainstream of local events for so long, I soaked it all up like a sponge, finding it incredible that so many of the young folks we knew were now serving in armed forces all over the world, and some even getting engaged or married.

That evening we visited the Standishes. Mr. Standish poured us all a glass of prewar sherry.

"Well, folks, here's to a lovely reunion. It's grand to see you both again."

We hardly had a chance to take a first sip, when William's Mom stood up and said: "Before we all get comfortable and before the blackout, let's take you on a tour of our new wartime backyard."

We all obediently followed her out the back door. The lawn and carefully tended flower gardens which had been Mrs. Standish's pride and joy had all disappeared; in their place were rows of peas and beans. Next to them stood a large chicken coop and wire-netted chicken run, across from the new outdoor air-raid shelter.

Mrs. Standish's full face was flushed from our quick trot around the yard. "Jim really went overboard when the Government called for home food production," she puffed, "but it's a bit of a nuisance having to feed those fowls so often. Don't throw away any of your table scraps while you're here, Ida," she added, looking Mom in the eye. "The fowls will be ever so happy to have them. They are marvelous egg-layers!"

I stared at the plump Rhode Island Reds in the chicken run. It was like seeing a reincarnation of "the girls" at Hove. "Just to think," I speculated to myself, "all that trouble I went to, making Mr. Dearborne's special mash recipe while all the time they would rather have had leftovers. No wonder they didn't lay any eggs!"

"SATURDAY, AUGUST 23RD: SOON AFTER BREAKFAST, MRS. WHITE CAME TO SEE US, THEN MR. WHITE ARRIVED WITH DAUGHTER BETTY. AFTER LUNCH MRS. BROWN, WHO'S HOME FROM EVACUATION TO SCOTLAND, POPPED IN TO SEE US. AT 2:30 PETER CAME, FOLLOWED BY WILLIAM AT 3 P.M. NEXT PAUL BATES ARRIVED! THE THREE BOYS STAYED TO TEA, THEN WE SANG, DANCED AND PLAYED SILLY GAMES LIKE 'CONSEQUENCES' UNTIL 10 P.M."

Such was our homecoming, brief as it would be. Friends and neighbors alike welcomed us back; Mom was teary as she hugged each one when they came in through the door. She made endless cups of tea and opened the sealed tin of cookies she had carefully hoarded for just such an occasion, hiding it on the back shelf of the larder before we had left for Wrexham a year ago. That evening in the warm, enveloping blackout, Peter, William and I walked Paul up the hill to catch the bus back to his new home on the other side of London. We returned to Bishop's Hill by the "scenic route," which took us about a mile out of the direct path home, giving us longer to chatter and laugh as we walked through the blackness. We were together again and I was in seventh heaven.

Invasion Practice

"MONDAY, AUGUST 25TH: BACK TO WREXHAM. IT'S ROTTENER THAN EVER! TOOK ROLL OF FILM TO CHEMIST'S SHOP TO BE DEVELOPED. BESSIE CAME TO SEE US AND WELCOME US BACK."

Britain didn't have "drugstores," back then. For decades they were called "chemists' shops," and that is where we went to buy film and have it developed. I hoped the old prewar film I had used still worked! It did. A week later I picked up the prints: Peter, handsome in his Home Guard uniform, William growing out of his suit, Paul tossing his floppy blond hair back from his blue eyes, and me--in the middle! I took the photos out of their envelope to show to Mom. She looked on in amusement as I romanticized and relived that week at home. The photos would be the last ones of us together.

"You know, Mom, apart from a few modifications like the blackout, no cream cakes for tea and the mess the house was in, those days at home seemed just like old times. We didn't even hear an air-raid siren. I guess another year of school ahead of me in Wrexham won't be so bad now, with those memories to keep me warm!"

Mom rolled her eyes. "Oh well, dear," she said. "If you can stand another year here, I guess I can, too. But I haven't had those kinds of memories for years!" I wondered what she meant.

Bessie had been very glad to see us back, so had Maggie and Bronwyn and Mr. Evans. Even little Davey stood up on his hind legs by way of a canine greeting. I realized that now I had two places I could call "home," but where, really, was "Home"? I would travel a long way further before I would find out.

"SUNDAY, SEPTEMBER 7TH: NATIONAL DAY OF PRAYER. WENT TO EVENING SERVICE AT ST. GILES'S PARISH CHURCH. BAD WAR NEWS FOR THE ALLIES, BUT GOOD NEWS ON OUR HOME FRONT, WITH U.S. AID ARRIVING."

Mom and I listened with Bronwyn and Mr. Evans to the radio as King George VI, struggling with his speech impediment, achieved the words to call hesitantly for another National Day of Prayer.

"Yes, indeed, things are going badly in the war." Mr. Jones looked more glum than usual. "I wonder what we'll be in for next?" During the past week I had forgotten the war in my delight at being home at Bishop's Hill, this time enjoying the comfort of a vacation without hearing "Moaning Minnie" heralding an air-raid. Not so comfortable was the realization that, with Hitler's attention now turning eastward instead of to the invasion of Britain, our reprieve had been at a terrible cost to our new allies the Russians, "strange bedfellows" though they might be. Events were going badly for their troops and civilians as the Nazi Blitzkrieg ground relentlessly on through a bruised and bloodied Russia. Newspaper photos of the agony inflicted by the Germans resembled those we had seen smuggled out of the collapsing countries across the English Channel a year ago.

"Oh, how terrible!" Mr. Jones sounded absolutely desperate: "I think Hitler is going to conquer Russia by the looks of it. We'll be next, I'm sure."

Since the arrival of "Desert Fox" Rommel and his Africa Korps in North Africa, the war was going badly for the Allies there, too.

We had quickly lost most of the territory captured from the Italians only months before.

Our spirits plummeted as we prayed at St. Giles's church. There was, however, one positive note; Britain was receiving increasing support and involvement from the U.S.: new equipment on the war fronts, new canned food in the shops, and two Eagle Squadrons had been formed, with American volunteers flying under R.A.F. command.

"SUNDAY, SEPTEMBER 14TH: I'M STILL SO BORED! AUNTIE BELLE HAS SENT ME ANOTHER TEA CLOTH TO EMBROIDER! WISH WILLIAM WAS HERE."

Auntie Belle, true to her sensitive, mothering nature, had evidently thought she had found the antidote to the boredom reflected in my letters. She responded by sending me embroidery projects. The 36-inch-square tablecloths were prewar fine linen, each stamped with an intricate design of flowers, accompanied by a color chart and embroidery floss to work them. I no sooner finished one than she sent me another. "Slave labor," I grumbled. "I wonder what she's doing with all these tablecloths--saving them for wedding presents?"

The latest tea cloth was magnificent, with a sheaf of flowers to embroider on each corner and a circle of them in the center. I loved the challenge of crewel embroidery, and after several weeks of work, I sent the finished cloth back reluctantly, feeling that part of me was going with it. It didn't enter my head that I would ever see it again.

"Wish William was here" preceded or ended so many of the remaining pages of my 1941 diary entries that there were two words that Pie Face would have used to describe them: "ad nauseam."

"THURSDAY, SEPTEMBER 18TH: KIEV FELL TO THE GERMANS. WE'RE BACK TO SCHOOL. I'M NOW IN FORM FIVE ARTS. DUG UP TWO SACKFULS OF POTATOES!"

The Russian front, to my mind reminiscent of those enormous oil paintings depicting the Napoleonic Wars, yielded commensurate statistics. In the battle for Kiev, Russian losses were estimated at more than half a million men. Ill-equipped as Britain was to help, R.A.F. pilots and planes were sent to aid the Russians as a goodwill gesture.

Maggie was ecstatic at our joint promotion into our final year of studies at Wrexham Park. "Just think, Bunty," she gushed, "we'll have another smashing year of larks together in the Fifth Form!" I tried hard to smile!

A smaller school than Ravenhurst, Wrexham Park had fewer forms, or classes. By our fifth year of secondary prep school education they were labeled "Arts" or "Sciences," according to the degree program we would pursue at university. Maggie, with her artistic talents, and I, with my abysmal non-grasp of arithmetic, had opted for "Five Arts." Bessie had chosen "Five Sciences," so once more we only saw her before and after the school day. Before the school year was over we would have to take the dreaded Central Welsh Board exams. If we passed, this would qualify us for higher education in college.

"'Ello there, girls," boomed Mr. Roberts, our school janitor, "indeed it is good to have you back. Look you, I'm ready to help you dig potatoes today!" Eager to escape classes, Maggie and I were ready, too.

All summer long we had harvested veggies, selling the excess to friends and neighbors, with the proceeds going to our school's charities. Mr. Roberts was as good as his word, so potatoes were added to our stock for sale. In the warm sunshine of those September weekends we also picked wild blackberries and hazelnuts for our mothers to use in baking and jam-making, and collected bunches of purple elderberries and ripe, red rose hips for the war effort as the autumn days sped by.

"SUNDAY, SEPTEMBER 28TH: WREXHAM STAGED A MOCK INVASION, PRACTISING HOW TO DEAL WITH TEAR GAS, FIRES, BRIDGES BLOWN UP, FIFTH COLUMNISTS ARRESTED, ETC."
This was the first and only invasion drill mentioned in my diary. The situation on the Russian front made us all realize that a German invasion of Britain was still very much a possibility, and our town didn't intend to be caught napping.

The drill had been intensively planned. It involved nearby Army and R.A.F. bases, hospitals, police, fire companies, and all the Civil Defence services. Trucks equipped with loudspeakers drove slowly through Wrexham's streets. "All civilians must remain indoors until the drill is over," they blared. Bronwyn, Mom and I looked in vain through our windows for signs of the invasion drill in our suburban surroundings, but it was evidently centered in the town itself. All day long we heard the sound of planes droning overhead. It was comforting to know they were from the two airfields just outside of town. Bronwyn looked up from her ironing: "I'll bet hundreds of people are involved out there. I heard that each organization has its own part to play: the Auxiliary Fire Service putting out fires, the Home Guard capturing enemy parachutists, and the Auxiliary Police arresting Nazi collaborators ..."

Mr. Evans looked at her quizzically. "Oh, go on, girl, you've got a good imagination! We've no spies in Wrexham. But all the same, I'd rather not think about it at all." And he went back calmly to reading his Sunday paper.

Deflated, Bronwyn busied herself with her housework until the loudspeaker trucks announced the drill was over several hours later. Mr. Evans looked up from his paper. "Well, all I can say is, I hope to God we won!" he growled.

"SUNDAY, OCTOBER 19TH: GERMANS ADVANCING ON MOSCOW. NICE SUNNY DAY. WENT FOR A THREE-MILE WALK IN THE AFTERNOON. DID SOME HOMEWORK AND WROTE TO WILLIAM."
Dad was home for the weekend from his latest job in Yorkshire, installing drinking water for an R.A.F. training camp. He looked worried as he read the war news in the Sunday paper. "I wonder if the 'Ruskies' can stop those bastards?" he asked.

Mom said quietly, "And if they can't, and Russia goes under, Hitler will probably turn back to Britain to deliver the 'coup de grace'; it will be the end of us, unless there's a miracle." But her miracle was about to happen.

The Nazi onslaught continued across Russia, and the German army was within a few miles of Moscow. But the first snow of the season had begun to fall. The Russians were able to hold the line until the bitterly cold Russian winter set in. The Germans became bogged down in their tracks, ill-prepared for the severity of the weather and immobilized for the duration of the winter, leaving the Russians time to regroup and prepare for a spring offensive. Once more we were to be spared, and Hitler's dream of strutting as a conqueror through the streets of London was never to come true.

I still had a tremendous crush on William. I worried when his letters didn't arrive as frequently as I thought they should, but, when one did, the "warm fuzzies" I felt for him were reinforced. I reported in my diary: "I THINK HE CRACKLES ABOUT ME A LITTLE, TOO!"

"Utility'

My diary for October listed schoolwork, an occasional movie with Bessie, Maggie or Mom and frequent letters to and from Peter, Paul and William. Peter and William were restless in their boring temporary jobs while they still waited to be called into the R.A.F. Paul complained about his humdrum life at the seminary.

Summer was over, its golden sunlight lengthening into autumn shadows. The remaining summer vegetables were harvested; I noted that Bessie and I delivered some to the local hospital. Mom and I, Maggie and Bessie spent as many of those fall days as possible outdoors, taking walks in the countryside and gathering fall plants on our herb list. The blackout began to intrude earlier and earlier into the shrinking daylight; soon the bitter winter would bluster into North Wales and confine us indoors. Restrictions were proliferating for us on the home front.

"Just think," Mom grumbled, as the list of rationed goods became longer and longer, "those days before the war really were the 'Good Old Days,' only we didn't know it. They've taken away our silk stockings and now they are going to ration our clothes and fabrics, too. And 'Utility'--ugh!"

Sewing had always been one of Mom's passions. Her old Singer sewing machine had been acquired before they came with an electric motor. I can remember her before the war humming contentedly as she worked the treadle with her feet to turn the belt that ran the machine, making most of her own clothes and some of mine, and sewing for St. John's annual church bazaar. But now the fabrics she used were labeled "luxury" and were rationed, if they could be found at all.

The government had introduced a new economy measure: its name was "Utility." Utility applied no-frills standards to consumer goods manufactured in Britain including clothes, gold jewelry, household appliances and furniture. Utility skirts had no pleats, only straight panels. Dresses and blouses were not allowed to have any "adornment." Utility clothing, scratchy sheets and skinny blankets were identified on the label by a stamped-on symbol: two small black circles resembling stylized capital letter Cs, with fifteen percent slices cut out of each circle, followed by the number 41. I later found out that the logo stood for "Civilian Clothing 1941." I had forgotten the Utility icon until "Pacman" came into the life of today's computer-happy generation, the spitting image of one of those little black Utility Cs zooming across the screen, gobbling up everything in sight!

The amount of gold used in jewelry was reduced to nine carats; brides and grooms had to be satisfied with plain, nine carat gold Utility wedding rings, skimpy clothes for the honeymoon, Utility sheets and blankets and plain, drab furniture with a thin veneer.

"MONDAY, NOVEMBER 3RD: SCHOOL CLOSED TODAY. I WENT BY TRAIN TO LIVERPOOL TO SHOP WITH MAGGIE AND HER MOM. BOUGHT SOME GORGEOUS SLACKS."

Liverpool had been consistently pounded by the *Luftwaffe* through-out the war. Its docks were the major wartime terminus of the transatlantic lifeline for the British, where ships that survived the U-boats in the convoys delivered troops, armaments and food from Canada and the U.S.

Dad raged: "Those filthy Nazis! How the Liverpool docks can keep functioning with all that bombing, I just can't imagine. They must have a whole army of men working night and day to keep salvaging the ships and repairing the damage. Remember that newsreel showing hundreds of oranges floating around covered in oil?"

I well remembered the newsreel. The movie camera slowly moved over a dock where hundreds of oranges from the U.S. had been spilled from a merchant ship as it sank at its berth from a direct hit. The oranges bobbed around in the dock, blackened by the dirty slime on the oil-soaked water, unfit for consumption. Most adults in Britain hadn't tasted or even seen an orange or a banana since the war; these oranges had been destined for use by the military, in children's hospitals and at the baby clinics. Sobbing could be heard in the audience as we watched helplessly.

For us in Wrexham there had been plenty of evidence of the air raids on Liverpool, twenty-five miles away. Nazi bombers could be heard overhead on their way to their target, sometimes triggering Wrexham's air-raid sirens, and if the wind was in the right direction, a series of thuds continued for hours, as bomb loads were delivered.

Hitler's all-out war to conquer the Russians, however, had diverted many of the air raids from Liverpool, and determination to "carry on" kept most of its remaining stores in business despite their depleted stocks of merchandise.

It was fun for me to take a train ride with Maggie and her Mom to a new destination. A short walk from the station was the shopping district, which Maggie's mother knew very well. We were soon in the largest of the department stores, trying our luck in the "Ladies' Apparel" department. Our annual clothes ration of sixty-six coupons per year didn't go far: fourteen for a lined raincoat, five for a pair of shoes. Today, however, I willingly parted with seven coupons for a pair of glamorous, dark green corduroy slacks. Not only was it a miracle to find them in my size, but in my rapidly maturing teenage mind they were equal to any I had ever seen worn by the glamorous heroines of American movies, which made them irresistible. I could hardly wait to model them for Mom. Maggie whooped triumphantly when she found a beautifully tailored wool coat that fitted her. My slacks and Maggie's coat must have been made before Utility struck; no little black circles were on the labels. We could hardly believe our good luck!

Maggie's Mom decided it was time to celebrate. "Girls, I'm going to treat you to lunch at a nice little tea shop I know," she announced. "It's a great place; you'll love it." Maggie and I trotted along after her, carrying our bundles and with our appetites ready. As we turned into the street the tea shop was on, her face fell when she saw the gaping space where it had been. She was a woman of few words: "Damn Hitler," she said, as we sat down in another tea shop that she considered a poor substitute.

Mom was duly appreciative of my new slacks. "Wait till the boys back home see those, Bunty. I'm just wondering what they'll say." "To heck with what they'll say," I thought, "I just wonder what they'll *do!*"

"TUESDAY, NOVEMBER 11TH: WE'VE SUNK TWO ITALIAN DESTROYERS AND NINE MERCHANT SHIPS IN THE MEDITERRANEAN. LORD HAW-HAW SAYS GERMANY SANK OUR *ARK ROYAL*--AGAIN! RUSSIANS BEGINNING TO ATTACK SUCCESSFULLY ON EASTERN FRONT."

Russian ships were now carrying raw materials to Britain for our war effort, returning to Russia with badly needed armaments. A fragile newspaper clipping attached to this page of my diary shows a smiling British sailor posing for a propaganda photo on a Russian ship unloading at a British port, flanked by a pretty Russian stewardess and a Russian seaman. The caption reads, "And So Is Unity Made," followed by a quote by the Russian Ambassador to Britain: "It is my country's wish that now and after the war our two countries should cooperate closely in the cause of peace." Brave words, but I couldn't help thinking again of the cartoon with Stalin and his pistol!

Dad grunted with satisfaction over the news of our naval victories over the Italians, but growled: "That bloody idiot Lord Haw-Haw should have been strangled at birth. This must be the umpteenth time he's boasted that the German Navy has sunk the *Ark Royal* It's getting to be a national joke!"

Two days later the British Royal Navy's aircraft carrier *Ark Royal* really was sunk by a U-boat in the Mediterranean. The fate of the *Ark Royal* however, paled in comparison with the news the world was to hear as the year drew to a close.

"MONDAY, DECEMBER 8TH: AMERICA AND JAPAN ARE AT WAR! YESTERDAY JAPS BOMBED PEARL HARBOR. SOME OF AMERICAN FLEET SUNK. AT SCHOOL, GENERAL DE GAULLE SENT OUR CERCLE FRANÇAIS A LARGE, PERSONALLY AUTOGRAPHED PHOTO."

Britain was stunned. Immediately after Roosevelt's official declaration of war, Churchill honored his promise that Britain would join the U.S. in the war against Japan. The following week nation after nation declared support for either the Axis or the Allies until thirty-eight nations, representing half the population of the world, were now at war. I thought of my two cousins with the British Army in Singapore, and wondered what the future would hold for them, now that a Japanese attack could be expected on the Malayan Peninsula.

Straight "As" attested to my affinity for the French language. As a member of Wrexham Park's French Club, the Cercle Français, I became an avid fan and supporter of General Charles de Gaulle, leader of the Free French, now exiled in England. Our club raised minuscule amounts of money to send to their headquarters. I still have one of the small lapel pins with its enameled Cross of Lorraine, emblem of the Free French, which our club members bought to raise money for them and wore proudly on our school uniforms.

The club president unexpectedly called a special meeting of the Cercle Français. She waved at us a large manila envelope which she had just received in the mail. In it was an impressive photo of the future President of France, autographed in his own handwriting, in recognition of our efforts to help his cause. As I read this entry in my diary, so many years later, I couldn't help wondering if that autographed photo of de Gaulle had survived, and if so, what it would be worth at auction today.

"WEDNESDAY, DECEMBER 10TH: JAPANESE HAVE SUNK BRITISH BATTLESHIP *PRINCE OF WALES* AND BATTLE CRUISER *REPULSE*. HAD A LETTER FROM WILLIAM. HE'S PASSED HIS FIRST PHYSICAL FOR THE R.A.F. 100 PERCENT."

Well prepared for the war, the Japanese had struck with lightning speed the day of their surprise attack on Pearl Harbor; in the days following they bombed Singapore, landed in Malaya and Thailand, and attacked Hong Kong and the Philippines. By Christmas they had captured Hong Kong, Wake Island and Guam.

The *Prince of Wales* had been dispatched to the Far East to protect Singapore. Britain now mourned the loss of two of her battle fleet. Less than a year old, the *Prince of Wales* took down with her more than eight hundred officers and men, some of whom had probably sung "Onward,

Christian Soldiers" on her deck only four months before, along with Winston Churchill and President Roosevelt.

Back at Upper Woodside, William must have been in a tizzy of excitement, one step closer to his dream of joining the R.A.F. I didn't know whether to feel glad or sad.

"FRIDAY, DECEMBER 19TH: TOMORROW BEGINS CHRISTMAS RECESS FROM SCHOOL. TODAY AT ASSEMBLY THE WELSH DRAGON SAID SOME ROTTEN THINGS ABOUT DAPHNE LEIGHTON. I COULD HAVE WRUNG THE OLD SOW'S NECK. DAPHNE HAS BEEN EXPELLED!"

To be expelled was an unthinkable disgrace in those days. Along with myself and several other girls, Daphne was an English evacuee. We had already felt resentment of this fact from our headmistress, and if there had been any really serious details of Daphne's infraction they were never told.

In later years, the shrewish behavior of the Welsh Dragon would probably have been dubbed "unprofessional." We sat in our rows of chairs, paralyzed with shock as she tiraded on, publicly holding Daphne up to ridicule and shame, possibly thinking her example would be a warning to others. I seem to remember phrases such as "disgraceful insubordination," "flagrant disobedience" and, after pausing for breath, "unacceptable scholarship." At the end of the assembly, after singing the Welsh National Anthem, the girls filed out silently, seething with resentment.

Poor Daphne! But now I had something more important on my mind: we were going to Sunderland for Christmas!

Sunderland for Christmas

"MONDAY, DECEMBER 22ND: LEFT AT 6:30 A.M. WALKED IN THE BLACKOUT TO WREXHAM STATION. HAD TO CHANGE TRAINS THREE TIMES TO GET TO SUNDERLAND! LONG DAY. ARRIVED ABOUT 4:30 P.M."

My excitement was at bursting point. Traditionally we always spent Christmas and New Year's in Sunderland, but we hadn't been to my parents' home town for the holidays since before the war.

It was still pitch black outside at Wrexham when we tiptoed downstairs so as not to wake Mr. Evans and Bronwyn. We ate a hasty breakfast. Mom packed some sandwiches and cookies to take with us, "just in case there isn't anything to eat on the train."

Dad had always had a "thing" about catching trains on time. His interpretation of "on time" was to be on the station platform *two hours* before the train left, so he had Mom and me trekking with our suitcases to Wrexham station in the blackout on this bitterly cold morning. But Mom and I didn't complain this time; we were so far ahead of the crowd that he found us a compartment on the train with three empty seats!

Gone were the prewar express trains we had known, with their luxurious dining cars and booked seats. To conserve fuel in wartime there were fewer trains. Packed to overflowing, they stopped at all the stations the express trains used to breeze through with just a hoot of their whistles. Passengers now had to switch trains to make connections for their destinations.

We had to change trains three times on our two-hundred-mile journey to Sunderland. Each time, Dad elbowed our way into the crowded waiting room, blue with cigarette smoke but warm and humid from the combination of sweaty bodies and steam from the large, shiny tea urns at the food counter. I remember standing in the crush of humanity, nibbling one of Mom's sandwiches and warming my cold hands on a cup of steaming tea, until the announcement of our train came crackling over the loudspeaker. After changing trains twice more, it was midafternoon by the time we boarded our final connection for the last leg of our journey.

Through the train window the scenery gradually changed from smoky factory towns to the beauty and isolation of the northeast coast. I watched cloud patterns moving over the rippling, silver-gray surface of the North Sea as our train clung to the edge of high cliffs above it.

The conductor walked through the corridors, shouting: "Next stop, Sunderland." We gathered our suitcases and stepped stiffly down the train steps; it was already almost dark.

Uncle Arthur Amiss, Dad's youngest brother, was waiting for us on the platform. He seized my suitcase and went charging away with it. Dad took off after him with the other suitcases, while Mom and I struggled to make our legs keep up with him; they felt pretzel-shaped after being cramped from sitting all day. In the distance we glimpsed Uncle Arthur stopping at his car, parked by the curb almost a block away. A small, elderly Vauxhall sedan, it was prone to regular breakdowns and was used rather sparingly in these days of stringent gasoline rationing. Mom and I caught up with the men to find them stowing the luggage. Uncle Arthur, short and jolly, peered up at us through his round, black-rimmed glasses. He had a pun for everything, and we knew his well-worn car joke was coming. "You know why this car is called a Vauxhall? Because 'them that owns one usually valks-all-the-vay!'" We snickered politely.

On our short ride through Sunderland in the waning daylight, Mom and Dad were shocked at the bomb damage to their home town, its dockyards a prime target. Mom wept when she saw the empty space once occupied by the church she had attended as a girl, but she cheered up when, minutes later, we were warming ourselves in front of the fireplace in a house full of welcoming smiles.

Ever practical, Auntie Belle already had the table ready for supper. When she hugged me, she cried: "How you've grown, Bunty. It's lovely to see you again." The only thing I hated about going to Sunderland was when my relatives told me how much I'd grown, but I managed a smile as she said to my young cousins, softly but firmly, "Come on, you two, give me a hand bringing supper in. These folks must be starving." The two little girls scampered to help.

Auntie Belle was one of my favorite aunts. Soft-spoken and kind, her presence felt as calming as a caressing breeze after a storm. But underneath that laid-back exterior, she was a capable businesswoman.

Adjoining the roomy, two-story house in a neighborhood a few blocks away from the sea front was the flourishing "Corner Shop" she owned with Uncle Arthur. Their little convenience store sold everything from shoe polish and cigarettes to candy, cakes and vegetables. Running the store took up the bulk of Auntie Belle's time so she had a house-keeper, her widowed neighbor, Mrs. Howland, whose daughter Tessie took care of my two cousins. Uncle Arthur was her invaluable partner in the business. They both were up in the mornings at the crack of dawn. Auntie Belle often headed for the kitchen and did some baking while Uncle Arthur walked across town pushing a cart, to load it with boxes of freshly baked bread, cakes and pastries from the bakery owned by Auntie Belle's brother; then he wheeled it the two miles back again to the store. With his quiet sense of humor, he was popular with the customers and loved to exchange local gossip with them as he filled their orders.

In addition to his "war work" as a volunteer ambulance driver, Uncle Arthur also supported the war effort by regularly donating blood to the Red Cross. Dad was skeptical about being a blood donor and cautioned Uncle Arthur with brotherly concern that his blood would be so depleted it could cause his early demise.

"Arthur, you'd better be careful how often you give blood, me lad. You don't want to drain your body; you might need that blood yourself some day."

Uncle Arthur grinned. "Oh, don't worry, Jack, I'll always have plenty left; I've hypnotized my body so it's trained to put more in as quickly as they take it out."

True to his conviction that he was always right, misconceptions and all, Dad was still unconvinced and always blamed the blood donations for any ailment Uncle Arthur had after that.

I can still remember the stockroom in back of the store, with its tantalizing smells of freshly cut ham, newly baked bread and hand-ground coffee. Before the war the stockroom shelves bulged from floor to ceiling with fancy, imported merchandise; now they were stocked with basic grocery rations for the registered customers with their coupon books.

"THURSDAY, DECEMBER 25TH: CHRISTMAS DAY. MONTGOMERY'S EIGHTH ARMY CAPTURED BENGHAZI IN LIBYA. RECEIVED SOME MONEY, A CALENDAR PLUS A NEW DIARY FOR NEXT YEAR, AND SOME PERFUME FROM WILLIAM. TOOK THE TRAM TO GRAM AND GRANDPA'S. THE AUNTS AND COUSIN ALAN WERE THERE TOO."
Halfway around the world from Sunderland, the British Eighth Army's offensive had pushed Rommel's Afrika Korps back along the Mediterranean coast of North Africa--a welcome, if temporary, Christmas present for the "folks back home."

This Christmas morning Auntie Belle's living room was filled with squeals of happiness as my two little girl cousins, Audrey and Dorothy, rapidly invaded the contents of their Christmas stockings and carefully wrapped presents. This was the third Christmas we would not be in our own home, but for the first time since the war began we were with our own family, together with the sounds, sights and smells of Sunderland that I remembered from my childhood.

That afternoon Mom, Dad and I took a bus into town and boarded one of the double-decker street-cars called "trams" to visit Mom's family, the Ditchfields. The home of my grandmother and grandfather was a beautiful old Victorian house, full of nooks and crannies, which held for me so many memories of this effusive, irrepressible family.

In the bustle of our arrival, I cringed again as one after the other of my aunts said: "Merry Christmas, Bunty, it's lovely to see you again, and look how you've grown!"

I felt myself blushing as, out of the corner of my eye, I saw my cousin Alan, four years my senior, with an amused look on his face, enjoying my embarrassment. I had never quite felt comfortable with him ever since he chased me with his water pistol when I was five years old. Alan was now in uniform. With his musical talent, he had managed to get himself a job in the R.A.F. playing in a dance band, entertaining the troops at concerts where he rubbed elbows with many of the well-known actors and musicians in Britain's show business world, while enjoying suspiciously flexible working hours.

We stayed for tea, with an invitation to come for New Year's Eve, a family tradition flooded with wonderful childhood memories. I could hardly wait.

"SATURDAY, DECEMBER 27TH: TOOK AUDREY AND DOROTHY FOR A WALK ALONG THE SEA FRONT IN THE MORNING. WHAT A NICE BREAK THIS IS FROM SCHOOL! SIRENS IN EVENING BUT NO AIR RAID."

It had been a long time since I'd seen this rocky coast of northeast England. With a jolt, I now I realized that the Nazis were just across the North Sea from it, in occupied Denmark.

Audrey and Dorothy, eight and four years old, were always ready for an outing. Muffled against the bone-chilling cold of the wind sweeping in off the North Sea, they hopped and skipped ahead of me like two overstuffed dolls on the promenade overlooking the beach and the sea. In the distance was the harbor entrance, with its lighthouse at the end of the long, curving, concrete fishing pier over which an occasional R.A.F. patrol plane flew looking for enemy submarines.

The shoreline was bordered by limestone cliffs, their edges battered for centuries by the winds and high waves of the North Sea. Here and there, erosion had left a grotesque pillar of rock or a limestone arch we could walk through at low tide. By the harbor entrance, ground-down rocks extended out from the beaches for more than a mile offshore, their tops hidden under water at high tide.

From my childhood I remembered tales of pirates and smugglers here in earlier centuries. They caused shipwrecks by hanging lanterns near the rocks hidden by the sea at high tide, to trick the crews of incoming sailing ships into thinking they were the harbor lights, so they ended up with their hulls torn apart by the rocks.

Once a ship was wrecked, the waiting pirates rowed out and plundered its cargo, stripping it of valuables and bringing them ashore. The loot was then smuggled through a chain of hollow caves in the cliffs, resurfacing several miles up the coast, where it could be safely bartered with no questions asked.

"Bunty, let's go and see 'Spottee's Hole,'" chorused the girls. We walked to the end of the promenade near the harbor and down onto the beach. One of our favorite places to visit was a large cave in the cliff face. Spottee was thought to have been a French sailor shipwrecked in the 1800's wearing his signature spotted shirt. He was reputed to have taken up residence in the cave, where he lived and died. Legend has it that his ghost is heard moaning periodically. It was fun to go inside and make ghostly noises, which would echo around its sides and ceiling. To my dismay, what had been the cave entrance was now boarded up, with a sign "Danger, Unsafe to Enter." Erosion had taken its toll, but the "coup de grace" had been dealt by a bomb intended for the harbor, which had landed near the cave instead.

That evening the air-raid siren sounded. We shivered as we made our way to the outdoor shelter, carting with us as many blankets as we could carry. But after a few distant thumps we heard the "All Clear" and hurried back to the warmth of the house. Hardened by the deluge of destruction from air raids the previous year, Sunderland residents now viewed these puny raids with some disdain, and nobody got excited any more about the air-raid warnings.

— ✼ —

Churchill in North America

WINSTON CHURCHILL HAD spent Christmas and New Year's three thousand miles away from Sunderland, after a rough eight-day crossing of the U-boat infested North Atlantic on the battleship, *Duke of York*. Addressing the U.S. Congress on December 26th, he had said: "I cannot help reflecting that if my father had been American and my mother British, instead of the other way round, I might have got here on my own!" The halls of Congress rocked with laughter; he had won their hearts. Two days later, Churchill declared to the Canadian Parliament that in 1940 he had told the French that if they surrendered to the Germans, Britain would fight on alone. He added: "Their (the French) generals told their Prime Minister and his divided cabinet: 'In three weeks, England will have her neck wrung like a chicken.' Some chicken! Some neck!" British radio audiences listening to his words across the Atlantic applauded delightedly, just as the Canadian Parliament did as they rose to their feet in a standing ovation while they roared with laughter.

"WEDNESDAY, DECEMBER 31ST: WENT ACROSS TOWN TO CELEBRATE NEW YEAR'S EVE WITH THE DITCHFIELDS. HAD TEA, THEN A TRADITIONAL FAMILY NEW YEAR'S PARTY IN THE EVENING. WONDERFUL! SO LONG, 1941 - SEE YOU IN NEXT YEAR'S DIARY, 1942!"

"Come in, come in!" Gram Ditchfield's face was alight with joy, her apple-pink cheeks flushed and blue eyes dancing as she opened the front door with its elegant stained-glass panels to welcome Mom, Dad and myself.

Small and plump, in her ankle-length dress, with her hair caught up into a little bun on top of her head, she looked the epitome of an Edwardian lady. We stepped across the brightly polished brass doorstep into the front hall. Next to the coat rack and its mirror was a magnificently carved, dark oak Jacobean storage bench, its high back resting against the wall, where I remember sitting as a child to have Dad take off my outdoor boots. Hugs and kisses were exchanged, and I took my suitcase upstairs to the little bedroom that would be mine while we stayed with the family for the next few days, before returning to Auntie Belle's.

Gram and my aunts must have hoarded food for months to be able to have a party, but New Year's Eve at the Ditchfield's was a long-standing tradition in the family, one not to be broken by those "filthy Nazis," as my grandfather called them. The lull in the intensive air raids on Sunderland had made it possible this New Year's for the family to gather in relative safety.

My diary entry was a long one; it continued on the extra lines available for notes at the end of the little book. I described arriving at Gram and Grandpa's in time for toasted tea cakes and hot, fragrant tea while I listened to the aunts catching up on local gossip, births, deaths and marriages.

As the evening approached, more people arrived, and soon there were twenty of us in Gram's high-ceilinged drawing room, three generations of Ditchfields: Grandpa's sister Auntie "Cis," and her husband, Uncle Hal McKenzie, Mom and her sisters, Alan and myself. There were also a few invited friends I had never met including some of Alan's cronies in their R.A.F. uniforms. My diary reported: "ALAN PLAYED SOME OF THE OLD NORTH COUNTRY FOLK SONGS ON THE PIANO, AND WE ALMOST RAISED THE ROOF WITH OUR SINGING! WE PLAYED THE OLD PARTY GAMES I REMEMBERED, AND A NEW ONE, PASSING A BALLOON FROM CHIN TO CHIN AROUND THE ROOM. HILARIOUS! WHEN IT CAME TO 'FORFEITS,' AUNTIE CIS PAID HER FORFEIT BY RECITING 'WHEN FATHER CARVED THE GOOSE.'"

No family party was complete without Auntie Cis reciting her "party piece," so we all sat back to listen. We knew it by heart; a very long, comic poem describing a family around the table at their Christmas dinner, and the misadventures of Father as he tries to carve the roasted goose. In one of the many verses he gets the carving knife stuck in it, and when he tries to shake it loose, the carcass whizzes across the table, landing in the lap of a horrified aunt. We all laughed at the right places. Auntie Cis eventually sat down, surrounded by energetic applause.

My diary continued: "AT FIVE MINUTES TO MIDNIGHT UNCLE HAL AND ALL THE MEN WENT OUTSIDE FOR FIRST-FOOTING. AFTERWARDS WE HAD A LOVELY BUFFET SUPPER AND TOASTED THE NEW YEAR WITH GRAM'S HOME-MADE GINGER WINE AND HER SPECIAL CHRISTMAS CAKE. IT WAS FOUR O'CLOCK BY THE TIME WE ADJOURNED TO BED!"

"First-Footing" is a tradition followed in the north of England and Scotland. When he was young, Grandpa's brother-in-law, Uncle Hal McKenzie, had become the family's official First Foot. With his neatly trimmed moustache and military bearing, he met all the criteria. A First Foot had to be tall, dark-haired, healthy and good-looking. As midnight struck, his foot was the first to step across the threshold in the New Year. The First Foot brought the household good luck for the year, and gifts to ensure plenty of food, drink and warmth to last all year long.

A few minutes before midnight, Uncle Hal and the men put on their coats and went outside into the cold, blacked-out night, then formed a line behind him, facing the door. The ladies lined up inside the front hall behind my grandmother. At the stroke of midnight there was a knock on the door, and Gram opened it. In peacetime all the church bells in Sunderland would have been heard "ringing out the old year and ringing in the new."

Uncle Hal stepped across the threshold, the first foot to enter the house in 1942. He gave Gram a hug and a kiss, and wished her a happy New Year. He handed her a piece of rock salt, representing plenty of food. Tucked under his arm was usually a bottle of wine, representing plenty to drink. Representing warmth for the New Year he gave Gram a large lump of coal, dressed as a Santa Claus in red crepe paper, which was later burned with ceremony in the dining-room fireplace.

This New Year's there were two things missing: wine was scarce, so Uncle Hal had nothing under his arm, and the blackout outside was silent; church bells would have been rung only as an alert for an invasion. Gram, always the gracious hostess, received Uncle Hal's gifts and said softly: "We can do without the bottle of wine, and I'm grateful we aren't hearing the bells this year."

The men filed into the house, small puffs of steam on their breath from the frigid midnight air. Each of them hugged and kissed the waiting ladies. We wished each other a Happy New Year, then trooped into the dining room to enjoy the buffet supper on the laden sideboard and to toast the New Year with Gram's traditional home-made ginger wine. The party continued for another few hours, ending at four o'clock with everyone joining hands to sing "Auld Lang Syne." The memory of that night has remained as bright and clear for me as if it had just occurred.

As he wished us "Happy New Year" on his way home, Uncle Lewis asked Dad: "How would you and Bunty like a visit to the docks tomorrow?" Dad was ecstatic: "Would we? What time shall we be ready?"

"THURSDAY, JANUARY 1ST: 'DECLARATION OF THE UNITED NATIONS' SIGNED IN WASHINGTON, D.C. WE STAYED THE NIGHT AT DITCHFIELD'S. SLEPT AS LATE AS POSSIBLE. WENT WITH DAD AND UNCLE LEWIS TO VISIT THE SUNDERLAND DOCKS."

The next step in the Atlantic Charter, originally drafted by Roosevelt and Churchill when they met in 1941, came about at the Arcadia Conference on New Year's Day, 1942. Twenty-six nations represented at the conference signed the "Declaration of the United Nations," affirming their support for the Charter in preparation for the formation of an international organization for mutual support. Eventually, forty-seven nations would sign, in the hope of shaping a world forever without war.

One of my earliest memories as a young child, after we came home from Africa to live in Sunderland, was going to visit the docks with my

Dad to see a ship launched after being built in the sprawling Sunderland shipyards. I joined in the cheers as it slid slowly down the "ways" and into the River Wear.

Dad's family had strong ties with the sea: a great-grandfather who was master of his own sailing ship trading in the Far East, a father and brother who were employed in the shipyards, and his own record of being a Chief Engineer on ships in the Merchant Marine, an officer in the Royal Navy, and, in the 1920s, captain of a merchant ship trading on Lake Victoria, the "inland sea" of Central Africa.

In wartime the shipyards were off-limits to visitors, but Uncle Lewis Dent was manager of the Payroll Department at one of the largest shipyards in Sunderland and pulled the strings for us to visit. We went aboard a damaged cargo ship that was being refitted. My diary reported: "CLIMBED ALL OVER THE SHIP, ESCORTED BY A LOVELY SAILOR WITH A LONDON ACCENT AND A RED MOUSTACHE. SAW CREW'S AND OFFICERS' QUARTERS, ENGINE ROOM, AND THE SHIP'S BARRAGE BALLOON, ANTI-AIRCRAFT GUNS AND MACHINE GUNS. GOT MY CLOTHES FILTHY!"

I couldn't have cared less about my clothes; exploring a real ship with my inherited love of the sea made getting them dirty seem insignificant. I couldn't resist asking our escort about his war experiences.

"How did your ship get damaged?" I asked. The red-headed sailor scratched his head. His weatherworn face had a pained look as he spoke carefully: "Well, Miss, it's loike this 'ere. I ain't allowed ter tell ya where we've been, but you moight say it was jest the wear and tear of being in a convoy. We ran into a pack of U-boats. One of 'em got the next ship to ours wiv a diyrect 'it wiv a torpedo, and we 'appened to be close enuff to be clobbered by some bits of the ship wot 'ad blown apart and took them pore brave lads down with 'er." His red moustache fairly bristled with emotion. "Pore bastards, they didn't stand a chance."

Chastened, I asked no more questions.

Disaster in the Lab

"FRIDAY, JANUARY 9TH: LEFT SUNDERLAND AT 7 A.M. IT WAS 5 P.M. WHEN WE GOT BACK TO WREXHAM. LOTS OF CHRISTMAS CARDS AND LETTERS WAITING. WAR NEWS IS TERRIBLE!"

No, we didn't "valk-all-the-vay," but Uncle Arthur's ancient Vauxhall wheezed all the way to Sunderland station with us and our baggage in the early morning blackout. After changing trains four times, we finally arrived back at Wrexham. Bronwyn, Mr. Evans and little Davey were all at the front door to welcome us.

"Welcome home, my dears," said Bronwyn, with a hug. "We've missed you. Had a quiet Christmas here, just the two of us. Supper's ready. When you get settled, come down and tell us all about your holidays with your family. A Happy New Year to you all!"

I took a small pile of envelopes up to my bedroom. Christmas cards and letters had come from Peter, Paul, William, George and also Bruce Ferguson, who was expecting to be promoted to midshipman in the Royal Navy and had suddenly begun to write to me, much to my surprise. My old Ravenhurst buddies Molly and Jessie sent greetings, as well as neighbors back at Bishop's Hill. My eyes filled as I opened each one of these messages of affection reinforcing the bonds of friendship that had been woven into the tapestry of my life.

Dad relaxed in the Evans' living room. He had been catching up on his mail and the accumulated newspapers. "Well, I'm off again on a new job on Monday. This time it's drinking water for a new airfield being built for the U.S. Air Force in the southeast of England. The 'Yanks' are coming, alright!"

Mom was worrying about the latest news broadcast: "What a way to start the New Year! The Japs are close to overrunning Singapore, and in North Africa that awful Desert Fox has pushed our Monty out of all the territory he had recaptured before Christmas! And the newspaper says that in the North Atlantic the number of Allied supply ships sunk by the "wolf packs" has soared. Oh dear, won't we ever hear something good for a change?"

"WEDNESDAY, JANUARY 14TH: BACK TO SCHOOL. GOOD NEWS! AT ASSEMBLY, ONE OF THE 6TH FORM GIRLS ANNOUNCED THAT IN A FEW WEEKS A COURSE IN BALLROOM DANCING WOULD BEGIN IN THE EVENINGS AT THE LOCAL HOTEL. MOM SAYS I CAN GO IF ONE OF THE GIRLS GOES WITH ME."

"Ballroom dancing classes! Whoopee!" I effervesced to Bessie on our way home. "I'd give my eye teeth to go. Don't you just love those Fred Astaire and Ginger Rogers movies? I'm wondering what Mom will say. Hope it's 'O.K., Bunty, off you go.'"

Maggie said she wasn't interested, but Bessie was thrilled at the prospect. "But I don't think Dad would allow it." She was the picture of dejection; her blonde braids actually seemed to droop. "He's a straight-laced Welsh Baptist, you know, and he doesn't hold with men and women dancing together like that. Says it's tempting the devil!"

I was surprised to find Mom wasn't a pushover, either. She was adamant. "You can go, Bunty, but only if you have another girl to go along with you. I don't want you running around alone in the blackout."

"Bessie's longing to go, Mom, but her father's a stumbling block that his children never seem to dare to challenge. After supper I'll go over to Bessie's and see if there's any hope."

"All right, but don't you upset Bessie's Dad, and don't forget to take your flashlight."

I was on a crusade: I had to somehow get Bessie into that class or I couldn't go either. When I came home, Mom couldn't contain her curiosity.

"Mom, I don't know how it happened, but Bessie's Dad is going to let her try the ballroom dancing lessons with me! Bronwyn says she is coming with us, too. Surprise!"

Mom capitulated. "O.K., you win this time." But she had to deliver a parting shot: "But don't let it interfere with your school-work."

"TUESDAY, JANUARY 15TH: DISASTER! THIS AFTERNOON IN CHEMISTRY CLASS NELLA LET ME DEMONSTRATE HOW TO MAKE

DISTILLED NITRIC ACID. THE RETORT I WAS HEATING EXPLODED AND THE MIXTURE OF BOILING SULPHURIC ACID AND POTASSIUM NITRATE FLEW IN ALL DIRECTIONS. MY RIGHT HAND IS BADLY BURNED. THANK GOODNESS I WRITE LEFT-HANDED!"

Another shortage caused by the war was the manufacture of new chemistry lab equipment. I was thrilled that my favorite teacher, "Nella," had singled me out to carry out the chemistry demonstration for the class. Neither of us realized that the glass retort I was heating with my right hand was old and worn dangerously thin. In peacetime it would have been replaced long before this. It suddenly exploded, splashing boiling acid over my right hand, which was holding the Bunsen burner on a low flame. I dropped the burner, and Nella rushed me to the sink and ran cold water over my hand. She probably saved it. Strangely, there was no blood, but I remember feeling faint as I saw the skin on two of my fingers split open under the stream of cold water, peeling like ripe red bananas. The index finger was burned right down to the bone. I could see it, white and glistening, in a bed of scalded flesh. I can still remember Nella making me lie on the floor and covering me with a blanket, while my stunned classmates retrieved the Bunsen burner and began cleaning up the broken glass.

The school nurse came and put a large wad of absorbent cotton on my hand, then covered it with a loose bandage before calling my local doctor for an appointment early the following morning. Nowadays I would have been rushed to the hospital emergency room, but back in 1942, given the shortage of doctors and hospital beds, my condition was evidently not considered serious enough. I don't remember how I got home, but Maggie and Bessie walked with me, and after an eternity I wobbled through the door into the arms of my shocked mother. Mom sat by my bed all night as waves of pain engulfed me. This had finally tapered off to a steady throbbing as the two of us walked to the doctor's office the next morning in the cold, crisp air.

"FRIDAY, JANUARY 16TH: WENT TO DOCTOR FIRST THING IN THE MORNING. HE BEGAN TREATMENT ON MY HAND. NO MORE PAIN. HAD TO HAVE INTERVIEW WITH THE 'WELSH DRAGON' TO EXPLAIN WHAT HAPPENED. MAGGIE CAME TO VISIT WITH USUAL RESULT."

As the doctor gently took off the temporary dressing, I was scared to death. I forced myself to look at the scorched fingers, an angry red color where the skin had opened; they were grotesquely swollen to twice their size. It was impossible to bend them; I described them in my diary as feeling like "liquid wax gone solid."

"Will I ever be able to use that hand again?" I wondered miserably. I wasn't at all hopeful that I would. I began to shake uncontrollably. "What will he do to me, and will it hurt?" I wondered. Then, "Oh, stop it, Bunty, you're behaving just like you do when you go to the dentist! Better try to get hold of yourself."

My inward struggle was interrupted by a quiet voice. "Can you feel any pain, my dear?" asked the doctor.

"No, there's no pain now," I whispered, still shaking.

"Well, that's a good sign, anyway. You've already been through a lot, I know, but I'm going to begin your treatment today in consultation with a colleague of mine who is a burn specialist. It should take a few weeks, but I think there's hope we can save the movement in your fingers."

My shaking eased as I saw the compassion in his eyes, and his graying hair was somehow comforting to me, too. He was one of the civilian doctors who had not been called into war service because of his age, and I surmised that under normal circumstances he would now be enjoying retirement. His quiet words gave me the confidence that I wouldn't lose the use of my hand. As he was speaking, another man came in to the examining room and was introduced to us. This was the burn specialist consultant whom the doctor had just mentioned. He began work immediately, bathed my hand with warm saline solution, then clipped away some of the dead skin before finishing up with a large padded dressing. On the daily visits to the doctor that followed, treatment was always in consultation with his specialist colleague. Mom had told the doctors about her service as a nurse's aide with the V.A.D. (Volunteer Aid Detachment) at Sunderland Hospital in World War One, when she had helped care for the wounded men returning from battlefields in France. Both doctors were delighted and showed her how to apply warm saline baths to my hand three times a day, then how to put on a new dressing. The next ten days in my diary recorded slow but steady improvement, as Mom followed their instructions at home in between our daily appointments at the doctor's office.

Maggie came to visit me shortly after the accident, but rather unfortunately at a time when Mom was being a V.A.D. with the saline solution. Maggie regarded my injured fingers with horror, and true to form, passed out on the floor. I was used to Maggie's routine; she would have recovered on her own, but Mom said proudly: "It's a good thing I had all that V.A.D. training in World War One; I knew just what to do for her." There was no point in bursting Mom's V.A.D. bubble--Maggie and I just smiled at each other.

The Welsh Dragon had demanded that I come for an interview. Her dour appearance wasn't enhanced by the glare she gave to Nella, who seemed somehow shrunken, sitting in a chair in the school office.

I explained as well as I could what had happened, emphasizing that I had been well instructed by Nella on how to demonstrate the experiment, but that both of us were unprepared for the explosion of the thin glass retort, in view of the fact that I had kept a very low flame on the Bunsen burner. My headmistress dismissed Mom and me, but insisted that Nella stay in the office. As Mom and I walked home, I said a quick prayer that the accident wouldn't cost poor Nella her job. Luckily, it didn't.

"SATURDAY, JANUARY 24th: WAR NEWS IS ROTTEN, EXCEPT FROM RUSSIA. THEY SEEM TO BE HOLDING THE NAZIS, BUT ROMMEL HAS TAKEN MORE TOWNS IN NORTH AFRICA, THERE ARE MORE BRITISH WITHDRAWALS IN MALAYA, AND THE JAPS HAVE LANDED IN NEW

GUINEA, POSING A THREAT TO AUSTRALIA. THE ONLY GOOD NEWS IS THAT MY HAND FEELS BETTER EVERY DAY."

There were long faces everywhere in Britain as territory was lost day by day to the Germans in North Africa and to the Japanese in the Far East. On the Eastern Front, the Russian winter had immobilized both armies.

The specialist was now applying some thick yellow ointment to my hand, and I could move my fingers a little bit. At today's visit, both doctors were so pleased with my healing that they allowed me to go back to school after changing the dressing. My diary reported: "IT'S A BIT OF A PROBLEM HAVING ONLY ONE HAND TO USE WHEN I COULD DO WITH HALF A DOZEN, BUT MAGGIE HELPS ME ON AND OFF WITH MY COAT. I'M GLAD I HAVEN'T MISSED MUCH AT SCHOOL; IT WON'T BE HARD TO CATCH UP."

"TUESDAY, JANUARY 27TH: A SCHOOL INSPECTOR OBSERVED US IN OUR FRENCH LESSON, AND ANOTHER CAME TO OBSERVE OUR BIOLOGY CLASS. NICE LETTER FROM PETER WITH AN ADORABLE BROOCH ENCLOSED."

In Britain, education was a serious business, and from elementary schools to prep schools inspectors visited to check on the quality of instruction in the classrooms. Private schools like Ravenhurst and Wrexham Park welcomed these visits, because the excellence of the reports would insure healthy numbers of enrollments and income from school fees.

Peter was working in the daytime and going to night school at a technical college in a nearby suburb. Enclosed in his letter was a beautifully crafted pin he had made from leftover metal from the industrial arts shop. It was in the shape of a small figure-skating boot, and on the back he had engraved his and my initials. As Mom pinned it on the lapel of my tweed coat, she said: "There, Bunty, you're not losing the boys, after all."

My diary entry continued: "MY HAND IS BEGINNING TO RETURN TO NORMAL. I CAN NOW BEND MIDDLE FINGER AND THUMB, BUT NOT INDEX FINGER YET." To everyone's relief, I was healing quite quickly from what might well have been a catastrophic loss of the use of my right hand. I breathed a hasty prayer: "Thank you, dear Lord, for sending good doctors to work your miracle!" Again, I felt blessed.

"THURSDAY, JANUARY 29TH: AMERICAN TROOPS LANDED IN NORTHERN IRELAND. MY HAND IS MUCH BETTER. BACK TO SCHOOL IN TIME FOR TESTS! UGH! AT 7 P.M BRONWYN, BESSIE AND I WENT TO OUR FIRST DANCING LESSON".

The first Americans to land in Britain were tough, regular Army men. A contingent arrived in Sunderland to man the coastal guns. They quickly found the local pubs, also some of the less virtuous local girls. Brawls were common. Girls from Sunderland's "nice" families were hustled indoors before dusk by their concerned parents. Gram Ditchfield wrote scandalized letters to Mom about the goings-on of "those dreadful Yanks." Her mental image of the heroic American male projected by Hollywood had been shattered forever.

While the first Americans were arriving on British soil, Bronwyn, Bessie and I, now with my hand minimally bandaged, were heading for the Wynnstay Arms Hotel to enroll in "Miss Price's Dancing Academy." The elegant hotel ballroom had oak-paneled walls and a highly polished parquet floor. A crystal chandelier hung from the center of the sculpted plaster ceiling. Surprisingly, young males outnumbered the handful of schoolgirls and older women. Miss Price was tall and sinewy, resembling a rejected ballet dancer, with her hair scraped back into a bun. She surveyed the motley collection of students as we sat in chairs on the edge of the dance floor. Her voice was firm and very loud.

"Well, class, let's get to it. I've no doubt I can shape you all up into good dancers by the time our course is finished if you pay attention and follow my instructions." She then wound up an ancient phonograph, and carefully inserted the needle into its holder at the edge of the ten-inch record.

Yanking an embarrassed young man from his chair, she demonstrated a few basic waltz steps, then, barking like a drill sergeant, she ordered us to choose partners. I found myself grabbed convulsively by a brawny, unkempt youth named Eric, who looked as if he had just come in from the hayfield. In time with the music, Miss Price shouted: "a-one-and-a-two-and-a-three-and BEGIN. One two three, one two three, twirl your partner, one two three."

The waltz tune was one that I had danced to on the ice at Brighton ice rink, and for a moment I was lost in memories. My mind jolted back to the present as Eric's foot landed squarely on my toes.

Bronwyn Enlists

"MONDAY, FEBRUARY 9TH: BRONWYN BEGAN HER NATIONAL SERVICE AT THE ROYAL ORDNANCE FACTORY. SHE HATES GETTING UP AT 5 A.M. FOR THE DAY SHIFT! SOAP RATIONING BEGAN. ROGER WHITE IS IN SOUTH AFRICA, TRAINING FOR AIR CREW AND ENJOYING LOTS OF BANANAS, LUCKY DUCK."
Bronwyn looked gloomy after opening her call-up notice. "Dammit," she groaned, "the bloody Government has caught up with me at last! I'll have to do war work or join the women's armed forces."

Needed by her father at home to run the household, Bronwyn decided to apply for war work at a nearby Royal Ordnance factory, making munitions. Her time available for housework severely curtailed, she set the neighbors gossiping when they saw her hanging wash on the outdoor clothes line and scrubbing the front steps in slacks and an old sweater on Sundays, violating their pious taboo against work on the Sabbath.

Shift work at the factory put an end to Bronwyn's dancing lessons. After class on Thursdays I made notes on the new dance steps we had learned so we could practice them together when she had the spare time to turn on dance band music on the radio or phono-graph. We made a notebook, which I still have, illustrated with little footprints showing the steps.

Soap was now rationed, a victim of the shortage of fats and oils. Mom sewed little pouches from thin pieces of plastic sponge cov-ered with netting, cut to fit a bar of soap. Once sewn into the pouch without any means of escape, a precious bar of soap could be used down to the last sliver without any being wasted.

Mrs. White wanted us to know that "our Roger" was safe and enjoy-ing an unlimited supply of bananas in South Africa while he trained as an R.A.F. navigator/bombardier, leaving us full of envy for warm sun-shine and our mouths watering for the bananas.

"MONDAY, FEBRUARY 16TH: CHURCHILL ANNOUNCED THE FALL OF SINGAPORE. WHAT AN UNWELCOME SIXTEENTH BIRTHDAY PRESENT. BUT MOM GAVE ME A LOVELY BIRTHDAY TEA. PETER SENT ME A GREETINGS TELEGRAM. WILLIAM SENT A SWEET LITTLE NECKLACE. HE HAS BEEN ACCEPTED FOR TRAINING AS AN R.A.F. FIGHTER PILOT!"

In a radio speech, Churchill morosely announced the Japanese capture of Singapore, along with sixty thousand British troops. He called this "the worst disaster and largest capitulation in British history." His tone was sombre as he asked for national unity in the face of this disastrous defeat. This was not the ebullient, defiantly cheerful Churchill we knew, now compelled to report such huge losses in the Far East, as well as in North Africa and on the Atlantic Ocean.

"Happy sweet sixteenth birthday, my love," said Mom, giving me a hug as I sat down to breakfast.

"Nothing much to celebrate," I thought. But I brightened up when the boys remembered my birthday. The mailman delivered a small package, a little jewelry box containing a pretty necklace from William. Folded inside the box was an ecstatic letter. William's dream of being accepted by the R.A.F. for training as a fighter pilot was a reality. He would receive orders five months from now to begin pilot training, and he hoped this would take place in Canada.

Later that day, a birthday "Greetings Telegram" arrived. Peter, as usual, was doing things with a flourish. He hated writing letters, and he knew this special, colorfully decorated telegram would be a better birthday surprise. He was right.

Mom's priorities were clear. Maggie and Bessie had insisted on walking me home from school. As they followed me through the door they joined in the chorus of "Surprise!" Along with Maggie and Bessie, Mom had invited their mothers and Bronwyn to a surprise sixteenth birthday tea, with dainty little sandwiches and cakes made from hoarded rations. It was a gesture of love, worth more to me than any number of fancy presents.

"THURSDAY, FEBRUARY 19TH: DANCING CLASS. ALL FOURTEEN OF US TURNED UP. THERE'S A NEW CHAP FROM LONDON, KEN KNIGHT. HE ESCORTED BESSIE AND ME HOME IN THE BLACKOUT." After our next attempt at the waltz, Miss Price exploded: "Good grief, class, you sound like a herd of elephants thumping around! Now, this time I don't want to hear your feet when you dance. Once again, one-and-a-two-and-a-three, glide, glide, glide."

After that we danced with less exuberance and there was no more stomping on the polished floor. "Miss P." insisted that we change partners for each dance, and when it came time for the slow foxtrot, I found myself face to face with Ken Knight.

What a relief from my other partners! Ken and I danced together very well. He said: "You know, I believe I can learn how to dance now, after all!" I was flattered, and his English accent was music to my homesick ears. He asked if he could escort Bessie and me home. We dropped Bessie off and I invited Ken to come in, standard procedure with all my friends. Mom looked a bit surprised, but bustled into the kitchen and made some hot cocoa.

"Well, what are you doing here in North Wales, Ken?" Mom was understandably curious about the sudden appearance of a new young man on the scene with a cultured London accent.

"I'm working on an assignment for a London engineering company. It's 'essential work' that would exempt me from military service, but I've volunteered for R.A.F. flight crew training and now I'm waiting to be called up."

My diary noted: "WE TALKED AND TALKED UNTIL ELEVEN O'CLOCK!" Ken was on his way to becoming a fixture in my life.

"SATURDAY, FEBRUARY 20TH: NEWS FROM SUNDERLAND. ENOCH WALKER, MOM'S COUSIN, HAS BEEN LOST AT SEA. THE TWO MCKENZIE BOYS ARE LISTED AS MISSING AFTER THE FALL OF SINGAPORE."

"Bad news from Sunderland, Bunty." Mom was reading a letter from Gram which had just arrived. "Your Uncle Enoch Walker has been drowned at sea. He was just like a brother to me. But praise God, the McKenzie boys are not reported killed at Singapore."

Enoch was named after Grandpa Ditchfield. His mother was a Ditchfield, Grandpa's younger sister; he and his brother Ernie were orphaned when they were very young and Gram and Grandpa had raised both boys along with their own six children. Enoch's ship had been sunk by a U-boat in the North Atlantic. By some miracle he was the only one of our family to die in World War Two.

The two sons of Uncle Hal McKenzie, the Ditchfields' perennial First Foot, were war correspondents with the British Army in Singapore and had been reported as missing. Although their escape left them unhurt, it would be months before their parents would know they had been taken prisoner by the Japanese. They would eventually survive horrific experiences in Japanese prison camps and come safely home to England after the war to write about them.

"THURSDAY, FEBRUARY 26th: WENT TO BESSIE'S TO PICK HER UP FOR DANCING CLASS, BUT SHE'S NOT FEELING WELL, SO I WENT

ON ALONE. KEN ASKED TO SEE ME HOME, A BIG HELP IN THE BLACKOUT."

Miss Price was steering us through the ballroom dancing lessons like a commando sergeant with a drill team. She still insisted that we change partners for each dance. Ken and I struggled through some new dance steps together when he turned up as my partner. He asked me if he could escort me home, and I was surprised and glad. Mom was on hand with the hot cocoa soon after we rang the doorbell.

For a mere sixteen-year-old schoolgirl to have captured the attention of an "older man" of twenty-one was rather flattering, and I was fascinated. At dancing class, Ken's muscular, compact body moved with the strength and grace of one who has spent much time out of doors. His brown hair had an irrepressible tendency to curl, his face was bronzed from sun and wind, and the humor in his brown eyes was sobered by the dark rims of his glasses. Ken was interested in anything and everything; he could speak knowledgeably on an enormous variety of subjects. His hobbies included hiking, rock climbing, sketching and photography, and he was writing a novel! He had volunteered as a Wrexham fire watcher and had already become a blood donor for the Red Cross. I had a new hero! William began to fade into the distance.

"THURSDAY, MARCH 5TH: IT SNOWED ALL NIGHT, BUT DIDN'T FREEZE. WE'RE HAVING A WEEK OF EXAMS TO PREPARE FOR THE CENTRAL WELSH BOARD. WENT TO DANCING CLASS TO RELAX. ONLY EIGHT OF US THERE!"

At school I was up to my armpits in exams. Designed as practice for the Central Welsh Board exams in July, each one was two hours long, consisting entirely of essay questions, some requiring maps or diagrams. Based on what we had learned in all five years of secondary school, the exam results of the Central Welsh Board would determine if we would qualify to enter university.

Bessie and I waded through the melting snow to dancing class. Only eight of us were there. Ken arrived late, but I had most of the dances with him, and he came home with me for another visit after we saw Bessie safely to her front door.

With the unexpected arrival of Ken, my social life improved one hundred percent. When we came home after dancing class, Mom had the usual cups of steaming hot cocoa ready, to warm us after our chilly walk through the slush in the blackout. Ken looked at me intensely over his cup. I wondered what was coming.

"Bunty, you're having a grueling week in school with exams, you really deserve a reward. Mrs. Amiss, I thought I'd reserve seats at the movies on Saturday for Bunty and me. Is it O.K. with you?"

This "older man" was asking me for a date! I held my breath.

Mom said: "That's very nice of you, Ken. Yes, it's O.K."

It was customary for reserved seats to be sold for special high-quality movies that were expected to fill up the movie theaters on weekends. This time it was the movie spectacular, *King Solomon's Mines*. I was impressed and felt very grown-up; what a perfect antidote after a week of those exhausting exams!

"SATURDAY, MARCH 7TH: DAD IS AWAY FOR A FEW WEEKS ON A NEW JOB.
THE JAPANESE HAVE TAKEN JAVA. AUSTRALIA IS IN DANGER OF INVASION! KEN TOOK ME TO THE MOVIES - RESERVED SEATS!"
The Japanese seemed unstoppable in the Far East and were now threatening the Australian mainland, shocking news for Britain, on top of the defeats of the past weeks. Seen from our reserved seats, *King Solomon's Mines* was all the previews had promised.

Ken was the breath of fresh air I had longed for, ever since we came to Wrexham. We found in each other the good companionship we had been missing. He and I talked for hours, walked for miles and rode our bicycles to explore the lovely little villages and beauty spots in the surrounding countryside. Mom had missed the boys at Upper Woodside with their happy enthusiasm for life and their appreciation of her cooking, so Ken soon found with us a home away from home.

Most weekends he went off on his own to explore North Wales, staying at youth hostels, hiking, and climbing some of the smaller peaks in the mountains. He often "popped in" for a visit on his way back from his trips, entertaining Mom and me with stories of his adventures, and if he happened by at dinner time, we shared whatever we were eating with him. "Mother hen" Mom had found a new chick.

Ken was currently working on the draft of his first novel, which, to my surprise, he gave to me to read. My respect for him knew no bounds. I felt like a sponge, soaking up his grownup views and philosophy of life. Evidence of Ken's existence must have seeped through the pages of my letters to William. Little did I dream what the consequences would be!

The National Loaf

"WEDNESDAY, MARCH 11TH: NO MORE WHITE BREAD!"
Ever resourceful, the Government had added an innovation to our sparse wartime diet in order to offset the shortage of wheat. It was called "The National Loaf." Wheat and all other grains were pooled together, ground into unbleached flour, and baked into loaves of bread. To say that it contained plenty of healthy roughage would be pure British understatement: the remains of semi-ground husks were in every slice!

Each morning housewives waited in line at bakeries for the warm, newly baked, beige bread which had no preservatives. Delicious when fresh, it was usually eaten before it had time to spoil. If not, after a day or so it became a hard, moldy, light green substance, fit only to be recycled into the gizzards of the National Hens waiting to gobble it up in millions of British backyards. I caught Mom disposing of a greenish, brick-shaped chunk in the garbage can one day.

"Well," she said defensively, if Mrs. Standish lived closer, I would have given it to her for her 'fowls'."

"SUNDAY, MARCH 22ND: DARWIN AND OTHER TOWNS IN AUSTRALIA HAVE BEEN BOMBED BY THE JAPS. THE RUSSIANS ARE ADVANCING

AGAINST THE NAZIS. PETROL IS BEING CUT TO HALF THE PRESENT RATION FOR GOVERNMENT EMPLOYEES. NO MORE PETROL AT ALL FOR CARS FOR PRIVATE USE."

The war had temporarily left our own doorstep, but we could identify with those families on the other side of the world in Australia, who were now on the receiving end of air raids, possibly a prelude to a Japanese invasion. Our hearts went out to them.

On a brighter note, we could see the tide turning in Eastern Europe as the Nazi war machine failed to recover from the punishing harshness of the Russian winter. However, in Britain the shortage of gasoline was at crisis point. In the next few weeks, family cars went up on blocks in driveways and garages. There they would remain, like stranded porpoises, for three more years, or even longer.

"SATURDAY, MARCH 28TH: BRITISH COMMANDOS HAVE RAIDED U-BOAT DOCKS AT ST. NAZAIRE IN FRANCE. KEN TOOK ME TO CHESTER TO SEE MY FIRST REAL LIVE OPERA."

This was a banner day. A daring Allied commando raid had tweaked Hitler's tail by landing in Nazi-occupied France, dealing a successful blow to his U-boat fleet, which was decimating British shipping. The main gate of the submarine pens had been blown up and the pens themselves also sustained considerable damage.

On the home front, I had one of the greatest thrills of my teenage life. After dancing class on Thursday, Ken had announced: "Guess what, Bunty? I've got reserved seat tickets for us at the opera house in Chester. You said you had never seen an opera, well, there's no time like the present!"

In my surprise, I could only manage one word: "Wow!" My excitement was at boiling point; I could hardly eat the noontime meal Mom had prepared for us before we took the bus to Chester about ten miles away, the nearest large town across the border in England, to see a matinee performance of *I Pagliacci*. It was performed, as most theatricals were in wartime, by a substitute male cast too old or too young for the armed forces.

I empathized with the tragic clown hero, weeping copiously into my handkerchief in all the appropriate places. We walked back to the bus stop. "Well, how did you like Pagliacci?" asked Ken.

"Oh," I sobbed, "I thoroughly enjoyed every minute. He reminded me of my grandfather."

"WEDNESDAY, APRIL 1ST: CLASSES HAVE RECESSED FOR THE EASTER BREAK. FINISHED KNITTING ANOTHER PAIR OF SOCKS FOR R.A.F. FLIGHT CREWS. TOOK THEM BACK TO THE W.V.S. AND GOT SOME MORE WOOL TO KNIT NEXT PAIR. DANCING CLASS TOMORROW--YIPPEE!"

The welcome break from school gave me time to attend to my war effort knitting; another pair of khaki socks for the Free French and the next pair of greasy, raw wool ones to go inside the flying boots of some R.A.F. air crew member. I was also wading through the draft of Ken's novel. I never did hear if it was ever published, but I was, of course, duly impressed.

Ken and I had by now become steady partners at dancing class, in spite of Miss Price's disapproval, and were learning our ballroom dancing steps pretty well. Each dance had a different set of steps to be memorized and followed--a mixed blessing, as I was to find out much later.

By now Ken had met Dad, who came home sporadically at weekends. Dad had said: "You know, Bunty, he's far too old for you to be running around with, but he seems to be a decent enough type, not the kind to pull any funny stuff. And you're getting old enough to know the difference."

I realized I was only sixteen, and Mom hadn't said anything about "funny stuff." "What difference?" I wondered.

"SATURDAY, APRIL 4TH: DOUBLE BRITISH SUMMER TIME BEGINS AT MIDNIGHT. KEN CAME BACK EARLY FROM HIS LATEST ROCK CLIMBING ADVENTURE."

"Time to put the clocks ahead another hour," sang Bronwyn, as she rushed from room to room to set them before bedtime. With Double British Summer Time came the flowers of spring. We gathered wild primroses and daffodils to fill the vases in the Evans' front hall, where they greeted visitors with their fragrance and sunny yellow flowers as the days began to lengthen. Next afternoon Ken dropped in, soaking wet from his latest rock-climbing weekend in the Welsh mountains. Mom gave him Dad's bathrobe and, in those days before electric clothes dryers were invented, put his clothes to dry on a wooden rack in front of the dining-room fire. She was all "mother hen": "Where on earth have you been, Ken, to get so muddy, and what have you done to your arm?"

Ken grimaced sheepishly. "Well, it was pouring with rain, and I slipped and fell twenty feet down a rock chimney. Fortunately there was another chap there to help me. I just grazed my arm a bit."

Mom, the ex-V.A.D., examined it, cleaned it up, and pronounced it not to be seriously injured.

During his work week, Ken often dropped in with little gifts. One lunch hour it was a packet of scarce cookies for Mom, another time a small jar of peanut butter, which he remembered I had said I'd never tasted. One evening when he picked me up for dancing class, his gift was a pin he had bought for me to wear on my Donegal tweed coat, made out of tiny acorns, beechnut burrs and small fir cones crafted into a beautiful little bouquet. Jewelry in wartime was often made from anything that came to hand: dried seed pods, lacquer-coated leaves and flowers, and also scraps of plexiglass left over from the aircraft factories and fashioned into earrings, pins and bracelets.

"SUNDAY, APRIL 19TH: YESTERDAY JIMMY DOOLITTLE AND HIS SQUADRON BOMBED TOKYO!"
The bad news coming from the war in the Pacific was offset by a daring air raid when American Lieutenant Colonel James Doolittle led a flight of sixteen B-25 bombers, launched from the modified flight deck of the aircraft carrier U.S.S. *Hornet* to attack the Japanese mainland. The

folks back in the U.S.A. needed this boost as much as we did in Britain. History books tell us that this raid gave impetus to Japanese Admiral Yammamoto's proposal to attack Midway and crush the American fleet, but that his ultimate defeat in the bitter naval Battle of Midway restored command of the Western Pacific to the U.S. Navy.

"SATURDAY, APRIL 25TH: KEN HAS TO GO BACK TO THE LONDON OFFICE FOR A WEEK. HE WILL SOON BE GOING BACK FOREVER. BOO-HOO! THIS AFTERNOON I WENT TO THE WREXHAM LABOR EXCHANGE TO SIGN UP FOR MANDATORY YOUTH REGISTRATION." The last of our ballroom dancing lessons on Thursday was followed by Ken's announcement of his recall to London. His face was glum when he stopped in to see us and tell us the news.

I thought to myself: "So this is the end of my reprieve from the humdrum existence in Wrexham. I wonder if I'll ever see Ken again?" His disappearance for a week left me time to spend with Maggie and Bessie, not half as exciting, but good company nevertheless for trips to the movies and long bike rides and walks in the country, to offset the intensifying pressure at school as tests and exams continued.

Youth registration was mandatory now that I was sixteen. Between now and my eighteenth birthday, when I would be eligible for the armed forces, I would become part of a pool of young labor that could be tapped for help in factories, offices, or on the farms, when school was in recess.

"SUNDAY, APRIL 26TH: STAYED IN ALL DAY DOING HOMEWORK. TODAY IS EMPIRE YOUTH SUNDAY, SO IN THE EVENING WENT WITH MOM, BESSIE AND HER MOM TO A YOUTH SERVICE AT ST. GILES'S CHURCH."
The gray stones of the church sanctuary echoed as hundreds of young people marched in from all over Denbighshire, dressed in the brightly colored uniforms of boys' and girls' youth organizations which had counterparts throughout the countries of the British Empire. They filled

the front pews with a rainbow of color. Bessie and I were particularly proud to see Maggie among their ranks, decked out in her full Girl Guide regalia.

Late afternoon sunlight streamed in through the ancient stained-glass windows, making little pools of red, gold and purple on the worn flagstone floors of the church. In the quiet hush, as the service was about to begin, I felt the protective reassurance of the old walls surrounding me, and in their presence, peace.

A Sad Farewell

"FRIDAY, MAY 8TH: CANDY AND CHOCOLATE TO BE RATIONED JULY 27TH. (CANDY RATIONING MEANS LESS CAVITIES. WILL THE DENTISTS EVER SURVIVE?) IN THE PACIFIC, JAPS NOW DOMINATE THE BURMA ROAD (BOO!) BUT HAVE RETREATED AFTER THE BATTLE OF THE CORAL SEA (YAAY!)."

I thought wistfully of the little boxes of chocolates that Dad always brought for Mom and me when he returned from one of his jobs away from home. They might soon be just a memory, like bananas!

More bad news from the Pacific: the Japanese had severed the Burma Road, vital supply route for the Allies. But there was good news, too. Among the names of far-off places becoming war zones was a new one to me. The Coral Sea, off the coast of northwest Australia, was where air combat was now being fought between Japanese and U.S. carrier-based aircraft battling for supremacy. The Japanese finally were forced by the U.S. Navy to retreat, their first reversal since Pearl Harbor. History records the U.S. victory in the Battle of the Coral Sea as the first turning point of the war in the Pacific.

"SUNDAY, MAY 10TH: KEN STOPPED BY THIS EVENING ON HIS WAY BACK FROM ANOTHER HIKING WEEKEND, WITH SOME BEAUTIFUL WILD RHODODENDRONS FROM THE WELSH MOUNTAINS FOR MOM. HE STAYED FOR SUPPER, AND GAVE ME A JAR OF HIS SPECIAL 'JAM.'"

Ken had a knack of leaving reminders of himself with us at all times. Fat buds were bursting into big pink and purple blossoms in the armful of wild rhododendrons he presented to Mom. They would soon be spectacular flowers. Mom rushed them into a vase of water, and as the days went by I reported: "RHODODENDRONS OPENING UP NICELY. I TOOK SOME AND MADE A FLOATING BOWL FOR THE LIVING ROOM TABLE, PER KEN'S ORDERS."

I thanked him for my gift, a little jar full of jam that had no identifying label. I held it up to the light: it was a nondescript brownish color. "What kind is it, Ken?"

"Well, this is "Knight's Delight." It's my own special blend. When I have enough jam jars with just a bit left in the bottom, I put them all together in an empty jar, give them a good stirring, and there you have it: "Knight's Delight." Thought you'd like to try some." Obviously straining to be kind, my diary said: "I GUESS IT TASTED O.K, AFTER YOU GOT USED TO IT--MAYBE HE SHOULDN'T HAVE INCLUDED THE MARMALADE!"

"TUESDAY, MAY 12TH: NEWSPAPERS ARE FULL OF POSSIBILITY OF POISON GAS BEING USED BY THE NAZIS ON THE RUSSIANS ON THE EASTERN FRONT. IF THE NAZIS GAS THE RUSSIANS, AND IF THE ALLIES GAS THE NAZIS, THEN THEY WILL PROBABLY GAS US!"
The Welsh Dragon looked more severe than ever as she addressed us at morning assembly: "Girls, I have been instructed to tell you to practice wearing your gas masks at home. You must carry them at all times, and bring them to school every day for a daily gas-mask drill."

When we moved to Wrexham we had all but forgotten about our gas masks. But now, even in the comparative safety of Wrexham, the war had found its way to our doorstep!

"WEDNESDAY, MAY 13TH: HAD A LETTER FROM WILLIAM. HE DARKLY HINTS AT BRINGING HIS BICYCLE TO WREXHAM FOR A VISIT, BETWEEN JUNE FIRST AND JUNE FIFTEENTH! WOW! WENT WITH

MOM AND KEN TO SEE THE THREE PRIZEWINNING PLAYS IN THE NORTH WALES DRAMA FESTIVAL. WONDERFUL PERFORMACES."
It dawned on me that my letters to William lately must have mentioned the arrival of Ken upon the scene. Had this galvanized him into action? But to think of him coming on a visit threw Mom into what my diary described as a "minor hurricane" of panic. Spilling out worried thoughts, she asked: "Whatever will I do with him? Where can he stay? He can't stay here with us; there isn't enough room. And for two weeks, how on earth will we keep him entertained? And what will I feed him? There's so much of him to fill up! And it's the wrong time for you, Bunty, to be distracted from studying for the Central Welsh Board. Oh dear, oh dear!"

Mom forgot her troubles for a few hours as she lapped up the performances of the talented amateur players who had brought home such honors to Wrexham from the annual Drama Festival, hanging onto their every word with total concentration. She had played in many amateur dramatic productions in her younger days in Sunderland, and also in the Townswomen's Guild Drama Group back in Upper Woodside. Being in the audience for a change, she had become a happy drama critic, reveling in every minute.

The following day Mom and I both wrote to William, asking him for more details for his plans. Bringing his bicycle with him would insure bike rides in the country, there were plenty of interesting walks, and Wrexham's two movie theaters would take care of a lot of the "entertaining" that Mom was worried about. She rushed around making advance plans for his proposed visit. Maggie's mother offered to let him stay in her spare bedroom, so that eased Mom's anxiety no end. I didn't mind; I didn't think Maggie was his type, anyway.

"SATURDAY, MAY 16TH: U.S. CONGRESS HAS PASSED A LAW CREATING WOMEN'S AUXILIARY ARMY CORPS (WAACS). THE U.S. FIRST ARMORED DIVISION HAS ARRIVED IN NORTHERN IRELAND. WENT FOR A BIKE RIDE WITH KEN IN THE EVENING."

The British women's "Auxiliary Territorial Service" (A.T.S.), had caught the eye of U.S. Chief of Staff General George Marshall, who advocated that a similar service be modeled after it in the U.S. forces. Soon the first contingent of eight hundred WAACS, as they were now called, were doing basic training at Fort Des Moines in Iowa. By the end of the war their numbers would have swelled to one hundred and fifty thousand. Meantime, U.S. troops had been trickling into Britain since January. In the next two years the trickle would become a flood, and by the end of the war, four million men would have been shipped to the E.T.O. (European Theater of Operations).

Life in Wrexham was brightened considerably by the addition of Ken. He was a talented story teller, and Mom and I made the perfect audience. We were equally enthralled by his story telling and then convulsed with laughter as he dramatized his experience after one of his days of rock climbing.

It went like this: "I had just come down from a Welsh mountain, complete with rope and ice axe, when I saw a chap in a Home Guard uniform coming toward me, brandishing his rifle. He said, in a thick Welsh accent: 'Halt, look you!' I halted.

'Hadvance and show your Hidentity Card, then,' he barked. I advanced. 'I can't show you my Identity Card, I left it back at my lodgings,' said I.

'Hand where, hindeed, is your gas mask?' he demanded 'I'm awfully sorry,' said I, 'but it's at my lodgings, too.'

'Then, look you, start marching,' shouted the Home Guard, bayonet at the ready.

I marched. The Home Guard escorted me at bayonet point to the local police station for two hours of interrogation under a naked electric light bulb, and I finally convinced them I was not a German spy by reciting the British cricket and soccer team scores for the past season. I was in luck. One of the local constabulary was a sports fan, and we all ended up at the local pub for a beer."

"TUESDAY, MAY 19TH: NICE SUNNY DAY. TOOK MY GAS MASK TO SCHOOL FOR FIRST TIME THIS YEAR. WE ARE EXPECTING TO BE GASSED BY THE GERMANS ANY MINUTE! AT SCHOOL THE WELSH DRAGON HAS SCHEDULED GAS MASK DRILLS EVERY DAY FROM NOW ON. MOM STILL RUSHING AROUND PREPARING FOR WILLIAM'S VISIT. HAD A LETTER FROM PETER, WHO SAYS HE'S 'DYING FOR US TO COME HOME.'"

Fortunately no poison gas was used in World War Two, but rumors were persistent. In retrospect, it is thought that the idea of using poison gas was probably propaganda put out by the Nazis to keep the Allies off balance. My gas mask smelled as pungent as ever, and there wasn't the fun with drilling at Wrexham Park like the hilarity we had experienced at Ravenhurst.

After a few weeks with no sign of anyone using poison gas on anyone else on the war fronts, the Welsh Dragon dropped our drills, much to everyone's relief.

Peter's letter was a surprise. I thought by now he would have found a steady girlfriend, but evidently he hadn't. He was still working, going to night school, and "doing his thing" with the Home Guard, but sounded bored with life. Mom said: "Thank goodness *he's* not planning a visit!"

"TUESDAY, MAY 26th: KEN HAS TO LEAVE WREXHAM. HIS ASSIGNMENT HERE IS FINISHED. WILL I EVER SEE HIM AGAIN? AT SCHOOL WE ARE HAVING ANOTHER ROUND OF INTENSIVE TESTS TO PREPARE FOR THE CENTRAL WELSH BOARD EXAMINATION."

Ken's departure would probably have hit home harder with me if I hadn't been preoccupied with preparations for the Central Welsh Board exams looming ever closer; they would determine whether or not I was qualified to enter college.

"I couldn't leave without bringing you a farewell gift, Bunty, and I promise to write," Ken said, as he handed me small, neatly wrapped box. In it was another sample of wartime jewelry, and I marveled that such a pretty bracelet could have been fashioned out of factory Plexiglass left over from the gun turret of a fighter plane. I gave Ken a hug and held out my arm to let him put the bracelet on for me. Sadly I realized once again how transitory my wartime relationships had been with so many people who had come into my life, touched it, then passed out of it again. They were what Dad called "ships that pass in the night."

A salty, down-to-earth engineer by nature, with a life history of travels on many oceans and interactions with many people, Dad often quoted from a poem by Henry Wadsworth Longfellow, written back in the nineteenth century:

"Ships that pass in the night, and speak each other in passing,
Only a signal shown, and a distant voice in the darkness;
So, on the ocean of life, we pass and speak one another,
Only a look and a voice;
Then darkness again and a silence."

I have never forgotten it.

The Central Welsh Board

"WEDNESDAY, MAY 27TH: THE GERMANS ARE ON THE OFFENSIVE IN LIBYA. TANK BATTLES RAGING ALL OVER THE DESERT. HAD A LETTER FROM PETER, AND ONE FROM MRS. STANDISH. WILLIAM IS VERY UPSET."

The war seesawed back again from British victories to British defeats in North Africa, now that "the Desert Fox" Rommel and his Afrika Korps had taken over from the Italians. British spirits seesawed up and down with these developments.

Peter had written that he was "dying for us to return home" after my exams. Mom said, with a smile: "He's probably broken up with his latest girlfriend!"

For two weeks there had been no further letter from William since he had announced his proposed visit, and I was furious that he hadn't followed up with any details. The letter from Mrs. Standish made it clear why we hadn't heard from him; he was nursing a bruised ego.

Both Mom and I had presumed that William would be coming to Wrexham by train, bringing his bicycle with him in the baggage car. His mother's letter said that he had planned to come on his bicycle! Now we could understand why he said he would be coming between June first and June fifteenth; it might have taken him that long to get here!

Reading between the lines, there must have been a lively battle of words and wills going on at the Standishes over William's determination to ride his bicycle to Wrexham. Both parents had finally managed to persuade him that such a risky venture was foolhardy; the thought of their only child pedaling alone from dawn to dusk for two hundred miles on major highways, at the mercy of traffic and the capricious British climate, and in the middle of a war, was simply unthinkable. Having lost face over the whole business, probably William was too mortified and embarrassed to write and tell us that his parents refused to allow him to come, and had called the whole thing off. Mom heaved a sigh of relief. "Thank goodness," she said, "he'll never know how much trouble he could have caused for us all!"

Out of compassion I stopped calling William uncomplimentary names in my diary for not writing.

"SUNDAY, MAY 31ST: TREMENDOUS SLAUGHTER GOING ON AT KHARKOV IN RUSSIA. THOUSANDS ARE BEING KILLED ON BOTH SIDES EVERY DAY. MEXICO HAS DECLARED WAR ON GERMANY! IN LIBYA THE TANK BATTLE IS STILL RAGING, THE FOURTH DAY WITHOUT A BREAK. WE HAVE WITHDRAWN NEARLY ALL OUR TROOPS FROM BURMA. LAST NIGHT THE ALLIES SENT MORE THAN ONE THOUSAND AIRCRAFT TO ATTACK INDUSTRIAL TARGETS IN THE RHINE VALLEY."

The war continued to fulfill its name as the Second World War with the addition of Mexico's commitment on the side of the Allies. U.S. aircraft with their flight and ground crews were pouring into Britain; air bases sprang up like mushrooms all over the landscape to accommodate them. Joint missions over Germany were now being flown by U.S. and R.A.F. aircraft numbering over one thousand planes at a time, to cripple Hitler's factories and his war machine.

The catalog of war news in my diary was probably the result of listening to the radio at breakfast time. Today I added, as an afterthought: "DID PILES OF HOMEWORK THIS EVENING." The Central Welsh Board examinations would begin on July first, not much time was left to review five years of learning.

In retrospect, the vacuum left in my life by Ken's departure and William's aborted attempt to cycle to Wrexham probably saved me from abysmal academic failure!

"WEDNESDAY, JUNE 3RD: ESSEN AND COLOGNE POUNDED BY U.S. AND R.A.F. BOMBERS. COUSIN LEW ACCEPTED FOR AIR CREW TRAINING. MY BEDROOM IS VERY HOT. DID MY LATIN HOMEWORK DRESSED ONLY IN MY WRISTWATCH!"

Germany's war production was being slowed down by the massive Allied air raids on its factories, due to the combined efforts of the R.A.F. and the U.S. Eighth Air Force.

My cousin Lew would soon send me a photo of himself by the Great Pyramid; his flight training would be in Egypt!

When I look back and remember those hours I spent propped up in bed in my small, stuffy room doing homework, I wonder how I ever achieved anything scholastically! In those days before central air conditioning, my bedroom *must* have been hot for me to mention in my diary how I coped with the soaring temperature!

"TUESDAY, JUNE 9TH: HAD A SUPER LETTER FROM KEN. HE HAS AT LONG LAST RECEIVED HIS CALLING-UP PAPERS FOR THE

R.A.F.! I'M GETTING NERVOUS ABOUT MY FRENCH ORAL EXAM ON THURSDAY."

Excitement filled Ken's letter; his dream of being inducted into the R.A.F. would become reality in two weeks' time. I thought to myself: "You know, Bunty, this is the perfect time for Ken to disappear from your life if he wants to. I wonder if I'll ever hear from him again?"

My gloom wasn't helped by the thought of the French Oral exam coming up in two days' time.

"THURSDAY, JUNE 11TH: "CENTRAL WELSH BOARD FRENCH ORAL. MY NAME WAS FIRST ON THE REGISTER, SO I WAS THE FIRST LAMB TO THE SLAUGHTER. THE EXAMINER WAS A FUNNY OLD LADY WHO CONDUCTED THE EXAM WHILE DRINKING A CUP OF TEA. SHE HAD A SET OF PROMINENT FALSE TEETH, HORN-RIMMED SPECTACLES, AND SMELLED OF MOTHBALLS. WE CHATTED LIKE OLD FRIENDS FOR ABOUT TWENTY MINUTES IN FRENCH, THEN WE PARTED ON THE BEST OF TERMS."

There was an oral as well as a written exam for modern foreign languages. Although my diary was quite critical of the state examiner's appearance and behavior, I thought to myself: "I really enjoyed that! She was a nice old bird, but I wonder how tough she is when she grades our exams? I'm so glad Latin isn't a modern language. It's dead as a door-nail--no oral!" The following day my diary reported: "BOY, AM I GLAD I HAD MY FRENCH ORAL YESTERDAY. TODAY I HAD THE SAVAGE AND CALLOUS SATISFACTION OF SEEING THEM ALL DITHERING AND ON THE BRINK OF HYSTERICS AS THEY WAITED THEIR TURN FOR THE EXAM. MARGARET JONES ACTUALLY DID HAVE HYSTERICS AND HAD TO BE TAKEN HOME!"

With the French Oral out of the way, I now had to wait until July to begin the Central Welsh Board series of written exams. The next days were spent nervously cramming (or "swotting" as we called it) for them.

"TUESDAY, JUNE 16TH: AT SCHOOL THE SECOND FORMS ARE VERY BUSY, HARVESTING STINGING NETTLES FOR OUR HERB-GATHERING PROJECT. THEY HAVE MADE A 'NETTLE STACK' IN THE CLOISTER, THEREBY OUSTING US FIFTH FORMERS FROM OUR HANGOUT. LITTLE STINKERS! WE WERE GIVEN THE SCHEDULE FOR THE CENTRAL WELSH BOARD WRITTEN EXAMS, WHICH CAUSED MOST OF US NERVOUS PROSTRATION. THEY BEGIN JULY 1ST. UGH!" Stinging nettles were high on the list of herbs to be collected. Their long fibers were valuable for weaving as a substitute for cotton and linen, to make clothing. Rich in vitamins A, B, C and K, as well as calcium, magnesium and other minerals, their leaves were edible when boiled. They could then be used as a nutritious substitute in recipes calling for spinach or kale. There was only one drawback. If the growing leaves touched your bare skin their tiny hairs left an unwelcome calling card, a sting that burned like hot needles, leaving itchy little welts on whatever skin surface they contacted. Wrexham Park's senior classes took full advantage of the school's pecking order, assigning the sixty or more twelve-year-olds in the second forms the miserable task of collecting stinging nettles for the war effort. But these kids were smart enough to figure out their own revenge. Grimly scratching themselves all over from the itchy "nettle rash," they spread out and stacked the nettles they had collected in an enormous pile, which took up all the sitting space in the sunny school cloister, a surefire way to keep us upper-class girls away from our favorite hangout at break and lunch time.

Maggie was even more stressed out by the thought of the exams than I was. Trying to be helpful, I said: "Just think, Mag, when the exams are over, it'll mean 'goodbye' for us to Wrexham Park and the Welsh Dragon forever. We might even have forgotten her a few months from now!" Maggie shrugged and looked scared. Luckily, she didn't faint.

"SUNDAY, JUNE 21ST: ROMMEL HAS PUSHED THE ALLIES OUT OF LIBYA; HIS AFRIKA KORPS IS 50 MILES INTO EGYPT. JAPS HAVE

OCCUPIED THE ALEUTIAN ISLANDS OFF ALASKA. RUSSIAN CITY OF
SEVASTOPOL STILL IN A STATE OF SIEGE."
Bad news for the Allies from all war fronts: the Nazis were clearly winning
in North Africa. On the Eastern Front, the Russians were once more trying to stem the German onslaught; the starving citizens of Sevastopol
were still barely holding out under a Nazi siege which had lasted for
several bitter months.

And now the U.S., too, had another headache: occupation of the
Aleutian Islands by the Japanese brought the threat of invasion to
North America.

"WEDNESDAY, JULY 1ST: CENTRAL WELSH BOARD WRITTEN EXAMS
BEGAN. HAD A LETTER FROM DEAR OLD KEN WISHING ME GOOD
LUCK. NOTHING FROM WILLIAM OR PETER OR PAUL! PHOOEY ON
THEM! JAPS TOOK GUADALCANAL IN PACIFIC."
If I achieved good results in the Central Welsh Board exams, I would
achieve my goal of entrance into Wales's prestigious Bangor University.
To qualify, my scores would have to be high enough in English, science
and languages. My ambition was to earn degrees in French and English
to qualify me to teach French in England or to teach English in France
after the war. My exams were in seven subjects: English, French, Latin,
History, Biology, Chemistry and Math. Each exam was timed, with two
to three hours of essay questions (no multiple choice); we needed every
minute of time allowed before the closing bell rang.

We got up stiffly from our desks after each exam, staggering out of
the examination hall in varying degrees of despair, which worsened when
we met outside the room to compare notes and comfort each other.

"TUESDAY, JULY 7TH: NASTY, RAINY DAY. SO FAR EXAMS NOT BAD,
BUT WE ARE ALL NERVOUS WRECKS, NEVERTHELESS. I'M TIRED!
HAD BIOLOGY EXAM THIS AFTERNOON--NOT NICE! OH WELL, I
DID MY BEST. LETTER FROM KEN. HE HAS BEEN TAKING VARIOUS
TESTS FOR FLIGHT TRAINING. SO FAR PASSED THEM ALL."

So Ken wasn't disappearing from my life, after all! He forwarded his new R.A.F. address to me, and our friendship continued.

The biology exam required essay answers, along with diagrams to illustrate them. When I came to a question on the anatomy of a frog, I almost burst out laughing, remembering my partnership with Maggie in the biology lab. One day our biology mistress went around the lab benches with a large jar and a pair of tongs, dispensing to each two-some in the class a formaldehyde-soaked frog to dissect. Maggie looked the other way. "I just can't bear to look at it, let alone touch the awful thing," she hissed under her breath.

"Oh, I'll dissect it, don't worry," I replied, remembering the days when I was about eight years old and relished looking under the rocks in Mom's rock garden for creepy crawlies, including small frogs that I enjoyed collecting in jam jars as pets.

I accepted our petrified frog with gusto, and laid it on the examining board between where Maggie and I were standing. The biology mistress told us to take what we would need from the drawer in the bench- -scissors, a small hammer, pins for securing the frog to the board, and a sponge to wipe our hands on. I spread out the frog on the board, and began to hammer it in place.

"Boy, Mag, this is really fun," I said, and turned to look at her to see if I had cheered her up. To my surprise, she wasn't there. It took only a minute to find her, spread neatly on the floor in a dead faint! Maggie had "done it again," in her own words! She soon revived, but was hurried off to the nurse's office for observation, so I had the doubtful honor of doing the dissection without her assistance.

Suppressing the desire to giggle at the memory, I dragged my mind back to my exam.

Home to Stay!

"MONDAY, JULY 13TH: WE ARE PACKING TO LEAVE WREXHAM. HELPED MOM AND BRONWYN WRESTLE WITH A BIG BOX (PROVIDED

BY THE W.V.S.) FULL OF OUR CLOTHES. IT WILL BE SHIPPED TO UPPER WOODSIDE JUST BEFORE WE LEAVE."

Bronwyn looked in frustration at the large box from the W.V.S. depot, filled with our winter clothes.

"Oh, Mrs. Amiss, it's so full I can't get the top down." She stood in front of the box, both arms straining to squash the folded clothes down further, but they still persisted in overflowing.

Mom replied: "Well, Bronwyn, it's the only box we have; maybe if we all push at the same time we can get the top down."

We arranged ourselves in a line and, at the count of three, we pushed down with all our strength. Still the lid wouldn't close. Mom wailed:

"Oh, Bronwyn, whatever will we do?"

Bronwyn thought for a moment. "I know, I'll sit on it!" Shift-work at the factory hadn't diminished her ample figure, and this time it worked. The lid closed over the top of the box, and Mom quickly tied it down with the ends of the rope already around the bottom and sides.

Bronwyn laughed triumphantly. "There, I knew there must have been a reason for putting off going on that diet!"

"TUESDAY, JULY 21ST: CENTRAL WELSH BOARD EXAMS ARE OVER! TOOK THE BUS TO LLANGOLLEN FOR A PICNIC WITH BESSIE, MAGGIE AND OUR MOMS TO CELEBRATE. A LETTER FINALLY CAME FROM WILLIAM. HE IS FULL OF NEWS ABOUT HIS SUCCESS AS LEADING MAN IN A PLAY GIVEN BY THE LOCAL REPERTORY COMPANY."

Our mothers came up with a fitting farewell celebration for Bessie, Maggie and me. They packed a picnic lunch, and we all took a bus to Llangollen, a place noted for its beauty. We picnicked by a bridge over a picturesque canal where barges, pulled by horses on a tow-path, stopped to take people for rides.

After eating our Spam and tomato sandwiches and draining the last drop of tea from the thermos bottles, we hailed a passing barge for a ride. The horse stopped, and we lined up to get aboard. Mom had picked a bunch of wildflowers to bring home. They made a hit with the barge horse, who saw the bouquet as a tasty snack and lunged toward her, trying to get a mouthful.

Clutching her flowers, Mom made a flying leap onto the barge in the nick of time. To our relief, the horse didn't try to follow her! With a look of resignation, it obeyed the proddings of the barge owner and began to tow us down the canal. We floated lazily along, admiring the beautiful scenery without further incident, and Mom boarded the bus back to Wrexham with her bouquet still intact.

William hadn't been letting the grass grow under his feet during his months of waiting to be called by the R.A.F. The local amateur dramatic club was struggling to find a suitable leading man for the play they were rehearsing. Most of the available males were either too old or too young to be called up for military service. They pounced on William, whose six-foot frame and good looks made him a natural candidate. The play was a hit. William's rise to stardom had left him, as Dad put it, "with a swelled head."

"Oh, Mom, I complained," I'll be a nervous wreck until I hear the results of the Central Welsh Board exams."

I would have to chew my nails for many weeks before the results were published and I would know if I had done well enough to be accepted at Bangor University. If I qualified, preparatory courses in the elite sixth form would have to be taken at Wrexham Park. Maggie's mother had already told us she would be glad to have me stay in her spare bedroom. In the meantime, I was going back to Upper Woodside, to live again in our own home, and to wait for news of my grades.

"FRIDAY, JULY 24TH: SCHOOL IS CLOSING FOR SUMMER VACATION, AND ALSO CLOSING MY LIFE IN WREXHAM. TEARFUL FAREWELLS TO FRIENDS AND TEACHERS. I'VE ALMOST FINISHED PACKING."
My diary added: "COULDN'T HELP WEEPING, AS I WENT AROUND THE SCHOOL SAYING 'GOODBYE' TO ALL MY MISTRESSES. PINKY

(English teacher) SHOOK MY HAND UNTIL I THOUGHT IT WOULD DROP OFF. MISS DAVIES (French) HUGGED ME. 'NELLA'(Chemistry) BURST INTO TEARS, AND MISS LLOYD (Latin) WAS ON THE BRINK. I SIGNED AUTOGRAPH BOOKS AND WROTE MY HOME ADDRESS SO MANY TIMES I HAVE 'WRITER'S CRAMP'!"

The diary entry continued: "I PLACED FIRST IN MY CLASS, WITH THE HIGHEST SCHOLASTIC RATING FOR THE YEAR! WILL WONDERS NEVER CEASE? MEGAN DAVIES WAS SECOND, AND BETTY HILL, THIRD."

Betty Hill and I were English evacuees, among several other English girls who happened to do well at Wrexham Park. To our great embarrassment, the Welsh Dragon lashed out at the Welsh girls at morning Assembly. "You Welsh girls should be ashamed," she ranted, allowing English evacuees to get the top honors in the school." I wrote in my diary in disgust: "WE'RE ALL BRITISH; THIS IS SUPPOSED TO BE THE 'UNITED' KINGDOM, BUT NO THANKS TO HER!"

Once more in those war years we were packing. I busied myself cleaning the mud off my bike, Percival, ready for him to be picked up and sent to Upper Woodside by train.

My last few days at Wrexham were full of genuine regret, a total about-face from my feelings when we first moved there two years before. The town I had viewed as a symbol of separation from my home had really *become* my home for the past two years, enriched by close friends and the dedication of good teachers. At last my secondary education was over. It was time to move on. We were going home to Upper Woodside, this time to stay. It would be just like the good old days ... or so I thought!

"MONDAY, JULY 27TH: 'CARTER PATERSON' PICKED UP OUR TWO SUITCASES AND PERCIVAL IN THE MORNING. MOM, BRONWYN AND I TOOK THREE IMMENSE CARTONS TO THE POST OFFICE. WE'LL STAY WITH MRS. WHITE WHEN WE GET TO UPPER WOODSIDE. HAD A LOVELY LETTER FROM KEN--ALMOST A BOOK! HE'S FED UP

WITH HIS BASIC TRAINING. SAYS HE DIDN'T JOIN THE R.A.F. TO FILL SANDBAGS, BUILD ROADS AND PEEL POTATOES!"

As the brawny Carter Paterson driver loaded his truck bound for the train station, I felt a tingle of excitement in anticipation of tomorrow's journey home.

I counted the blessings I'd found in Wrexham; "Ken was certainly an unexpected one," I mused. Then, with a grin, I thought: "Sounds just like him, after joining the elite who had been picked for flight crew, only to be subjected to the indignity of basic training with hard labor and the further insult of becoming a potato-peeler. But one thing is for sure: this is one place where he can't complain to the management!"

"TUESDAY, JULY 28TH: LEFT WREXHAM ON THE TRAIN AT 9:15 A.M. ARRIVED AT UPPER WOODSIDE AT 4:30 P.M. BESSIE AND MAGGIE CAME TO SEE US OFF AT THE STATION. NICE TRIP. NO OVERCROWDING. AFTER A CUP OF TEA AT MRS. WHITE'S WENT ON A RECONNAISSANCE TOUR TO SEE THE HOUSE. AWFUL! WHAT A MESS. WEEDS SIX FEET TALL. STAYED WITH MRS. WHITE, AS ARRANGED."

Bessie, Maggie and I exchanged hugs, tears, and promises to write before Mom and I climbed aboard the waiting train. It took all day, with all the stops and changes, but Mrs. White had the kettle on for tea when we rang her doorbell later that afternoon. Before we left Wrexham, she had written to invite us to stay with her until we could get our house opened up and fit to live in again.

Her ample body seemed to be perennially covered with a large flowered apron. In her motherly North Country way she bustled about, the kindness in her eyes embracing us.

"E'ee, lasses, it's good to see the two of ye. I'll have dinner on't table as soon as ye are settled - a loovly bit of roast beef and Yorkshire puddin'."

There was plenty of daylight left when we walked the two blocks to Bishop's Hill to see our house. It reminded me of a picture in my old nursery story-book: Sleeping Beauty's castle, almost hidden in weeds and vines that had grown during her long sleep while she waited for Prince Charming's kiss. Our windows were still boarded up. The Anderson shelter was full of stagnant water again. I was too tired to think about it. We walked sadly back to Mrs. White's.

I fell asleep that night almost as soon as my head touched one of Mrs. White's best feather-filled pillows.

"WEDNESDAY, JULY 29TH: BEGAN TO CLEAN UP THE HOUSE - IT'S IN TERRIBLE SHAPE. OUR SUITCASES AND ONE BOX CAME, FOLLOWED CLOSELY BY WILLIAM ON HIS LUNCH HOUR.   EVERYTHING IS DIFFERENT. WHAT HAS HAPPENED TO THE GOOD OLD DAYS?"
I was back home, but not for a visit this time, as we began the painstaking business of moving back into our neglected, bomb-damaged house. Our front and back doors had been replaced; now they could be opened to air out the house and get rid of the stench of mildew. Dad had arranged to have the doors put back on, but the windows were left boarded up until we came home to stay, when it would be safe to put glass back into them.

A Carter Paterson truck delivered the large box of clothes. The other boxes of belongings that we had sent off by mail before we left Wrexham slowly began to arrive.

Mom took charge: "Bunty, I think we should leave the garden for later, and concentrate on unpacking and getting our things put away. You can start in the front bedroom."

I put our clothes away in the bedroom chest of drawers. The furniture had deep scratches in it, left by flying glass blown across the room when bombs had shattered the windows. By lunch time I was feeling tired and depressed. Mom came in from the backyard, where she had been trying to find her prize gooseberry bushes under the tangle of weeds, and put the kettle on to boil for cups of tea. The doorbell rang, and I rushed to answer it. There stood William, looking taller and more handsome than ever in his business suit. The boyish grin I had known was still there, but something had changed.

"Well, hello again, Bunty," he boomed, "welcome home, this time for keeps. Where's your Mom? I must give her a hug." The moment I had dreamed about was here, but he brushed past me into the kitchen to greet Mom. I heard him say loudly, "You'll have to come to our next performance. The repertory company are a smashing crowd!"

As he had come into the front hall, I noticed William had grown a small moustache, and his raincoat was slung casually across his shoulders in typical Hollywood-leading-man style. There was an air of sophistication about him that I didn't recognize, which made me feel awkward and childish. After only a few minutes of desultory conversation, he rushed back to Croydon to his office job. My diary recorded: "HE STOPPED IN AGAIN ABOUT SIX P.M. AND HAD JUST BEGUN TO PLAY 'VALSE TRISTE' ON THE PIANO AND LOOK SOULFUL WHEN PAUL ARRIVED! WILLIAM RUSHED OFF TO A REHEARSAL OF HIS LATEST PLAY. PETER POPPED IN A FEW MINUTES LATER, AND HE AND PAUL WALKED MOM AND ME BACK TO MRS. WHITE'S."

Paul's arrival was a surprise. The seminary was a train journey away, and even his new home was a bus ride away from Bishop's Hill, on the other side of London. "I say, I just *had* to come and welcome you home," he exclaimed, "and anyway it was a good excuse to get away from the seminary for awhile. I'd hoped I would never see another classroom after those years at St. Oswald's Prep. Just for kicks I practiced wearing a cassock the other day. There must be a knack to doing it without tripping over it and landing face down in a mud puddle as I did."

Peter had come directly from work; Mom busied herself making sandwiches and cups of tea. Peter and Paul talked non-stop as they munched, and we caught up on each others' lives since we had last met. It felt more like old times, having them around again and being escorted back to our temporary lodgings for the night.

While William's feet floated slightly above the ground from his successes in amateur theatricals, Peter's remained planted firmly on it. He was still the brother I'd never had, and he was to be my mainstay as I made the slow adjustment to a new life after two years away from Upper Woodside. Peter helped Mom and me in his spare time as we cleaned up the house and garden. He went two miles on the bus when Percival arrived from Wrexham at the train station in a neighboring suburb, and rode him home for me. Was Peter my new hero?

"FRIDAY, JULY 31st: LEFT MRS. WHITE'S AFTER BREAKFAST AND MOVED BACK INTO OUR OWN HOUSE. 'MOANING MINNIE' WOKE US UP ABOUT 3 A.M. THE NAZIS ARE STILL BOMBING LONDON, ALSO OTHER CITIES IN BRITAIN."

I listened to the warning sirens with a sinking heart. "Is this really what the good old days back at Bishop's Hill are going to be like?" I wondered. The *Luftwaffe* had been operating at a distance while we were in Wrexham, but now they were back overhead again.

Mom said wearily: "There's really nowhere for us to go for shelter, with the Anderson full of smelly water. At least our beds are still downstairs, so we might just as well turn over, try to go back to sleep, and hope for the best." Luckily, no bombs fell nearby again.

The Morrison Shelter

"SATURDAY, AUGUST 1ST: ORDERED NEWSPAPER DELIVERY TO RESUME. CHOPPED DOWN PRIVET HEDGE OVERSHADOWING THE DINNG ROOM FRENCH DOORS THAT WAS THREATENING TO MAKE US LIVE IN SEMI-DARKNESS. PETER CAME WITH A STIRRUP PUMP AND PROCEEDED TO PUMP THE WATER OUT OF THE ANDERSON SHELTER MOST EFFICIENTLY."

Each day Mom and I scrubbed, vacuumed, and slashed at the overgrown backyard until we were too tired to do any more. Peter came from time to time and helped. He arrived this afternoon with a large stirrup pump, sweating profusely until the stagnant water in the Anderson shelter was all pumped out. A day or two later, after another rainstorm, the shelter again had a couple of inches of water in it. Peter looked at it in disgust.

"Never mind, Peter," said Mom, "I think Dad's getting us an indoor shelter; at least I have my fingers crossed! An indoor shelter--where on earth would we put it?"

"FRIDAY, AUGUST 7TH: GANDHI AND FOLLOWERS ARRESTED IN INDIA. GERMANS STILL ADVANCING IN RUSSIA. DAD CAME HOME FOR TWO WEEKS' VACATION. THE THREE OF US CLEARED REMAINING DEBRIS FROM BEDROOMS SO DAD CAN REFINISH THE FLOORS TOMORROW."

According to the news report, Gandhi and some of his Congress Party followers were arrested after demanding British withdrawal from India. In the next few days, I recorded: "RIOTS BROKE OUT IN BOMBAY, INDIA. PEOPLE BEING KILLED RIGHT AND LEFT."

The events in Bombay (now Mumbai) were making headlines, but at that point in time it would have been unthinkable for us to perceive that this was the beginning of India's struggle for independence from Britain. Meantime, on Europe's Eastern front, Nazi Panzers were still driving the Russians back. Soon they would be at the gates of Stalingrad.

That morning I ran down the front garden path to welcome Dad home for his two weeks' vacation. He hugged me. "Well, Bunty, how does it feel to be back? You and Mom must be tired out with all the work there is to do. This will be a working holiday for me too, by the look of it." Dad looked tired out himself. He pulled a banknote out of his pocket. "Here's a little 'attagirl' for being top of your class this year, Bunty. I'm proud of you."

Always short of cash, I said a happy "Oh, thanks, Dad," but I thought to myself: "He's probably thinking those school fees were finally worth it in the long run, after all! Now I wonder if he'll let me go to Bangor University?"

In the bedrooms Mom gazed with tears in her eyes at her prized deep-pile Indian carpets, which Dad had rolled up and tied, ready for disposal. Encrusted with lumps of plaster, then embedded with bits of glass when the windows were blown in, they were beyond rescue. Mom finally had accepted the fact that they had to be thrown away, casualties of a war that seemed as if it would never end.

"FRIDAY, AUGUST 14TH: DAD ERECTED OUR NEW INDOOR MORRISON SHELTER IN THE DINING ROOM! NOW ALL THE DINING-ROOM FURNITURE IS IN THE FRONT BEDROOM."
"Oh well,"rationalised Mom, "even if Peter *had* pumped it dry gain, the outdoor Anderson shelter would have been too cold to use in winter. But I wonder where Dad will put the Morrison?"
By 1941 the government had made an indoor air-raid shelter available, named for Home Secretary Herbert Morrison. The Morrison shelter was designed to withstand the falling weight of a two-story house full of furniture, without collapsing. Dad had bought us a Morrison, and decided to erect it before he went back to Wales after his vacation. The three of us heaved our heavy, oak dining-room table upstairs into the front bedroom to join the dining-room chairs, then Mom and I beat a hasty retreat, leaving Dad to figure out how to assemble the new shelter and to give him plenty of freedom for as many cuss words as would be needed. Surrounded by wrenches, nuts and bolts, and with a sprinkling of nautical epithets and uncomplimentary remarks about Mr. Morrison, Dad finally managed to get the new contraption erected. Measuring six and a half feet long and four feet wide, it stood at table height against the inside wall between the dining room and kitchen; it was a rectangular steel cage with a thick slab of steel for a roof, and steel mesh sides. Barely high enough to sit up in, it was designed for sleeping. Mom, Dad and I could barely fit, lying down on the old mattress which had been squeezed into

it. Mom rounded up all her spare blankets to put over the mattress, then covered the roof with one of her best tablecloths. We used it as a dining-room table with folding chairs, but in between meals, without the tablecloth, it was great for ping-pong!

"WEDNESDAY, AUGUST 19TH: The B.B.C.REPORTS THAT A LARGE-SCALE RAID HAS BEEN MADE ON DIEPPE, FRANCE, BY CANADIAN, BRITISH, AMERICAN, FREE FRENCH AND POLISH TROOPS. HEAVY CASUALTIES ON BOTH SIDES."

It was thought that if a major French channel port could be seized and held, it would boost Allied morale, sagging from defeats in North Africa and Russia. It was decided to send a combined Allied force including tanks and infantry to the French coast on a daring raid. Spearheaded by Canadian units, the Dieppe raid lasted nine disastrous hours. A full report, not released for thirty years, states that of the five thousand Canadians, almost three thousand were killed, wounded or taken prisoner. My diary reported: "THE R.A.F. SHOT DOWN 95 GERMAN AIRCRAFT AND DAMAGED ANOTHER HUNDRED. ALLIED LOSSES WERE REPORTED AS 98 AIRCRAFT WITH 80 FIGHTER PILOTS SAFE."

The raid had been carried out at a terrible cost. However, in retrospect, it was considered that it had tested the feasibility of a cross-channel landing, revealing weaknesses in training and equipment which would later become invaluable for D-Day planning.

"SATURDAY, AUGUST 22ND: BRAZIL DECLARED WAR ON GERMANY AND ITALY. ENJOYED A HOT BATH IN OUR NEWLY SCRUBBED BATHTUB. PETER TOOK ME TO MY FIRST DANCE, AT ST. JOHN'S HALL. SAW LOTS OF PEOPLE I HADN'T SEEN SINCE EVACUATION IN 1939. QUITE A LITTLE GANG THERE FROM OUR DAYS AT RAVENHURST. PAUL AND FRIEND FROM SEMINARY TURNED UP! HAD A SIMPLY MARVELLOUS TIME."

World War Two was still expanding. With Brazil's declaration, we now had allies in South America!

During our evacuations from Upper Woodside, the bathtub had been left half-filled with cold water, to comply with the Air Raid Precautions regulation that water from a half-filled bathtub should be available at all times to put out any incendiary bombs that fell through the roof. By the time we came home to stay, the tub had a brown ring of sediment that defied all our scrubbing; it was never quite white again. In those days of electric power shortages, government posters exhorted the public to take cold baths in summer, and not to run more than five inches of hot water in winter. Five inches of water barely covered my legs. To erase any unpatriotic guilt, I rationalized: "After all those socks I've knitted for the R.A.F., the Army and the Free French, the herbs I've collected, and the veggies I've grown for the government, I'm going to reward myself!" I emptied some scented bath salts into the shallow five inches, and turning on the hot water, I filled the tub without suffering one twinge of conscience.

That evening the church hall at St. John's was packed with young folks, many in uniform. Peter was an excellent dancer. Oddly, Ken's absence wasn't making my heart grow fonder. I hardly gave him a thought as I put into action the steps we had learned together at Miss Price's Academy in Wrexham. In the middle of a waltz, Peter suddenly shouted: "My gosh, look who's here--it's Paul!"

I had forgotten to tell Peter that in one of my letters to Paul at the seminary I had mentioned the dance, never dreaming that he would turn up with a fellow student priest, both without their "dog collars." We never asked if they were A.W.O.L. They were having too much fun dancing with the female "wallflowers," who in turn were delighted with two such handsome strangers!

"WEDNESDAY, AUGUST 26TH: I ENROLLED IN COLLEGE NEAR UPPER WOODSIDE. THERE GOES MY BID FOR BANGOR UNIVERSITY! IN THE EVENING WENT TO SEE WILLIAM IN HIS NEW PLAY."
The Central Welsh Board exam results were still not published. Mom and Dad had sat me down after we settled back into our home and told me of their decision about my future.

Dad looked serious. "Bunty, Mom and I have talked this over very carefully, and you know we only want the best for you. Even if you qualify for entrance into Bangor University, it's too far away for us to be separated, with a war on and a Nazi invasion still possible. We'll have to find you a college closer to home."

My heart was broken, but in retrospect it later appeared the best thing that could have happened in order to make possible the incredible story of the rest of my life's journey.

A daytime branch of one of London's colleges had opened just a bus ride away, offering a Bachelor of Commerce degree course. I enrolled. The first year curriculum was loaded and tough: Economics, Commerce, Mercantile Law, Commercial Engish, Accounting, Commercial French, Commercial Geography. Serious stuff! I added optional courses in Shorthand and Typing, both of which carried accreditation from the prestigious Royal Society of Arts; I thought: "Probably they are easy enough, and you never know, some day they could be useful."

While we were in Wrexham, I once shared my teaching ambitions in a letter to Mom's sister, Auntie Lil, a teacher in Sunderland. She wrote to my mother: "Ida, don't let Bunty be a teacher. You should encourage her to go into business. She's not the 'old maid' type, and she would have to give up teaching when she marries." In Auntie Lil's day, this was true. In 1942 we didn't know that the rule would end after the war, so I listened to Auntie Lil and abandoned my dreams of teaching in favor of the business world. I began classes the following week.

The disappointment of my compromise was offset that evening when Mr. and Mrs. Standish took Mom and me in their car to see William the Thespian in his latest starring role. The play was good, and he took two curtain calls. I was proud of him, but I groaned inwardly: "Oh Lord, he'll be even more insufferable than ever, after this!"

"THURSDAY, AUGUST 27TH: VERY WARM DAY. FELT PATRIOTIC WHEN I TOOK A LUKEWARM BATH IN FIVE INCHES OF WATER TO COOL OFF. WILLIAM CAME FOR A VISIT IN THE EVENING TO SEE HOW WE

LIKED THE PLAY, AND WAS SHOCKED WHEN I LEFT WITH PETER TO GO TO A DANCE IN CROYDON."

My diary oozed satisfaction when William's inflated self-image was punctured. He didn't seem to notice that Peter and I were obviously dressed ready to go out somewhere. Peter listened politely for a few minutes to William's appraisal of his performance, then held out my coat for me to put on, rolled his eyes at me and said: "If you'll excuse us, William, we have a date in Croydon for a dance at the Grand Hotel." Peter stretched out the words "Grand Hotel," and I could see a small smile of triumph light up his face as we went off to the dance, leaving a somewhat deflated William behind, still discussing the play with Mom.

College Life

"SATURDAY, AUGUST 29TH. PETER IS ON MANEUVERS WITH THE HOME GUARD THIS WEEKEND. DAD IS HOME FROM WALES FOR A COUPLE OF DAYS. IT POURED WITH RAIN ALL DAY. PAUL CAME TO SEE US THIS AFTERNOON IN A TERRIBLE STATE. HE IS FED UP WITH THE SEMINARY AND WANTS TO QUIT AND JOIN THE R.A.F.! MOM, DAD AND I ALL TALKED TO HIM. HE CALMED DOWN AFTER AWHILE AND FINALLY TOOK THE BUS HOME AFTER DINNER."

Mom left the pot of tea she had just made to answer the doorbell as a summer rainstorm beat down on Bishop's Hill. To her surprise, Paul stood on the doorstep, dripping wet, his distress almost palpable.

"Oh, Mrs. Amiss, I need to talk to someone. May I please come in?" He was already in the front hall before Mom could reach out and haul him in, soaked and shivering. Taking his wet raincoat, she hung it up to dry. Then, bringing him a steaming cup of tea, she sat him down in a comfortable chair by the dining-room fireplace next to Dad, who happened to be home for the weekend.

Dad looked puzzled. "Now, son, tell us what has happened." He put his hand gently on Paul's shaking shoulder. "Well," blurted Paul, I'm fed up with being at the seminary. I don't know if I'm on the right path for the priesthood or not. I really want to leave it and join the R.A.F." Paul's cheeks flushed and his blue eyes brimmed.

Dad asked bluntly: "Paul, what would you do when you came out of the R.A.F. after the war?"

A little frown appeared on Paul's face. "I really don't know what I want to do to earn a decent living; I'm not fit for anything much. Never was really a good student at St. Oswald's Prep., and my aunt convinced me that my destiny and duty to the family was with the priesthood. Maybe she was right -- after all, I've never seen a hungry priest!"

Dad spoke slowly, trying to choose the right words. "Go home and think it over well, lad. Don't rush into something you might regret by leaving the seminary. It's going to have to be your decision, but you know we're here for you any time you want to come and talk to us about it again. Now stay awhile and have some dinner with us."

Paul showed no indication that he wanted to go home, but having shed his deepest worries, he calmed down and stayed on to join us for dinner. The rainstorm was over by the time he left.

Paul didn't quit the seminary, after all. Several years later he was ordained into the Roman Catholic priesthood, and I came from America to accept his invitation to attend the ceremony. After his ordination I didn't hear from him again, but I heard that he had become a Monsignor, and, ironically, had pioneered a program for counseling young seminarians who were in doubt as to their future with the church.

"TUESDAY, SEPTEMBER 1ST: FIRST DAY AT COLLEGE. ONLY TWELVE IN MY CLASS- TEN FEMALES, TWO MALES. IT'S NICE TO GET BACK TO SCHOOL! COFFEE BREAK, NICE HOT LUNCH, LOVELY COMMON ROOM TO RELAX IN, WITH A RADIO, DARTBOARD AND PING PONG TABLE. RAVENHURST AND WREXHAM PARK WERE NEVER LIKE THIS!"

The college building was old but dignified. For me this was a new atmosphere, refreshing and uncluttered, no more daily assemblies with their accompanying admonitions from an irritable and impossible headmistress. Almost all my courses were taught by men--another novelty!

Mr. Cohen was one professor I'll never forget; he was a short, swarthy man with dark curly hair, whose expressive face was never far from laughter, but always looked in need of a shave. A declared conscientious objector, he taught Commercial Geography and Commercial French with such passion that he was often short of breath. He was a great admirer of the Russians, who were then our allies, and lost no time teaching us to sing the rousing "Red Flag," and also the "Internationale," national anthem of what was then the U.S.S.R. Mr. Cohen had translated them into French and we learned them as French folk-songs! Both smacked of the Russian Revolution; they sounded to me like good background music for a trip to the guillotine. I often wonder what became of Mr. Cohen!

The boys in Mr. Cohen's classes were two nineteen-year-olds. Whether they were conscientious objectors or unfit for military service I never found out, but neither one mentioned wanting to be in the armed forces and I asked them no questions.

Bernard was a candidate for the Intermediate Bachelor of Commerce (associate degree) at the end of the year. Stocky and verbose, he was almost completely without inhibitions, possibly because of his musical talent with the violin, on which he had been performing concerts since childhood. I tolerated Bernard's overt precociousness with what I hoped was good humor, but my diary yelped: "BERNARD PERSISTS IN CALLING ME 'SWEETHEART' OR, EVEN WORSE, 'HONEYBUNCH.' HE SITS BEHIND ME IN CLASS AND BOTHERS THE LIFE OUT OF ME. UGH!"

Bernard knew I didn't take teasing too well. He delighted in sitting behind me in class and hissing: "Bunty, dear, let me whisper sweet nothings in your ear." He would lean forward and I would feel warm breath in my ear and hear a hoarse whisper:

"Sweet nothings"!

Oh, well. I decided I'd have to "grin and bear it".

Manuel, on the other hand, was almost the exact opposite of Bernard: slightly built, studious, courteous, quiet--and dull. He and his family had fled to England to escape the Spanish Civil War. Maybe the trauma of this experience had helped create his retiring personality.

The most unassuming of the girls in my classes was Hannah, a twenty-year-old refugee from Austria who had arrived in England with her family just before Hitler pounced upon her country. With her pretty dark hair and eyes, she had a quiet dignity about her. One day she brought in one of her national instruments, a zither, shedding her shyness as she charmed us all with her musical talent in the Common Room after lunch.

The most outgoing of the girls was Carmen, whose family, like Manuel's, had left the civil war behind in Spain. Petite, olive-skinned and dark-eyed, she came to class dressed as if expected on a Hollywood movie set, makeup and all. I'm sure she must have had a stack of beauty aids. One day she brought in an eyelash curler, the first such contraption any of us had seen. For the next few days, Carmen basked in popularity, as each of the girls tried out the curler. It took me almost a week to get my eyelashes back into shape again so they wouldn't stab my upper eyelids when I fluttered them!

There was good reason for a bit of eyelash fluttering; our spare classrooms and teaching staff had been loaned to the Royal Canadian Air Force for air crew candidates, far from home and eager to fraternize.

"THURSDAY, SEPTEMBER 3RD: NATIONAL DAY OF PRAYER. WE LISTENED TO THE 11 O'CLOCK CHURCH SERVICE ON THE RADIO IN THE COMMON ROOM. PETER CAME IN THE EVENING TO INSPECT OUR NEW CEILINGS."

The nation had once more turned to God, this time to mark the beginning of our fifth year of war, to pray for peace, and to remember those who had lost their lives in this horrible world conflict. We listened in silence to the radio broadcast of the Church of England service, joined by as many Canadian air crew cadets as could squeeze into the Common Room with us. Again I felt the unity that war generated among perfect strangers. In that moment, we all were one.

A work crew from the War Damage Commission had appeared earlier that week and we now had new plasterboard ceilings in all the upper floor rooms. Peter was becoming quite proprietary, now that William was increasingly absent from the scene. He had already expertly repaired Mom's kitchen faucet. Today, hands on hips, he surveyed the new ceilings and pronounced them a "first-class job." I hoped Dad would agree on his next trip home.

A few days after the ceilings had been replaced, more workmen had our windows and French doors gleaming again with glass. With these welcome changes, the house was almost its old self again!

"THURSDAY, SEPTEMBER 10TH: I'VE PASSED THE CENTRAL WELSH BOARD WITH MATRICULATION INTO BANGOR UNIVERSITY! PETER HAS HAD HIS CALLING-UP PAPERS FOR THE R.A.F."

I didn't know whether to laugh or cry. "With Matriculation" meant that my Central Welsh Board scores were with honors, high enough to exempt me from the entrance exam for Bangor University. Mom and Dad were delighted with my results, but Dad was direct and to the point: "Bunty, Mom and I are proud of you, but we can't let you go back to North Wales to be on your own two hundred miles away from home. You're only sixteen, and don't forget there's still danger of an invasion."

After much argument and many tears of frustration, I agreed to stay on at the college in London.

At last the R.A.F. summoned Peter; he would be going in three weeks. I felt a pang of real regret; it was like saying goodbye to a brother. And what would I do for a dancing partner at St. John's dances?

Mom would miss him, too. Peter's seemingly inexhaustible supply of energy had spilled over into our house. In addition to fixing the leaky faucet in the kitchen, he had installed an electric light in the Anderson shelter, "just in case," he said. He took our ailing doorbell and Mom's malfunctioning electric iron apart, fixed them and put them together again, restored to perfect working condition. Peter had appeared almost every evening after work for a quick game of ping-pong played on top of the Morrison shelter, or to go with me for a bike ride or to practice some dance steps ready for the next hop at St. John's Hall. The house would be sad without him.

"MONDAY, SEPTEMBER 14TH: ARRIVED HOME FROM COLLEGE TO A BIG SHOCK. MRS. WHITE'S SON, ROGER, IS MISSING AFTER A BOMBING RAID OVER DUSSELDORF IN GERMANY."

Roger was a navigator/bombardier on an R.A.F. bomber. It was as if someone in our own family had been lost. There was little hope for air crews "missing in action." Mrs. White's husband was away on government work when the telegram had come. Mom quickly made up the guest room beds and brought Mrs. White and Betty home to stay overnight with us. I felt helpless, but tried to say something positive: "He's just 'missing,'" I began, struggling to hold back the tears, "and unless something worse is confirmed, let's just hope he's somewhere safe and we'll soon hear he's been found." I knew the words sounded trite and inadequate but I felt as if I had grown up in that moment, trying to comfort the two stunned women.

The White family never recovered from the weeks of waiting in vain for news of Roger's survival. At last came the "Lost: presumed dead" telegram. He had been so closely knit into the fabric of their lives that part of them died with him. Betty and Mrs. White came to stay overnight with us many times in the next weeks, when the pain of Roger's death became too great for them to bear.

Terror in a London Fog

"SATURDAY, OCTOBER 3RD: IT FEELS LIKE PREWAR TIMES! AUNTIE LIL IS VISITING FROM SUNDERLAND. WENT SHOPPING IN LONDON.

USED FOURTEEN CLOTHING COUPONS TO BUY A NEW RAINCOAT. LOTS OF 'YANK' SOLDIERS IN TOWN, ALSO POLISH, BELGIAN AND FRENCH SERVICEMEN."

With the lessening of air raids throughout Britain, civilians began to think of a normal life for the first time in years. Mom's older sister, Lily, was itching to resume her prewar visits to London, having come from what Londoners called "the provinces." I took the day off from classes to go with Mom and Auntie Lil on the one-hour bus ride into the city, where I was hopeful of finding a new raincoat. We waited for a bus longer than usual; most of them sailed past us, full up. As a result of the latest gasoline restrictions, fewer buses were running and on curtailed schedules. We were lucky to get a seat when a bus finally did stop. A sign inside urged civilians to travel between ten in the morning and four in the afternoon to allow seats for workers during rush hours.

The big department stores in the city bulged with cosmopolitan shoppers. Auntie Lil was fascinated by the multilingual chatter of men and women in the uniforms of Free France, Belgium and Poland. Periodically one heard a nasal American twang. "I've never heard so many different accents," Auntie Lil commented. Then, wiggling her rather long Ditchfield nose, "We've got some dreadful Yanks in Sunderland but it's always the rowdy ones you hear about, isn't it? I don't think they can *all* be *that* bad." This was the first time my diary reported the presence of Americans in London. It wouldn't be the last!

Our sixty-six clothing coupons had been reduced to forty-eight per year. Clothes rationing and scanty supplies would continue for years after the war. Finding the right size in clothes was a near miracle; I felt triumphant coming home with a new raincoat.

"SATURDAY, OCTOBER 10TH: THIS MORNING WENT TO LONDON TO SEE AUNTIE LIL OFF ON THE TRAIN FOR SUNDERLAND. BEGAN KNITTING A SWEATER FOR PETER IN R.A.F. BLUE. WENT TO THE FELLOWSHIP DANCE WITH HIM AT ST. JOHN'S, THE LAST

ONE BEFORE HE LEAVES TOMORROW TO JOIN THE R.A.F.! WHO SHOULD BE THERE BUT BRUCE FERGUSON! HADN'T SEEN HIM SINCE WE WERE EVACUATED TO HOVE! HE ASKED ME FOR THE 'FLIRTATION WALTZ.'PETER WAS NOT AMUSED! BROUGHT THE OLD RAVENHURST GANG BACK TO OUR HOUSE AFTER THE DANCE. THEY STAYED UNTIL MIDNIGHT."

After the dance, Mom took the invasion of my friends in stride; it was probably the largest party our house would ever see.

Although Peter was "not amused" when I danced with Bruce Ferguson, he was not annoyed either. The American custom of "going steady" was not part of our social code in England. Boys and girls had the freedom to "play the field" without breaking any of the social rules of the day until they became officially engaged. Even then, broken engagements were common. Marriage itself was a serious business, and as our Anglican prayerbook stated, "not to be entered into lightly." Divorce was still uncommon, living together before marriage was considered indecent, and there were many who had second thoughts before tying the knot.

The following day Peter left to join the R.A.F. His mother came and spent the evening with us. She was inconsolable. "My baby's gone off to the war," she sobbed." Mom and I shared her sadness and concern, and she soon became almost as frequent a visitor as Peter.

Weeks went by, and life fell into a routine. I was enjoying life at college, Peter was enjoying life in the R.A.F., William was enjoying his amateur dramatics. Mom was enjoying being in her own kitchen. Letters continued to flow from Maggie and Bessie; both were bored with life in Wrexham. Paul dropped in whenever he came home to see his family from the seminary.

Ken's letters became sporadic. Eventually he wrote to announce that he was engaged, rendering him just another "ship that passed in the night."

A ship that had returned from such passage was Bruce Ferguson! Sacrificing his Saturday mornings to attend R.O.T.C. when he was at

Ravenhurst had paid off. He was now looking handsome as ever in a midshipman's uniform, on his way to becoming an officer in the Royal Navy. Dad was delighted. "I've had about enough of the R.A.F. Nice to have a chap around from the Royal Navy for a change."

"SATURDAY, OCTOBER 24TH: THE R.A.F. BLITZED TURIN, MILAN AND SAVONA IN ITALY. FINISHED KNITTING PETER'S PULLOVER. TOOK IT OVER TO SHOW HIS MOM BEFORE I MAIL IT TO HIM. SAW MY FIRST FLYING FORTRESS!"

An intensive bombing of Italy by the Allies had begun. Winston Churchill had warned Italy that the R.A.F. would begin heavy bombing of its cities unless Mussolini withdrew from the Axis powers.

I kicked myself for keeping Peter's sweater as a surprise instead of measuring it properly for him before he left. What if it didn't fit? Oh well, too late now.

The American Eighth Air Force had arrived in Britain, and my diary showed excitement about the first B-17, the biggest plane I'd ever seen. There would be many more to come in the days ahead.

"THURSDAY, OCTOBER 29TH: THE RUSSIANS ARE STILL HOLDING OUT AT STALINGRAD. WE ARE ADVANCING IN EGYPT; MONTOGOMERY HAS LAUNCHED AN OFFENSIVE AGAINST ROMMEL! TOMORROW COLEMANS ARE COMING BACK FROM EVACUATION TO LIVE NEXT DOOR AGAIN."

In North Africa the Allied steamroller was gaining momentum to push back the Germans and Italians, but war news from the Pacific testified to the continuing seesaw between the U.S. and the Japanese, each winning and then losing territory.

The siege of Stalingrad continued in Russia. We could only guess at the agony of its citizens.

Mom opened a letter that morning with a gasp of surprise. "Guess what, Bunty, the Colemans are coming home to stay! Won't it be nice to hear children's voices in the neighborhood again?"

Our next door neighbors were moving back to Bishop's Hill after three years of voluntary evacuation. When war was declared, Mrs. Coleman had taken their two young children to live with relatives in the west of England near where her husband, a school teacher, was evacuated with his school. Like so many others, the school had now reopened in London. The Colemans stayed several nights with us while they reclaimed their deserted home from neglect and made it fit to live in again. My diary complained: "SPENT ALL MY SPARE TIME GIVING NANCY AND DENNIS RIDES ON MY GARDEN SWING. I'M EXHAUSTED!" The *Luftwaffe* was absent from our skies; the wailing voice of "Moaning Minnie" was silent. The war now seemed to have receded far from Bishop's Hill instead of being on our doorstep.

"THURSDAY, NOVEMBER 5TH: GERMANS AND ITALIANS ARE IN FULL RETREAT FROM EGYPT, WITH THOUSANDS TAKEN PRISONER INCLUDING SOME GENERALS. BRUCE FERGUSON CAME TO INVITE ME TO ST. JOHN'S FELLOWSHIP DANCE."
Humor peppered true stories in newspapers and on the radio about the flood of German and Italian surrenders in North Africa. I read aloud to Mom from the morning newspaper while she was having her breakfast: "Two German officers came to give themselves up to a captain who was leading his advancing British troops in the desert. The captain said: 'Can't you see I'm too busy to take you prisoner? You'll just have to walk to the nearest town, get on a train to Eighth Army Headquarters, and surrender there!'"

A cartoon in the newspaper illustrated another true story, a sweating British army corporal staggering into headquarters from the desert, closely followed by a winding trail of fifty trucks packed with German and Italian soldiers, all with their hands up.

I was flabbergasted when Bruce Ferguson dropped in to invite me to the next dance at St. John's Hall. My diary reported: "HAD A SMASHING TIME. BRUCE IS QUITE A GOOD DANCER--AT LEAST WHEN YOU GET USED TO HIS STYLE!" Bruce improvised rather wildly; he would have driven Miss Price, with her prescribed dance steps, up the proverbial wall. He was waiting to be posted to active duty by the Royal Navy, but in the meantime there were dances to be enjoyed.

"SUNDAY, NOVEMBER 8TH: YANKS AND BRITISH TROOPS LANDED AT ALGIERS AND OTHER POINTS IN NORTH AFRICA."
Allied "Operation Torch" was launched in Algeria and Morocco in North Africa under the command of an American general whose name we were hearing for the first time: Dwight D. Eisenhower. Under his command was another general not to be forgotten, George C. Patton.

"WEDNESDAY, NOVEMBER 11TH: ALL OF ALGERIA AND MOROCCO NOW IN ALLIED HANDS. I ALMOST DIDN'T MAKE IT HOME IN THE WORST FOG IMAGINABLE."
"Operation Torch" in North Africa was a success! Our spirits rose again. Far from the searing heat of the desert, it was a cold November day in London. The chilly air, saturated with dampness and smoke from coal fires in homes all over the city and its suburbs, created a notorious "pea soup" or "killer" fog. I caught a bus from the college at four o'clock, expecting to be home in forty-five minutes. Visibility on the roads was almost nil. About a mile from Bishop's Hill, the bus driver stopped. "Orl right, you lot, off yer get; I carn't see to bloody well drive no further. Sorry, but that's it."

Clammy and cold, the thick fog engulfed me in greenish yellow swirls, its chemical fumes so heavy that I dreaded my next breath. I began to walk; I could see only a few inches around me. Each time I came to a side road, I groped my way to the edge of the sidewalk to check its name sign with my flashlight. At last through the gloom I saw the sign "Green Lane." St. John's Church was almost a mile along Green Lane, but with a huge sigh of relief, I knew I was on the way home!

The fog was now too thick for me to see my feet. Missing the curb, I fell into the street, picked myself up and began walking in the road, surrounded by a hollow silence. All traffic had stopped. A raincoat-clad shape almost bumped into me; a woman's voice asked, "Is this Norbury High Street?" I had to tell her she was on the wrong road. The bus had left me on the corner of the street she was looking for. I said: "Just keep walking and you'll find it." She sat down on the sidewalk and I heard her sobbing. It was getting dark; I just had to go on and leave her there.

With the blackout closing in, my flashlight was now useless to penetrate the thick fog. My steps had become shorter, to avoid stumbling and falling again. After what seemed like a lifetime, I finally saw through the murk the outline of St. John's Church. The fluorescent numbers on my watch dial told me I had been walking for two hours. Turning at the church, I trudged the familiar last few blocks into Bishop's Hill. Mom was waiting outside the house; we both wept with relief.

Cellphones had not been invented yet. If I'd had one, poor Mom would have been spared a lot of worry! By next morning the fog was gone. Years later, the "pea soupers" would be gone forever when London became part of a "Smoke-Free Zone."

"SUNDAY, NOVEMBER 15TH: CHURCHILL HAS LIFTED BAN ON RINGING CHURCH BELLS TO CELEBRATE ALLIED VICTORIES IN NORTH AFRICA."
The bells of St. John's pealed joyfully to join others all across the country in a symphony of thanksgiving, after two desperate years of silence. But after today they would be silent for another year, again waiting to announce news of a Nazi invasion.

"WEDNESDAY, NOVEMBER 25TH: THE RUSSIANS HAVE ENCIRCLED GERMAN ARMY AT STALINGRAD. CLAIM TO HAVE KILLED HALF A MILLION NAZIS. AT COLLEGE I PASSED FIRST LEVEL OF THE ROYAL SOCIETY OF ARTS EXAMS. TWO MORE LEVELS TO GO FOR FIRST CLASS PROFICIENCY CERTIFICATE."
The battle for Stalingrad continued until the end of January 1943, with enormous losses on both sides, but it has gone down in history as one

of the most important turning points of World War Two. Our hearts went out to the suffering civilians in that beleaguered city.

I cornered Mom after dinner. "Mom, I've been thinking. I'm happy my college grades are good--so far all "A"s and "B"s--but I'm not sure I want to stay on for a Bachelor of Commerce degree. When I'm eighteen, I'll have to leave anyway to go either into the women's forces or a 'reserved occupation.' If I can earn first class proficiency certificates from the Royal Society of Arts, I can probably get a good secretarial job somewhere covered by the Essential Works Act. What do you think?"

I already knew that Mom and Dad didn't want me to go into one of the women's services, and I had heard the Ravenhurst girls at St. John's dances talking about the miserable experiences of some of their female friends and family members who had joined the "ranks."

The Royal Society of Arts was a well-recognized institution all over Britain. Along with shorthand and typing courses, I was also taking "Secretarial Practice," which was, in fact, a grooming course to become a professional secretary. If I met the R.S.A. examiners' standards of excellence at all three levels of proficiency, I would have acquired top credentials for a decent career. It sounded like a good alternative.

"FRIDAY, DECEMBER 25TH: DAD IS HOME FOR CHRISTMAS, THE FIRST ONE WE HAVE SPENT AT BISHOP'S HILL IN THREE YEARS! CHRISTMAS CARDS FROM SUNDERLAND FAMILY, WREXHAM FRIENDS AND ALL THE BOYS INCLUDING ONE FROM BRUCE SAYING 'ALL MY LOVE'! WOW! BITTERLY COLD DAY. WALKED OVER TO SEE MRS. WHITE AND BETTY. IT MUST BE A VERY SAD CHRISTMAS FOR THEM. BROUGHT THEM BACK WITH US TO BISHOP'S HILL."

Christmas Day of 1942 was the first we had spent in our own home since the war began. We hung our family ornaments on the small artificial tree perched atop the Morrison shelter, and exchanged small gifts. Then we went to visit Mrs. White and Betty. With Roger's death, this must have been the worst Christmas in their lives. We brought them home to stay the night.

"THURSDAY, DECEMBER 31ST: WENT TO NEW YEAR'S PARTY AT COLLEGE. SOME OF THE CANADIANS JOINED US. DANCED, ATE, AND SANG AROUND THE PIANO. DIDN'T STAY TO CELEBRATE NEW YEAR. LAST BUS AT 10 P.M.!"

Hours of work had gone into preparing for the party. The Common Room had been festooned with prewar paper decorations strung across the ceiling; sprigs of red-berried holly and a bunch of mistletoe hung over the doorway to complete the transformation. The ping pong tables and overstuffed chairs had been pushed back to leave room for a dance floor, and an impromptu stage had been erected at the opposite end of the room from the buffet table. Everyone brought treats from home for the buffet. There were finger sandwiches with savory fillings, cookies, little mince pies, a hoarded fruit cake, and fruit flavored gelatin with artificial cream. The Canadian air crew cadets added their share: goodies and soft drinks that we hadn't seen since before the war.

Bernard, with the flourish of a show-biz professional, acted as Master of Ceremonies. "Laydeez and Gents," he bellowed, "take your partners for the conga." The conga line wound through classrooms and the cafeteria back to the Common Room, where we all collapsed into the chairs lining the room to catch our breath. We nibbled at the buffet, then danced and sang along with the college trio: Bernard on his violin, Hannah on her zither, and one of the Canadians on the piano. Four girls from one of the classes did a funny skit, and three others belted out a series of popular songs worthy of the Andrews Sisters. Some of the cadets sang solos. Another used his artistic talent to draw a caricature portrait for those who wanted one. My diary recorded: "DANCED WITH A TALL CANADIAN FROM ALBERTA, WHO TOLD ME ALL ABOUT HOW THEY GROW WHEAT. WHAT A BORE, BUT AT LEAST I DIDN'T HAVE TO FIGHT HIM OFF!"

I ran to catch the last bus home. Mom, Dad and I hugged each other at midnight. Dad was our First Foot, in our own house at last.

∽

The Lost Diary

NINETEEN FORTY-THREE'S DIARY was nowhere to be found, but there was no use "crying over spilled milk," as Mom would have said, so I sat quietly and tried to reconstruct and jot down some of the events of that year in the war and in my life, as they would have been recorded in that missing diary. Even after all these years, some of the events, both tragic and humorous, stood out clearly. The array of historical data released since World War Two helped me pinpoint events in the war throughout the year, so I could begin to put both happenings together into words.

"SUNDAY, JANUARY 10TH: RUSSIANS SUCCESSFULLY ENCIRCLING THE NAZIS AT STALINGRAD. DAD IS HOME FOR THE WEEKEND. AS IN OLD TIMES, WE WENT TO EVENSONG AT ST. JOHN'S."
Whether Churchill was comfortable with it or not, the Russians had become our Allies after being attacked by Hitler's armies. Our press did full justice to the heroic struggle taking place in Eastern Europe. The words "scorched earth policy" crept into the news reports. In retreat, the Russians systematically destroyed anything that would be of use to the advancing Germans, burning acres of precious crops to deprive the enemy armies of a food source as their supply lines stretched out longer and thinner.

Battered since the previous summer by Nazi Panzer divisions and the full force of the *Luftwaffe*, the Russians had been beaten back through their vast tracts of land as far as Stalingrad, the "city of steel," pride of Russia's industrial might. Our newspapers and radio reported huge battles, with enormous losses of life on both sides.

The Battle of Stalingrad began in the summer of 1942, lasting through the bitter Russian winter, when besieged citizens suffered terrible hardships including starvation. Having succeeded in holding the line at Stalingrad, the Russians were now successfully counterattacking. A hysterical Hitler ordered his troops to fight to the last man. The Battle of Stalingrad lasted another month until there was no longer any other option left but surrender for the encircled Germans.

Dad's work was centered in the southeast of England now, and he was home for the weekend quite frequently. He probably would have said: "Things are beginning to look shipshape for us in the war at last, and there's certainly been a windfall of business for my company with these new American army camps and airfields springing up like mushrooms all over the map. But you know, Bunty, I've missed going to church; very often there hasn't been one anywhere near these places out in the middle of nowhere. Let's go down to St. John's for Evensong."

The little brick church had been like us; it had known the terror of the London Blitz, been damaged by its fury and immobilized by delayed action bombs, but it had survived. The congregation was still sparse, with so many parishioners scattered by the war, but St. John's stood, a symbol of our faith, waiting for better times.

This Sunday Mom opted out; she would have said, "I'll stay home and make our Sunday dinner; going to church only makes me feel guilty!"

"THURSDAY, JANUARY 14TH: CHURCHILL AND ROOSEVELT HELD A CONFERENCE AT CASABLANCA. COLLEGE STUDIES STILL INTERESTING. LOTS OF CANADIANS PASSING THROUGH. MOM AND I TOOK DOWN OUR CHRISTMAS DECORATIONS."

The Prime Minister and President were joined by French Generals Charles de Gaulle and his rival, Henri Giraud, U.S. Field Marshal Eisenhower (later to become General Eisenhower) and British Field Marshal Alexander, for a conference at Casablanca in North Africa. They discussed future strategy for the war, and it was agreed that Germany must surrender unconditionally. Plans were formulated for the Allied invasion of Sicily. Stalin had been invited, but his presence was required in Russia at the crucial turning point in his war against the Germans.

While Churchill and Roosevelt were deciding on how to proceed with the war in the two principal Theaters of Operations, Mom and I were taking down our Christmas decorations and storing them in their boxes in the attic, hoping that next time we saw them it would be peacetime again. Although I did most of the climbing into the attic, I can remember Mom's expression as she huffed up the attic stairs: "Gosh, every year the stairs seem longer and the boxes get heavier." I had hardly realized she and Dad were getting older.

Early in January I went back to college classes, having added "Secretarial Practice" to my curriculum. Doing secretarial classroom work felt like being an apprentice in a law practice--I'd never realized that so much knowledge would be necessary to make me a professional secretary.

Even with the heavy load of ten college courses, I was still enjoying the change of pace from the classical education I had had at Ravenhurst and Wrexham Park. To crown it all, I was getting good training to fit me for the working world, something that Caesar's *Gallic Wars*" and Ovid's *Metamorphoses* and all that Latin homework could never have done, although I grudgingly had to admit it *had* helped me understand English a lot better!

To add a bit of zest, our college Common Room was always packed with Canadian flight-training cadets; I was learning how to lose graciously at ping pong!

"TUESDAY, FEBRUARY 2ND: THE GERMANS FINALLY SURRENDERED TO THE RUSSIANS AT STALINGRAD. HERE AT HOME THE *LUFTWAFFE* ISN'T LETTING US FORGET WHAT AN AIR RAID FEELS LIKE."
The Battle of Stalingrad has been called the greatest military disaster in human history. It was certainly the worst defeat ever for Hitler's armies. Labeled by some historians the bloodiest battle ever fought, with an

estimated one million, two hundred thousand casualties, it was hailed by some as the most significant turning point in World War Two. We heard the news of the Russian victory with relief, but mourned the human cost.

In Upper Woodside we were confident that the unrelenting daily air raids we had endured were now a thing of the past, but periodically during those first few months of the new year we received reminders that the *Luftwaffe* still had a sting in its tail. History records that there were thirteen large raids on London between January and the end of March, referred to as "the Little Blitz." During this time we slept all night in the Morrison shelter, having abandoned the Anderson to its own soggy domain in the backyard. Fortunately, no bombs fell near us in Bishop's Hill.

Sometimes the air-raid sirens wailed when I was on the bus going to or from college. If the bombs and ack-ack fire sounded close, the bus driver stopped in front of a public shelter and the conductor would yell: "'Orl right, laydees an' gents, ev'rybody off--shayke a leg there, fowks!"

Followed closely by the bus driver and conductor, all the passengers piled as quickly as they could into a street-corner shelter, a rectangular concrete structure with sandbagged entrance, flat roof and no doors or windows. Sitting in the gloom inside on two long wooden benches facing each another, we were reminded once again of our frailty against the destruction raining down from the skies.

I think every woman in Britain was a "bag lady" during the war, with an extra appendage growing from her arm - a large tote bag. Mine contained a lightweight, rolled-up raincoat, collapsible umbrella, purse, identity card, gas mask, flashlight, knitting, and a magazine to read. But my favorite diversion in a public air-raid shelter was to make conversation with my shelter-mates and listen to their stories. Shared wartime experiences drew us close, people so diverse yet so much a part of each other's lives joined together in common danger. All signs of traditional English "reserve" melted away as life histories were swapped with gusto. When the "All Clear" sounded, we wished each other good luck, gave a cheery "V" sign, then headed back to the bus to pick up our lives again where we had temporarily left them.

"MONDAY, FEBRUARY 8TH: U.S. TROOPS COMPLETED CAPTURE OF GUADALCANAL IN THE PACIFIC."
The Japanese were finally forced to give up Guadalcanal, another significant turning point in the war in the Pacific for the Allies.

"WEDNESDAY, APRIL 7TH: MONTGOMERY'S BRITISH EIGHTH ARMY LINKS UP WITH AMERICANS IN TUNISIA. IN OUR BACK GARDEN SPRING IS HERE AT LAST!"
There was great celebration, for the end of the Nazi victories in North Africa was now in sight. "Monty" had become a national hero as he led his Eighth Army from one victory to another.

He's done it," exulted Mom, "he's joined up with the Yanks! There'll be no stopping the Allies now."

Mom looked out over the backyard, welcoming the shafts of early spring sunshine lighting up the sprouting shoots in her flower borders. She added: "Well, these arthritic hands and feet of mine have made it through another winter; it's time to put them to work again." And pulling on her "Wellies," she headed out to do some weeding. We had both been feeling despondent after so many gray winter days without sunshine, but today a hint of pink and white blossom was showing on the pregnant buds of our three apple trees: Granny Smith, Cox's Orange Pippin and Russet. The bright pink flowers on the almond tree would soon burst into bloom to join them. Spring was on its way, war or no war.

"MONDAY, APRIL 19TH: NAZI SS TROOPS ATTACK JEWS IN WARSAW GHETTO UPRISING. LETTERS FROM PETER, PAUL AND BRUCE."
After the war, the story came to light that about seven hundred and fifty Jews remaining in the Warsaw Ghetto in Poland fought off Hitler's troops for almost a month to avoid another series of deportations. I

don't remember any editorializing about the Warsaw uprising in the British press or on the radio. However, there were rumors of messages smuggled through occupied Europe's underground telling of the brutal annihilation of the Jews in the Warsaw Ghetto, and later we heard of Himmler's order to liquidate all Jewish ghettos in Poland. We also heard rumors filtering through the underground in Europe about the deportation of large numbers of Jews to "work camps." We had already heard of the Germans deporting men and women from occupied countries to forced labor camps to enable the German war factories to operate continuously, day and night. I don't recall reports of any "extermination camps," nor was it revealed that Hitler had planned the systematic elimination of all the Jews in Europe, his "ultimate solution." The truth about death camps like Buchenwald and Belsen would not be fully known to the British public until after D-Day in 1944, when newsreels recorded pictures of horrified Allied troops as they liberated the death camps with their piles of skeletal bodies and survivors in pitiful, near-death condition.

At Bishop's Hill the arrival of letters from the boys always felt like a lifeline. Bruce's letter began: "I knew you wouldn't write unless I did, so here I am, on an L.S.T. somewhere on the sea. Tell me all the latest neighborhood news - I wish I could tell you more of mine!"

I had a feeling he was sidestepping the censor's black pencil. I wondered where he was, and said a quick prayer for his safety.

Peter hadn't the educational requirements for air crew, so he had settled for acceptance as a dispatch rider with the R.A.F. instead. He and Bruce sounded a bit "down," so I decided to spend the evening writing letters to the boys. Paul announced he would be visiting us at the weekend and to get my walking shoes out because he wanted to see Spring Glen Park now that the weather was better. At least I didn't have to worry about *him*!

"THURSDAY, MAY 13TH: ALL AXIS TROOPS SURRENDER IN NORTH AFRICA. HAD A LETTER FROM WILLIAM IN CANADA."

That the war in North Africa was over, became official. But how would we feed all those prisoners? Would our food rations be cut?

By this time William was off in Canada, doing his R.A.F. training to become a fighter pilot. He had come to say goodbye to us, excited at the prospect of realizing his dream, but leaving behind two worried parents. According to his sporadic letters, he was having a "wizard" time, wreaking havoc with his charm among the local girls. He had outgrown our old life in Upper Woodside, as an adult, just as I had as a college student. My disenchantment with William knew no bounds.

"MONDAY, MAY 31ST: JAPANESE END OCCUPATION OF ALEUTIAN ISLANDS."
To the relief of the Allies, Japan's dream of invading North America had failed.

To Thine Own Self ...
"SATURDAY, JUNE 12TH: ALLIES BOMBED RUHR VALLEY INDUSTRIAL TARGETS AGAIN, ALSO CAPTURED ISLANDS IN THE MEDITERRANEAN AND PACIFIC. WENT TO DINNER AND A SHOW WITH ARCHIE SILVERSMITH."
The war news in the European Theater included massive strategic bombing attacks by R.A.F. and American aircraft on industrial cities in the Ruhr valley, one of the main sources of supply for Hitler's war machine. In the Mediterranean, several islands between North Africa and Sicily had been captured by the Allies, and in the Pacific, U.S. forces were beginning to reclaim islands occupied by the Japanese.

On the home front, I was feeling depressed. The novelty of college had worn off and classroom work now became monotonous. After final exams at the end of the college year, I could look forward to trying my wings in the working world, but that was still a month away. My social life in Upper Woodside was nil, in a neighborhood deserted by young people now serving in the armed forces. Periodic letters arrived from

William and Bruce, both overseas. They seemed detached and remote. Peter was stationed in England, but I saw him rarely, when he had leave and took me to St. John's dances.

In this barren desert of a social vacuum I was about to experience something that would give me a lesson in values I would never forget. A tall, aristocratic but awkward young man had joined our college class. I will call him Archie. His blue-blooded ancestry stemmed from Lord Aubrey Silversmith, an aristocrat whose forebears had received land grants and titles from William the Conqueror back in the eleventh century. Left behind in the good looks department, poor Archie had the air of a dismal Great Dane. For weeks he had been asking me to go out with him. By this time, bored with my nonexistent social life and in a "what the hell" mood, I relented and agreed to a Saturday dinner and theater date in London's posh West End. Air raids had temporarily stopped. In the spirit of "Stay Calm and Carry On," city restaurants and theaters were struggling back to some semblance of their prewar activity in the unexpected lull.

I took a train to the city. Archie was waiting on the station platform, and as I stepped off the train he leaped forward, clutching a small box. I took off the lid, and gasped when I saw three perfect little pink "sweetheart" rosebuds fashioned into a lovely corsage. Archie pinned them to my well-worn coat with a flourish. He surprised me by his success in hailing a taxi, and we were soon being ushered by a uniformed doorman into an exclusive restaurant. Waiters hovered over the white, linen-clad table with its silver vase of fresh flowers and daunting lineup of cutlery.

I was painfully conscious of my plain woolen "utility" dress, unpolished nails, hastily polished shoes and thick lisle stockings, which we had to wear now that silk ones were off the market. At this time, we had never known nylons. I tucked my feet under the chair to hide them and tried to look sophisticated. Archie rattled off a series of French phrases to the waiter, who bowed and brought a bottle of wine for Archie's inspection.

"Aha," I thought, "so that's what he's up to. He's going to get me drunk and I'll end up in some exclusive apartment with him for the night." But one look at Archie's harmless, mournful face put my mind at rest.

Dinner was an extravagant treat, the theater seats were in a private box, the show was entertaining. I should have felt bubbly and excited, but each time I looked at Archie, I liked him less. After an awkward grab or two at me in the theater, he gave up any romantic advances, and we parted at the train station with a handshake and a hurried peck on the cheek.

On the hour-long journey back to Upper Woodside, I had time to think about the evening. I felt sorry for Archie; he was lonely. Unattractive as he was, I now understood why he wanted so badly to have a girl go out with him. His breeding and background were obvious, as was his apparent abundance of spending money--"quite a catch," as some of my mother's friends would say. I could have had it made as his girl-friend, but I simply felt out of place with him!

I pondered over the greed of women who effectively played a part to hide their indifference to a wealthy man in order to enjoy the luxury and status he could provide. Was I one of those? As I thought about continuing a relationship with Archie, I knew I had the opportunity to develop it to my own advantage, but strangely some words I had mem-orized from English Literature classes at Wrexham Park kept popping into my mind:

"This above all: to thine own self be true,
And it must follow, as the night the day,
Thou canst not then be false to any man."

I had never quite understood what Shakespeare meant, but now it was so clear to me. By the time I arrived home, I had decided that I would stay where I belonged--not with the aristocracy, but in the middle class!

Archie tried to make a date with me a few more times, but it was now with relief and without one pang of guilt that I could tell him I had other plans.

"FRIDAY, JULY 9TH: LAST DAY OF COLLEGE; THE R.S.A. EXAM RESULTS WILL BE MAILED TO US. FINGERS CROSSED! I'VE SIGNED UP TO GO AND HELP BRING IN THE HARVEST, ALONG WITH OTHERS FROM MY CLASS."

A few weeks earlier a government recruiter armed with pamphlets and a clipboard came to collect the names of those of us who would volunteer to help. The pamphlet had a list of items we should bring with us, and a magical sentence: "Bicycles allowed." I was thrilled. "Wow," I thought: "Here's a chance to help the war effort, escape from boredom in Bishop's Hill, and enjoy a week's free vacation in the country! And I can take Percival with me!"

Five from our class signed up: Bernard, Hannah, Carmen, my new friend Pat, and myself. Archie, to my great relief, decided that anything as plebeian as becoming a farm laborer was not for him, and he opted not to volunteer. The recruiter said we would be notified when we were needed to "bring in the sheaves," probably in August.

The British Government had anticipated with alarm that the thousands of farm-workers who had joined the armed forces would leave the country's farmers unable to cope with the annual chore of harvesting the grains and vegetables needed so badly to supply food for Britain. Even the Women's Land Army would be unable to supply the number of farm-workers needed during the crucial months of harvest.

To avert a sure catastrophe, early in the war an organization was set up to construct Harvest Camps for older schoolchildren who would be urged to volunteer as farm-workers during their summer vacation. Postwar statistics estimate that over a thousand camps were set up, and over two hundred and fifty thousand young people were housed in their tents, under somewhat primitive conditions, between 1940 and 1950.

On the last day of school, Bernard quipped: "Well folks, I'll see you when they send for us. Sounds like fun!"

The five of us went home for the summer to wait for the summons --the wheat harvest would probably be due in August.

"SUNDAY, JULY 25TH: MUSSOLINI HAS BEEN DEPOSED! I WONDER WHAT WILL HAPPEN TO ITALY NOW AND TO 'IL DUCE'?"
On July twenty-fifth Italian dictator Mussolini was deposed by his own government and sent into exile in the Italian mountains. With amazement we read the story of how Hitler's paratroopers had rescued him from his imprisonment, after which he headed a puppet government regime for the Germans in Milan. History records that, largely due to British and American diplomatic delays, the Allies missed the opportunity to secure an unconditional surrender from the Italians after the overthrow of Mussolini. Hitler's troops quickly moved in and took over. The costly, bloody war in Italy dragged on until 1945.

"WEDNESDAY, AUGUST 11TH: CHURCHILL AND ROOSEVELT HELD FIRST QUEBEC CONFERENCE. MOM MAY BE CALLED UP!"
Announcement of the Quebec Conference was probably not made public, but it has gone down in history, along with several other meetings in Quebec. At this one, Canada was represented by its Prime Minister, MacKenzie-King. We now know that plans were made for the invasion of Italy and France, to take place in 1944, and cooperation in the development of an atomic bomb was discussed.

There were rumors in Britain that the conscription age for older women would soon be increased. We hadn't anticipated that Mom would ever be involved, but now, at forty-seven, she might be whisked away for National Service. Dad's reaction was: "What a revolting development that would be!"

"TUESDAY, AUGUST 17TH: ALLIES HAVE SUCCESSFULLY TAKEN SICILY! BEGAN PACKING TO GO TO WILTSHIRE TO HELP WITH THE HARVEST."

The Allied invasion of Sicily was apparently well planned and executed, culminating in the capture of its capital, Messina, and giving the Allies a springboard for the invasion of Italy.

I was excited about going to Wiltshire for a new adventure. Everything I would need would fit into a small suitcase, and I was soon packed and ready to go. I took Percival down to our local railway station and made the arrangements for him to be delivered to the village hall where we would be staying in Wiltshire, a county I had never seen before, to the west of London.

"SUNDAY, AUGUST 22ND: TOOK THE TRAIN FROM LONDON TO WILTSHIRE. GLAD PAT IS GOING WITH ME."
Our little group from the college joined hundreds of other young people our age under the bomb-damaged roof of the London terminus whose trains went to the "West Country." Pat and I found two empty seats in a passenger carriage. Pat was bubbling over with excitement. "You've sent your bike on ahead, haven't you, Bunty? It will be so great having wheels of our own to get around when we have free time; I can hardly wait!"

"Me, too, Pat, this is really going to be something new!" We didn't realize just how new! I hoisted my small suitcase up onto the luggage rack above our heads, and memories of my first evacuation came flooding back as I heard the sound of young voices singing popular songs in the crowded train carriages. After rattling through many unmarked stations we arrived in Wiltshire and were met by special buses. We sped through country roads dotted with thatched cottages, passing fields of golden-ripe wheat, rye and barley, rippling in the breeze and sunshine near farm buildings and whitewashed farmhouses.

Good fortune smiled on Pat and me; we were spared the ordeal of being in one of the Harvest Camps sleeping on damp groundsheets in a small tent city. We were dropped off at a village church hall, whose bare wooden floor had straw-filled mattresses spaced at intervals around its perimeter; girls on one side, boys on the other. There was no sign of Hannah or Carmen; they had been on a different bus, but

I found myself next to Pat; at least, among all the strange faces, hers was one I knew.

Depositing backpacks and suitcases at our assigned mattresses, we headed for the kitchen, ravenously hungry, bringing back loaded plates to the rough tables at the far end of the hall.

Bringing in the Sheaves

"MONDAY, AUGUST 23RD: WOW! NOBODY TOLD ME IT WOULD BE LIKE THIS! I ACHE ALL OVER!"

After a restless night on unaccustomed lumpy straw mattresses, we were up at dawn to wash, dress and devour a prewar breakfast: thick slices of home-cured ham, freshly laid eggs, home-baked bread.

A small bus picked us up and took us to a nearby farm, where we were divided into squads of a dozen workers each. As new farmhands, our squad's first task was to learn how to "stook" sheaves of wheat ready for threshing (a procedure that would be outdated after the war and done by machine).

We burst into song, the old gospel hymn "Bringing in the Sheaves," as we rode the bumpy, horse-drawn hay cart on the way to the wheat fields. Rows of fat bundles of harvested wheat were lying where they had been dropped by the binder in neat rows all over the field. Pat and I picked each other as partners, glad that we could stay close to someone we knew. An elderly farmer bellowed instructions at us as we stood together with our partners. "Now listen 'ere, all yew lot. Fust of all ye stands about a good three feet apart. Then yew lifts these 'ere sheaves, one under each arm. When oi shouts, 'one-two-three,' yew walks t'ward each other and stacks yore sheaves in a stook."

We hadn't a clue what a stook was, but Pat and I took up our positions. Watching each other struggle to lift the heavy bundles and tuck them under our arms, we giggled so much that, after staggering a step or two, we both dropped our sheaves and had to start all over again. I tried to suppress a giggle. "No more laughing, Pat," I admonished my partner, "or we'll be here all day and still not have made a silly stook, whatever that is!"

The farmer hid a smile as Pat and I stumbled toward each other once again with a sheaf under each arm; then he roared, "Now then, one-two-three," at which we stacked them together, making a self-supporting group of four. Taraah, a stook! Our joyful whoop was cut short as the stook promptly leaned over and fell back on the ground. By the end of the morning we had perfected our stooking, but with red, blistered hands to show for our efforts.

"Oh gosh," wheezed Pat, "I'm exhausted already. It isn't even lunch time, and my hands hurt something awful."

"Oh well," I replied, "they told us we'd have a lunch break in the middle of the day, so let's keep at it and remember nothing lasts forever!" We blew on our blistered hands and made another stook.

The sun was high in the blue summer sky when a farm cart appeared and turned off the lane into the field where we were toiling. The farmer's wife brought the big cart horse to a stop by a small row of trees at one side of the field. A tall, buxom woman with skin ruddy from the summer sun and wind, she wiped strands of hair from her damp forehead, tucking them under her kerchief with the corner of her flowered apron. She then began to swing a large handbell. As if by magic, our fellow workers materialized from all over and converged upon the cart. The farm wife heaved her ample figure upright, stood up in the cart and shouted: "Now all of yew goes over and sits down in the shaide, 'ear me?" Putting down the bell, she continued: "Oi've brung yer lunch out to yer."

After several hours in the hot sun, the welcome coolness of the shade, the ham sandwich made with thickly cut, fresh bread spread with creamy butter, the crisp apple, and the foamy cup of milk seemed like heaven. Hour after hour we somehow worked our way through the afternoon's stooking and were collected by the cart for the bus ride back to the village hall.

Pat and I splashed cold water on our hot faces and throbbing hands, then joined the lineup for supper. The cook filled our bowls with hearty stew and handed each of us a crunchy chunk of freshly baked, crusty white bread (in this village they must not have heard of the National Loaf, thank goodness). Another apple was our dessert. We wolfed it all down, put on our pajamas and flung ourselves onto the unyielding straw mattresses, to become swiftly and blissfully unconscious until the sun's rays and the smell of sizzling bacon woke us next morning.

"TUESDAY, AUGUST 24TH: SOME VACATION IN THE COUNTRY! NOBODY TOLD ME IT WOULD BE LIKE THIS; I'VE NEVER WORKED SO HARD IN ALL MY LIFE! AND ON TOP OF IT ALL, I ITCH LIKE BLAZES." Next morning we noticed a rash of tiny red welts around our waists and under our arms. As we washed, we itched, and began to scratch. The cook at the village hall took one look at us as we gyrated through breakfast. Hands on hips, with stray strands of hair escaping from the bun she had scraped up to rest precariously in a nest of hairpins on top of her head, she knew immediately what to say: "Oh, aye, them's 'arvest mites. Them little buggers burrows under the skin and itches yer. But don't ye worry, them goes awaie, later."

She didn't say how much later! For the rest of the week, scratching at the harvest mites became a way of life, always good for a laugh as we watched each other become contortionists to get at the itches.

Ever the opportunist, Bernard charmed the farmer into teaching him how to drive the horse and cart, neatly avoiding the heavy field work. After two days of stooking wheat, the farmer addressed us again: "Now listen 'ere", he yelled, "oi thinks yers good enuf to 'ave a go at bringing in the 'ay. Bernie 'ere will taike yer out to the 'ay field; it ain't fur."

We hadn't yet seen any hay to bring in, but Bernard drove us to a distant field where the long grass had been cut and strewn all over it in a series of ragged rows. Bernard maneuvered the horse and cart close to the edge of the field, and we began our new job, each equipped with a long-handled, sturdy pitchfork. With a load of hay on it, all my strength was needed to get it off the ground, but after a few tries, I was able to figure out how much hay to put on it so I could lift it high enough to pitch the hay off it and into the cart.

Bernard prodded the enormous cart horse forward, ready for the next batch of hay. I looked away for a minute to say something to my fellow sufferers, and felt a stab of pain in my right foot. Turning to look, I saw, to my horror, that it had disappeared under a giant, hair-covered hoof. I shouted at the horse, and beat it on its shin with my fist. It simply twitched its ears, and remained immobile, quite oblivious of the fact that it was pinning a human being to the ground. I tried grinding my foot into the loose soil, hoping to pull it out, but as it sank, so did the horse's hoof, still squarely planted on top of it. By now, we were all yelling at Bernard to move the horse. After what seemed like a lifetime of agony, the great beast heaved itself forward and I thankfully retrieved my foot. Fortunately nothing was broken, but I still have a calcified lump on the bruised bones, to remind me.

That cart full of hay was irresistible. We clambered up on it, and lay back on its yielding softness. Bernard took us on an impromptu hayride down one of the country lanes, eventually arriving back at the hayfield to face the irate farmer, who had lost about an hour of our labor and thought he had lost his horse and cart, too.

Having filled the cart with hay, we now learned how to pitch it into the hayloft in the barn. It was hard enough pitching hay up from the ground to the cart, but this next exercise was the ultimate challenge. Standing on the pile of hay in the cart, we took careful aim at the small open door in the hayloft above it, groaning as we heaved the pitchfork up and shook its load of hay off, with a quick jerk. Each jerk was torture, and by the end of the day, our arms felt like lead pipes. At breakfast next morning, the village hall echoed with laughter as we watched each other trying to lift forks to our mouths with protesting muscles that even refused to function enough to scratch our harvest mites.

"WEDNESDAY, AUGUST 25TH: PAT AND I WENT FOR A BIKE RIDE AND MET TWO YANKS. THEY SPEAK RATHER UNGRAMATICALLY, BUT IT WAS FASCINATING TALKING TO THEM. WONDER IF WE'LL EVER SEE THEM AGAIN?"

Our young bodies were adapting to the unaccustomed heavy labor. By midweek Pat and I had enough energy left at the end of the working day to explore the country lanes around the farm on our bicycles. On Double British Summer Time, daylight lingered where it once had been night. One beautiful evening Pat and I were riding our bikes, the wind on our faces and the setting sun making shadow-patterns on the fields.

We rounded a bend to see two uniformed figures walking ahead of us in the middle of the narrow lane. We gave a warning tinkle on our bicycle bells, to be greeted by wolf whistles, and "Hey, girls, slow down!" Stopping our bikes, we came suddenly face to face with the first American soldiers we had ever met, presumably from a nearby army camp. The big one introduced them: "Ah'm 'Butch' from Kaintucky an' this yar is 'Dook' from Noo York."

We shook hands politely, then all sat down by the fragrant hedgerow at the edge of the road while they told us about their home states, which they each referred to as "God's Country." Pat and I were fascinated as they described a life so different from ours in England, speaking in strangely foreign American accents that intrigued us.

Reluctantly we cycled back to the village hall in time for our ten o'clock curfew, still in broad daylight. We rode down that lane the following day, and the day after, and each time the same two soldiers happened to be sauntering along. When they heard we were from London, Butch and Duke asked for our addresses, probably thinking London was a small enough town for them to look us up on their next pass there. We were sure we would never see either one of them again. I, at least, was wrong!

"SUNDAY, AUGUST 29TH: TOOK THE TRAIN BACK TO LONDON. WHAT A WEEK! BUT I'M GLAD I DID IT; IT WAS FULL OF SURPRISES! MY R.S.A. EXAM RESULTS ARRIVED WHILE I WAS AWAY. GREAT NEWS!"

The week had flown by and I was back in London, complacently proud of my latest contribution to the war effort. Mom greeted me with: "Oh Bunty, how tanned you are; all that fresh air and rest must have done you a world of good!"

I didn't have the heart to say: "What rest?" Or to show Mom the blisters on my hands or the itchy red welts around my waistline until the following day, when I wouldn't be too tired to make it an amusing story. My own bed felt heavenly that night.

In the mail that had arrived during my adventures in Wiltshire was a letter from the Royal Society of Arts announcing that I had been awarded their first class proficiency certificates in Shorthand and Typing. Another letter from the college contained a battery of very respectable grades for my remaining college courses including an "A" in Secretarial Practice!

"MONDAY, AUGUST 30TH: FREE FROM SCHOOL AT LAST! TIME TO THINK ABOUT GETTING A GOOD FULL-TIME JOB. MEANTIME, I WONDER WHEN I'LL BE CALLED FOR NATIONAL SERVICE?"

My work/study program in the secretarial course had netted me a part-time clerical job in the welfare office of a small factory a few miles from Bishop's Hill, which suited Mom and Dad fine; it was only about half an hour's ride on Percival.

The job lacked challenge and the office offered no opportunities to try out the procedures I had learned in Secretarial Practice. In other words, it was boring and had no class! However, it occupied me only for a few hours, several times a week. Many and various managers and factory foremen kept me busy with short letters and memoranda, and it was good shorthand and typing practice to get me up to the speed needed for the R.S.A. exam.

The Welfare Officer (these days she would be known as the Personnel Director) was temporarily without a secretary. She seemed to like me. One morning she called me into her office. "Bunty, if you produce satisfactory records of your secretarial education from the college, I'll offer you a full-time job to fill the vacancy."

My Royal Society of Arts certificates and good grades clinched the deal. I decided to stay on and give it a try, beginning in two weeks' time.

Dad, who had been paying hefty private prep school and college fees ever since I was twelve years old, was delighted at the prospect of a wage-earning daughter. "Well, Bunty, it might be a good idea at that. It's nice and close to home; and just think, you'll be getting your first pay check! And besides, you never know what's around the corner."

Little did Dad or I guess what life had in store for us.

Called Up

"TUESDAY, AUGUST 31ST: SOMEBODY MUST HAVE READ MY DIARY! MY NATIONAL SERVICE PAPERS CAME TODAY!"

Evidently the British Government heard me wondering when I would be called up for National Service! The summons to register had arrived. I had said to Dad when he was home for the weekend: "When my papers come, I think I'd like to volunteer for the W.R.N.S. (Womens' Royal Naval Service) officer's training, just to keep Royal Navy officers in the family, you know. Don't you think I'd look smashing in a 'Wren's' uniform?"

Mom gave me a worried look. "Well, Bunty, you'd have to go up to the recruiting office in London and see about volunteering, but I think you should stay on at the factory, now that you've been offered a full-time job there. You'd be doing just as much to help the war effort, and you're now fully qualified for secretarial work. In the Wrens they would put you just anywhere, most likely some job you hadn't even been trained to do!"

"WEDNESDAY, SEPTEMBER 1ST: TOOK THE BUS TO LONDON TO THE ROYAL NAVY RECRUITING OFFICE. NO LUCK. DISGUSTED, SO I REGISTERED FOR AN ESSENTIAL WORKS JOB. LONDON IS FULL OF AMERICANS; THEY REALLY HAVE ARRIVED!"
Volunteering to join the Wrens had always appealed to me. With my National Registration papers in my purse, on the bus to London I had no idea how naive I was as I rationalized: "After all, not only is their uniform the most attractive of all three of the women's services, but of course I'll train to become a Navy officer, just as Dad had been in the first World War."

From behind a shabby desk an unsmiling, hard-boiled W.R.N.S. recruiting officer listened to my reasons for wanting to enlist. "My dear girl," she barked, "you haven't had any R.O.T.C. You will join the Wrens at the lowest non-commissioned entry level, just like everyone else, and there will be no guarantee you will ever make it to officers' training!"

Deflated, I huffily turned my back on the Royal Navy, and decided to register for a job under the "Essential Works Act," which, translated, meant doing work considered essential to the war effort. The factory was already in that category, and I would be close to home with a nice promotion. I resigned myself to reporting for my new job in two weeks.

American servicemen were pouring into Britain in preparation for D-Day, beginning the build-up of men and materiel for the Allied invasion of the European mainland. They impacted the lives of British civilians in many ways. Their warm-hearted generosity was evident, particularly in their concern for war orphans and for poor children in the cities; they gave parties for them at American Red Cross clubs and in local town halls.

The "G.Is" were easygoing, fun-loving and also wealthy by British standards. This fostered jealousy and resentment among some British servicemen, especially when British girls began to go out with them.

Their now-famous saying went: "There are three things wrong with the Americans; they're overpaid, oversexed, and over here!"

In Sunderland the tough, regular army Americans who had arrived in Britain earlier in the war to help fortify and defend the northeast coast, had not yet been followed by milder enlistees recruited from farms and small-town high schools, many of whom had left their home towns for the first time.

Letters to Mom from my grandmother and aunts were full of gossip about the local rugged Americans: the drain on the beer supplies in the Sunderland pubs, rowdy fistfights and rumors of the rape of some local females. Along with the lurid details, Gram's letters stressed to Mom the need "to make sure Bunty doesn't get involved with these sex-crazed Americans." But Upper Woodside was far enough away from the city of London that not one American serviceman had yet been seen in our suburb.

"WEDNESDAY, SEPTEMBER 8TH: ITALY HAS SURRENDERED TO THE ALLIES.THE GERMANS ENTERED ROME. A LETTER FROM BUTCH! HE WANTS TO COME AND VISIT!"

When the Italians surrendered, the Germans immediately occupied all of Italy by force. The Allies paid dearly for the Salerno landings and faced seasoned, crack German divisions in Italy on the entire long and bloody uphill struggle north to Rome. What Churchill had called "the soft under-belly of the Axis" was now what an American general called a "hard gut."

Mom took Gram's concern for my virginity seriously. When I arrived home from work, she handed me an envelope. "The postmark on this letter is Wiltshire, and it's from an American army post office. Bunty, is this the fellow you told me you met when you were helping with the harvest?"

"Yes, Mom," I replied, tearing open the envelope. "Wow, he says when he gets a forty-eight hour pass he would like to come and see me! Is it okay for him to come and stay with us?"

There was a pause. Two little lines appeared on Mom's forehead; she was looking a bit shaken at the prospect of entertaining a total stranger of suspicious origin. But then, in her normal hospitable way, she said: "Of course you can, dear; I've always trusted your judgment, you know."

Mom and Dad had an iron-clad recipe for judging my judgment of the opposite sex: they insisted I bring them home for inspection! So I dashed off a short note to Butch, telling him he was welcome to spend his next weekend pass with us at Bishop's Hill.

Pat and I had given the two soldiers our addresses more as a joke than anything; I never dreamed that Butch would want to visit Upper Woodside! In the next few days, Mom began her usual nervous reaction by worrying about what to feed our visitor and starting to get the guest bedroom ready.

"THURSDAY, SEPTEMBER 9TH: AMERICAN, BRITISH AND CANADIAN TROOPS HAVE LANDED IN FULL FORCE IN ITALY. BEACHHEADS AT SALERNO AND BRINDISI. ALLIED BOMBING RAIDS CONTINUED ON HAMBURG, GERMANY."

Holding the beachhead at Salerno in southern Italy was vital; the harbor port would be the main landing point for the further invasion of Italy. After a bloody struggle, the Americans secured it as the Nazis pulled out in retreat to the north.

Post-war statistics estimated that 33,000 were killed in the R.A.F. raids on Hamburg. Mutual hatred was spreading like a cancer, filling our world as the war progressed. The *Luftwaffe* blasted London and other large British cities in retaliation for the Allies' enormous raids on the important port of Hamburg, a center of production for Hitler's war machine. And so it went on: "An eye for an eye; a tooth for a tooth," throughout 1943.

The air raids on London couldn't compare in intensity with the London Blitz, but we spent many nights shoehorned into the Morrison shelter, falling asleep in the cramped space from sheer exhaustion.

We experienced the viciousness and hatefulness of war all around us. Occasionally, a single Nazi renegade fighter pilot would leave his formation and sweep low over our suburban streets, to satisfy a bloodlust to gun down any moving civilian target. Dad was home one weekend, reading his morning newspaper in the dining room. I had just come down to breakfast, and Mom was grumbling in the kitchen: "That milk delivery is really late today. You'll have to do without it in your tea, Jack, if it doesn't get here soon. I wonder where he's got to?"

Our milkman had a small, electric battery-powered truck, which he usually drove down our street as if competing in the Grand Prix, stopping periodically with a screech of brakes to rush back and forth across the street, carrying full bottles of milk and returning with the "empties." Suddenly we heard the whine of a diving plane and the stutter of machine-gun fire. We rushed in the direction of the sound to our living room window on the street side of the house, just in time to see a German plane zoom by at rooftop level. It seemed to fill our whole bay window for an instant before it screamed upward and away, narrowly missing St. John's church tower. The plane had chased the milkman down the street but had missed hitting his little truck, which arrived unceremoniously at our front door a few minutes later. The shaken driver tottered up the front walk to deliver Mom's two bottles of milk. Mom opened the door and urged: "Won't you come in and have a nice cup of tea to steady your nerves?"

The milkman was still in shock. "No thanks, madam, I'll be too late with the deliveries if I do that!"

Dad said: "Well I'll be damned, that man deserves a medal!"

Until they were repaired months after the war, holes from machine-gun bullets could still be seen in the stuccoed outer walls of houses across the street that had been in the path of the plane--a grim reminder of this senseless incident of revenge.

It had been a happy escape for our milkman, but not for the elementary schoolchildren walking across their playground in southeast

London earlier in the year. A lone Nazi plane dived down from the sky, machine guns blazing. This time the bullets found their mark and some of the children were hit. The plane then dropped a bomb on the school, where other children were having lunch. One side of the school wall collapsed and more tots were buried under the rubble. Two teachers and thirty-eight children were killed, many more injured. Thirty-one of the children and one teacher were buried in a communal grave, all innocent victims of insane, barbaric hate.

There were other reports such as these, involving renegade Nazi pilots taking it upon themselves to machine-gun civilian targets. Churches, schools and hospitals were systematically singled out as targets by Goering's bombers as part of Hitler's strategy to break the spirit of civilians on the British home front. In reality, these deliberate attacks ignited indignation and anger, strengthening our resolve to resist. The wording of my diaries showed that I had learned hatred in those days, one of the evil by-products of the greater evil that is war itself.

"MONDAY, SEPTEMBER 13TH: THE GERMANS HAVE NOW FORMALLY OCCUPIED ROME. MY FIRST DAY AS A FULL-FLEDGED SECRETARY! I WONDER IF BUTCH REALLY MEANT IT ABOUT THAT 48-HOUR PASS?" The fact that Hitler's army had occupied Rome didn't register with me particularly, but as the Allied campaign in Italy developed into a bloodbath for Allied troops, now up against Hitler's seasoned storm troopers, the news began to hit home. Churchill's "soft under-belly of the Axis" was soft no longer.

I was now a working woman! The factory was located a few miles outside the residential suburb of Upper Woodside. I could easily ride Percival to work when it wasn't raining, which would save waiting at the bus stop while buses already full of commuters sailed past me. Outside the building was a large sign that I thought was rather odd: "THE HYGIENIC WIRE WORKS." I wondered how or why wire could be hygienic. It was an unattractive, noisy place, working on government contracts under the Essential Works Act. What it actually produced was a classified secret, which must have been the reason for its ambiguous name; nobody really knew what the thousands of gadgets turned out by this factory actually did for the war effort. Whatever they were, they must have been in great demand; the machinery hummed twenty-four hours a day.

The Welfare Office was a haven of peace away from the clanking of machines and the smell of hot oil. I was kept busy from nine to five typing letters, compiling endless reports, answering phones, making cups of tea. The Welfare Officer was besieged all day long with tales of woe from the long line of employees waiting their turn in the outer office near my desk.

I felt the distress of wives on the assembly lines whose husbands were reported missing in action, and of mothers having to report for work with sick children at home. A young woman in her twenties buttonholed me on my way back from the ladies' room. "Aw, what a lucky girl yew are, Miss," she began, "wiv 'ardly a care in the bloomin' world, I'll bet. Now me and me 'usband is on different shifts and we 'ardly ever sees each uvver these doiys. But oi counts me blessins. 'Ee's got flat feet, and 'ee's not fit to go in the Army."

I was learning how sheltered I had been from the real world. But I thought: "Surely this wasn't the kind of job they intended to prepare me for, in my course on Secretarial Practice. I feel more like a "gofer" than a secretary! Oh well, I'll give it a fair trial, and if it doesn't improve, I can always look around for something more challenging.

Butch's 48-Hour Pass
"SATURDAY, SEPTEMBER 18TH: BUTCH MEANT IT ABOUT THAT 48-HR. PASS! WENT UP TO LONDON TO MEET HIM AND BRING HIM HOME. DISASTER!"

The fateful letter from Butch said: "Dere Ida, I have a forty-ait hour pass. If it's still okay, can you meet me in London at the raleroad station?"

I wondered at the spelling, but wrote a quick note to say it was okay. The weekend found Mom ready with the rations and the guest room bed made up for his visit. "I'm curious to see our first American, dear, and I hope he's had a good upbringing."

I eagerly took the bus to meet Butch's train and spotted him among the milling crowd on the platform. He looked burly and muscular, more of a "tough guy" than I had remembered, the peak of his army cap pulled rakishly over one brown eye. Catching sight of me, he bellowed: "Hyar, Bunty gal, thought you wuz never comin.'"

Sitting in our dining room, Butch attacked Mom's tea sandwiches, regaling us with raunchy army jokes and tales of life in backwoods America. Mom didn't utter a word, but her eyes rolling up toward the ceiling said it all! Later, she cornered me. "I don't think he's had too good an upbringing, Bunty, but I'm glad you've brought him home. You can see him more clearly from here." I had a feeling she was rereading Gram's letter in her mind.

Next day, Butch and I took the bus to London. I dutifully showed him the usual tourist sights, but he was obviously bored by the historic buildings. "Hey Bunty," he said, "I heerd they had good nite clubs an' bars – oh, sorry, pubs, in this hyar siddy. "Oh maybe," I replied, a prickly sensation at the back of my neck, "but I've never been interested in that kind of thing." (Actually I had never been allowed inside a pub, let alone a night club!)

As I was going up the stairs that evening, Butch reached out and caught me in a vise-like grip, pressing his hard body against me and squeezing one of my breasts so hard with one huge hand that tears of pain came to my eyes. Terrified and angry, I twisted free. "Don't *ever* do that again!" I exploded. I locked my bedroom door that night! Mom had been right! I thought to myself: "Good thing Dad hasn't been home this weekend; he would have thrown him out bodily!"

After Butch had wolfed down several days' worth of our rations for breakfast next morning, I walked him up Bishop's Hill to catch the bus that would take him back to London. As the bus slowed down at the bus stop, he looked at me with resignation and growled: "Too bad you didn't have an older sister, kid."

Exit Butch, leaving one more important lesson for me. I muttered to myself as he hopped aboard the bus and out of my life: "I hope he finds himself a "good nite club in the siddy."

Shortages Increase

"TUESDAY, SEPTEMBER 28TH: WAR NEWS IS GREAT FOR ALLIES. NAVY HAS DISABLED GERMAN BATTLESHIP *TIRPITZ*. GERMANS IN RETREAT ALL ALONG RUSSIAN FRONT. U.S. HAS RECLAIMED GILBERT AND SOLOMON ISLANDS FROM JAPANESE. PETER IS HOME ON LEAVE."

The *Tirpitz* had been a threat to British Arctic shipping routes. In a daring raid, the Royal Navy employed several midget submarines to cripple her in her berth in Norway, which put her out of commission for six months. Next time, it was hoped she would sink.

At enormous cost, the Russians were winning back territory lost in the Nazi onslaught of the past years. Newspaper editorials again compared the full-scale German retreat with that of France's Napoleon in the previous century, with hundreds of thousands of casualties on both sides.

In the Pacific, the U.S. had reclaimed islands in the Solomon and Gilbert chains from the Japanese, inch by painful inch.

The doorbell rang as Mom and I were beginning to get ready for bed. There stood Peter, smiling, on our doorstep. He stepped in and hugged us both. "Here I am, home on leave! I know it's a bit late, but I want you to pack a picnic lunch and be ready by about ten o'clock tomorrow morning. I have a surprise for you both."

Thinking we would be going to Spring Glen Park, where there was a picnic area, Mom packed a basket with sandwiches, some of her little wartime "rock cakes" (aptly named, but fortunately we all had strong teeth), and a few apples, plus a thermos of tea.

Next morning bright and early, there was Peter. Behind him, waiting at the curb, was a prewar four-door Austin sedan, all shined up and wheezily waiting. Peter clicked his heels, saluted with a flash of humor in his eyes, and announced: "Your chariot awaits, mesdames, we're off to Chipstead Valley."

We both stood, paralyzed with surprise. Peter took the picnic basket out of Mom's lifeless hands and stowed it expertly away in what the English call "the boot." Somehow he had managed the impossible: to procure a car with enough gasoline to take us on a surprise trip for a picnic in the country. We asked no questions!

Once free of the suburban streets and houses south of Croydon, the road opened up into the countryside and we were soon in lush Chipstead Valley, a favorite local beauty spot for picnics, a medley of green and gold. We drove along roads flanked by tall trees, still heavy with summer leaves, whose branches met overhead to form a cool green tunnel, punctured here and there by shafts of golden sunshine in an ever-changing pattern of light and shade. Peter was an excellent driver, and Mom and I relished every mile. After our picnic lunch we filled Mom's basket with plump, ripe blackberries and hazel-nuts from the hedgerows to make blackberry jam and pies, and to store the nuts to share as a Christmas treat. I still have the photo Mom took of Peter and me standing up on the front seat of the car, heads and shoulders sticking out through its open sun-roof, with his protective arm around me.

"FRIDAY, OCTOBER 1ST: "NAPLES FALLS" was the cryptic newsstand headline. Naples was reputed to have been the Italian city most heavily bombed by the Allies in World War Two. It was also the first Italian city whose people rose up against their Nazi occupiers. On this day they were free at last. After the Salerno landings in September, Allied troops faced stiff resistance from the Nazi forces in control of Italy. The Allies now occupied Naples, as they continued their bitter fight northwards toward Rome. By winter they were stalled at a place called Cassino.

"WEDNESDAY, OCTOBER 13TH: ITALY DECLARED WAR ON GERMANY, HAS NOW JOINED THE ALLIES! MOM GOT HER CALLING-UP PAPERS! ETHEL WATKINS IS AT BANGOR UNIVERSITY, LUCKY DUCK!"
Our "strange bedfellow" allies, the Russians, had moved over to make room for another unlikely bedfellow, Italy. It was one more quirk of developments in World War Two. The tide of mistrust had turned against dictator Mussolini and his Nazi allies, and the Italian people had welcomed the Allied invasion of Italy as an act of liberation. On this day the new Italian government presided over by Marshal Badoglio had formally declared war on Germany.

At home, Mom was about to embark upon a new career: she was to become a working woman. In July 1943, conscription of women for National Service had been extended to age fifty-one; still in her late forties, Mom had already had to register for National Service. Back from the registration office, she had wrinkled her nose as she shrugged. "Well, I don't know what use I could ever be to the government! I've never had a job outside my home, except before I married your Dad, and even then it was just to do window dressing for Grandpa Ditchfield's three tailor shops."

Rather than become a factory worker, she applied for an office job. Now came the summons: she was assigned to an office in the City of London, at the headquarters of Cable & Wireless Ltd. Catching a bus daily from Upper Woodside to the big office building in the city, she now spent her day as a filing clerk for the British War Office. Her job involved helping to sort the thousands of cables that came through Cable & Wireless, reporting servicemen and women killed, missing in action or having become prisoners of war. The cables then had to be filed in alphabetical order. Not the most cheerful or challenging of occupations, but as Mom put it: "Someone has to help do the job, and I suppose it has to be me."

Mom's daily journey to and from work involved changing buses on several different bus routes, which was exhausting enough, but was coupled with long hours of sitting and considerable eye-strain at the office. In spite of it all, Mom enjoyed the novelty of being employed. She hoarded her small pay check to use for "luxuries": little surprise presents for Dad and me, a bunch of hothouse grapes or flowers, or a lunch out with her coworkers at one of the city restaurants near the office. Several of her fellow conscripted clerks lived in the City of London, and they became her closest friends.

Jennifer Thompson, a twinkling little woman a few years younger than herself, was her best friend. Jenny's husband was an Inspector in the London Metropolitan Police, which exempted him from military service. Their apartment was not far from the office, and sometimes Jenny invited Mom home for lunch to give them both a break from the monotony of their work.

Mom often arrived home after I did. A wry grin on her face, she said: "I know I should be teaching you how to cook, Bunty, but with all due respect to your ability, accidents will happen, and I can't afford to waste the rations! I'll make our dinner ahead of time, and you can warm it up for us if I'm late getting home."

This I could do. On days when she arrived home late and bone-tired, I felt happy to be useful, making it possible for Mom and me to sit down to a hot meal served on the top of the Morrison shelter, spread with a pretty tablecloth and sporting a little vase of flowers.

Dad continued to be moved around the country, installing water purification plants in new factories and at the airfields and military camps being built to hold the burgeoning numbers of Americans arriving all over the British Isles. He was seldom home for more than an occasional weekend until his annual vacation, and this was usually spent catching up on household repairs which, with Peter's magic touch now absent, had languished while he was away.

Maggie and Barbara were still sending me news of Wrexham. I was green with envy when they reported that one of our friends and my former rival from schooldays, Ethel Watkins, had gone on to Bangor University, after her sixth form year at Wrexham Park.

I thought of how our two paths had divided since those days. Our paths would cross again, but not for another two years.

"SATURDAY, OCTOBER 16TH: SHORTAGES OF EVERYTHING INCREASING. WILL THIS WAR NEVER END?"

Hitler's creation of U-boat wolf packs had caused horrendous losses of merchant ships carrying crucially needed supplies to Britain across the Atlantic. Postwar statistics show that in 1942 more than one thousand Allied merchant ships were sunk. History tells us that, after failing to bomb the British into submission, Hitler changed tactics in an all-out effort to starve them into suing for peace. With a substantially increased U-Boat fleet, groups of Nazi submarines operated under encoded orders which pinpointed the positions of supply ships in Atlantic convoys. The wolf packs then could attack and destroy them.

1943 saw the climax of the Battle of the Atlantic. The pendulum at last swung in favor of the Allies, helped by the enhancement of merchant ship convoy protection, and also by the capture of intact Nazi Enigma and other coding machines and their codebooks. The resulting huge U-boat losses convinced Hitler to withdraw the wolf pack attacks, whereupon Allied supply ship losses dropped significantly.

On the home front we were being squeezed by ever-increasing shortages. Now that Mom was working, her weekends off kept her busy doing the week's laundry and preparing meals ahead as much as she could for the following week. I found myself standing in line with housewives and working men and women on Saturday mornings hoping that the shopkeepers wouldn't run out of our weekly rations before it was my turn. Our local butcher had resorted to selling unrationed revolting-looking dark red lumps of horse and whale meat, which were eagerly bought up by customers with large families to stretch their meat ration. I said to Mom later: "Just the look and smell of it made me sick to my stomach." We never bought any!

Shoes were already rationed and sometimes the largest supply a store had was in its window display. The shortage of leather for shoes created a new women's fashion rage in London: the "sabot." With their chic French name, sabots had a curved, thick wooden sole with an open heel, held on by strips of fabric or leather across the top. After I saw several fashionable sabots left behind in the street as their owners leaped aboard London buses, I decided not to risk a pair. I was glad I didn't; as time went by, sabot wearers began to develop foot ailments due to the rigidity of the wooden soles. In an effort to save the sabot market, a model was developed with a metal hinge in mid-sole, allowing it to bend. Unfortunately it also allowed the hinge to protest with a series of loud squeaks. The newspapers poked fun by suggesting that, with each pair of hinged sabots, shoe shops should sell a small oil can!

Rope-soled summer sandals became a national mania. Mom and I decided to try our hand at making some, sewing coils of thin rope together to form the soles. We raided Dad's toolshed for brightly colored strips of canvas that he kept to repair worn lawn chairs, crossing them from side to side to hold the rope soles on our feet. These creations, like the sabots, were somewhat inflexible; I felt my calf muscles protesting the penguin-like walk needed to keep them on. Home for a weekend, Dad looked at my new rope-soled sandals and said gruffly: "What will these daft women think of next?" Then, relenting a little, he added: "Oh well, I suppose something on your feet is better than nothing at all."

It's well-known that nothing can perk up the female psyche more than wearing a new outfit, but between the reduced number of clothing coupons per year and the difficulty of finding clothing in the right size, buying new clothes had become a near-impossible venture. As the war ground on, our prewar clothes became more and more shabby.

Government posters everywhere exhorted us to "Make Do and Mend," personified by a wide-eyed, doll-like figure in a striped apron called "Mrs. Sew and Sew." In her hand was a needle with a long piece of thread embedded in whatever garment she was mending, a chore she appeared to be thoroughly enjoying. As I bicycled past one of her posters on my way to work, I stuck out my tongue at her smiling face and looked down with disgust at all the mended runs in my thick lisle stockings.

In summer it became fashionable to draw a line with eyebrow pencil down the center of the backs of our bare legs to make believe we were wearing the sheer prewar stockings we remembered and yearned for. I never could draw a straight line, so I simply went to work bare-legged on warm days.

"SATURDAY, NOVEMBER 6TH: RUSSIANS LIBERATED KIEV IN UKRAINE."

The battle for Kiev, capital of Ukraine, was a bitter one. The city was taken by the Germans in 1941. On this day, two years later, history tells us that by its greatly superior numbers (almost three quarters of a million men) the Soviet Army overwhelmed the German garrison after six days of onslaught. The Germans, however, took time to burn the city and destroy its historical artifacts before they withdrew, leaving the Russians a smoldering ruin with shattered antiquities. Such is the utter heartlessness and brutality of war.

"THURSDAY, NOVEMBER 18TH: LARGE RAID BY R.A.F. BOMBERS ON BERLIN."

This was the first in a series of eight heavy air raids by the R.A.F. launched in November and December, now known as the beginning of the Battle of Berlin. Much of the city was reduced to rubble. These first two raids reportedly killed over four thousand Berliners and made half a million homeless. Many more subsequent R.A.F. raids on Berlin were joined by the U.S. Eighth Air Force and lasted through April 1945. The carnage of World War Two went on.

"SATURDAY, NOVEMBER 27TH: TEHERAN CONFERENCE BEGINS, WITH CHURCHILL, ROOSEVELT AND STALIN."

Although we didn't know it at the time, this conference determined the target date for the Second Front invasion of Europe by the Allies as May, 1944. At home, my missing diary would probably have reported the usual November fogs. I felt that my life was gray just like them, everything in it immobile and stagnant. In those closing cold, days of 1943, I can remember staring out our bay window into an empty street, listening for the footsteps of the mailman, only to see him pass by. But then a surge of romantic optimism would bubble to the surface, making me sure that somehow more than just letters would soon come into my life.

"WEDNESDAY, DECEMBER 22ND: ANOTHER CHRISTMAS, BUT THIS ONE IS AT BISHOP'S HILL AGAIN, HOORAY! I WONDER WHAT THE NEW YEAR WILL BRING?"

Dad came home for the Christmas holidays, and once again we brought the cardboard boxes with their assortment of holiday decorations down from the attic. The dining room, the only room our winter coal ration would allow us to heat, soon looked bright and cheerful. Multicolored paper chains crisscrossed the ceiling, suspended from each corner. Mom cut red-berried boughs of holly from the bushes outside to decorate the mantel above the fireplace. A twig of mistletoe was hung above the door. It was my job to decorate the small, artificial Christmas tree that stood on a corner on top of the Morrison shelter. I remember unwrapping each fragile glass ornament with care. None of them could be replaced. In the firelight they twinkled with flashes of color as they danced slowly on their hangers when I hung them on the tree. The sight of the decorated room brought to the three of us a comforting feeling of family tradition and reassurance that there was some permanence in life, after all. Once more we felt lucky to be alive and to know again the joy of being in our own home.

"FRIDAY, DECEMBER 24TH: HOW LUCKY WE ARE THAT ST. JOHN'S WASN'T DEMOLISHED BY THE BOMBING. WHAT A YEAR THIS

HAS BEEN, AND NOW WE HAVE ONE MORE CHRISTMAS TO BE THANKFUL FOR."

On Christmas Eve we put on our shabby coats and walked to St. John's Church for the annual carol service. The little church was full to capacity, decorated for Christmas with boughs of evergreens and prewar red ribbon. Candles from a hoarded supply were sparingly lit around the sanctuary. We raised our voices to sing the beloved, familiar words and music, with full and thankful hearts for our survival and freedom to worship.

By the end of the old year, the Russians had reclaimed Ukraine, the R.A.F. "dam busters" had crippled Nazi war factories in the Ruhr, North Africa was under Allied control, and the Battle of the Atlantic against Hitler's submarine "wolf packs" had been won. In the Pacific the Japanese were facing the sting of defeat as, one after the other, the islands they had captured were being retaken by American and Australian troops.

"FRIDAY, DECEMBER 31ST: ROMMEL IS APPOINTED TO OVERSEE 'THE ATLANTIC WALL.' A NEW YEAR--WONDER WHAT IT WILL HOLD FOR US?"

At the end of December, Nazi General Rommel was commissioned by Hitler to inspect and improve the German fortifications along the English Channel coast of Europe: "the Atlantic Wall." Both the Allies and the Nazis were preparing for a Second Front, the expected Allied invasion of Europe.

Back home in Upper Woodside, New Year's Eve was almost like old times. Our neighbors on both sides were home again. They came in to share with us a glass of wine saved from before the war. Dad was once again our First Foot. Best of all, the skies were studded with stars instead of probing searchlight beams and flashes from anti-aircraft guns. We had a sense of what peacetime could be like. That we were on the threshold of a new and terrifying ordeal, we fortunately neither knew nor could imagine.

YEAR SIX -- 1944

✿

Beginning of the End

AFTER THE ALLIED victories in North Africa in 1942, Churchill said, at the Lord Mayor's Banquet: "Now this is not the end. It is not even the beginning of the end, but perhaps the end of the beginning."

And now it was two years later. At the beginning of this new year, civilians in Britain were "war-weary," and so was I. Most of the houses on Bishop's Hill needed a coat of paint. It had become a drab street. Housewives made the daily trek to the shops with their wicker shopping baskets over their arms to stand for hours in line, first to wait for the bus to take them to the shops in Croydon, then to tack onto the end of the line at the butcher's shop, or the bakery or the little barrows where fruit and vegetables were sold in Croydon's outdoor street market.

Our clothes were worn and colorless. Even our lisle stockings were tubular, shapeless affairs. Repaired to please Mrs. Sew and Sew, smiling at us from her "Make Do and Mend" government poster, they always seemed to end up in folds around our ankles; pantyhose hadn't yet been invented. "Nylons" were something we saw only in American movies, or maybe they could be found on London's black market, but for me, that was not a legal option - I viewed it as helping the underworld!

Scattered air raids still plagued London, but the tide of war had turned against the Nazi war machine, and there was a feeling of hope that maybe this year would mark the end of the war.

Our little island was by now groaning under the weight of millions of extra people. For years Britain had been sheltering refugees from Nazi persecution: kings, queens and heads of state of Western Europe, as well as many others fleeing to the comparative safety of Britain. With them came the remnants of their armed forces. In addition, we were now seeing uniforms from all over the British Empire and were hosting millions of American servicemen and women in the build-up for D-Day. The latest national joke was:

"I say, if one more person sets foot on Britain, the whole bloody island will sink into the sea!"

Meanwhile, in my new diary for 1944, the story of Bunty's war was still unfolding.

"SUNDAY, JANUARY 2ND: CHURCHILL IS RECOVERING FROM PNEUMONIA IN MARRAKESH. PETER CAME TO VISIT THIS MORNING, THEN PAUL ARRIVED. WROTE TO BRUCE. WONDER WHERE HE IS?"
The headline in Dad's Sunday paper was worrisome. This was the second bout of pneumonia for Churchill in the past twelve months. Dad put down the paper with a sigh. "Thank God, he's recovering. For a man of his age he's been overdoing it with all this traveling around in different climates and time changes. We can't afford to lose him now, the captain at the helm of our ship. He's been keeping us all afloat with his grit and determination and we'll need him to see it through to the end. Let's hope his doctors can knock a bit of sense into him and slow him down."

But, as we found out when the history of World War Two was written, true to form, "Winnie" was not wasting a minute of his recuperation in North Africa. From his sick bed he was planning directives for the Allied landings in Italy at Anzio, south of Rome.

My childhood friends and I had grown up. Bruce's letters usually began with: "I knew if I didn't write, you wouldn't either, so here I am again." His latest letter enclosed a photo of himself in his Royal Navy midshipman's uniform on his way to becoming a second lieutenant. Reading between the lines, we figured he must be somewhere in the Mediterranean.

Peter was home on Christmas leave, now a dispatch rider in Royal Air Force blue. Mom and I were sure he had a steady girlfriend somewhere, but he still came to our house almost every day.

Paul visited us frequently. These days he was never without the black suit and white "dog collar" of a student priest.

William was back from Canada; now a sergeant pilot, the recent non-commissioned creation of the R.A.F.to fill its need for more pilots through relaxing the requirement that they must be officers. He was still very much involved with his friends from the repertory theater.

And the flighty and flirtatious tomboy that I had been was now a working woman.

"TUESDAY, JANUARY 4TH: HAD A 'BUSY' DAY AT THE FACTORY, PREPARING FOR A KIDS' PARTY. THIS IS THE LAST STRAW!"
Making paper hats and wrapping toys for a Welfare Department New Year's party to be given to the factory workers' children, I thought grudgingly of the years of mind-crunching study in exile at Wrexham and of my Central Welsh Board and college exam results.

"This is absolutely not what I want out of life," I grumbled to myself, "I'm in a real rut here!"

I called the Headmistresses Association that day, to ask them to provide interviews for a job which would require better use of my hard-earned credentials. The factory had served its purpose: a "work experience" to add to my resume. My next goal, however, however, was to shed it and move on.

"SATURDAY, JANUARY 15TH: MOM TOOK THE DAY OFF FROM HER OFFICE AND WE WENT INTO CROYDON TO SHOP. FOUND A 'UTILITY' SKIRT AND BLOUSE IN MY SIZE, READY FOR THE JOB INTERVIEWS I'M HOPING FOR. TWENTY-FOUR CLOTHING COUPONS GONE! LAST NIGHT THE DAVIS THEATRE IN CROYDON GOT A DIRECT HIT, AND OTHER BOMBS FELL IN GEORGE STREET. WILL IT NEVER STOP?"
An entire day's shopping in Croydon yielded a new outfit! This alone boosted my spirits and my resolve to get a better job. We skirted carefully around George Street and the Davis Theatre, where demolition crews were working in the rubble. The random air raids had hit close to

home once more, but were so sporadic that we now slept in our beds instead of crawling into the Morrison shelter in the dining room. We worked, shopped and lived as normally as possible, but the raids were a constant reminder that we were still a favorite target of the *Luftwaffe*.

"WEDNESDAY, JANUARY 19TH: WENT FOR AN INTERVIEW AT REUTERS NEWS AGENCY. EXCITING--BUT IT'S SHIFT WORK, AND UP IN THE CENTER OF THE CITY OF LONDON. SETTLED FOR BRITISH OVERSEAS AIRWAYS."

This week I had a series of interviews. First came one with a publisher, followed by two others conducted entirely in French with companies where I could use my beloved "second language." Both of these job offers had to be disqualified because they weren't scheduled under the Essential Works Act.

The interview that excited me most was for a job as a junior editor at Reuters News Agency. I took the bus up to Fleet Street in London, where most of the big newspaper offices were located. Knees knocking, I was ushered into the office of the manager of the editorial staff, after navigating through a large room littered with desks at which people were pecking away at typewriters or huddling together over a tickertape machine (now they would have been huddling over a computer screen). I was ecstatic when the big boss said I qualified for the job! Then he added: "You realize, of course, Bunty, this is an international news agency, and our staff works around the clock. You'll have to start on the night shift."

Undaunted, I thought: "I'm not going to let anything stand in the way of a terrific opportunity like this!" I cast what I hoped was a determined look at the managing editor. "Oh yes, I'd love to work for Reuters. The last train to Upper Woodside is at ten o'clock, and the first one out isn't until six in the morning, but I'm sure Reuters will find me a place to stay in the city if I need one."

Dad was home early for the weekend. I burst in the front door and yelled, "Guess what? I got the job at Reuters!" My bubble was punctured when I saw his and Mom's faces after I told them my working hours.

As always, Dad and Mom gave each other "that look." Dad said: "Now Bunty, calm down. Your Mom and I will have to talk this over. We'll all discuss it again tomorrow."

Next day I wasn't surprised at the verdict. Dad looked up from his breakfast. "Bunty, we can't agree to letting you be in that building all night in the middle of the city. I'm sure you understand, especially now, when bombs are still being dropped on London."

"Rats," I thought to myself, "if only I were twenty-one, they couldn't do this to me!" But I was still only seventeen, and I sat down and wrote a note of regret to Reuters. So ended my career as a journalist, before it even began.

"FRIDAY, JANUARY 21ST: HAD A SUPER INTERVIEW AT BRITISH OVERSEAS AIRWAYS CORPORATION; THINK I'LL TAKE THE JOB! I CAN BEGIN ON MONDAY."

British Overseas Airways Corporation, as British Airways was then called, was operating under the direction of the government's Air Ministry for the duration of the war; a job there would qualify under the Essential Works Act. I was offered a secretarial job at Airways House, the company's glamorous white-stuccoed headquarters building in London, with its signature clock tower, a few blocks away from Buckingham Palace. I decided to accept the job, and was told to report for work on Monday.

Airways House could easily be reached by bus or train from Upper Woodside. There were good prospects for advancement, travel, and a chance to use my French with some of the passengers. What more could I ask? I bounced back home with the good news. This time there were no objections. I sat down and wrote a letter of resignation to the Hygienic Wire Works.

"SATURDAY, JANUARY 22ND: RADIO NEWS SAYS THE ALLIES HAVE ESTABLISHED A BEACHHEAD IN LANDINGS AT ANZIO, ON THE ITALIAN MAINLAND. PETER IS HOME ON LEAVE. HE TOOK MOM AND ME TO THE MOVIES LAST NIGHT. JUST GOT HOME IN TIME FOR MOANING MINNIE. AIR RAID FROM 9:30 TO 11:00 P.M. AND

ANOTHER THIS MORNING FROM 4:30 TO 6:00 A.M. NOTHING SERIOUS. WENT BACK TO BED. PETER WOKE US UP RINGING THE DOORBELL AT 10:30 AND STAYED FOR BREAKFAST."

Due to a series of misjudgments, Anzio has been called one of the biggest blunders of World War Two, and resulted in a year of agonizing losses and delays for the Allied forces. Its American commanding general was eventually relieved of his command.

On this day, it was announced that the road to Rome was opened by the Allies. In reality, the road to Rome wouldn't be open until May, after the Allied troops who landed at Anzio finally linked up with the main invasion force. Nevertheless, history tells us that Anzio had actually begun the end of the war in Europe.

Peter seemed to grow more handsome every time I saw him in his R.A.F. uniform. "Let's go for a walk in Spring Glen Park just for old times' sake," he begged.

"O.K., I'll be ready in a jiff. Need to bundle up; I have to find my hat and gloves."

It had been many months since we had visited the Glen. This time it wasn't the same, somehow. Hand in hand, we walked through the rose garden with its encircling flower beds lying dormant under a light covering of snow, where the skeletons of last year's roses slumbered quietly, awaiting resurrection with the signs of spring. In the center of the garden, the fountain was now turned off for the winter, topped by its green-coated bronze statue, looking forlorn and cold. Peter looked at it wistfully: "Remember when we used to catch newts and tadpoles in that fountain, Bunty? God, what a childhood we had; every day was a holiday, then."

I looked at him thoughtfully, with more maturity than I knew I had. "Let's face it," I said to myself, "my old boyfriends are now men, and we can't bring back our childhood by visiting Spring Glen." Shaking myself out of such memories, I said brightly: "How about a cup of hot coffee at the Manor House, Peter?"

The mood was broken; we were back in the present.

Career Woman

"MONDAY, JANUARY 24TH: TOOK THE TRAIN UP TO LONDON. BEGAN WORK AT B.O.A.C. AT THREE POUNDS, TWO SHILLINGS AND SIXPENCE A WEEK. DID NOTHING ALL DAY EXCEPT RUN OFF STENCILS. DISGUSTING!"

I felt quite worldly, traveling to London with the "business set" on the commuter train. After a short walk down Buckingham Palace Road from the train station, I easily found Airways House, with its imposing white clock tower. Suddenly I felt nervous, especially when I saw an armed guard at each of the entrance doors. I showed my new B.O.A.C. pass to the doorman, who smiled and said, "Good morning, Miss--a lovely morning, isn't it?" He waved me into the building. Feeling reassured, I sat down to wait for someone to come and collect me. I looked around curiously at my new surroundings.

The prewar interior had a lavish passenger reception lounge, tastefully furnished with color-coordinated "Art Deco" upholstered chairs and sofas. Opening into the lounge I could see the entrance to a ladies' restroom decorated with a chandelier and mirrored walls. The whole scene reminded me of the beautiful sets in a Fred Astaire and Ginger Rogers movie.

When I accepted the job offer at B.O.A.C., I had fantasized that I would be introduced to V.I.Ps and celebrities galore, becoming instantly invaluable in helping frantic, French-speaking passengers to understand the procedures at the passenger desk. On my first day at Airways House, my only introduction was to a pile of stencils and an evil-looking Ormig duplicating machine, which used bright purple ink. To my disgust, I had been assigned to the clerical pool with other prospective secretaries to go through "assessment," while doing unpleasant clerical chores and filling in for sick or vacationing secretaries somewhere in the building, until deemed ready to accept a full-time secretarial position. I grumbled to myself: "Bunty, you should have joined the Wrens!"

My diary added: "I GOT COMPLETELY COVERED WITH PURPLE COPYING INK! BUT I GUESS ANYTHING IS BETTER THAN SITTING

TWIDDLING ONE'S THUMBS OR BLOWING UP BALLOONS FOR KIDS' PARTIES AT THE HYGIENIC WIRE WORKS!"

"WEDNESDAY, JANUARY 26TH: MORE ORMIG STENCILS, BUT I'M GETTING USED TO THEM. POOR MOM ISN'T! SHE SAYS SHE'LL HAVE TO DYE MY WHITE BLOUSE PURPLE SO THE STREAKS WON'T SHOW! GUESS WHAT? PAT IS WORKING HERE! I FEEL 100 PERCENT BETTER. SPENT ALL MY SPARE TIME WITH HER. HOPE I GET A SECRETARIAL ASSIGNMENT SOON."

"Pat, is that really you?" I had looked up from toiling over the duplicating machine to see my college friend and harvesting partner rush over to hug me, purple ink and all; she was working at B.O.A.C. too. Giggling over lunch, we reminisced about the blisters and harvest mites at the farm in Wiltshire, and our first brush with the American army.

Pat looked much older in a new, tailored dress and with her pretty face sporting makeup. She listened soberly to my account of Butch's visit: "Gosh, Bunty, now I know what they meant by those wolf whistles! I suppose we should have known better than to give them our addresses, but what a rotten experience you had! I'm glad I didn't hear from Duke. Birds of a feather and all that, you know."

After a few weeks of basic training I must have qualified for a promotion, and my salary doubled after a few forays as the temporary secretary to a Director of B.O.A.C. in the hallowed executive suite, where I felt young, inexperienced and uncomfortable. Then I had an interview with the head of the Air Cargo and Diplomatic Mail department. Here I instantly felt at home!

Air cargo was pretty self-explanatory, but I found diplomatic mail to be something totally new to me.

Carrying this mail were couriers--elderly men, long since retired, who had been recruited back to work when their young counterparts went into uniform. Their job was of the utmost importance to the war effort. They traveled alone in a specially reserved first-class compartment on the long-distance trains to and from airports, where they collected and delivered red pouches containing highly secret war dispatches, reports and diplomatic correspondence. The pouches were chained to their wrists for security while they traveled. Our office kept track of these pouches, documented their whereabouts, and oversaw their safe delivery to the appropriate government entities. Long after the fact, we learned that, among other documents, the secret orders for the Anzio landings in Italy had gone through our office in one of those red pouches.

In wartime, air cargo was restricted to emergency freight sanctioned by the government as essential to the war effort and requiring special handling, followed by speedy and accurate delivery. Some of the shipments were unusual, to say the least. Just to name a few: crates of bananas to sustain the lives of children suffering from a rare disease at the famous Great Ormond Street Children's Hospital in London; live fruit flies and fleas for medical research; top-secret weapon parts for military use; and, on one occasion, a small package of fresh oysters packed in dry ice, a gift to "Winnie" from the prime minister of New Zealand.

Truckloads of mysterious special supplies arrived regularly for the U.S. Navy. One of my duties was to make phone calls to let them know of their arrival at the loading dock below the cargo department office, presided over by a small army of elderly porters. I added new words to my vocabulary: waybills, consignment notes and bills of lading. These documents had to be checked by me and signed to authorize pickup. After my phone call to the U.S. Navy office, one or more of the U.S. Navy men would show up with a truck from their London headquarters and produce the appropriate pieces of paper. These were more like visits than business transactions; the men didn't seem to be in a hurry and always stopped to chat at my desk. Their story is woven into my diary entries with great regularity.

A pared-down wartime staff of five of us ran the department. Supervising all of us in his spiffy, tailored, navy blue airline uniform was my boss, the department head, Fred Keene, whose film-star good looks and brusque military manner concealed a pleasant nature that allowed us to call him "Freddy." He was supported by two uniformed male assistants, Sydney French and Graham Bradley, "Syd" and "Brad."

Short and bouncy, with a mop of blond, curly hair, Syd was the ultimate Cockney comedian. Why the London stage had never discovered him escaped me. Brad, his counterpart, was tall and slender, his thinning hair carefully parted to hide his bald spot. He reminded me of "Eyore" in the Christopher Robin books; his long face wore a perpetual look of suffering and resignation, and he spoke in a slow Yorkshire drawl, the exact opposites of Syd's round-faced grin and rapid, machine-gun Cockney patter. Brad's melancholia may have been due to the fact that he was living alone in his home in London while his young wife and baby were stowed away in a safe area of Yorkshire, living with relatives. In his sad, dark brown eyes I saw such kindness that he immediately became my favorite.

As Freddy's secretary, I was put in charge of Buzz, the office boy who made tea and ran errands--my first experience of management! With only an elementary school education, Buzz was happy in his job, and bore no resentment for the menial tasks he was usually asked to do. Cheerful and willing, he was a delight from the top of his unruly hair, with its persistent cowlick, down to his rather large feet, which he would probably grow into some day, just like a puppy I once had.

From the day I set foot in the office, I was welcomed into an atmosphere of congeniality and mutual respect. The days flew by, and I always came home with amusing stories to tell. I loved it.

"WEDNESDAY, FEBRUARY 16TH: MY EIGHTEENTH BIRTHDAY. GOSH, I'M GETTING OLD! RECEIVED A LEATHER HANDBAG FROM MOM AND DAD, AND SILK STOCKINGS FROM AUNTIE BELLE (BLACK MARKET). WELCOME CASH FROM THE DITCHFIELDS. THE ALLIES HAVE BOMBED MONTE CASSINO ABBEY."

A real leather pocketbook was a rare and expensive treat. Not so expensive but just as rare was the pair of silk stockings, since the government had removed them from our store shelves. Why I thought Auntie Belle must have accessed the black market for silk stockings I don't know; it was more likely they were prewar ones she had been saving as gifts. In any case, I wasn't going to ask! My birthday presents gave a lift to what would otherwise have been just another working day.

In far-off Italy, the date went down in history to mark another blunder of World War Two. A stalemate had developed for the Allies in their drive toward Rome after the Anzio landings. Rome had not yet been taken from the Nazis; winter and a rocky mountain, Monte Cassino, stood in the way. Not released until years after the war, the account of the Battle of Monte Cassino relates that, mistakenly believing the Germans to be using the historic mountaintop abbey as a fortress, successive assaults by Allied bombers reduced it and the small town of Cassino below it to rubble. In reality, the abbey was being used by the townspeople to shelter their women and children. After the air raids, however, the Germans moved into the ruins, which gave them a strategic position to effectively block the Allied advance on Rome for three more months.

"SATURDAY, FEBRUARY 19TH: YESTERDAY DAD BROUGHT HOME U.S. ARMY STAFF SERGEANT BOB ROBERTSON FOR THE WEEKEND. BOY, CAN HE TALK!"

Dad had begun what Mom and I jokingly said was his personal campaign to thank America for Lend-Lease! He was now supervising the installation of water purification plants at American army and air force bases, where he met and talked with many homesick G.Is. Some of these young men struck a responsive chord in Dad, and he would write to say he was bringing one of them to our home for a soft bed and home-cooked meal on his next forty-eight-hour pass.

Mom would launch her usual routine, bustling around to make up the beds in the guest room, setting out towels and worrying about how to stretch the week's rations for an extra male appetite. My job was to take our guests up to London and act as a tour guide. I never tired of showing them my beloved landmarks which still stood in spite of years of pounding by Nazi bombs. Our first such visitor was Bob Robertson, a great talker, so absorbed in what he was saying that he hardly glanced at the sights of London. As if in retaliation, London unexpectedly gave him the experience of his first air raid. He never came back!

Air raids continued from December, 1943 through March, 1944, but never again with the magnitude of the Blitz. Croydon was hit repeatedly with random bombs, and in London gas and water mains were wrecked. Airways House had no gas one morning, and small fountains of water spurted through manholes in Buckingham Palace Road from a broken water main. From our backyard in Bishop's Hill one evening, we saw a familiar red glow on the horizon from fires burning in the city of London after an incendiary bomb attack.

"FRIDAY, MARCH 7TH: ONE THOUSAND U.S. AIR FORCE BOMBERS DROPPED TWO THOUSAND TONS OF BOMBS ON BERLIN. THE NAZIS ARE GETTING A TASTE OF WHAT WE HAD IN 1940."
Next day, I wrote with my newly learned American slang: "U.S.A.F. DID IT AGAIN! BOY, ARE THESE JERRIES GETTING A LICKING! BERLIN MUST LOOK A MESS. RUMOR IS THAT THE SECOND FRONT WILL BE ANY DAY NOW."
At last the tables were turned in the air war. News of the air raids on Germany was received by British civilians with a joy born out of suffering and hatred; I found myself reveling in the satisfaction of revenge. The magnitude of the bombing raids on Berlin caused speculation all over Britain that they were a prelude to the Second Front, heralding the Allied invasion of Europe. Rumors ran wild about the date; bookies were even taking bets on it! We were convinced it would happen within weeks or even days, which history tells us was all part of the Allied strategy of spreading rumors to keep the Germans off-balance as to when the landings would take place. Information released long after World War Two revealed many of the other deceptions used to confuse the Nazis; in the meantime they were confusing us, too.

Three New Uniforms

"SUNDAY, MARCH 19TH: GERMAN TROOPS OCCUPIED HUNGARY. CAN HITLER NEVER BE STOPPED?"

In spite of Hitler's defeats at the hands of the Russians and the devastating damage now being done to his war production by the Allied air forces, his conquests still continued. Northern Europe, Western Europe, Eastern Europe--was the Nazi juggernaut still unstoppable?

"TUESDAY, MARCH 21ST: VERA LYNN CAME TO AIRWAYS HOUSE TODAY. WENT OUT TO PASSENGER LOUNGE TO MEET HER. SHE GAVE ME HER AUTOGRAPH. AT HOME, THE ALMOND AND APPLE TREES ARE IN BLOOM. BRUCE IS HOME ON LEAVE."

V.I.P. passengers such as diplomats, high-ranking military personnel and "show biz" troop entertainers, were given preference by the Air Ministry to fly in wartime. Other would-be travelers had to wait hopefully for vacancies on passenger lists, which seldom appeared. With my newly elevated position at Airways House came a special privilege: to go to the passenger lounge and meet some of the celebrities. I was thrilled to shake hands with singer Vera Lynn, the famous English "Sweetheart of the Forces." I wonder whatever became of the autograph she gave me?

These days I was feeling more cheerful. My job was fun and rewarding. Spring was here, with Mom's flower borders and fruit trees in bloom. Best of all, Bruce was home on leave, now a Royal Navy second-lieutenant, to fill my empty social life for a few days.

But it wouldn't be empty much longer.

"THURSDAY, MARCH 23RD: IT NEVER RAINS BUT IT POURS! DAD WROTE FROM ESSEX TO SAY HE IS BRINGING TWO YANKEE FLIERS HOME FOR THE WEEKEND. BRUCE PICKED ME UP FROM THE OFFICE AND WE WENT TO THE WEST END FOR DINNER AND A SHOW. JUST MADE IT HOME IN TIME FOR A FIRE BOMB RAID."

"Ready, Bunty? Tarrah! How do you like it?" Bruce appeared in the doorway of my office, dazzling the impressionable Buzz, who was just returning from an errand; his mouth hung open as he gazed in awe at all the gold braid on the Royal Navy uniform. Bruce literally sparkled; he was now Second Lieutenant Ferguson, R.N. I was speechless. I thought: "Could this be the same boy who lived across the street when we were evacuated to Hove, who was too shy to speak to me? And I thought he was *so* unattainable!"

I almost danced down Buckingham Palace Road as I left the office on the arm of the handsome naval officer he had become. Dinner in London's Theatre District, escorted by Bruce, was a real treat, and the show that followed was a good one, too. But there came a reminder that this was still wartime as "Moaning Minnie" announced an air raid just as we arrived back at Upper Woodside. Bruce said a hurried farewell and went off at a trot to his home a few blocks away. Within minutes incendiary bombs fell in the next street to Bishop's Hill. Houses blazed--so close that from our Morrison shelter Mom and I could hear the crackling roar of the flames that lit up the blacked-out neighborhood with leaping fingers of fire. Would the next stick of bombs hit Bishop's Hill? We held our breath and clung to each other in the confined space of the shelter. At last we heard the "All Clear." Once more we had escaped.

"SATURDAY, MARCH 25TH: GOT UP EARLY AND RODE PERCIVAL TO COLLECT HALF A DOZEN NEW-LAID EGGS FROM MRS. POPE. DAD ARRIVED WITH TWO U.S. NINTH AIR FORCE SERGEANTS, GUNNERS IN THE SAME FIGHTER-BOMBER."

When Mom read Dad's letter, she went into her usual tailspin. "He's done it again, Bunty," she wailed, this time it's *two* Yanks instead of just one!" The first thing she did was to order six eggs from the wife of one of Dad's workmen, Charlie Pope.

The Popes lived not far from Upper Woodside and had a large chicken coop with very productive hens. The official egg ration was still only one egg per week per person, if we were lucky enough to get one, so the Popes had no trouble selling their surplus eggs to friends and neighbors. For this special occasion, Mrs. Pope had saved us half a dozen ready for our guests' breakfast.

Dad and the two Americans arrived: Bill Baer, from Wisconsin, blond and stocky, twenty-one and single; Frank Kopeck, short, muscular and twenty-three, had left a new bride behind in Ohio. This would be the day they became part of our family from March through September, 1944.

Next morning after enjoying Mrs. Pope's eggs for breakfast, the boys and I took the bus up to Westminster. As they said later, "Bunty almost walked our legs off!" But they loved London. We got off the bus and explored the ancient beauty of Westminster Abbey, then walked by the Houses of Parliament and Big Ben, through St. James's Park to Buckingham Palace. Bill and Frank were enchanted to see the pictures in their history books come alive, but our feet were aching by the time we boarded the bus for home. Back at Upper Woodside, we collapsed on the dining-room chairs just in time for tea, served to our guests' amusement, from the top of the Morrison shelter.

Dad returned with Bill and Frank to the air base early on Monday morning. I felt as if we were saying goodbye to three family members. Frank hugged Mom on their way out the door. "You've made us feel just like we had come home, and that bed sure felt to me like I was sleeping on cloud nine. Thanks, Mom."

Bill said shyly: "And Bunty showed us so many places I have pictures of in my encyclopedia back home. Now I'll never look at them again without remembering her taking us on that grand tour." He squeezed my hand. "Thanks, Bunty."

Bill and Frank had found a home away from home, and we were happy to adopt them. They came "home" on their forty-eight-hour passes as the weeks went by, quickly learning to navigate the two-hour train and bus journey from their base without Dad's help. As our bonds with them grew stronger, we shared their joys, fears, dreams and hopes. We became good listeners, and, literally, their surrogate family. They were the sons my parents never had. Frank mused: "I've told my folks how Pop is there at the edge of the runway, watching for us to come back from a mission and counting the planes as they come in to land. Bill and I each try to be first to spot him, it makes us feel so good."

I was thrilled when Mom let me use some of our rations to bake cookies for the boys to take back after their visits. Some of those cookies looked a bit odd, but Bill and Frank never once mentioned that, just commented how good they tasted!

"SATURDAY, APRIL 1ST: DAD CAME HOME FOR WEEKEND BRINGING LETTERS FROM BILL AND FRANK, ALSO BILL'S SHIRT. I OFFERED TO SEW ON HIS STRIPES AND NINTH AIR FORCE INSIGNIA--DIDN'T THINK HE'D TAKE ME UP ON IT BUT GLAD HE DID. THEY ARE REALLY JUST LIKE FAMILY! FRANK SENT SOME AMERICAN MAGAZINES AND THE 'STARS AND STRIPES' NEWSPAPERS, ALSO SOME AMERICAN CANDY."

A new chapter had dawned in my story of World War Two with the arrival of Bill and Frank, two very special people who brought their lives into ours to share, even if only for a little while.

We soon began to receive letters from Frank's family. His father was a doctor of Eastern European ancestry, whose letters were warm and chatty. He told us that a dear friend of his, whom he had met during his army service in World War One in England, lived not far from Croydon. They had kept in touch over the years, and Dr. Kopeck said he would be coming back to England to visit him again after the present war was over. Frank's mother was a stay-at-home Mom while raising him and his older brother, Bob. She took care of the household with the help of their housekeeper, "Tillie the Toiler," who had served the family faithfully for many years. She wanted to know if there would be any food we couldn't get that she could send. Frank's pretty young wife, Kate, was grateful to hear he was safe and welcomed any news we had of him; she also wanted to know if there was anything we needed that she and the family could send to us.

Bill's widowed mother's letter was much more formal. His blond hair and fair skin must have been inherited from her Teutonic background, and I sensed a certain reluctance on her part to be too relaxed in her manner when she wrote to thank Mom for her kindness toward Bill. She enclosed a note from Bill's sister and included me in the last paragraph of her letter.

Bill and Frank flew in an A-20 fighter-bomber. There was a three-man crew, a pilot and the two gunners. Undoubtedly under orders, they never spoke of their flying, but historical records tell us that they flew twenty-nine combat missions before June first in France and Belgium to soften up targets in preparation for the Second Front. The A-20 airplane was designed for low-level flying to bomb ground targets such as railroads, highways, factories and coastal defences, which made it vulnerable to flak from anti-aircraft fire. A high concentration of raids were made on the Pas de Calais area, at the shortest distance between the English and French coasts--part of an elaborate mass of diversions to convince the Germans that this would be where the invasion on D-Day would take place. At this time it had been planned for a date in May, but even that had not yet been officially decided.

"MONDAY, APRIL 10TH: MANAGED TO GET BILL'S SEWING DONE AND SENT BACK WITH DAD LAST WEEK. BEGAN TO FEEL NOT SO GOOD ON SATURDAY. DOCTOR SAYS I'VE CAUGHT GERMAN MEASLES FROM SOMEWHERE! BEEN IN BED EVER SINCE. HAD A LETTER FROM FREDDY WISHING ME A SPEEDY RECOVERY; I HOPE THEY WON'T ALL CATCH THIS AT THE OFFICE! GOOD NEWS FROM THE RUSSIANS; THEY HAVE RECAPTURED ODESSA."

In another few days, I was up and around; Mom thought I must have picked up the German measles on the bus or the train. So far there wasn't any I knew of at Airways House; I prayed that I hadn't started an epidemic!

The Russians continued to push back the Nazis in Ukraine and had now retaken the crucial port city of Odessa. The monumental struggle for Russia to reclaim her homeland from the Nazis was almost over.

"SATURDAY, APRIL 15th: DAD BROUGHT LETTERS FROM THE BOYS AND MORE MAGAZINES AND CANDY, PLUS A PAIR OF BILL'S OVERALLS. BADLY WORN AT THE KNEES AND NEED PATCHING. IS HE TESTING ME OR SOMETHING? HE MUST DO A LOT OF GROVELING IN THAT GUN TURRET!"

Fortunately my case of the German measles was a light one; the doctor had released me to go back to work on Monday.

Reinforcing Bill's overalls with knee patches had proved to be more of a job than I had anticipated. My diary observed: "NEARLY HAD TO TURN A SOMERSAULT TO GET AT THE WORN PARTS." I took out his letter again and read what he would have been too shy to say: "I hope this isn't too much of an imposition, but I will feel like you are right here with me, keeping me company on our missions."

"I wonder what the size of that gun turret is?" I closed my eyes. "Just think of how it must feel, being squeezed on one's knees into what must be a very small space, immobile and helpless under fire from an attacking plane or from the showers of flak spraying skywards from ack-ack guns." The thought made me feel sick to my stomach. I tucked a note for Bill into the pocket, gave one of the new knee patches a quick kiss, and folded the overalls to give back to Dad.

A Full Life Again

"MONDAY, APRIL 17TH: BACK TO WORK. ROYAL WELCOME FROM THE OFFICE. NO SIGN OF GERMAN MEASLES OUTBREAK, THANK GOODNESS! LETTER FROM BESSIE FROM WREXHAM; THEY HAVE AMERICANS THERE NOW, TOO, ALSO A POLISH AIR FORCE SQUADRON."

The office was buzzing with activity. Everyone looked very healthy; I was greatly relieved that I hadn't started a German measles epidemic at Airways House.

My desk was loaded with work. I was absorbed in catching up on the pile when Syd wandered into my office, a cup of tea in his hand. He perched on the corner of my desk and said with a straight face: "'Mornin', Bunty. Hey, d'you know wot 'appens wen an 'and grenade goes off in a field of cows?"

I looked up a little impatiently. "I really don't know, Syd; tell me what happens when a hand grenade goes off in a field of cows."

Syd shook his mop of blond curls: "Aw, Bunty, you c'n do better than that! Carn't yew guess what'appens wen an 'and grenade goes off in a field of cows? Udder destruction, of corse!" He left my office fast, before I could throw an eraser at him.

Bessie's letter was the first I had heard from her in months. She sounded excited about the influx of new servicemen at the nearby airfield. Near the end of her letter, she darkly hinted that Maggie might be beginning to have a fling with one of them. I resolved to write to Maggie and find out her latest news. Maybe now she had done something with her hair and fixed her glasses so they wouldn't keep sliding down her nose. I also hoped she'd given up fainting.

"WEDNESDAY, APRIL 19TH: HAD A VISIT FROM WILLIAM, BACK FROM CANADA. HE'S TURNED INTO A PROPER JERK, WITH WOLFISH TENDENCIES. LONDON BUS DRIVERS AND CONDUCTORS ARE OUT ON STRIKE."

A little after dinner, William rang our front doorbell. Now twenty-one, he had returned from Canada as Sergeant Pilot Standish, with three stripes and R.A.F. wings on his uniform. The old William I had known had changed. Both of our worlds had changed. Gone was the dear, boyish lad I knew, with his "two left feet"; now a mature man, he was poised and more self-confident than ever. Listening to him, I sensed his transformation with an objectivity and remoteness that rose above the childhood crush I'd had on him.

William's vocabulary was peppered with R.A.F. slang. "I'll never forget the wizard time I had in Canada," he enthused from the depths of an armchair in the dining room, "and learning to fly a crate has been a gung-ho experience. It's a jolly huge country over there--unbelievable! The people are smashing; wizard girls, so open and friendly, especially toward me. I was invited to dinner at some of their pukka homes, even though they didn't know me from Adam." He went on at great length about his adventures in Canada, but his voice receded as my mind stubbornly wandered to the weekend ahead when Bill and Frank were due for their next pass.

William soon went off to an R.A.F. training camp, where he was stationed as an instructor for the remainder of the war. We saw him one more time before he left. Incredibly, he had become just another "ship that passed in the night." But then, I realized, I had passed *him* in the night, too.

A bus strike was on in London. To keep them running, the buses had been taken over by the Army. Much to the amusement of the passengers, the khaki-clad substitute conductor often resorted to asking them to identify the bus stops: "What the 'ell's the name of this 'ere street, Mum?" Then he would yell out its name when the bus came to a halt. Riding the bus route to work, I just hoped the driver had a map!

"SATURDAY, APRIL 22ND: U.S. MARINES LANDED ON NEW GUINEA. DAD ARRIVED HOME WITH LETTERS, CANDY AND MAGAZINES FROM BILL AND FRANK. THEIR LEAVE HAS BEEN POSTPONED FOR A WEEK. WILLIAM PUT IN AN APPEARANCE AGAIN, AND SO DID DORIS BOYNTON."

Half a world away in the Pacific, in 1941 the Japanese had taken New Guinea, a jumping-off place for the invasion of Australia. Although some Australian cities had been bombed by them, there was never a Japanese invasion. On this date U.S. forces carried out successful amphibious landings, but the battle to win New Guinea from the Japanese dragged on until the end of World War Two.

Letters continued to come via Dad from Bill and Frank. Weekend passes decreased, as more missions were flown in the all-out "softening-up" process on military targets in France and Belgium in preparation for D-Day and the Allied invasion of Europe. Log-book records released after the war indicated that Bill and Frank's squadron sometimes went on two missions per day and that losses were light but fairly frequent. I worried in my diary about their safety. Among the famous magazines Dad brought home were pared-down, overseas editions of *Look*, *Life* and *The Saturday Evening Post*, also the official newspaper of the U.S. forces, *The Stars and Stripes*. Some of these always accompanied me in my tote bag, and I read them on the bus to and from work, familiarizing myself with life in Bill and Frank's faraway homeland.

William evidently was bored, so he came over to visit before leaving for his new assignment. I was becoming equally bored with him, and it was a diversion when Doris Boynton came over to relieve the monotony of his stories about his conquest of Canada.

I wondered what had motivated Doris's visit. "Oh Bunty," she gushed, in her uncultured accent, "I jest thought I'd pop over and say 'ello."

Doris had never been a close friend; I had been snobbishly aware, as I was in those days, that she lacked the polish of a prep school education. She lived a few blocks away, further up Bishop's Hill from William. Had she or her snoopy mother seen him come to our house in his R.A.F. uniform and had she come to be introduced? Had she or her mother seen Bill and Frank coming and going? Doris and I had never had much in common. What was behind this sudden bid for friendship? I introduced William to her. His conversation dried up but he didn't budge, and eventually Doris left after I promised to go for a bicycle ride with her the following day. But this wouldn't be the end of Doris.

"MONDAY, APRIL 24TH: SYD CALLED THE OFFICE; HE HAS - GUESS WHAT? GERMAN MEASLES! BOY, AM I GETTING TEASED! FREDDY IS AWAY, ONLY BRAD AND I IN THE OFFICE HOLDING THE FORT. ALL OVERSEAS TRAVEL FROM BRITAIN HAS BEEN BANNED BY THE GOVERNMENT."

The incredible had happened--Syd had developed the scourge that I had so confidently concluded hadn't gone any further than myself. My diary went on: "HAD A HECTIC DAY AT THE OFFICE; BRAD AND I HAD TO COPE WITH A BUSY DAY AND SEVERAL CRISES. VERY TIRING."

Preparations for D-Day were becoming more and more obvious to us. The British Government was taking extreme precautions to guard the secrecy of information associated with Operation Overlord, the proposed invasion. In April, to plug any possibility of an invasion infor-mation leak, the entire population of the island was virtually sealed off. An overseas travel ban prevented civilians from leaving the country, and a travel ban on a five-hundred-mile stretch of the southern and south-eastern coasts of Britain was imposed. It was also later revealed that all letters written by the armed forces stationed in Britain were intercepted and held by the censors until after D-Day, also that high wire fences had been erected around marshalling areas, sealing in military personnel and materiel being gathered to take part in the invasion.

"FRIDAY, APRIL 28TH: FREDDY BACK AT THE OFFICE. TONS OF LETTERS TO DO FOR HIM. HE LET ME COMPOSE A LETTER TO SEND TO SYD FROM ALL OF US TO WISH HIM A SPEEDY RECOVERY. I LAID IT ON THICK! GOT HOME FROM WORK TO FIND BILL AND FRANK ALREADY THERE! HUGS AND KISSES ALL AROUND. I LIKE MY NEW FAMILY. THIS TIME I'LL SHOW THEM THE CITY."

The boys wanted to explore more of London; I was thrilled. We had "done" the City of Westminster by now. This time I took them to the City of London, England's center for business and trade. First we visited the historic Tower of London, then my beloved St. Paul's Cathedral, a brave symbol of hope which still stood intact, except for one small area of bomb damage, in the midst of acres of burned-out ruins from the *Luftwaffe*'s fire bombings.

While Bill was putting his hand in mine as we strolled around the City enjoying our weekend, we had no idea that a tragic event was playing itself out at a place called Slapton Sands, on the coast of southwestern England. The story was suppressed for many years after the war, but now it can be told. Back in 1943, three thousand residents had been relocated away from villages around Slapton Sands beaches, so that the area could be used to practice amphibious landings in preparation for the eventual Allied invasion of Europe the following year.

The American "Operation Tiger," a dress rehearsal for D-Day, took place on the night of April 28, 1944, with four thousand American troops participating. Unfortunately, American communications about the planned exercise had been picked up at listening stations by the Germans, who dispatched nine motor torpedo boats to attack the eight L.S.T landing craft packed with hundreds of men and vehicles heading for the beaches. Another glitch caused protection from two Royal Navy escort ships to prove ineffective. Several of the landing craft sank, and seven hundred and forty-nine American men were drowned. It was the costliest training exercise of World War Two, whose story was kept hidden for forty-three years after it happened.

After their weekend with us, Bill and Frank returned to base. We worried about them. When it rained for several days on end, I wrote hopefully in my diary: "I'M GLAD IT'S RAINING. IT MIGHT KEEP THE BOYS GROUNDED."

"MONDAY, MAY 1ST: BEGAN WORKING LONGER HOURS AT THE OFFICE, 9 AM TO 6 PM. STILL HAVE TO WORK EVERY OTHER SATURDAY, TOO. SYD IS BACK AFTER HIS BOUT OF GERMAN MEASLES, WITH SOME COFFEE TO SELL. PAUL IS WRITING TONS OF LETTERS THESE DAYS. GLAD I CAN BE TRUSTED WITH HIS PROBLEMS AT THE SEMINARY. BILL AND FRANK'S LETTERS ARE

SHOWING THE STRAIN OF TOO MANY MISSIONS, BUT NO SIGN OF GERMAN MEASLES, THANK GOODNESS!"

German measles is notoriously contagious. After Syd had called up with the news that he had developed it, we grimly awaited the next victim in the office, but thankfully no one else succumbed. Bill and Frank seemed to have escaped, too. I shuddered to think what might have happened to the Ninth Air Force if I had unwittingly infected an entire U.S. air base!

I looked up from reading the latest letters Dad had brought from Bill and Frank. "Oh Mom, I feel so helpless. The boys sound so tired and depressed. I hope they'll be given some R&R soon." Stress was showing in Bill and Frank's letters. They had a quota of sixty-five missions to fly, after which they would be eligible for rotation back to the U.S., but although their low-level sorties over France and Belgium were nearing the peak of their quota, there was no sign that they would be rotated in the near future.

Rumors and more rumors continued to circulate that D-Day was near. This morning Syd came skipping into the office. Back to his usual ebullient self, we heard him before he came in the door, bellowing: "Never fear, Sydney's here." He was brandishing a large bag containing two pounds of coffee, which he proceeded to try to sell to everyone within earshot. Real coffee was almost nonexistent during the war, but sometimes it showed up on the black market. Did Syd have a connection to this? My diary observed: "THE STUFF SMELLED LIKE GROUND ACORNS TO ME, SO I DIDN'T SPLURGE ON IT AS A SURPRISE FOR MOM. IT WOULD HAVE BEEN THE KIND OF SURPRISE SHE WOULDN'T APPRECIATE!"

It wasn't unusual for roasted ground acorns to get passed off as coffee in those days of shortages. In fact, most of the "coffee" sold contained ground chicory root, and tasted terrible.

Paul's voluminous letters were obviously an outlet for his frustrations and inner feelings. He sometimes wrote more than twenty pages of nonsensical tales about life in the country, where a working farm, complete with various species of livestock, was operated by the seminarians. He illustrated these stories with funny cartoons depicting himself slipping on the mud in a pigpen, being kicked by a cow, or with a goat chewing at something in his pocket; his drawings always made me giggle. His letters always ended on a more serious note. A less-than-studious student, he griped about his struggles with Greek and Latin classes at the seminary, sometimes ending a letter: "I'm so fed up some days I feel like walking out of here and never coming back." Periodically he was allowed free time to come home to see his family, and would end up on our doorstep at Bishop's Hill. He would air his problems as we walked around Spring Glen Park. My diary commented: "IF FLOWER GARDENS COULD TALK, WHAT A STORY THEY WOULD TELL!"

D-Day--at Last!

"MONDAY, MAY 8TH: THE RUSSIANS HAVE RECAPTURED SEVASTOPOL. TARGETS IN FRANCE UNDER CONTINUOUS ATTACK BY ALLIED AIRCRAFT. HOPE THE BOYS ARE O.K."

On the Eastern Front, Hitler's invasion of Russia had now collapsed. The Russians had driven his armies into the Black Sea at Sevastopol; almost all of Russia had now been reclaimed.

American and British bombing of targets in Germany, Belgium, Holland and France had been increased. Could D-Day be any day now? Unknown to us, the date for D-Day had been set for June 6th.

"SATURDAY, MAY 13TH: BILL AND FRANK CALLED AT 7 P.M. TO SAY THEY HAD ARRIVED AT TRAIN STATION IN LONDON. COMING TO UPPER WOODSIDE BY BUS. I MET THEM OFF THE BUS AT TOP OF BISHOP'S HILL. FRANK VERY SHAKEN UP. BILL GAVE ME A BEAUTIFUL BROOCH TO WEAR--SILVER WINGS."

Frank was obviously showing the strain of recently stepped-up missions. A large band-aid was visible above his right eye. "We got too close to a German ack-ack gun this time," he said shakily. A burst of enemy anti-aircraft fire had exploded just outside the plane. Fragments of shrapnel had pierced the gun turrets and a piece flew across Frank's eyebrow, grazing it with a cut as it went. He said the blood dripped into his eye and he was sure he had been blinded. "It was the most terrifying feeling I've ever had, not being able to see through that red curtain of blood. For the first time in my life, I knew what the word 'panic' means. When we got back to base, the doc cleaned it up and put in some stitches; he said if it had been a fraction of an inch lower, I would've lost that eye. The C.O. says I'll be getting a Purple Heart, but I really don't feel I qualify for such an honor, when I think of the boys who have really terrible injuries."

Bill, too, had been hit by shrapnel, but also had escaped serious injury. He wasn't as shaken as Frank, but clung to my hand as if he would never let it go. He pulled a small box out of his pocket. "Hon, I want you to wear this for me," he said, his blue eyes clouding with tears.

I let him pin the small silver wings onto my dress, and kissed him quickly. I had a scary feeling that he was getting too serious, but hadn't the heart to discourage him and hurt his feelings. I had just thought of the little silver wings as a nice present. What I didn't realize was that to Bill they represented a commitment.

Ever practical, Mom soon hustled them both off to bed with cups of hot cocoa. The following morning we tiptoed around while Bill and Frank slept late. On their passes to Upper Woodside in the following weeks, sightseeing trips to London were replaced by naps, quiet strolls in the tranquility of Spring Glen Park, a jigsaw puzzle or a board game played on the steel top of the Morrison shelter. The lines of stress and tension had usually been smoothed out of their faces by the time they left us to go back to base. We were glad to see our R&R working!

"SATURDAY, MAY 27TH: IN ITALY, THE GERMANS HAVE RETREATED FROM ANZIO. ALLIED TROOPS HAVE JOINED UP AFTER THE BATTLE OF MONTE CASSINO. MY SATURDAY ON AT THE OFFICE. WE'RE ON

EXTENDED WORKING HOURS. BILL AND FRANK WERE ALREADY
RELAXING IN THE BACKYARD BY THE TIME I ARRIVED HOME."
Victory in the bloody battles against the Nazis on the Italian front had
taken longer and been more costly than anticipated, but the stalemate
had been brought to an end in the rubble of Monte Cassino monastery
and its little town. The Allied armies had now joined up and were finally
on the road to Rome.

Was it my imagination, or had the boys lost weight? Their faces
betrayed the overwhelming stress of their additional missions. When
would it ever be over? We did our best to cope with their weariness and
didn't mention the war.

"SUNDAY, MAY 28TH: SPENT TODAY IN LAWN CHAIRS ON THE
LAWN, SOAKING UP THE SUN. BRUCE IS ON LEAVE. HE CAME TO
CHECK OUT THE BOYS! SEEMS TO APPROVE."
Bill and Frank were sunbathing in lawn chairs in our backyard when
Bruce, on leave, decided to come and visit. They all had a great time
exchanging stories. When he left, Bruce conceded to me: "Not bad
chaps at all; first Yanks I've ever met, you know." He added: "They've
got a rotten job, and they deserve all the R&R they can get, but I hope
you won't get too fond of them, Bunty."

"THURSDAY, JUNE 1ST: B.O.A.C.IS ASKING FOR VOLUNTEERS TO FILL
SOME SECRETARIAL VACANCIES IN THE CAIRO (EGYPT) OFFICE. IT'S
FOR THREE YEARS. THAT'S A BIT OF A WRENCH, BUT SHOULD I TRY
IT? MY CAREER IS GOING NOWHERE IN ENGLAND!"
Looking back, I wondered where on earth I had thought my career
could be going when I had only been employed for five months! But at
the time, my spirit of adventure was tempted. As I reasoned back and
forth with myself, I thought: "Wow, what an opportunity! But will I be
happy being away from Mom and Dad for three years, after all we've
been through together? The three of us is all we have, and three years is
a long, long time. Oh, but think of being in a glamorous place like Cairo!

On the other hand, what if I don't like it? Will I be stuck there? And if they do bring me home, a failure, will that damage my chances of getting ahead at B.O.A.C.? And what about Bruce and now Bill? It's exciting to be noticed and appreciated by them! And what about the office? If I stay on, maybe I can get another promotion to a better job without going overseas at all! And after all, there is still a war on; anything can happen anywhere!" And it did.

"SATURDAY, JUNE 3RD: DAD CAME HOME FOR THE WEEKEND WITH LETTERS, CANDY, MAGAZINES, 2 PACKAGES COFFEE, SUGAR CUBES, 1 BAR LUX TOILET SOAP AND A DOLLAR BILL FROM THE BOYS, AND A NEW SHIRT FROM BILL THAT NEEDED TO HAVE HIS STRIPES AND HIS NINTH AIR FORCE PATCH SEWN ON. DAD ALSO BROUGHT HOME A PIECE OF A PARACHUTE!"
We had never seen an American dollar bill before, which the boys had sent to us as a souvenir along with the special grocery treats and candy, magazines and letters. There was also a new shirt of Bill's. I had offered to sew on his staff sergeant's stripes and insignia.

"Now here's a surprise for you, Mom," said Dad, and he fished out from his suitcase a large piece of a white nylon parachute, given to him by someone in the parachute packing shed on the air base. Mom immediately pounced on it with a whoop of joy. A week later, working on her old treadle sewing machine, she had produced a white nylon blouse for me with a jaunty bow at the neck. It turned out to be almost indestructible, and whenever it was admired, the story of its origin was told and retold. It was far from worn out when I donated it to a church rummage sale after countless washings and wearings, ten years later.

I was still mulling over my career opportunity with B.O.A.C., but when I told Dad about my chance to go to Cairo, he gave me his "well-travelled sailor" look and as usual didn't mince words: "Positively no. Dammit all, that's no place for a decent girl; Cairo is one of the worst cesspools in the world! You're only eighteen. If we set you adrift there, you might be scuppered without a life jacket."

"Oh rats," I thought, "all Dad has ever seen of Cairo must have been years ago in the Merchant Navy on shore leave, when his ship docked at Alexandria. I bet he and his shipmates only saw the seamy side of Cairo in the dockside bars or hunting for souvenirs in the bazaar." I wailed: "But just think, Dad, it could be the chance of a lifetime for me."

Although I'd had my own doubts, as usual when something became "forbidden fruit," it always looked much more attractive. But Dad was adamant. I knew better than to try to sell him on Cairo any longer. The die was cast. I still wasn't twenty-one, so my mind had again been made up for me, but this time it was a secret relief. On Monday morning I passed the volunteer list on to the girls in another office.

"MONDAY, JUNE 5TH: THE ALLIES HAVE CAPTURED ROME WITH COMPARATIVELY LITTLE OPPOSITION. AT THE OFFICE FREDDY'S OUT SICK, BRAD ISN'T BACK FROM HIS WEEKEND OFF. ONLY SYDNEY AND I TO RUN THE SHOW. FELT DONE IN BY THE END OF THE DAY."
U.S. forces took possession of Rome on June 4, 1944. However, an official German surrender in Italy would not take place until May 2, 1945.

At the office I was beginning to realize the meaning of "work load." At least young Buzz was there to run errands and keep Syd and me afloat with cups of tea, but there was no time for lunch, and I often came home so tired that I tottered off to bed without even being tempted to eat supper.

"THURSDAY, JUNE 6TH: D-DAY! ALLIED FORCES TODAY INVADED EUROPE AT SEVERAL POINTS ON THE NORMANDY COAST OF FRANCE. WROTE TO BILL AND FRANK. THEY MUST BE INVOLVED IN AIR SUPPORT. HOPE THEY'RE O.K."
Between 130,000 and 156,000 Allied troops were landed on three beaches in Normandy, France--the largest amphibious military operation in history.

I shall never forget D-Day. At dawn Mom and I were awakened by what sounded like a horde of angry hornets above the house. Mom and I threw on coats over our night clothes, and rushed downstairs and out the back door into the yard. Over our heads in the sky was a sight that has been burned indelibly into my memory. Instead of a sky full of airplanes heading toward London to bomb us, this time the sky was filled with planes all headed in the opposite direction! Transfixed, we watched as the first rays of the early morning sun glinted on squadron after squadron of American Flying Fortress and Liberator bombers as far as the eye could see, flying south in formation toward the coast. Mom and I stood looking up, tears streaming down our cheeks. We realized that here at last was the day we had suffered and waited for all those years: D-Day! People were watching from their yards all over the neighborhood, their cheers almost drowned out by the throbbing drone of aircraft filling the sky.

I hugged Mom, who closed her eyes, then said quietly: "Please God, be with them, today and in the days to come." We went back indoors to get dressed, shaking with a combination of excitement and relief.

"SATURDAY, JUNE 10TH: PAT AND I WATCHED MOVIES OF D-DAY LANDINGS."
Pat and I worked on the same alternate Saturdays at the office. Today we skipped lunch to find a news theater showing the first newsreels of the D-Day landings in Normandy. The audience sat in silence as the drama of mixed tragedy and triumph unfolded before our eyes. Most of us wept.

Years later, in a letter I still cherish, Frank responded to my request for him to write down his description of the once-in-a-lifetime scene as he and Bill saw it when their aircraft flew low across the English Channel and the landing beaches on D-Day:

"The English Channel was choppy, and swarming with ships of all sizes. Landing craft by the hundreds rushed back and forth, loading men from larger ships in the deeper waters offshore, discharging them on the beach, then returning for another load. Some landing craft were blown up by German coastal gun batteries before they reached the beaches, spewing men into water too deep for them to wade ashore. We could see some floundering and others floating, face down among the whitecaps. The beaches, also under heavy fire, were scenes of total chaos: men staggering ashore under their load of equipment, some never making it before being hit and drowning in surf already red with blood. Many reached the beaches, their full packs now water-soaked and heavier from the struggle ashore from their landing craft, only to be mown down by German machine guns before they could run across the beaches to shelter at the base of the cliffs beyond. Watching all of this from our plane can only be described as 'gut-wrenching.' Bill and I both threw up, we just couldn't help it."

Living With Doodlebugs

"SATURDAY, JUNE 10TH: DAD ARRIVED HOME WITH THE USUAL CANDY, ETC., ALSO LETTERS FROM THE BOYS."

Dad unloaded the usual things from the boys. I opened Frank's letter:

"I want to ask you a favor, Bunty. Please write to Kate for me. I know she will be worried sick now that D-Day has come and she knows we will be flying support missions. An air-mail letter from you will probably reach her earlier than mine, and it would put her mind at ease. Tell her that I love her and that I'm safe. I'm sure she will share your letter with the family."

Bill wrote: "Bunty, would you please write to my Mom and Mary? They will be wondering what has happened on D-Day, and if I'm okay."

The following day I carefully composed the letters. Kate's letter was pretty straightforward, but I felt unsure of how to write to Bill's mother. She was the daughter of German immigrants, and Bill had told me she still spoke with a German accent. Would she resent my letter? After all, I was English.

I felt I was reaching out with hands across the sea as I slid my letters into the red mailbox at the corner of Bishop's Hill. They would be on their way within a few hours. To our surprise, "thank-you" packages soon arrived from Frank's family, luxuries that dazzled and delighted us. For me there were nylons, lipstick and nail polish; for Mom, three beautiful aprons and some delicate handkerchiefs edged with their housekeeper Tillie's exquisite tatting; for Dad, a squeezable coin purse for his change, and a key ring that said: "City of Cleveland, Ohio."

"TUESDAY, JUNE 13TH: I'VE BEEN GIVEN A NEW ASSISTANT AT OFFICE, BERT BONNELL. HE'S A SWEET KID, MUCH SHARPER THAN BUZZ. HE'LL HELP ME A LOT."
Bert turned out to be all that he seemed to be, a willing worker with a sunny disposition. What a relief it was to be able to show him how to compile the weekly reports which had taken me away from my secretarial duties and kept me at the office late for so many evenings. I now had a staff of two! "Not bad," I thought, "only eighteen years old, and here I am learning management skills on the job and getting paid for the experience!"

Buzz and Bert got along fine; it was an easy matter to delegate their work so each was responsible for a different aspect of the job to call his own, and I was glad to see they helped each other out when necessary, too.

"FRIDAY, JUNE 16TH: NOW WHAT'S GOING ON? MOANING MINNIE WENT OFF AT 11:30 LAST NIGHT AND WE DIDN'T HEAR THE ALL CLEAR UNTIL 9:15 THIS MORNNG. MOM AND I DIDN'T ATTEMPT TO GO TO OUR OFFICES. HITLER IS SENDING OVER PILOTLESS, REMOTE CONTROLLED PLANES THAT EXPLODE. THEY CONTINUED TO COME OVER ALL DAY. THE KIDS ARE CALLING THEM 'BUZZ BOMBS.'"
As the Allies struggled to consolidate and advance from the Normandy beachheads, Hitler again turned his vengeance on London. With Allied air supremacy, never dreaming that we would ever have to sleep

downstairs again, we had taken the beds back up to the bedrooms. Mom reacted quickly to Moaning Minnie's wails. "Come on, Bunty, grab your blankets and let's get into the shelter."

Above the house we could hear what sounded like a sputtering motor cycle approaching. It stopped abruptly, and after a moment of silence, there was an ear-splitting explosion. Accustomed to manned aircraft, we thought at first that a Nazi plane had been hit by ack-ack fire and had exploded with a full bomb load. Mom said: "Oh those poor young men. Even if they are our enemies, what a terrible way to die."

The strange performance went on and on, all night. Moaning Minnie was silent. The two of us slept in fitful snatches in the claustrophobic Morrison shelter until morning. The B.B.C. news was cautious. Eventually it was announced that there was a new kind of attack on southern and southeastern England by Hitler's long-threatened vengeance weapon, a flying bomb. It was officially known as the V-1.

"SATURDAY, JUNE 17TH: "SPENT ANOTHER HECTIC NIGHT IN THE MORRISON SHELTER. AIR RAID ALERTS AND BUZZ BOMBS ALL DAY TODAY. DAD ARRIVED HOME FOR THE WEEKEND IN THE MIDDLE OF AN ALERT, WITH LETTERS FROM BILL AND FRANK AND ONE FROM FRANK'S WIFE, KATE. SHE SEEMS VERY NICE. MURIEL PRATT GOT MARRIED TO HER R.A.F. FIANCE DURING A LULL IN THE BUZZ BOMBS! THE AMERICANS ARE CALLING THEM 'DOODLEBUGS.'"

I heard Mom's voice from the living room: "Bunty, Jack, come to the window, hurry!" Mom didn't very often sound *this* excited. Dad and I rushed to the big bay window and looked across the street where Mom was pointing. "Muriel's getting married in spite of the doodlebugs. Isn't it wonderful?" Mom was on the brink of tears. We had known Muriel Pratt since she was a little girl. She and her family were keeping her wedding date as scheduled. The shiny black limousine with white ribbons stretched across its hood arrived on time, and Muriel looked lovely as she floated in her white gown and veil into the waiting car.

Dad exclaimed: "Well, I'll be jiggered! Talk about 'Keep Calm and Carry On!' I wish Old Adolf could see Muriel looking calm as a cucumber, on her way to St. John's to marry her R.A.F. sweetheart in spite of his blasted buzz bombs! That would give him something to think about, the Nazi bastard!"

"SUNDAY, JUNE 18TH: SPENT ALL DAY TRYING TO GET A LITTLE SLEEP. SLEPT FOR A FEW HOURS IN THE AFTERNOON. MANAGED TO REPLY TO BRUCE'S LATEST LETTER. FINISHED ONE TO PAUL, AND MAILED THEM BOTH. TODAY NO BUZZ BOMBS FELL CLOSE BY, BUT THEY KEEP COMING. WE NEVER KNOW WHEN OR WHERE." Unknown to us, Hitler had been manufacturing thousands of what he called "vengeance weapons," guided missiles to rain down on civilians in the south of England and the London area. He was convinced that the resulting terror, demoralization and destruction could win the war for Germany, even at this late date. Hidden underground were factories, difficult for Allied bombers to detect from the air and impossible to penetrate and destroy with bombs. The completed V-1s were now being flung at London and south-eastern England from launching ramps in northern France, which had not yet been reached by the Allied armies after D-Day. Postwar information showed that, at the peak of the V-1 attacks, more than a hundred per day were fired at London and southeastern England. As in the London Blitz in 1940, we fought our battle against the V-1s by going about our business as normally as possible.

Housewives stood in queues for food. Office workers rode buses and trains to and from the city. Bus routes sometimes had to be changed if they happened to coincide with the pre-set paths of V-1s; the trains had to take their chances. Dad went back to his job; Mom and I went to work at our offices. The days went by, and we learned to live with this new unstoppable onslaught. V-1s were low-flying and easily visible, with a twenty-seven-foot long body and short, stubby wings, looking like black crosses spouting flames from the jet engine mounted on their backs. They streaked across the sky at about four hundred miles an hour on a gyroscope-guided path aimed at London.

Dubbed "Doodlebugs", by the Americans, they had enough fuel to last for roughly one hundred and sixty miles from their launching ramps. When the fuel was running out, they could be heard "putt-putting" like a motor bike, until the motor stopped. A moment or two of silence was followed by an ear-splitting explosion as they plummeted to the ground and the warhead containing two thousand pounds of amatol fragmented on contact to destroy everything around it. Like the bombs in the London Blitz, the V-1s that fell short of their main target fell on us in London's southern suburbs.

Many of the V-1s were shot down or tipped off-course by R.A.F. fighters intercepting them over the English Channel. Barrages of ack-ack guns were set up along the southern and southeastern English coast-line. But the V-1s that got through these defences caused tremendous damage and casualties. We heard of London's hospitals and the Old Age Pensioners' Home being hit; not even Buckingham Palace escaped a V-1 that fell not far from where King George VI was sitting at his desk.

"THURSDAY, JUNE 22ND: I FEEL VERY TIRED. BILL AND FRANK HAVE 48-HR. PASSES! HOWEVER DID THEY DO IT? LONDON IS OFF-LIMITS! THEY PICKED ME UP AT THE OFFICE AT 5 P.M. BILL SAYS IT'S LIKE A 'DREAM WORLD' TO GET AWAY FROM THE BASE."
We hadn't seen Bill and Frank since before D-Day. I wondered if they would ever visit us again. Because of the V-1s, London had been put off-limits to U.S. personnel, but by some miracle, the boys had passes. I could hardly wait to ask them: "O.K., you two, how did you do it?"

"Simple," said Frank, with a grin. "We just had our passes made out for Cambridge! Hey, Bunty, how about us going up to London tomor-row? I have to see Madame Tussauds while we're still in England. Also I've heard about the Piccadilly Commandos - let's give them a look, too. What the heck--we've as good a chance of being hit by a doodlebug if we stay here at Upper Woodside all day as we will in the city."

When "Moaning Minnie" went off that night, the boys, Mom and I all squeezed into the Morrison shelter and, after we sorted ourselves out, remained in it all night, sitting up wrapped in blankets and propped with pillows against its steel mesh sides. In spite of the sputtering of buzz bombs and explosions outside, we were all so tired we managed to doze. Again, we came through the night unscathed.

"FRIDAY, JUNE 23RD: MOM WENT TO HER OFFICE. BILL, FRANK AND I HAD A LATE BREAKFAST, THEN CAUGHT THE BUS TO LONDON'S WEST END. WENT TO MADAME TUSSAUD'S, THEN TOOK THE TUBE TO PICCADILLY, SAW THE COMMANDOS, RELAXED AT A GOOD MOVIE ON OUR WAY HOME."

The boys were very impressed with London's famous waxworks, Madame Tussauds. In the basement they were thrilled by the "Chamber of Horrors," a dimly lit, scary series of lifelike wax figures being tortured by every horrible instrument possible, along with figures of famous murderers wielding their murder weapons.

I couldn't imagine why Bill and Frank were so delighted to see such gruesome sights. "O.K., boys, you've seen the worst Madame Tussauds has to show you; now let's go find a Commando or two." We took the train in the Underground, or Tube, to Piccadilly Circus station, then resurfaced on the sidewalk. We walked past miniskirted girls lounging in doorways or sitting on the steps of the island in the center of the traffic circle, under the famous statue of Eros, Ancient Greek god of love, now boarded up for protection for the duration of the war. As we walked, I accidentally brushed against one of them. She bristled: "'Oo the 'ell d'you think you are, girlie? Git the 'ell out of my spot."

The boys cracked up laughing. Bill was particularly tickled: "Well, Bunty, who'd have thought you looked like one of *them*? It just goes to show, some things simply go with the territory!"

I playfully hit him with my new handbag; he put his arm around me and gave me a conciliatory hug. I thought to myself: "I'll bet she's wondering what's my secret--two G.I.s, and she hasn't even got one!"

We got off the bus at our neighboring suburb and let our sore feet recover with a good movie at the Astoria: Ginger Rogers and Ray Milland in *Lady in the Dark*. It has now become a classic.

"SATURDAY, JUNE 24TH: VERY TIRED BUT IT'S MY SATURDAY "ON" AT THE OFFICE. THE BOYS CAME WITH ME AS FAR AS LONDON. COULDN'T HELP CRYING WHEN WE SAID 'GOODBYE.'"

We were all so tired, having spent another night of fitful sleep sitting up in the Morrison shelter. As I left the boys on the bus to continue on to the railroad station, I wondered if we would ever see each other again. Bill forgot his dogtags when they left. I put them in the mail, hoping nobody would notice the postmark was London, not Cambridge!

A Failed Assassination

"TUESDAY, JUNE 27TH: THE ALLIES HAVE CAPTURED CHERBOURG. HAD A NOISY NIGHT. DOODLEBUGS IN GREEN LANE, ABOUT 500 YDS. AWAY. ONLY HEARD TWO DURING THE DAY, NOWHERE NEAR THE OFFICE."

By the end of June it must have been clear to the Nazi generals that they were losing the war. The Allies had occupied Rome, and now we were cheered by a prize capture, the large, deep-water port of Cherbourg on the Normandy coast. Once restored, after the battle damage was repaired, it would be ready to receive shipments of men and materiel directly from England and the U.S. to boost the advancing Allied armies in France.

On Britain's home front, Hitler's V-1s were still pounding England, their launching ramps not yet overrun by the Allies. We were learning that war is a double-edged sword; while we cheered the turning of the tide of war in our favor, at the same time we mourned the terrible cost in human lives on all sides.

"SATURDAY, JULY 1ST: IN PACIFIC THE JAPANESE HAVE GIVEN UP SAIPAN TO THE ALLIES. THE RUSSIANS HAVE BEGUN A SUMMER OFFENSIVE TO WIPE OUT REMAINS OF GERMAN ARMIES. WE ALL FEEL SO TIRED. BUZZ BOMBS DAY AND NIGHT, ALL OVER LONDON. SEVERAL BIG OFFICE BUILDINGS IN LONDON HAVE BEEN HIT, AND MRS. ORCHARD'S OFFICE BUILDING IN CROYDON WAS WRECKED. SHE IS BADLY HURT."

While overseas news was good, the war was still striking home to us in Upper Woodside. There was no respite from the V-1s. All day and all night they streamed endlessly across southern England from launching ramps still out of reach of the advancing Allied troops. Mom and I complained to each other about trying to stay alert throughout the working day at our offices, after so little sleep. The buses and trains running to and from London were filled with sleeping passengers. More of the town of Croydon was demolished; postwar statistics revealed that more V-1s fell on Croydon than on any other town in England! According to statistics released after the war, a total of 9,251 V-1s were launched against England. The R.A.F. brought down around 2,000; anti-aircraft guns shot down almost that number, and barrage balloons snagged 278. The gyroscopes on the 5,000 that got through kept them on a straight route, along which they dropped and exploded at whatever point their fuel ran out.

One of Mom's close friends who, like her, had been called up into the wartime workforce, was badly injured when she was pinned under the wreckage of her office building. After a long recovery, her bodily injuries were repaired, but her mind bore the scars of her ordeal for the rest of her life.

"MONDAY, JULY 3RD: POURED WITH RAIN ALL DAY. GOT HOME AHEAD OF MOM FROM WORK. HAD A VISIT FROM PETER WHEN I

HAD JUST CHANGED MY WET CLOTHES. HE'S ON A WEEK'S LEAVE. HE WAS SHAKING ALL OVER FROM THE SHOCK OF SEEING THE CASUALTIES WHEN A V-1 DROPPED ON AN APARTMENT BUILDING. MOM ARRIVED HOME LATER FROM HER OFFICE, COVERED WITH MUD!"

The doorbell rang. Peter stood on the doorstep in the rain, shaking from head to foot. Shedding his drenched R.A.F poncho, he flung himself into one of the armchairs in the dining room while I filled the teapot.

"Oh, Bunty," he said, teeth still chattering. "Remember I wrote to say I had seven days' leave? Well, about an hour ago, I arrived at the train terminal in London and caught a bus for Upper Woodside. We were on the bus route home when we were stopped by a man in a Civil Defence uniform. A V-1 had exploded just a short time before the bus came along, and our driver was told to turn around and find another route, to make room for emergency vehicles. Through the windows in the upper deck of the bus I could see that terrible scene: powerful lights focused on Civil Defence and Red Cross men and air raid wardens working feverishly, some with their bare hands digging through the wreckage of an apartment building that had received a direct hit. The building had been full of people. They were home from work, probably having their dinner, when it happened.

Peter seemed to need to tell the whole story, so I just sat and said nothing, while he went on. "It was horrible. When the bus was stopped, we could see them pulling bleeding bodies out of the wreckage, some without arms or legs, and blood, blood everywhere." He put his head down on his knees and sobbed. He calmed down after pouring out this terrible memory, and we sat in silence for awhile, comforted by our cups of hot tea. Next moment I heard a key in the front door, and in came Mom from her day at her office in the city. She was soaking wet from head to toe and covered with mud. Peter and I looked at her in dismay.

"Oh, Mom, what on earth has happened to you?" was all I could manage to say. Without a word, Mom went slowly into the kitchen and took off her mud-caked raincoat and shoes, leaving them on the floor. I heard the kitchen faucet running as she wiped the mud off her face and hands. She ran upstairs, then soon appeared in a bathrobe. Looking shaken, she sank into the armchair next to Peter without a word. I filled a teacup from the pot, handed it to her on her lap, and she began to drink the hot liquid. Peter came back for a second cup. Mom gradually recovered her composure. Peter and I looked at her expectantly, and she began her own saga. "Well, I had just stepped off the bus at the top of the hill when I heard a V-1 overhead. It sputtered, then its engine cut out. You know what the Civil Defence instructions are: 'You only have a few seconds to drop to the ground, face down, wherever you happen to be!' I just happened to drop face down into a large mud puddle! That wretched doodlebug exploded a few streets away, but it nearly burst my eardrums; in fact, I still can hardly hear properly--everything sounds like a faint echo. I practically ran down the hill, and just look at me!"

It was my turn to tell *my* story. "What a time *I* had getting home on the bus, too. My usual bus route from the city now evidently intersects with one of the doodlebug paths. The bus was stopped by Civil Defence workers because a doodlebug had exploded and left a crater in the road ahead of us. The conductor shouted: "Nah, let's orl of us keep calm and stay in are seats, mates. We'll 'ave to mike a bloody dee-tooer so's not to fall into that bloody big 'ole in the road made by that bloody doodlebug. And up a'ed the road's pretty well blocked by the bloody rekidge of all them 'ouses, too. Jest all of yer 'ang on and we'll try to stay as close to the proper rewt as we can." I paused for breath then took a gulp of tea. I continued:

"The driver took the bus a few blocks away from the regular route, stopping wherever he could to let passengers off. They, in turn, had to walk several streets out of their normal way home in the pouring rain to get there, probably frantic with anxiety, not knowing if they would find their houses still standing or their folks injured or even killed." I wound up my story. "The bus eventually got back on the regular route, but no wonder it took me an extra hour and a half to get back to Bishop's Hill!"

Living with the doodlebugs, Mom and I never knew when, or if, we would arrive home safely after work, or if our house would still be standing when we did. I still remember the taste of fear in my mouth each time I rounded the bend in Bishop's Hill after getting off the bus. I felt myself forcing my eyes open to look down the hill to see if our house containing everything we owned was still standing. I remember preparing for the worst by telling myself how foolish it was to put a value on "things," when being alive was so much more important. I shall never forget how Dad put it: "Even if you lose everything else, if you still have what's between your ears, that's what counts."

We were among the lucky ones: our house stood firm throughout the onslaught of this latest episode in Hitler's vengeance. I didn't know this would be the last time I would see Peter for many years. After his leave, he went back to his air force base, and his motor cycle collided head-on with a truck in a blinding rainstorm when he was delivering an R.A.F dispatch. His leg was so badly mangled that he spent almost a year in a hospital in south Wales, while doctors fought the possibility of amputating it. After many surgeries, they saved the leg, but it was immobilized at the knee, leaving him permanently unable to bend it. Meantime, Peter's life and mine had drifted apart; his was focused on a new girlfriend, mine on Bill.

"SUNDAY, JULY 9TH: PAUL IS HOME FROM SEMINARY FOR A FEW DAYS AND CAME TO VISIT. WE WENT FOR A WALK IN SPRING GROVE PARK. FLOWERS THERE ARE BEAUTIFUL. IN THE MIDDLE OF A WAR, IT'S COMFORTING TO KNOW THAT AT LEAST THE SEASONS STILL COME AND GO WITH RELIABILITY. IT TAKES OUR MINDS OFF THE BOMBING."

As the V-1 assaults continued, taking time to appreciate the unchanging beauty of nature in an ugly world did wonders to revive our spirits. Looking back, I believe that it must have been this kind of reassurance that carried me through my worst experiences in World War Two.

"WEDNESDAY, JULY 12TH: BUZZ BOMBS ALL DAY. BRAD IS BOMBED OUT. A V-1 FELL TOO CLOSE TO HIS HOUSE, WHICH HAD COLLAPSED WHILE HE WAS AT WORK. SEVERAL OTHER PEOPLE AT AIRWAYS HOUSE HAVE LOST THEIR HOMES. NONE OF THEM CAN COME IN TO WORK UNTIL THEY FIND A PLACE TO STAY."

Brad took a week's vacation time. He couldn't come back to work until he found another place to live. In the meantime, he busied himself sorting through the rubble of the attractive little house that had been their first home shortly after he and his wife were married. Today, in the rain, he was salvaging what he could from the wreckage. The atmosphere in the office that day was one of gloom; our hearts went out to Brad and his wife. But, as in so many wartime tragedies, we learned to look, as Mom often said, "on the bright side." Thankfully, Brad wasn't home when it happened, and his wife and baby were safe with relatives, where they had gone to live when war came. This was the "bright side."

"THURSDAY, JULY 20TH: LETTER FROM BRUCE, WORRYING ABOUT US AND THE V-1s SMASHING CROYDON. HE'S ON ACTIVE SERVICE ON AN L.C.T., FERRYING SUPPLIES AND VEHICLES ACROSS THE ENGLISH CHANNEL WHILE WAITING FOR ORDERS TO GO OVERSEAS. WISH I COULD GET SOME SLEEP. I FEEL TERRIBLY TIRED. WILL THESE BUZZ BOMBS NEVER STOP?"

Bruce had good cause to be worried. Croydon was only a few miles from Upper Woodside, and it was directly in the path of the V-1s. Much later, statistics were released, showing that V-1s had destroyed or damaged seventy-five per cent of the houses in Croydon.

"SATURDAY, JULY 22ND: ATTEMPT MADE ON HITLER'S LIFE."

With the Allies now in Europe, we were hearing news about what was happening there, for the first time in six years. The B.B.C. newscaster reported the bizarre events that occurred two days before. For awhile, some of Hitler's generals, among them "Desert Fox" Rommel, had plotted to assassinate him, convinced that the war was lost and should not be prolonged by allowing his idiotic and irrational commands to continue. They reasoned that Germany could be saved from total destruction through a negotiated surrender.

On July 20th, Hitler was sitting at a conference table with his high-level staff officers. A man casually placed a brief case containing a bomb on the floor near Hitler's feet, then left the room. The bomb exploded. It killed one attendee and blew some of the others through a window. To the disappointment of millions, Hitler was relatively unscathed. Two hundred suspected conspirators were rounded up and executed. Still convinced he could win the war, Hitler's insane orders as commander-in-chief would continue to plague the German armed forces until he died the following year.

AWOL Again!

"FRIDAY, JULY 28TH: AT THE OFFICE WE RECEIVED A CONSIGNMENT OF ETHER FOR THE AMERICAN RED CROSS, WHICH LEAKED AND ALMOST DID US IN! BILL AND FRANK ARRIVED ON ANOTHER 48-HR. PASS FOR CAMBRIDGE! PAUL CAME TO VISIT US IN THE EVENING TO CHECK THEM OUT."

The air cargo that flowed through our office was surprising enough, but this took the cake. How and where the American Red Cross ether sprang its leak we'll never know, but we felt "spacey" for the rest of the day! I took advantage of the chance to leave early, eager to see our two fliers again.

One by one, my childhood friends had arranged to stop by to check out these Americans they kept hearing about in my letters. They must have looked like an odd assortment to Bill and Frank: a Navy officer, a fighter pilot, and now a student priest in a "dog collar"! The curiosity cut both ways; they all had a great time swapping stories and enjoying the encounter. But each time there was a follow-up letter from Bruce, William and Paul, telling me not to get too involved!

"MONDAY, JULY 31ST: ON SATURDAY A V-1 HAS EXPLODED 15 YARDS AWAY FROM OUR OFFICE. GLASS EVERYWHERE. EMPTY WINDOW FRAMES ARE BEING BOARDED UP."

Back to work after a weekend off, I looked at Airways House in disbelief. There were armed guards behind coils of barbed wire all around the building; carpenters were nailing sheets of plywood to the empty window frames. My B.O.A.C. pass took me inside. Where was my desk? Glass and debris littered the floor, and two janitors were trying to sweep it up before the office workers arrived.

It had been Syd's Saturday "on". His usual grin was missing as he brushed away the covering of plaster dust on his desk and sat on the corner of it, one leg dangling dramatically, as he began his story. We gathered around to hear about it firsthand. "That was a close one, orl right. I heard the motor splutter, then cut orf, and that 'orrible moment of silence; then we could 'ear it 'issing as it fell through the air. I thought the bloody thing would make a direct hit on us, and I remember thinkin' 'O.K. Syd, your number's up this time, old lad.'" He shivered slightly as if reliving the memory. "It exploded bloody close, but lucky fer us nobody 'ere in the building was killed or seriously injured. But truth be told, I thort I was a gonner! You know Betty, that little clerk over in the Passenger Office? The poor kid, you remember she lost her 'ome to a V-1 not long ago? Well, she was on duty on Saturday, too. When the windows blew in opposite her desk, she got some cuts from the flying glass. Bleedin' something awful, she was and 'ad to be carted orf to the 'ospital, but they was only superficial cuts, thank God, and she was discharged after they patched 'er up. As if she needed any more troubles, poor little soul."

It had been my Saturday off. Once again, I had been spared! I wondered how much longer my luck could hold out. Night and day the V-1s continued to fall randomly on buses, houses, office buildings, hospitals and churches in London and its suburbs. The explosions robbed us of sleep and frayed our nerves. One early morning on my way to work, I peered through the blast-netted windows on the bus as we passed by a direct hit on a block of apartments. A mist of dust hung in the bright beam of a powerful searchlight over the rubble, where a rescue team was digging for buried victims. My face streamed with helpless tears of sorrow, horror and rage.

"FRIDAY, AUGUST 4TH: HAD A LETTER FROM BILL. HE SOUNDS VERY TIRED AND LONESOME. WISH I COULD SEE HIM. HE WANTS ME TO WRITE TO HIS MOTHER AGAIN AS SOON AS POSSIBLE TO REASSURE HER THAT HE'S O.K. SOUNDS LIKE THEY MIGHT BE SHIPPING OUT SOON."

By now, having satisfied himself there was plenty of pure drinking water on Bill and Frank's base, Dad had moved on to his next water purification job, so he was out of contact with what was going on in their lives. I had a sinking feeling that Bill wanted me to contact his Mom because he wouldn't be at the base much longer. Mail would be interrupted when he was moved, causing her to worry. I hadn't received an answer to my previous letter to his Mom, so I worded this one cautiously, wondering what this German lady was like, and whether she would appreciate an English girl writing on behalf of her only son. I included two photos of my family and one of myself, and addressed the letter to both Bill's Mom and his sister Mary.

"TUESDAY, AUGUST 8TH: ONE AND A HALF TONS OF AIR FREIGHT ARRIVED AT OUR LOADING DOCK FOR THE U.S. NAVY! DICK DONAHUE CAME TO COLLECT IT, AFTER CALLING ME FOUR TIMES TODAY TO CHAT. HE BROUGHT A SILLY LITTLE TRUCK, SO OF COURSE HE HAD TO MAKE TWO TRIPS. SECOND TIME HE BROUGHT HIS LIEUTENANT UP TO MY OFFICE TO SEE ME!"

Whatever it was that merited special handling by air transport from the U.S. for its navy in London we never really knew, but the frequent air freight shipments for the U.S. Navy kept the B.O.A.C. porters busy on the loading dock, and were a welcome diversion in my worries about the safety of Bill and Frank.

Chief Petty Officer Dick Donahue's jovial voice came through my telephone with clockwork regularity. Today was no exception. "Hey, Bunty, any sign of shipment number 20385N? It sounds to be real big! An' by the way, how about them lousy V-1s? We had one nearly busted through our door here at H.Q. office the other night, blast its hide. Be shore to let me know when that stuff arrives, hon."

When he and his helper brought their truck to collect today's huge shipment of who knows what, Dick left the helper on the loading dock and made his way to my office, as usual, to drink a cup of tea while perched on the edge of my desk, making nonstop conversation between gulps. "Guess I'll have to come back for another load, hon. That shore didn't all fit on our little truck." This performance was repeated two hours later, when he returned with the same small truck.

Dick's trips to Airways House and the length of time it took him to bring back the freight to London's U.S. Navy depot must have aroused his boss's curiosity, because on his second trip today the lieutenant himself came up to the office with him.

James Truman Oates, Lieutenant J.G., U.S.N. was in his mid-twenties, tall and very handsome. I felt myself blushing as Dick introduced us. Flashing his gold braid, the lieutenant put out a hand, which I shook as firmly as I could manage. He seemed surprised by my business-like handshake and to discover I was so young; obviously I was not a "femme fatale," which probably convinced him I was harmless and that he had no need to save his chief enlisted man from a fate worse than death. Cheerfully accepting a cup of tea, he sat down in a nearby chair, crossed his long legs comfortably, and proclaimed: "Ah'm surely glad to meet ya, Bundy. Mah home state is Ioway, Gawd's Country, ya know." I was realizing that the home state of every American I had met so far was "God's Country." The lieutenant's corner of it sounded a bit boring when he described cornfields in Iowa as far as the eye could see; I hoped my boredom didn't show too much. "Anyway," I thought to myself: "I bet I never see *him* again!"

"TUESDAY, AUGUST 15TH: AMERICAN FORCES HAVE CRUSHED THE JAPANESE ON GUAM. BRITISH AND FREE FRENCH TROOPS HAVE LANDED IN SOUTHERN FRANCE. BILL'S LATEST LETTER SAYS ALL PASSES CANCELLED. I THINK THEY ARE GETTING READY TO BE SHIPPED SOMEWHERE."

From the faraway Pacific, we heard that Guam had finally been taken back by the Americans, after bloody battles lasting years. Things were moving more quickly now in Europe. In France the Allies were securing their new beachheads on the fashionable French Riviera, General Patch's American Seventh Army had entered Grenoble in the south. In the north, General Patton's Third Army was at the outskirts of Verdun, General Hodge's First Army was at the River Meuse, and the British under General Montgomery were at the River Somme.

The following day my diary reported: "HAD WONDERFUL LETTERS FROM BILL AND FRANK. THEY HAVE BEEN SENT TO A REST CAMP FOR A DAY OR TWO. FEEL SO THANKFUL THEY'RE O.K."

"SATURDAY, AUGUST 19TH: BRUCE IS HOME ON SEVEN DAYS' LEAVE AND CAME TO VISIT IN HIS NEW OFFICER'S DRESS UNIFORM. DOES HE EVER TAKE IT OFF?"

It was the beginning of a hectic week on the social calendar. First came Bruce, looking elegant in his Royal Navy "whites." Mom was appropriately dazzled. I think she fancied that things could be getting serious between Bruce and myself, but all his visit did was to help me feel worried that I might never see Bill or Frank again. As if to consolidate his advantage in their absence, Bruce visited again the following evening. It was a beautiful summer evening, so we walked around Spring Glen Park for old times' sake. I wished he had been Bill!

Bruce popped in again the following evening, but I had to be up early next morning for work, so I begged off going to the movie he wanted to see.

The following day I heard from Bill that they were practicing moving. My diary commented: "I'M FEELING DECIDEDLY DEFLATED."

"TUESDAY, AUGUST 22ND. SUDDENLY BILL ARRIVED, UNAN-
NOUNCED. HOW DID HE DO IT? BETTER NOT ASK! MAYBE HE
HAS ESCAPED FROM THE REST CAMP!"
Bill's nerves were jangled. He called me at the office, and as soon as
he arrived to pick me up I left with him for Upper Woodside. He talked
very little about the war and his part in it, but etched on his face was
the strain from the missions he must have endured since I had last seen
him. When we got home I called the office. Syd answered the phone:
'Ello, 'ello, 'ello"-—his greeting was typical as soon as he knew who was
calling.

"Hey, Syd," I began, and could hardly hide the excitement in my
voice. "I'm going to take the next two days off. We didn't expect Bill,
and I think he may be A.W.O.L. I believe he and Frank are going to be
shipped out. This could be the last time I'll ever see him – and I can't
leave him home alone for two days, anyway!"

"Go to it, Bunty," warbled Syd, his usual self, "but be good, and if
you can't be good, be careful, and if you can't be careful it's your own
fault! Not to worry, I'll tell Freddy for you."

Lately the V-1 attacks had tapered off, with the Allied advance in
Europe now closing in on their launching sites. After weeks sleeping
in the Morrison shelter, we could get a good night's rest in our own
beds once more. I said to Bill: "Good news. We don't need to be
cramped in the shelter any more. You can have your own bed back in
the guest room." He looked at me with a weary grin and said: "Aw,
shucks!"

When Mom came home she asked pointedly after Frank: "Well,
what a surprise, it's good to see you, Bill. Where's Frank?"

"Oh, he went to look up an old friend of his Dad's, so he won't be
coming this time, but he said to say 'hello' and give you a hug."

The quiet at Upper Woodside did wonders for Bill, with rest, regular meals, a movie, and leisurely walks around Spring Glen Park. As the
hours passed, his face gradually lost its lines of stress, and he was more
like his old, happy self by the time he went off to catch the train back to

the air base. His next letter said they were getting ready to move, and reading between the lines I knew it would be to France.

I thought I was in love with Bill. But in the coming months I would discover that I had only been in love with love.

Sunderland Revisited

"THURSDAY, AUGUST 24TH: BILL DEPARTED IN A ROSY HAZE THIS MORNING. I THINK WE'RE IN LOVE! BATTLE OF NORMANDY ENDED AS TRAPPED GERMAN ARMY SURRENDERED. BACK TO WORK. CROYDON AIRPORT IS NOW IN FULL OPERATION AGAIN. NO MORE U.S. NAVY FREIGHT AT AIRWAYS HOUSE!"

In Frank's absence, Bill blossomed romantically. On one of our strolls around the park. he announced that he wanted to marry me after he was established in a good job back in the States. I was surprised and flattered, but something kept me from promising to marry him. Did I really love him enough? Time would tell, and I needed time.

Two months after the D-Day landings, the final chapter in the Battle of Normandy ended with the surrender of the surrounded German army. Despite Hitler's orders to fight to the death, fifty thousand Nazis were taken prisoner.

Freddy came out of his office. "Good news, Bunty. Now that Croydon Airport's back in operation, those U.S. Navy chaps will have to pick up their freight there instead of here at Airways House."

So it was goodbye to Dick Donahue and Lieutenant Oates, and all that U.S. Navy paperwork. Being polite throughout their chatty phone calls and visits was getting a bit wearing. I often needed to stay late to catch up on time lost from being kind to our Allies, although I'll admit it was always a good excuse for a cup of tea!

I heaved a sigh of relief--but too soon!

"SATURDAY, AUGUST 26TH: THE ALLIES HAVE LIBERATED PARIS. YAY, ALLIES! WE'RE OFF TO SUNDERLAND FOR A VACATION. TOOK

TRAIN FROM LONDON AT 7:30 A.M. WITH MOM AND DAD. HAD TO STAND FROM LONDON TO DARLINGTON (256 MILES), CHANGED TRAINS TO NEWCASTLE AND AGAIN TO SUNDERLAND. LONG DAY!" What better way to celebrate the liberation of Paris than with a trip to Sunderland to visit the family? The compartments in the steam train were already full when we boarded it in London. Dad left Mom and me and went off down the corridor to explore. "Come on, you two, bring your shoulder bags and follow me," he panted, "no seats, but I've found a place where we can all stand at the same spot in the corridor."

Under her breath, Mom sarcastically muttered, "Whoopee." We squeezed through the crush of civilians and uniformed servicemen and women already standing in the corridor. Dad stood our large suitcase up on the floor under the rail along its outer wall. The standing passengers all lurched in the same direction as the train gave a metallic screech and puffed out of the station, heading north. The hours dragged. We ate our sandwiches and drank the tea from Mom's thermos, taking turns perching on the suitcase to relieve our aching legs. It took eight and a quarter hours plus changing trains twice before we arrived at Sunderland Station, where Uncle Arthur was waiting on the platform. We exchanged hugs. He bellowed above the noise and bustle of the station: "Not enough petrol for me to bring the car, but come on, we'll soon be on our way home."

With that, he seized the heavy suitcase from Dad as if it was light as a feather and charged off to the bus stop, Mom and me puffing along behind him with our heavy shoulder bags. On the bus ride to the Sunderland suburbs, we looked out on a town that was bomb-scarred, with gaping spaces where stores and houses had been on our last visit. Fortunately, Auntie Belle and Uncle Arthur's house and "Corner Shop" were undamaged during the vicious air raids the *Luftwaffe* had inflicted on Sunderland's docks and factories accompanied by the customary extra "serving" of bombs scattered over shopping streets and civilian homes.

Supper consisted of a salad and thin slices of canned ham, with canned peaches from America for dessert -- treats that Mom found impossible to get from her grocery store in Croydon. Auntie Belle was an excellent cook who refused to be defeated by the meat shortages. She had found a local poacher who helped her add to the family meat rations with "game." We were never sure what lurked under the pastry crust on her delicious meat pies; rabbit we could handle, but at the next day's dinner came "Rook Pie." The top crust bulged ominously, and when Auntie Belle cut into it, we saw that the pie was filled with the lumpy, naked corpses of rooks, birds of the crow family, whose main purpose was to supply gravy for the vegetables surrounding them under the piecrust. Their small, bony bodies had practically no meat, but we politely busied ourselves trying to pry a shred or two off their skeletons before giving up and pushing them quietly to the side of our plates.

"TUESDAY, AUGUST 29TH: TOOK BUS ACROSS TOWN TO VISIT THE DITCHFIELDS. EVERYBODY IS WELL EXCEPT GRANDPA."
Mom's family had gathered to welcome us; Gram Ditchfield and Mom's four sisters crowded to the front door when Dad announced our arrival on the big brass knocker. My musical cousin, Alan, was there with four of his R.A.F. dance band members. He spent the war in his uniform entertaining the troops and revolving in British show-biz cocktail parties with movie starlets and fashion models, one of whom he married. Dad remarked scathingly, but with a hidden touch of envy: "Nice work, if you can get it!"

We went upstairs to see Grandpa. The six-foot-tall, jolly man I had known now looked shrunken as he lay in the ornate mahogany bed he had bought so many years ago at the Paris Exposition. He put his hand weakly over Mom's and his voice managed a whisper of welcome. She somehow held back her tears until we were safely outside the room again.

"WEDNESDAY, AUGUST 30TH: THIS MORNING I WENT FOR A 10-MILE BICYCLE RIDE WITH UNCLE ARTHUR. IN THE EVENING WE ALL WENT TO THE HIPPODROME THEATRE TO SEE A VARIETY SHOW STARRING VERA LYNN. NICE."

With no gasoline available to ordinary civilians, feet and bicycles were an alternative, and sometimes the best, form of transportation. Ten miles on either were quite common. Uncle Arthur was an outdoor exercise fanatic, delighted to find that I was willing to rise to the challenge. "Away, lass, let's get started," he roared in his North-Country accent, scarcely waiting for me to finish eating my breakfast. "Ye'll be ready for your lunch by the time we get back; a great way to work up an appetite, by gum! Let t'others sit about and get fat, eh?"

In the largest of Sunderland's theaters that evening, Vera Lynn's face shone out at the audience from under her heavy stage makeup. A great favorite of the troops, she traveled the length and breadth of the war zones to sing for them. Wartime songs had made her famous in person, on the radio, and on the phonograph records of her many hits. The theater echoed with hundreds of voices as we sang along with her. As Dad reminisced on the way home, "Good for Vera! We fairly raised the roof!"

On our way home from the theater, I casually mentioned to my two young cousins, Audrey and Dorothy, that I had met Vera Lynn at Airways House, and that she gave me her autograph. They were so overwhelmed with admiration that from then on they didn't hide hairbrushes in my bed for the rest of our visit!

"THURSDAY, AUGUST 31ST: DENTIST'S APPOINTMENT, BUT HE COULDN'T FIND ANYTHING TO DO, THANK GOODNESS."

Air raids on Sunderland had now stopped; a perfect opportunity for us to get an overdue checkup from the Ditchfield family dentist without interruption. I sat in his chair with some trepidation because I hadn't had a checkup since we returned from Wales two years ago. What a relief, nothing was needed in the way of repairs.

A forerunner of the British National Health Service had begun during the war and was very successful, raising the overall standard of the population's health, both medical and dental, from birth to death. Even though we didn't belong to the Sunderland dentist's panel (his network of patients), we were still eligible for his services free of charge. "No charge?" Dad exclaimed, his canny nature rejoicing: "God bless the N.H.S.!"

Our dentist in Upper Woodside had his office in a stately old Victorian house which I passed on the bus en route to work in London. Our dental appointments always seemed to coincide with air raids, so we missed one after the other. As the V-1s fell all around us, I passed by on the bus one morning and noticed the old house had been bomb-damaged, now showing a huge gaping hole in one wall.

A few days later we read a story in the local paper about a dentist who was in the middle of drilling his patient's tooth when a V-1 fell. The patient and the dentist's chair disappeared, along with half of a wall of the room. When the dust cleared, the dentist found himself on the floor of what was left of this room, still clutching his drill. Through the large hole in the wall, he saw his patient, unhurt but dazed, still sitting in the dentist's chair, now out on the front lawn, surrounded by fallen bricks and plaster.

The entire house eventually had to be demolished, and we never heard from our dentist again!

"SUNDAY, SEPTEMBER 3RD: FIFTH ANNIVERSARY OF THE WAR. TIME TO SAY GOODBYE TO SUNDERLAND. WENT TO SEE AUNTIE CIS AND UNCLE HAL BEFORE WE LEFT. THE ALLIES HAVE OCCUPIED BRUSSELS AND AMSTERDAM. THE AMERICANS TOOK LYONS IN SOUTHERN FRANCE. NAZIS RETREATING ALL OVER EUROPE."
I tried to remember where I had been on each of the five anniversaries of World War Two. Each one had found me in a different world as I evolved from a child into an adult. On this anniversary, for the first time, I was aware of my family members changing from larger-than-life

characters into faded, shrunken old people. I thought of Grandpa and how small he looked in that big bed.

Before we left Sunderland, we went to see Auntie Cis, Grandpa's sister. My diary said: "SHE IS PITIFULLY THIN, AND LOOKS SO ILL."

I closed my eyes. It was New Year's Eve again at the Ditchfields'. There was Grandpa, his laughing face ruddy from the cold, shaking the snow off his boots as he followed First Foot Uncle Hal through the front door. And I could see Auntie Cis, arms outstretched in a theatrical pose. reciting that voluminous, side-splitting poem: "When Father Carved the Goose."

That's how I'll always remember them.

"MONDAY, SEPTEMBER 4TH: WHAT A DIFFERENCE, TRAVELING SITTING DOWN! WE ALL HAD SEATS ON THE TRAIN TODAY! NICE, UNEVENTFUL JOURNEY. LETTERS HAD ARRIVED WHILE WE WERE GONE, FROM BILL, FRANK, BRUCE, PAUL, MAGGIE AND BESSIE FROM WREXHAM, AND FROM FRANK'S WIFE KATE AND HIS DAD IN OHIO."
Well, Mom," I said, after I had read my letters, "the boys are still in England, but it doesn't look as if we'll be seeing them again. Whatever will we do without them?"

Mom looked up from her own little pile of correspondence. "Of course we're going to miss them, Bunty, but when they first came we didn't think their tour of duty in England would even be this long. As to whatever will we do without them, if you ask me, our house will still be full of comings and goings. There's never been a dull moment, and probably never will be!"

I handed Mom the two envelopes from the U.S.A. "Kate sounds awfully nice, Mom, and the letter from Dr. Kopeck is lovely. Here, read them for yourself. Kay wants to know if there's anything they can send us that we can't get over here."

Mom laughed. "That's a good one, bless her heart", she said, "but let's not sound too pitiful or tell her about all our shortages. Maybe it

would be best just to mention that we've had trouble finding embroidery thread and linen to embroider, and let it go at that. I'm sure Frank
has noticed there are other luxuries we're missing but he has enough
on his mind, and if he doesn't mention them to her, I don't think we
should, either."

"THURSDAY, SEPTEMBER 7TH: V-1 LAUNCH SITES OVERRUN BY
ALLIED ARMIES AT PAS DE CALAIS. DOODLEBUGS NOW DEFINITELY
CEASED; HALLELULIAH! THE BLACKOUT IS TO BE RELAXED ON
SEPTEMBER 17TH!"
We were ecstatic that the stuttering sound of the V-1s and their devas-
tating explosions had disappeared from our lives forever.

There were sighs of relief all over Britain with the news of the coming
end of the blackout; I could hardly remember what our streets would
look like with the electric lights on again.

What we didn't know was that Hitler still had a surprise that he
thought could win the war for him--another "V" weapon.

Farewell, Ninth Air Force

"FRIDAY, SEPTEMBER 8TH: U.S. NAVY HAVE REFUSED TO GO TO
CROYDON TO PICK UP FREIGHT! LARGE CONSIGNMENT ARRIVED
TODAY AND DICK DONAHUE CAME IN HIS DRESS UNIFORM TO
COLLECT IT. BUSY DAY AT THE OFFICE. SYD IS ENGAGED! HAD THE
SHOCK OF MY LIFE WHEN BILL AND FRANK APPEARED AT AIRWAYS
HOUSE TO PICK ME UP! 48-HOUR PASS! WHEE!"
Whatever kind of politics had transpired to keep the U.S. Navy in busi-
ness at Airways House we never knew, but I must say Dick Donahue
looked a lot better in his uniform than he did in fatigues!

Syd had been engaged several times before, so nobody was very
impressed by his announcement. Freddy looked up from his desk when
Syd bounced in to announce the news to him, and said gruffly: "I'll drink
to your health when I hear the wedding bells, mate, but not before."

The sudden appearance of Bill and Frank took us all by surprise. There was general celebration at the office. Freddy said with unusual geniality: "I prescribe a weekend off for you, Bunty. I know it's your Saturday 'on,' but don't worry, we'll cover for you."

When Mom came home from work, she was astonished to see our two fliers installed in their favorite armchairs. She and I assembled a strange assortment of leftovers for dinner, but nobody minded. We all stayed up until after midnight, talking, laughing and just being together again.

Saturday flew past. Bill, Frank and I went for a nostalgic walk that morning in Spring Glen Park, stopping at the Manor House tearoom again, and sipping our cups of tea on the terrace overlooking the last blooms of summer in the rose garden. We used up another precious roll of film on views of the park as we walked along paths bordered with brilliant masses of chrysanthemums and dahlias. After lunch we relaxed in each other's company at a double feature movie at our favorite Astoria Theatre in the neighboring suburb, as we had done so often before.

We all knew this time together would be the last time. Once they were sent to France, Bill and Frank would be rotated directly back from there to the U.S. They were already over their quota of missions, so it probably wouldn't be long before this happened. Bill was almost in tears as we wished each other goodnight.

"SUNDAY, SEPTEMBER 10TH: WENT UP TO THE CITY WITH THE BOYS TO SEE THEM OFF AT LIVERPOOL STREET STATION ON THE TRAIN. FEEL ROTTEN. WHO WOULDN'T? WROTE A LONG AND SOULFUL LETTER TO KATE TO QUENCH MY MISERY."

This time I knew deep down that it would be the last time. All we could do now was wait to hear when and where Bill and Frank would be sent out of England.

"TUESDAY, SEPTEMBER 12TH: U.S. TROOPS HAVE ENTERED GERMANY. LE HAVRE HAS FALLEN TO THE BRITISH. CHURCHILL

AND ROOSEVELT MET AT QUEBEC CONFERENCE. HUGE GAS MAIN EXPLOSION REPORTED AS HAVING CAUSED DAMAGE ON THE OUTSKIRTS OF LONDON."

Mom and I were listening to the six o'clock news while we dined off the top of the Morrison shelter. We exulted in reports of the capture of Le Havre, closest French town to England's south coast, where many of the V-1 doodlebugs had left their ramps to attack us. The American army's advance into Hitler's Fatherland was another piece of welcome news. Newspapers carried pictures of Churchill meeting with an ailing Roosevelt in Quebec, Canada, to discuss strategy for the defeat of Japan after victory in Europe was complete.

We knew that the end of the war in Europe, though by no means over, was now in sight. But Hitler wasn't finished with us yet. B.B.C. radio began reporting gas mains exploding near and in London. I could imagine, if Dad had been with us, he would have grunted: "I could have told them they should have replaced those old gas mains before the war, the idiots!"

"FRIDAY, SEPTEMBER 15TH: USS *INTREPID* ATTACKED BY KAMAKAZI PLANES IN PACIFIC. RUMORS AT THE OFFICE THAT 'GAS MAIN EXPLOSIONS' MAY BE V-2s! HAD A LETTER FROM BILL'S MOTHER. SHE SOUNDS NICE, BUT A VERY SHORT NOTE AND NOT TOO ENTHUSIASTIC! I WONDER IF SHE'S BEEN LISTENING TO STORIES OF ENGLISH GIRLS SEDUCING NICE AMERICAN BOYS?"

While the E.T.O. troops were fighting their way through Hitler's Europe, the Allies in the Pacific were still battling the Japanese, a ferocious enemy determined to hold the upper hand. The aircraft carrier *Intrepid* was badly damaged but managed to make it back to San Francisco under her own steam; many years later I was able to stand on her deck when she became an exhibit at the Sea, Air and Space Museum in New York City.

On the home front in Bishop's Hill, without one wail out of Moaning Minnie, two loud crashes outside sent us scurrying from our beds into the Morrison Shelter. We began to suspect that the office rumor was true: Hitler's second secret revenge weapons, the V-2s, were finding targets. The B.B.C. couldn't hide the truth much longer.

Reading the letter from Bill's mother in America, I remember feeling rather more uneasy about its tone than I did about the V-2s. G.I. marriages to British girls were booming, the American newspapers must have been having a field day with "human interest" versions of these romances, no doubt striking terror into the hearts of many worried Moms across the Atlantic. I had the feeling that Bill's mother was probably one of these.

"SUNDAY, SEPTEMBER 17TH: BLACKOUT IN BRITAIN TO BECOME A 'DIM-OUT.' REGULATIONS TO BE MODIFIED TONIGHT. GLORIOUS SUNNY DAY. DAD HOME FOR WEEKEND. SPENT MOST OF DAY GARDENING AND KNITTING MY NEW SWEATER. REPORTS OF MORE FAULTY 'GAS MAINS' BLOWING UP. WHO DO THEY THINK THEY ARE KIDDING? BRITISH AIRBORNE TROOPS LANDED BEHIND GERMAN LINES IN HOLLAND TO TAKE BRIDGE AT ARNHEM. DISASTER!"

The blackout had caused countless accidents, but had been considered essential when Britain was under constant attack by the *Luftwaffe*. The government had now decided to relax the restrictions in Britain and to permit lights the strength of moonlight to be used. They were calling it a "dim-out". However, if an air-raid alert was sounded, the full blackout would be resumed.

Next day the newspapers showed photos of children being brought out into the streets to see the watery lights. The wonderment on their faces showed that many of them had been too young to remember or hadn't even been born when the blackout descended upon Britain. I don't remember a dim-out in London; maybe the Lord Mayor still didn't trust the *Luftwaffe* after the London Blitz. For whatever reason, my diary didn't record the official lifting of our blackout in London for another year.

News broadcasts told us about U.S. and British planes bombing targets ahead of the advancing Allied armies; we knew Frank and Bill would probably be taking part in these missions and would be in harm's way. This weekend Dad had busied himself around the house with touchup painting and other small chores. Over lunch he confided his worries to Mom and me about Bill and Frank. "I feel out of touch with them, now that they're in France. It isn't the same, not being there on the tarmac to welcome them back safe and sound after their missions, and I miss having an occasional beer with them at the pub on the base. Fine lads, both of 'em. With so many missions under their belts, they'll be getting sent home to the States soon, but I'm keeping my fingers crossed they'll be safe right through to their last mission." Dad was thinking of Mom's older brother, who was killed in action on the last day of World War One. Dad worked out his worries by keeping himself busy, and so did I. Gardening and knitting often found space in my diary, my favorite tension-reducing activities.

Listening intently to the six o'clock news, Dad leaned forward in his chair so as not to miss a word. War news on the B.B.C., like the rest of the media, was controlled in wartime by the Ministry of Information. The news was again reporting more gas main explosions. Dad's face was thoughtful but also indignant. "I'll be damned," he muttered, "when they started reporting faulty gas mains exploding, I used to blame poor maintenance. But now I think it's time they stopped trying to fool the public about this. Look at all the tales we're hearing from people in London and in Kent about some new kind of weapons falling out of the sky without any warning and exploding all over the place! Our news isn't reporting what they are, where they fall, or how extensive the damage is, and there must be deaths and injuries, too. The blasted things sound to me like some sort of self-propelled rockets."

"Well, Dad," I said, "the rumors are going around Airways House that they are V-2s."

"If they are, then God help us!" Dad looked glum. "We'll just have to hope and pray our army lads can get to wherever they're being launched in time to stop all the bloody hell they're causing."

Meantime, near Arnhem in Holland, British airborne landings behind enemy lines were being met with disaster: bad luck, faulty intelligence and organizational glitches resulted in their defeat and withdrawal after nine days of fighting. The costly, heroic story has gone down in history, and was even made into the movie *A Bridge Too Far*, which retold these tragic events.

"TUESDAY, SEPTEMBER 19TH: BRUCE IS HOME ON INDEFINITE LEAVE. THINKS HE'S GOING TO BE SENT TO THE PACIFIC!"
Bruce was in and out of our house periodically during the next several days, a little nervous on the one hand, but on the other hand itching for some action. "What I can't stand is the uncertainty, Bunty," he complained. "There's a possibility I'll be back on an L.S.T. again, but where it will be heaven only knows. The European war bash is almost over, but there's still plenty to do in the Far East."

He left the following week, stopping by on the last day of his leave to say goodbye. Mixed with my anxiety about his safety, I felt the familiar old sickening sense of being alone once more. Endless miles stretched between myself and each of the men in my life as one by one they were sent away. And gone again was my social life!

"THURSDAY, SEPTEMBER 28TH: A LETTER FROM BILL, WRITTEN TEN DAYS AGO AND CENSORED! THEY ARE STILL IN ENGLAND, BUT ALL LEAVES ARE CANCELLED. THIS MADE ME FEEL MORE MISERABLE THAN EVER. U.S. NAVY 'WOLF PACK' IS IN FULL HOWL. ONE OF THEM INVITED ME OUT TO DINNER!
Bill's letter looked like a surrealistic painting, blotched and splashed all over with censor's ink at the A.P.O. (American Post Office.) In between the blotted-out words and sentences, I gleaned the news that his squadron was still waiting to be shipped out of England.

At B.O.A.C. our loading dock was weighed down almost daily with shipment after shipment of assorted crates and packages for the U.S. Navy. By now I figured I had met all of James Truman Oates's group of opportunists at the U.S. Navy headquarters office in London. One by one they had appeared with Chief Petty Officer Dick Donahue when he came into my office to bring me the documentation for their air freight. I was beginning to feel like some kind of strange exhibit. Today's shipment was picked up by Don Ratchett, the seaman second class helper who had come with Dick on his last trip. When he ambled into my office waving the invoice in his hand, it confirmed my first impression of a somewhat cocky, unsavory type, in need of a clean shirt and a good shave. He shuffled up to my desk and uttered the words that would do him in, as far as I was concerned: "Hey, kid, how's about a dinner date tonite?" I was stunned. I not only didn't know him from Adam, but I didn't appreciate the way he leered at me or the way he worded his cryptic invitation. Stung by his approach, I thought huffily: "What a nerve! I wonder if the U.S. Navy wolf pack took bets on this? Maybe he won me in a poker game, or was it craps? Or did he just pull the short straw? They must think I'm one of those starving English girls who will do anything for a free meal or a bar of chocolate!"

Mustering a polite English smile, I dismissed him as graciously as I could, trying not to force the words from behind clenched teeth: "Thank you, but no thank you, Mr. Ratchett." My voice dripped with honey. "I have other plans, but it was so nice of you to ask."

And turning my back, I took my time putting his invoice into my filing cabinet until I heard the door close behind him. Yes, my social life had just collapsed again, but I wasn't *that* desperate!

V-2 Rockets, What Next?
"SATURDAY, SEPTEMBER 30TH: THE B.B.C. KEEP REPORTING MORE GAS MAINS EXPLODING, BUT THEY NEVER SAY WHERE. I WONDER HOW LONG THEY CAN KEEP THIS UP? IT'S TERRIFYING."

Gas main explosions continued to be reported by the B.B.C., but it was becoming obvious that something else was exploding! Rumors ran wild, but the existence of the V-2s was not officially acknowledged until November 8th. On November 10th, Churchill made the official announcement to the House of Commons that southeast England had been under rocket attacks for the "past few weeks."

Long after the war, more information was released about the V-2. This was the first human artifact ever to enter outer space. Shaped like a forty-six-foot giant torpedo, the rocket was five feet in diameter. It weighed twelve tons, had a warhead containing one ton of high explosive, and traveled through the upper atmosphere at more than four thousand miles per hour, faster than the speed of sound.

Moaning Minnie's sirens were silent; the V-2s dropped without any advanced warning being possible. Three times the size of the V-1s, and more sophisticated, the V-2s landed randomly on civilian "targets" with an immense explosion, followed by the eerie noise of the rocket speeding through the air as sound caught up with this supersonic ballistic missile. V-2s buried themselves in thirty-foot craters all over London and its suburbs as their warheads detonated, shattering everything in the areas where they fell.

Postwar statistics estimated that more than three thousand V-2s were launched against London, Paris, Antwerp and other cities in England, Holland and France over a period of eight months. Three hundred and fifty per week fell, killing almost three thousand civilians and injuring another six thousand, five hundred. Also killed were almost ten thousand laborers from German concentration camps who were forced to work to produce them, toiling for inhuman purposes and inhuman hours on their meager diet, some literally "working themselves to death."

Meantime, our daily lives had to go on.

"SATURDAY, OCTOBER 7TH: WENT SHOPPING WITH MOM IN CROYDON. STILL CAN'T FIND ANY SHOES TO FIT ME; EVERYONE MUST TAKE A SIZE FIVE! DEPRESSING, ISN'T IT? WE DID FIND SOME OTHER

NECESSITIES, THOUGH, GRIPPER FASTENERS AND HAIRPINS - BETTER THAN NOTHING! WENT TO PURLEY ICE RINK WITH DORIS BOYNTON THIS AFTERNOON."

The morning's shopping trip into Croydon speaks for itself. Mom looked crestfallen. "We'll just have to try a different town, Bunty, and see if they have those things we're looking for. It seems we spend all our weekends off from work these days looking for clothes to replace our worn-out ones." Exasperated, Mom added: "Let's go home. I can't waste any more time in Croydon when I should be home making pies for next week's dinners."

Mom had told me she'd had a visit from Mrs. Boynton, whose family lived some distance up Bishop's Hill. "Oh, Bunty," she said, "I felt so sorry for her. She must have been pretty desperate to come to me for help. Doris is worrying her to death, so depressed because all the young folks she knows have gone away that now she doesn't even want to go out of the house. Mrs. Boynton is wondering if you would take her with you next time you go somewhere!"

Doris Boynton was definitely not one of my favorite people, but at long last we now had something in common; we were the only ones of our generation left in the neighborhood!

"Aha," I thought to myself, "Ever since our own ice rink closed down at the beginning of the Blitz, I've been dying to try out Purley Ice Rink, but it's so far I didn't want to go alone. This is a perfect opportunity!" So here we were, on the bus going across to the other side of Croydon into unknown territory. I stepped on the ice for the first time in two years, gingerly trying out some of the figure-skating moves I had known so well. My diary reported: "MUSCLES VERY STIFF AND AWKWARD. I BET I'LL FEEL IT TOMORROW."

As my skating confidence improved, so did Doris's spirits. My diary entry concluded: "SHE SAYS IT WAS WORTH THE BUS FARE! I SUPPOSE THAT MEANS SHE ENJOYED HERSELF."

Little did I know that my association with Doris would soon change her life forever.

"THURSDAY, OCTOBER 12TH: LETTER FROM BILL FROM FRANCE! THE ALLIES HAVE LIBERATED ATHENS. HAD A LETTER FROM KATE. SHE CAN GET SOME LINEN AND EMBROIDERY FLOSS FOR ME! AT AIRWAYS HOUSE WE MOVED OUR OFFICE TO A LARGER ONE."

Bill's letter was brief. In reply to his last one, I had told him what the censor had done to it. Evidently Bill and his companions had been moved to their new airfield before it was ready to accommodate them; they were in tents, presumably near their airstrip, and he was writing by the unsteady light of a kerosene lamp. At least he was safe, an answer to my prayers.

The Allied advance in southern Europe continued. Greece was rapidly being liberated. On the war front it was tough going. But despite stiff resistance, unforeseen problems and tactical mistakes, the liberating armies were advancing nearer each day to the borders of the Third Reich.

I wrote to Kate, Frank's parents and Bill's mother, telling them the news that the boys were in France, in case they hadn't received letters yet. We hadn't been able to get linen for years, so it was exciting to know Kate planned to send some, and also some embroidery floss. I thought to myself: "Great, I'll be able to add crewel embroidery to the gardening and knitting, in all the spare time I'm going to have. I'm beginning to feel like an old maid!"

For some time the buzz had been going around the office that we were to move to more roomy quarters with fewer windows to pose a threat from flying glass when the V-2s were falling. After one false alarm, the day had finally arrived. Syd was having the time of his life supervising the Silent Workers, a nickname for our janitors that originated because they went so quietly about their duties. In the British class system of those days, this would have been due to "knowing their place" in society; lower-class workers were not expected to chat with their "superiors" who employed them. Although Syd didn't actually employ them, he enjoyed exercising his prerogatives in his higher place on the social scale. The four elderly substitutes who had been recruited to replace their strong young predecessors now in the armed forces, lined up in military fashion, facing him, without a word. Syd bellowed: "Now you lot, you can start with these boxes on yore right, then come back for the ones on yore left." He had raised his voice a couple of decibels, presumably taking it for granted that the current crop of Silent Workers were all old enough to be hard of hearing. The old fellows silently picked up the heavy boxes, put them on dollies and trundled them away for the next two hours, leaving us with an empty room and one telephone.

Suddenly the telephone bell rang. There was a general scuffle while we hunted to find the origin of the sound. The phone was eventually tracked down on the floor under an empty cardboard box protecting it while it waited to be disconnected and moved. Syd pounced on the ringing instrument. "The blarsted thing *would* ring now, while we're in this 'ere mess," he fretted, "but it's prob'ly important." Almost immediately, he announced: "Bunty, it's for you. It's that lieutenant from the U.S. Navy." Sheepishly, I took the phone from his hand.

The pleasant voice of Lieutenant James Truman Oates, U.S.N., came floating over the telephone. "Hi, Bunty. Just thought I'd call to fill you in on something I forgot to tell you about that corner of God's heaven, Iowa, last time we talked." I could feel the full force of Syd's curiosity beamed right at me. Trying to look as cool and businesslike as possible, I said into the telephone: "Oh yes, sir, I remember. I shall take it up with you as soon as we have moved into our new office later today, when I can get to my desk. Thank you for your query. Goodbye, and thank you for calling British Overseas Airways."

I could just imagine Jimmy Oakes saying to his crew: "You were right, guys, she's as nutty as a fruitcake!"

"SATURDAY, OCTOBER 14TH: GENERAL ROMMEL HAS COMMITTED SUICIDE. WENT WITH MOM TO STREATHAM. FOUND SOME DECENT UNDERWEAR TO BUY, WORTH THE CLOTHING COUPONS. STILL NO

SHOES MY SIZE. I'M WONDERING IF THEY HAVE DISCONTINUED MAKING SIZE FIVE."

Irwin Rommel, the brilliant Desert Fox of North Africa and commander of Hitler's Atlantic Wall fortifications, had swallowed poison and killed himself. On the one hand, the Nazis threatened him with condemnation for his participation in the failed plot to assassinate Hitler, which would result in imprisonment or death, and his family would be stripped of his pension and his estate. On the other hand, after the Allies won the war, he would also again face trial and punishment, this time as a war criminal. The handwriting on the wall all spelled his doom; he took the only alternative left to him.

The endless hunt for replacements of our worn-out clothing continued, as Mom and I combed other suburbs. At least after today we could use our old underwear to polish the furniture.

"TUESDAY OCTOBER 17TH: ANOTHER LETTER FROM BILL! ONE LONG GRIPE: COLD, TERRIBLE CONDITIONS, MISERY. POOR DEAR. BUSY AT THE OFFICE."

There wasn't one word censored in Bill's letter. Evidently, no national secret was involved in his litany of complaints! Presumably, his company were camped by their airstrip. Bill's letter could be titled: "The Original Unhappy Camper." He wrote: "The wind whistles through our cold tent all night; I can't get warm so I can't sleep; I'm tired all the time. We have to walk through mud outside to get to the latrine and the mess tent. The latrine is so cold it nearly freezes our butts off. Food isn't that good, either. No electricity. Kerosene lamps for light. They smell up the tent and make it even harder to get to sleep. No mail. I want to come home to you at Bishop's Hill!"

Unable to help poor Bill, I threw myself into work at the new office. Several good things had come from the move; Syd had found me a nice desk lamp and a small electric heater, so I could work more easily in the dim lighting while I kept my feet warm. Buzz found a small unclaimed portable radio in the Lost Property office, so we now had music while we worked. It was surprising what this did for our morale. "Music While You Work" was a special B.B.C. program instituted by the government to improve morale, lasting several hours at a time during the working day. It broadcast a flow of music to factories and offices without interruption, airing the songs and dance music so popular on both sides of the Atlantic during the 1940s. Slightly off-key humming could be heard throughout the office, even from behind Freddy's door; Syd alternately annoyed and entertained us by bursting into song along with the radio. I thought to myself: "This 'war work' isn't half so bad, after all!"

"MONDAY, OCTOBER 23RD: BATTLE OF LEYTE GULF IN THE PACIFIC IS UNDER WAY, WITH JAPANESE KAMIKAZE ATTACKS TAKING A TOLL ON AMERICAN WARSHIPS. NASTY, FOGGY MORNING, YELLOW STUFF THAT CLOGS UP MY THROAT."

The battle of Leyte Gulf is recorded as the largest naval battle in history. For the next three days, the U.S and Australian navies battled the Japanese, for the first time experiencing the deadly fury of suicidal Japanese kamikaze pilots crashing their planes loaded with bombs onto the decks of Allied warships. The story has been immortalized in documentary films and excellent postwar movies.

Remembering last year's ordeal, I dreaded fog season. The gentle mists of October were beginning to change into the thick "pea soup" fogs of November that would paralyze bus travel and make breathing a chore, their thick, damp, yellow air invading our noses and throats with chemical-laden fumes.

Today, while we ate breakfast, Mom listened with some alarm to the B.B.C. weather forecast for dense fog in the London area. "Oh dear," she said, wrinkling up her forehead, which was her usual distress signal, "It won't be any bargain getting lost in a 'pea souper,' but I suppose I'll have to give it a try. What do you think, Bunty? Should I stay home?"

I was in the mood for a bit of whimsy. "Just think, Mom, fighting a pea soup fog to get to and from a job in wartime is part of your patriotic duty. The government will be so proud of you. In fact, they might even create a 'Pea Soup Veterans Medal' in your honor!"

I dodged her slipper as she playfully aimed it at me. We both left earlier than usual to get to our offices. Luckily, this time the fog dispersed by lunchtime. The winds mercifully blew it out to sea and it didn't come back.

Rainbow Corner

"MONDAY, OCTOBER 30TH: WE'RE HAVING PRETTY FREQUENT ROCKET ATTACKS NOW. DAD TOOK AN EXTRA DAY OFF TO PAINT THE DINING ROOM. VERY BUSY DAY AT THE OFFICE. LIEUTENANT OATES STOPPED IN FOR A VISIT. WHAT A BORE!"

The V-2s continued to plague us. One fell close to St. John's Church, destroying several nearby houses, its blast blowing out some of the church's stained-glass windows. Luckily, when the dust settled, St. John's was still standing.

We had practically lived in the dining room ever since the war began. Dad decided to take an extra day off to give it a sorely needed facelift with some paint he found in his toolshed. With Mom and me safely stowed away at work, I could imagine him reveling in the freedom to air some of his favorite nautical epithets as he worked.

At the office I was up to my eyebrows with work. My diary said: "IN THE MIDST OF IT, IN WALKS JAMES TRUMAN OATES, TO TELL ME HE HAS BEEN PROMOTED TO FIRST LIEUTENANT!"

James Truman Oates III perched on the corner of my desk as Buzz scurried away to get him a cup of tea. I thought he had been overdoing the telephone chats lately; maybe he'd fallen out with his girlfriend back in the States. At any rate, I found him very boring, although it **was** kind of flattering that he came in person to tell me the good news of the promotion he expected!

"MONDAY, NOVEMBER 6TH: AXIS FORCES IN GREECE HAVE SURRENDERED. BUSY DAY AT THE OFFICE. PAT TOOK ME TO RAINBOW CORNER RED CROSS CLUB AFTER WORK. VERY IMPRESSIVE. MET MY FIRST TEXAN."

The war in the Mediterranean was winding down. Allied victories in Italy and southern France contributed to the Nazi withdrawal from Greece; Hitler's troops were needed in Western Europe to bolster his defences. The Allied liberation of Greece was a release from the terrible hardships endured under Axis occupation; forty thousand civilians had died in Athens alone from starvation, and tens of thousands more in reprisals for supporting the Greek Resistance. But Greece's troubles would continue with her economy in ruins and bitter internal political strife.

The departure of Bill and Frank had left a void in my life, but also gave me the opportunity to spend more time in the company of the other secretaries at Airways House. Over lunch with Pat, my old stooking partner from college, I complained to her how bored I was at home without the boys' forty-eight-hour passes to look forward to.

Pat said: "Hey, Bunty, I had a hole in my social life, too, but I heard that the Rainbow Corner American Red Cross Club was looking for volunteers. I go there a couple of nights after work to serve coffee and doughnuts and stop by at the dance. How about coming with me next time? The girls they accept as volunteers are so nice; the Red Cross folks are fussy about that."

So after work today Pat and I took the Tube across London to the West End. Rainbow Corner occupied a grand five-story building on Shaftesbury Avenue in the Theatre District that had housed two restaurants. After three months of remodeling, it was ready for the thousands of American non-commissioned servicemen (G.I.s) who passed through London in World War Two.

Above the reception desk was a signpost with a large arrow pointing due west, indicating "New York, 3,271 miles." Pat's pass took us to "Dunker's Den" in the basement, where we dispensed coffee and doughnuts to a noisy, wisecracking line of G.I.s.

After awhile Pat said: "I'll take you up to meet the club director now, Bunty. Let's leave this job to another couple of volunteers.

"Businesslike and petite in her tailored Red Cross uniform, Elsie Celli looked me over and held out her hand. A smile crinkled the laugh lines around her warm, brown eyes. "I see you're a friend of Pat's, Bunty. Welcome to Rainbow Corner." She outlined the rules and objectives of the club. "Thanks for helping with the coffee and doughnuts; now go on up to the ballroom and see what our dances are like. If you'd like to be a volunteer, here's an application form to think about, and there will be a few other formalities. At Rainbow Corner we're proud of our volunteers." Pat and I climbed the ornate staircase to the large ballroom.

I took in the sight before me: a polished parquet floor packed with dancing couples; a "big band" of G.I. professional musicians on the stage playing a Glenn Miller melody; soft lights brightened by the tiny mirrors reflected from a slowly spinning witch ball hanging on its stem from the ceiling; little tables and chairs surrounding the dance floor. Pat and I found a table and sat down.

Miss Price's ballroom-dancing lessons weren't much help when "Tex," a hefty G.I., lumbered over and asked me for a dance. There had been nothing like the Jitterbug at the Wynnstay Arms or at St. John's. I simply relinquished myself to the wild gyrations of my partner as he flung me out at arm's length, then deftly retrieved me, barely in time to save me from crashing into the nearby couple who were happily bouncing up and down to the music. At last it was over. Out of breath, I headed back to the table with "Tex" at my heels. He rumbled: "Say, ma'am, can I get you a cold Coke?"

Hot and perspiring, I said: "Oh yes, please", wondering what on earth a cold Coke could be. Tex handed me a glass full of brown liquid with a head of foam. Did Elsie Celli say "no alcoholic beverages"? It looked like one to me. Ugh! With a shrug, I closed my eyes and enjoyed America's favorite soft drink to the last drop.

I said goodnight to Pat, hurrying to the station just in time for the last train home at ten o'clock.

"TUESDAY, NOVEMBER 7TH: PRESIDENT ROOSEVELT ELECTED FOR A FOURTH TERM. THE V-2s KEEP COMING. MORE LETTERS FROM BILL AND FRANK FROM FRANCE. FILLED OUT APPLICATION FORM FOR RAINBOW CORNER. 'CHARACTER REFERENCES' ARE NEEDED FROM MINISTER AND DOCTOR."

Our newspapers expressed joy over Franklin Roosevelt's winning an unprecedented fourth term as President of the United States. It meant that Britain still had a friend across the Atlantic who, in spite of worsening illness, was still willing to provide continuity to a situation in which he was better versed than any other American statesman the British could identify.

V-2s continued to fall on the London area at the rate of eight per day. We wondered how much longer it would be before the Allies would reach their launching pads and we would be free again. It would be awhile. After the war we learned that, unlike the V-1s, the V-2s were movable, they could be pulled by truck to launching sites ahead of the Allies as they advanced.

Letters to and from Bill and Frank crossed the English Channel in a steady stream. Great chunks were obliterated by the censor, but enough was left for us to read. A letter from Bill sent from Paris enclosed a delicate lace handkerchief. He wrote that they would be going home soon to the U.S.

The application form for Rainbow Corner asked for endorsement by my minister and doctor. The Vicar of St. John's Church replied promptly, and wrote some nice things about knowing me since I was a child. Luckily, he didn't mention the time I brought a frog to my Sunday School class and let it loose, with disastrous consequences! The following Saturday, Dad came and sat with me while I waited my turn with other patients in the doctor's office, so I could go in and get the other magic signature. I got a clean bill of health.

Mom had been openly opposed to my becoming a volunteer at Rainbow Corner, but she was impressed by all the formalities. "After all, Bunty," she admitted, "I must say the Red Cross seem to be very thorough and reliable, and it'll probably be good for your morale now that Bill and Frank are going home. You never know, once they settle into life back in the U.S., we may never hear from them again."

"FRIDAY, NOVEMBER 10TH: NO MAIL. HOPE BRUCE IS O.K. AND NOT INVOLVED IN THE WALCHEREN LANDINGS. V-2s CONTINUING, BUT NOTHING VERY CLOSE, THANK GOODNESS."

In September the key port of Antwerp in Holland had fallen to the advancing Allies. A strong German garrison was still holding fortified Walcheren Island in the river estuary outside Antwerp, effectively blocking the route for shipping which had to travel past the island to access the port. The B.B.C. announced that on November 1st, three thousand British and Canadian troops had made amphibious landings on Walcheren in order to clear the path to Antwerp, a crucial port for the flow of supplies needed to guarantee the momentum of the Allied advances through Holland into Germany. The Walcheren landings had been costly; about one thousand men were lost or wounded. Four out of every five landing craft were lost; one had received a direct hit. I worried about Bruce's safety; his Navy duties involved landing craft. I needn't have worried, though; Bruce's next letter talked about coming home on leave for Christmas!

"MONDAY, NOVEMBER 13TH: WE'VE SUNK THE *TIRPITZ*! HOORAY! VERY COLD DAY. ICE ON THE BIRDBATH. PAT AND I WENT TO RAINBOW CORNER AFTER WORK, TAKING MY APPLICATION FOR MISS CELLI. ENJOYED OUR EVENING. I STAYED OVERNIGHT AT PAT'S APARTMENT".

Over the years, repeated attempts by the R.A.F. and the Royal Navy had failed to destroy Germany's *Tirpitz*, sister battleship to the *Bismarck* and a menace to Allied shipping. On November 12th, thirty R.A.F. Lancaster bombers attacked the *Tirpitz*, moored in a fjord in German-occupied Norway. About ten minutes after the first bomb struck, the *Tirpitz* capsized, only the hull remaining visible from the air. She took down one thousand of her crew with her. The bombers all returned safely to base.

Winter was nipping at us as I went again with Pat after work to Rainbow Corner. This time I felt more comfortable in the beautiful ballroom. As I told Mom when I came home: "Every partner I had told me more about "God's Country"! I'm even getting so I can handle that tricky Jitterbug! It's fun, Mom!" For the first time in weeks I was bubbling with excitement. Mom heaved a sigh of relief.

Two days later, Elsie Celli called me. "Your application to become an American Red Cross volunteer has been approved, Bunty," she said with that lilting voice of hers, and I could visualize the corners of those warm, brown eyes crinkling in her pert face. She added: "The House Committee just voted you in."

I was to discover that the House Committee ran Rainbow Corner's social events. They met regularly, and consisted of English girl volunteers, balanced with the same number of GI.s who were stationed in London. Their input was valuable to the running of the club, and they could be relied on as a core work group when special events took place.

"THURSDAY, NOVEMBER 16TH: DORIS BOYNTON CAME UP TO THE OFFICE WITH ME TODAY. SHOWED HER OVER AIRWAYS HOUSE. BUSY DAY. NO LETTERS FROM ANYONE. BOO! WONDER IF BILL HAS GONE BACK TO THE U.S. YET. AND WHERE IS BRUCE?"

Doris Boynton was out of a job. Her mother had visited Mom before to ask if I would take Doris out with me to lift her sagging spirits, which resulted in our trip beyond Croydon to skate away an afternoon at an unfamiliar ice rink. Taking the unattractive, silent Doris with me had made me feel rather noble, and I figured my duty had been done. Now a distraught Mrs. Boynton had come again to see Mom, and had burst into tears over her cup of tea.

"Oh, Mrs. Amiss," she sobbed, mopping her eyes with a well-used handkerchief. "I don't know what I'm going to do with our Doris, she's that depressed. She's lost her job, and we don't want her to be called up into the armed forces. That's no place for my sweet little girl. She's been going to night school to learn typing, and I wonder if your Bunty knows of anywhere at B.O.A.C. where she might get employment?" She mopped her eyes again; Mom sympathetically refilled her teacup. After a third cup of tea and reassurances from Mom, Mrs. Boynton went home.

As planned, Doris came with me on the bus to Airways House. She had made an attempt to improve her looks; her hair was newly waved, she had applied a little lipstick, and her outfit was in good taste and quite attractive. When I showed her around the lavish passenger lounges she was duly impressed, but my workday was beckoning and I left her with a "V" sign at the Personnel Office, and a promise to take her with me to Rainbow Corner the following day.

Hands Across the Sea

"FRIDAY, NOVEMBER 17TH: ALBANIA LIBERATED BY PARTISANS. DORIS CAME TO THE OFFICE AS ARRANGED, TOOK HER WITH ME TO RAINBOW CORNER."

By the time of its liberation from the Nazis by partisans after a twenty-day battle, Albania was one of the most devastated of all countries in Europe, with sixty thousand houses demolished and one tenth of the population homeless.

Mom was pensive as she ate her breakfast toast, her mind on things closer to home. "Poor Mrs. Boynton--I think I feel more sorry for her than I do for Doris," she murmured, "but I really don't know what I can do for her."

"Well, Mom, I'll keep up the momentum with Doris and see if I can shake her out of her doldrums," I replied. "As a matter of fact, I've offered to bring her to Rainbow Corner with me after work today."

Good luck, dear." Mom put her arm around my shoulders. "Just don't let Doris's gloom rub off on you!"

Doris turned up at my office on the dot of six o'clock. We had a sandwich at a nearby coffee shop, took the Tube to Piccadilly, then walked over to Rainbow Corner. I signed Doris in as my guest, and we followed the sounds of dance music up the stairs to the ballroom. Doris soon calmed down, and I sat with her awhile until two G.I.s came and held out a hand to each of us to invite us to dance.

I had never seen Doris enthusiastic about anything, but now she was thrilled when I found her sitting at our little table at the edge of the dance floor. "Oh, Bunty," she effervesced, "I've met such a nice boy from Boston. He seems so lonely, and neither of us really knew how to dance, so we just sat and talked. He's stationed near London and he wants to see me again!"

I didn't see Doris much after that. We went together to Rainbow Corner one more time and she ignored me, spending the entire evening with her Boston boyfriend. She joined Rainbow Corner's volunteers, but she never stopped in to visit Mom and me, nor to tell us the outcome of her bid for a job at B.O.A.C. Disgusted, I huffed to Mom: "Well, how d'you like that? I'm washing my hands of *her!*"

"THURSDAY, NOVEMBER 23RD: FREDDY IS AWAY. SYD IS AWAY. BRAD DEPARTED AT NOON, LEAVING ME "IN CHARGE." TERRIFYING! FORTUNATELY, NO FLAPS, AND NO U.S. NAVY. CLOSED OFFICE AT 6 P.M. CAME HOME EXHAUSTED!"

As usual, I survived. Luckily for me, the afternoon went fast, without any "flaps," my name for office emergencies. The telephone had been strangely quiet, without the usual chatty calls from the U.S. Navy. I had forgotten this was Thanksgiving Day in America, which meant that Jimmy Oates and his crew were probably celebrating the holiday with a day off and a Thanksgiving dinner.

"FRIDAY, NOVEMBER 24TH: ALLIES CAPTURED STRASBOURG. FIRST B-29 RAID ON TOKYO. DAD IS BRINGING ANOTHER G.I. HOME THIS WEEKEND."

The Allies captured Strasbourg on the German border. We hoped the German retreat would soon bring us relief from the V-2s, but they were moving them ahead of the Allied advance, and it would be the following year before we were free of them.

The uphill battle of the war in the Pacific was slowly turning in favor of the Allies. Flying the new B-29 "Super Fortress" bomber, the American air force could now attack the Japanese mainland from its air bases for the first time, a landmark date in World War Two. One hundred and eleven B-29s made their first raid on Tokyo, with only one aircraft lost.

From his most recent letter, I gathered there was hope that I would see Bruce again before he left for overseas. Time would tell.

Meantime, Dad was still doing his "Reverse Lend-Lease" on the latest American air base that he had supplied with purified drinking water.

He was bringing another G.I. home for the weekend. I remarked rather wearily to Mom: "He really bombed with the first one, but redeemed himself with Bill and Frank. I wonder what this one will be like?"

"SUNDAY, NOVEMBER 26TH: HAULED LARRY BRIDGES AROUND ALL OVER LONDON TODAY. I WAS BORED STIFF WITH HIM. WHAT A DRIP! IF THAT'S TEXAS, GIVE ME WISCONSIN EVERY TIME!"
Dad's latest "thank you" for Lend-Lease left me without any enthusiasm. Larry Bridges was from Texas, and getting conversation out of him was like wringing it out of a dry towel. My diary summed it up: "*What a drip!*" He showed little or no interest in famous London landmarks, but did remember to thank Mom for her hospitality when he left. His name never appeared again in my diary.

"TUESDAY, NOVEMBER 28TH: ALLIES CAN NOW USE ANTWERP AS A MAJOR SUPPLY PORT. HEAVY RAINS HAVE OUR TROOPS BOGGED DOWN IN ITALY. ADVANCE THERE IS AT A STANDSTILL. AT THE OFFICE BRAD IS SURE WE HAVE A RAT!"

Thanks to the Allied victory in the fight for Walcheren Island in Holland and to successful repairs to the sabotage damage done to the port of Antwerp by the Nazis as they retreated, it was now possible for the large quantities of supplies needed to support the advancing Allies to flow unchallenged into Europe. Sunny Italy became muddy Italy as once more the battered Allied armies were halted by the weather in the face of stiff opposition from Nazi defenders.

At the office, a different battle was looming. As usual, Syd had to make a joke out of it. Dancing around Brad's desk, balancing a cup of tea in one hand, he chuckled: "'Ere,'ere, Brad, wot's all this about a r-a-t? And at rat-proof B.O.A.C. 'eadquarters, no less? 'Ooever 'eard of such a thing? Brad, I think you're sufferin' from him-a-jin-ayshun over-load'! Wot you need is some time off! A rat, indeed!"

Brad had been even more melancholy since losing his home to a V-1. He raised sad brown eyes from his desk, piled with paperwork. Then he waved a limp hand to the side of the room. "O.K., Syd," he intoned in his usual monotone, "just you go and have a look in that fil-ing cabinet. You can see some droppings, and some of our file folders have been chewed. And unless *you* did it when you'd had too many beers, I think we have a rat!" The Silent Workers were summoned. They swarmed all around the evidence, clucking quietly at each other, with-out a word, as they removed the droppings and the chewed file covers and prepared for battle by putting down rat poison. In the next few days, the rat poison went untouched, and there were no more drop-pings. This was very smart rat!

Syd couldn't resist another dig at Brad. Popping his head around the door of Brad's office, he chortled: "Ha, there you are, Brad, me lad. Your rat 'as disappeared like greased lightning. 'E must've 'ad such a bellyache arfter chewin' them folders that 'e never came back to try out the rat poison!"

Brad shrugged, refusing to give Syd the satisfaction of a reply. Syd, deflated, retreated back to his own office, muttering to himself: "That chap 'as no sense of yewmer."

"THURSDAY, NOVEMBER 30TH: WENT TO COLLECT A PACKAGE AT POST OFFICE FROM KATE IN THE U.S.A. WROTE TO THANK HER AND TELL HER THE LATEST NEWS ABOUT BILL AND FRANK."

"Old Charlie," our mailman, delivered only letters and packages small enough to fit through the front-door mail slot. Too old to serve in the armed forces, he had been recruited out of retirement to fill the shoes of a younger man of conscription age. In all weather he trudged three times a day up and down Bishop's Hill with a heavy mail sack over one shoulder, making his deliveries.

During the war, most civilians still relied heavily on letters to stay in touch. Telephone calls were expensive, so they were reserved for emergencies and limited to very few words without much chitchat. For those without a home phone, there was a bright red public telephone booth at the corner of Bishop's Hill, containing a pay phone and a fat telephone directory dangling at its side on a long chain.

Charlie had left a slip with the mail. A package was waiting for pick-up at our nearest post office in West Woodside. I had come home early from work, so there was plenty of time to get there before it closed. I took the bus to West Woodside and picked up a neatly wrapped package from America. Kate had sent the items I had said we could use: several yards of linen fabric and a rainbow of colored embroidery threads. I thought to myself: "It's just like prewar; crewel embroidery fixings! First I'll make a cushion cover for Kate and Frank--a little housewarming present for when they settle down."

Tucked between the folds of linen in the package was a surprise bonus: nail polish, eyebrow pencil, mascara, and what my diary called "a pair of fully fashioned nylons." I impulsively kissed them--what a welcome contrast to the shapeless Utility lisle ones I had to wear. These actually were shaped like a human leg!

"SATURDAY, DECEMBER 2ND: BRITISH HOME GUARD HAS BEEN DISBANDED. ANOTHER PACKAGE CAME, THIS TIME FROM FRANK'S

MOM AND DAD. THREE PRETTY APRONS, GORGEOUS UNDERWEAR, MORE NYLONS, CANDY AND POPCORN!"

An encouraging sign that the war ending was the announcement of the disbanding of the 1.5 million Home Guard volunteers, largely composed of men too old for the armed forces and of youths too young, from the ages of seventeen to sixty-five. Uniformed and well-trained, they were dubbed "weekend warriors" or "Dad's army." As our second line of defence in the event of a Nazi invasion in the dark days after Dunkirk, they also performed many duties with regular army units and assisted civilian defence organizations.

The second package from the U.S.A. was for Mom and Dad as well as for me. Mom unwrapped three aprons, delicately made of organdy edged with wispy lace. "I'll really 'wow' the old girls next time I have them here for tea," she said, proudly modeling them, one by one. But this wasn't all; there were candy bars and a box of popcorn for Dad, a pair of nylons and two pretty slips for me.

Tears came as I ran my fingers gently over the two slips frothing with lace. "Just look at these, Mom: aren't they beautiful? I can't remember ever seeing anything like them."

I felt as though I could almost touch the hands of this loving family who had packed such beautiful gifts. Next time I looked out of the bus window at the Lend-Lease poster proclaiming "Hands across the Sea," I now fully appreciated what it meant. After supper Mom and Dad went into the kitchen, and I heard Dad reading the instructions on his box of popcorn while Mom heated up the frypan. We munched our way through the six o'clock news, then out came pens and paper. Heartfelt "thank-you" letters were soon ready to mail to Kate and to Frank's parents.

"MONDAY, DECEMBER 4TH: HAD A LETTER FROM KATE. SHE'S UPSET BECAUSE SHE ISN'T GETTING FRANK'S MAIL FROM FRANCE. BRUCE CAME HOME ON LEAVE. HE PICKED ME UP AT THE OFFICE FOR DINNER AND A SHOW."

I felt so sorry for Kate. She seemed to be clinging to us like a lifeline to hear news of Frank, which was so slow in coming from France through the A.P.O. channels. They had tried so hard to start a family before Frank went overseas, but were unsuccessful; Kate still said how badly she wanted a baby in case Frank didn't return, so she would still have part of him. I didn't have any idea that I would be meeting with Kate and the Kopeck family in the not-too-distant future!

While I was waiting at the office for Bruce to arrive for our date, I took a trip down memory lane. I remembered the prewar days when he used to roller skate by my home in Bishop's Hill, too shy to stop and say "hello." When our schools were evacuated at the beginning of the war, and I found he was billeted across the street, he became my first serious crush as a fourteen-year-old schoolgirl. In my wildest dreams, how could I have imagined that in a few years this shy schoolboy would have become the handsome, self- assured man escorting me to dinner and the theater in London's posh West End? No doubt conscious of his naval officer's uniform, Bruce chose an upscale restaurant and one of the best stage shows in London. I thought I was in seventh heaven!

A few days later Bruce left for duty in the Far East. Little did I know about surprise events to come, or that I would never see him again.

A Music-World Tragedy

"SATURDAY, DECEMBER 16TH: GLENN MILLER IS MISSING IN SMALL PLANE OVER ENGLISH CHANNEL. CHRISTMAS CARDS ARE ARRIVING. GERMANS HAVE LAUNCHED A COUNTEROFFENSIVE IN THE ARDENNES. BITTER FIGHTING. HEAVY CASUALTIES."

What a shock! Famous bandleader Glenn Miller went missing in a small private plane on his way to Paris to prepare a morale-boosting concert for the Allied forces there. The mystery of the plane's disappearance with its three passengers remains. There are several theories, but no trace of plane or passengers has ever been found.

Glenn Miller, brilliant arranger, composer and band leader, was admired and loved by millions on both sides of the Atlantic. As a U.S. Army Captain, he came to England in 1944. His American Band of the A.E.F.(Allied Expeditionary Forces) was legendary; to the dismay of watching generals, he revamped the "Saint Louis Blues" into a march, a delight to his band and to those who march ever since.

Instituted with the cooperation of the B.B.C., the American Forces Network broadcast his music not only to Britain but also eventually beamed it to Europe and the U.S.A. In October and November of 1944, Glenn Miller collaborated with General Eisenhower's Psychological Warfare Division in creating "Music for the Wehrmacht" programs beamed to Europe for the German armed forces, hosted by a female, German-speaking announcer and with Miller's greetings and propaganda conveyed in his halting German. Miller also broadcast from Rainbow Corner's "Dunker's Den" in a series of weekly programs called *An American Eagle in Britain* masterminded by the B.B.C.'s ace producer Cecil Madden, during which a segment was set aside for G.I.s selected in the Club to send greetings to their families and friends back in the U.S. In 1944 a homesick twenty-year-old G.I. from New Jersey was interviewed on Thanksgiving Day, using most of his allotted time to describe every item on Rainbow Corner's Thanksgiving Day dinner menu. He brought the tape home with him, and I get it out periodically just to hear his voice again. You guessed right: he became my husband!

Christmas cards from Old Charlie's mail sack were arriving. Paul's was the first. Peter's had no return address; we had no idea where he was; William's came from the R.A.F. training camp where he was now an instructor. Cards came from the family in Sunderland, the girls in Wales, Bill and Frank in France, my cousin Lew with the R.A.F. Bruce sent all his love from heaven-knows-where. But the card that would mark another turning point in my life was from "all at Rainbow Corner."

As we prepared for Christmas at Bishop's Hill, American troops were pinned down under enemy fire in the snowy Ardennes mountains. Pouring his remaining Panzer divisions into the attack, Hitler personally ordered the desperate offensive which he fantasized could win back the Allies' supply port of Antwerp. This turning point in the war would be known as the Battle of the Bulge.

The winter of 1944 was the coldest on record in Europe in fifty years. We shuddered at the newspaper photographs of American soldiers as they struggled against the intense cold in the Ardennes mountains, battling not only crack Nazi troops, but weather that froze both their bodies and their equipment. The Battle of the Bulge lasted more than a month. After the war, the estimated cost in losses was published: 89,500 Americans killed, 47,500 wounded, 23,000 captured or missing. British losses: 1,408 killed or wounded, 239 missing. German losses: 84,834 killed or wounded; other estimates put German losses at between 60 to 100,000 killed, wounded and missing. It was the largest and costliest battle for the Allies in World War Two.

"SATURDAY, DECEMBER 23RD: BILL'S LETTER TODAY SAID THEY ARE GOING BACK TO THE STATES. THIS WILL BE BEST FOR BOTH OF US, I BELIEVE."
Although I had expected this news, there was a finality about Bill's letter from France. In a way, I felt a sense of release. I was beginning to realize that my life could be what I made it; the possibilities were exciting and promising. I wasn't ready yet for a commitment to anybody. But my story and Bill's wasn't over yet!

"MONDAY, DECEMBER 25TH: WHAT A STRANGE CHRISTMAS. MAY I NEVER HAVE A WORSE ONE! FEEL DEPRESSED AND MISERABLE. WEATHER IS TERRIBLE, FOGGY AND COLD. BUS, TRAIN AND TUBE STRIKE IS ON IN LONDON. WENT WITH MOM AND DAD TO SPEND THE EVENING WITH MR. AND MRS. POPE."
For me, this was the loneliest Christmas I can remember. We put up the usual decorations, but somehow my heart wasn't in it. We exchanged little gifts; among mine was a new diary for 1945. Dad said it all when

he put his arms around Mom and me. "The best gift of all this Christmas is that the three of us are together and the war has left us unscathed. There's so much for us to be thankful for." It was a good reminder.

Knowing we would be alone on Christmas Day, Dad's employee, Charlie Pope, had asked him if we would like to join his family for the evening. Tiny Mrs. Pope, her round face beaming, welcomed us at the door. She twittered: "'Appy Christmas, folks, come in quick, out of the cold." Mom handed her a small gift--an embroidered kitchen apron she knew Mrs. Pope could use. In the small living room decorated with paper chains hanging from the ceiling, the Pope family sat in a semicircle around the fireplace, cheerful Cockney people, all about the same age as my parents. I listened to their lighthearted banter and laughed at the appropriate places, but I felt like a spectator rather than part of the gathering.

I thought wistfully of the lively Christmas dance I was missing at Rainbow Corner, but although loyalty to my parents would probably have kept me at home anyway on Christmas Day, the heavy fog and a widespread transportation strike made travel on London buses, trains and the Tube impossible, so the decision was made for me! Mrs. Pope served the Christmas cake and glasses of wine. We toasted Christmas, 1944, and Charlie made a short speech, ending with: "Well, folks, may the good Lord bless us, one an' h'all. We've got through, safe this far, let's 'ope the war will soon h'end and that next Christmas we'll be at peace 'agin." A chorus of "'Ere,'ere," one last toast to the New Year, and it was time to leave.

As Charlie helped us into our coats, Mrs. Pope handed Mom a brightly wrapped package. She warned: "'Old it carefully, Mrs. Amiss, h'it's frajile." Sure enough, when Mom unwrapped it at home, it contained six fresh eggs from Mrs. Pope's chicken coop.

When I saw the newspaper photographs of American soldiers miserably huddled in the sleet and frozen mud on the Ardennes battlefront, I felt ashamed that I had grumbled about the weather and lack of excitement on Christmas Day.

"WEDNESDAY, DECEMBER 27TH: WENT TO RAINBOW CORNER DANCE AFTER WORK. MET HANK MORTON, DECENT FELLOW FROM NEW ORLEANS. HE'S VERY INTERESTING; THINK I'LL BRING HIM HOME FOR THE WEEKEND."

It was my turn to rescue a homesick G.I., and also my chance to re-deem my misjudgment of Butch's character the previous year. Hank Morton was a shy sergeant from New Orleans. He was with the U.S. War Department's Transportation Corps, stationed on an army trans-port ship ferrying supplies and personnel across the English Channel to the Allied forces in Europe. Hank's ship was berthed at the London docks; Rainbow Corner had become his second home when he was in port. He was a lively and interesting conversationalist, and when we met at the Rainbow Corner dance, we had spent more time talking than dancing.

One of the topics we discussed, sitting at the edge of the dance floor, sipping our "cold Cokes," was the American game of football. I had never seen it played, and spontaneously Hank exclaimed: "Gee whiz, Bunty, yore education shore has bin neglected. How'd y'all like to come along with me to the football game on Sunday at White City Stadium?"

Then and there I decided to ask Mom if I could invite Hank for New Year's. Again she rose gallantly to the challenge. The fact that Dad would be home for New Year's probably reassured her that a mis-take like Butch would never be made again. "Yes, Bunty," she said with a smile, "of course it will be O.K. He must be a decent type, or he wouldn't be content with Rainbow Corner—instead he'd be out like that wild lot your Gram talks about in Sunderland, carousing and getting into trouble. If you like, he can stay over so you can go together to the football game on New Year's Eve."

"FRIDAY, DECEMBER 29TH: THIS MORNING HANK CALLED ME AT THE OFFICE TO MAKE SURE HE WOULD SEE ME TONIGHT AT THE CLUB. TOLD HIM ABOUT OUR INVITATION FOR NEW YEAR'S. HE'S

THRILLED. HE HAS MET SOME OF FRANK ROSATO'S E.T.O. BAND MEMBERS, ALSO FROM NEW ORLEANS. BROUGHT HIM HOME WITH ME ON THE TRAIN."

Hank was overcome when he called me this morning and I invited him to come to Upper Woodside for New Year's. His voice cracked with surprise, and he croaked: "Aw gee, Bunty, that's mighty nice of yore Mom. You bet I'll come! Oh, by the way, I just met some boys from New Orleans, my home town; they play in Frank Rosato's band here at Rainbow Corner. They-all will be in the big band at the game tomorrow. Chee, what a small world!"

The E.T.O. band and its bandmaster Frank Rosato, were fixtures in London. Frank had formed a smaller dance band with musicians picked from the larger one, who played regularly at Rainbow Corner. Part of the allure of the Club was its dance bands; small groups of professional musicians from U.S. Army, Navy and Air Force bands. The names of some of the groups were listed at the back of my diary: "The V-Mailers," "The Continentals," "The 36th Airborne," "The Gremlins" and "The Rosatos," led by Frank Rosato himself. Rainbow Corner really had the best!

Hank and I took the train home and he met Mom and Dad. He soon settled into a lively chat with Dad, home for New Year's, who in all probability enjoyed the change of pace with some male company.

"SATURDAY, DECEMBER 30TH: WENT UP TO LONDON WITH HANK TO THE QUEENS ICE RINK. HE CAN SKATE O.K. BUT OBVIOUSLY HASN'T FOR AGES. HAD LUNCH, THEN WENT TO MOVIES TO SEE *FRENCHMAN'S CREEK*. NOT AS GOOD AS THE BOOK, BUT VERY ENJOYABLE."

Our ice-skating session was a bit disappointing as Hank was not by any stretch of the imagination a skilled skater, but we had a pleasant morning, a tasty lunch, and saw an enjoyable movie.

Mom produced a traditional roast beef and Yorkshire pudding dinner with the small roast she had managed to find at the butcher's shop. She confided to me in the kitchen: "Now, that's more like a nice

American boy, Bunty. Rather an odd accent, but he's very easy to entertain. Good for you!" Dad was obviously happy with Hank's company, too. The two of them went off to "The Conquering Hero" after dinner for a quick beer in a typical English pub.

"SUNDAY, DECEMBER 31ST: WENT WITH HANK TO SEE MY FIRST AMERICAN FOOTBALL GAME AT WHITE CITY. WHAT'S IT ALL ABOUT?"

White City Stadium, in North London, had been built in 1908 for the Olympics, and had a capacity of one hundred and fifty thousand. I could hardly hide my excitement as Hank and I took the train to the football game. The stadium was packed with American servicemen; I began to realize just how many must be stationed in Britain! My diary continued: "COULDN'T MAKE MUCH OF AMERICAN FOOTBALL, BECAUSE IT SEEMS TO CONSIST MOSTLY OF THE PLAYERS THROWING THEMSELVES INTO PILES ON TOP OF EACH OTHER AT REGULAR INTERVALS. HANK DID HIS BEST TO EXPLAIN IT TO ME. THE HEADQUARTERS BAND OF THE E.T.O. SOUNDED GREAT AT HALF-TIME."

I'm sure I was too polite to tell Hank, but, for me, the half- time performance of the marvelous E.T.O. band was the best part of the game! We had brought Dad's binoculars with us, and from our perch high in the stadium Hank pointed out his new buddies. I thought I'd better prepare him for the First-Footing. "Hank, at midnight tonight you are going to witness a typical North Country English tradition. I won't spoil the surprise by telling you about it." Just before midnight Dad disappeared outside, leaving Hank with a look of concern on his face. As the dining-room clock struck twelve, Dad knocked on the front door, our First Foot for 1945. Mom answered the door, and Hank and I stood behind her in the front hall. Hank looked relieved that Dad hadn't left home for good!

"A Happy, Healthy and Prosperous New Year to the Lady of the House, and all Within," intoned Dad, in his best North Country accent. "Here's food, drink and warmth for the New Year." He handed Mom a box of salt, a half-empty bottle of sherry and a piece of coal wrapped in a small plastic bag, so as not to dirty Mom's hands. I explained this strange custom to Hank to prevent his concluding that we had all gone crazy. We all exchanged New Year's hugs, then "brought in the New Year" by drinking a toast to it with the remains of the prewar sherry.

I wondered what Hank would write home to his folks about First-Footing! As Hank joined us for our traditional midnight supper, he said quietly to Mom: "Thanks, ma'am, for letting me share a great New Year's Eve, with a real family in a real home."

Our guest room had its first occupant for 1945.

Not to Canada, but to Wales in my new tweed coat

Bessie, me and Maggie

Model of a 'Doodlebug' V-1

The love of my life, Al Greene

We Fight On

"WEDNESDAY, JANUARY 3RD: JUST AFTER I ARRIVED AT THE OFFICE, A V-2 EXPLODED ABOUT 100 YARDS FROM AIRWAYS HOUSE. DIRECT HIT ON CHELSEA PENSIONERS' HOME. HEAVY CASUALTIES."
Although not as frequently as before, V-2 rockets were still falling on London, and one fell too close for comfort to the office this morning. No air-raid sirens had sounded; flying faster than the speed of sound in the stratosphere, V-2s could not be detected, seen or heard until they landed and exploded.

As the rocket detonated we felt the blast, but this time we had no glass left in the windows for it to break. Airways House seemed to rock on its foundation, seconds after the earsplitting sound of the explosion. Then there was silence, followed by a strange whistling, moaning noise that we realized was the sound catching up with the supersonic missile as it had fallen through the air.

Freddy walked unsteadily out of his office and shouted: "Is everyone O.K.?" One by one, we pulled ourselves together and replied "Yes." After a few stiff cups of tea, we got back to work.

The rocket had landed nearby on the Chelsea Old Age Pensioners' Home for retired servicemen. Some did not survive the V-2; many more were injured. Newspaper photos of rescue teams digging them out of the wreckage made my heart ache for these poor old men who had served their country so well, losing the security of their only home. Again, I felt hatred for the Nazis, but relief that once more I was a survivor.

"TUESDAY, JANUARY 9TH: SURPRISE! TODAY A LETTER ARRIVED FROM FRANK'S BROTHER, BOB, A SERGEANT WITH THE U.S.

NINTH ARMY IN GERMANY, WRITTEN DECEMBER 11TH! HE SAYS IF HE GETS LEAVE HE WOULD LIKE TO COME AND VISIT US. WROTE BACK IMMEDIATELY, AS WE DIDN'T WANT HIM TO THINK WE HAD RECEIVED HIS LETTER AND IGNORED HIM."

The address on Bob Kopeck's envelope showed he was with an anti-tank company in an infantry regiment; judging from the date of his heavily censored letter, he might be involved in the Battle of the Bulge! He must have been wondering why we hadn't answered it. We mailed him an invitation to our home without delay.

"WEDNESDAY, JANUARY 10TH: WAR NEWS PRETTY GOOD, EXCEPT FOR BATTLE OF THE BULGE STILL CONTINUING. WENT TO RAINBOW CORNER IN EVENING. HAVE HAD MY SURFEIT OF HANK."

In the Ardennes, General Patton's tanks had failed to close a planned trap around the Germans, who would have been surrounded and cut off, had the plan succeeded. Savage fighting continued in the worst winter conditions imaginable.

The news was better in the Far East, in spite of increased Japanese kamikaze attacks on Allied warships. Japanese troops were retreating in Burma, and American B-29 bombers had again bombed Tokyo.

At Rainbow Corner this evening I decided I had had enough of Hank. In the days following our trip to see the football game, he had bombarded me with daily phone calls at my office. He insisted on coming there to pick me up after work, for dinner or to go to one of the Rainbow Corner dances--it was too much "togetherness" for me to handle! He was a nice boy, but I wasn't ready to be monopolized by his attentions, which were getting to be overwhelmingly possessive. As Dad would have said: "It's time for Hank to get the 'heave-ho.'" But Hank was not ready to be given the "heave-ho"!

"WEDNESDAY, JANUARY 17TH: BATTLE OF THE BULGE IS OFFICIALLY OVER. GERMANS HAVE SURRENDERED. HITLER RUMORED TO BE HOLED UP IN A BUNKER IN BERLIN WITH HIS STAFF AND EVA BRAUN. RUSSIANS ON THE OFFENSIVE AGAIN IN EAST PRUSSIA. BURMA

ROAD REOPENED. I WONDER WHERE BILL AND FRANK COULD BE? NO MAIL YET. THEY MUST BE BACK IN THE U.S. BY NOW! HANK ISN'T GIVING UP!"

The official date of victory in the Battle of the Bulge was announced on the six o'clock B.B.C. news, as well as rumors of Hitler's whereabouts. The clearing of the Burma Road, that essential link for traffic in the Far East, which had been under siege for so long, was wonderful news.

Mom's spirits had hit a new high. "Victory's in the air, Bunty; I can almost taste it," she said with a grin, then added more soberly, "but there's still a long way to go in the Far East." She was right, but after all the bumps we'd been through on the long road of the war in Europe, we were at last feeling hopeful that the "good old days" could really return.

My diary mentioned several times in the following days the fact that Hank was being persistent. The greatest challenge was his daily phone barrage. Fortunately, he always called at the same time, so I finally resorted to having Buzz answer the phone for me, and say I was busy and couldn't talk. After awhile Hank got the message. Exit another G.I.

There was no news of Bill and Frank, but as Dad said in a letter from across Britain written from his latest water purification plant: "Let's take a quote out of their own book, 'No news is good news.' But you never know, they might have just put us on the shelf with the rest of their wartime memories. Two more ships may have passed in the night.'" So we waited, and waited. Mentally, I wrote off Bill and Frank.

"THURSDAY, FEBRUARY 1ST: A LETTER FROM MAGGIE, INVITING ME TO SPEND A FEW DAYS IN WREXHAM AT EASTER. TOOK A TEST FOR A JOB UPGRADE AT AIRWAYS HOUSE. PASSED IT O.K. IT'S TIME I HAD A RAISE!"

At this point, a visit to Wrexham appealed to me; I needed to have a change of scenery. I accepted Maggie's invitation.

The result of my upgrade was to almost double my salary. It almost doubled my workload, too, but at least B.O.A.C. knew I was there! Maybe now I could still hope for a more glamorous career!

"SUNDAY, FEBRUARY 4TH: CHURCHILL, ROOSEVELT AND STALIN MET AT YALTA CONFERENCE. HAD A NICE HOT BATH, WASHED MY HAIR AND SPENT MOST OF DAY WRITING LETTERS."
One of the most important conferences of the war was taking place, but my diary was so preoccupied with everyday trivia that it only gave it a few words. At the seven-day conference at Yalta in Russia, Churchill, Roosevelt and Stalin met to discuss the postwar reestablishment of European nations. Newsreel and newspaper photos shocked us, showing how desperately ill Roosevelt had become. He looked like a dying man.

"FRIDAY, FEBRUARY 9TH: LETTER FROM FRANK'S MOM, TOOK 19 DAYS TO GET HERE! PRETTY BULKY, LOTS OF ENCLOSURES: TWO HANDKERCHIEFS WITH HAND-TATTED EDGES, PHOTOS OF BOB'S COTTAGE AND THE FAMILY HOME IN CLEVELAND. WENT TO CLUB DANCE AFTER WORK. GREAT BAND, FRANK ROSATO. MET A G.I. CALLED ARNOLD. NICE GUY. UNCOMPLICATED."
Mrs. Kopeck's letter was affectionate and the handkerchiefs were a touching little gift, edged with delicate tatted borders by Tillie, the housekeeper. The photo of Bob's cottage made us feel closer to knowing him.

A new chapter in my life began with my new friend, known affectionately at Rainbow Corner as "Little Arnie." Arnold Hoffman became a daily fixture for the next few months.

Arnie was what my fellow Red Cross volunteers and I had come to call a "non-wolf." Only two or three inches taller than my five feet, he was comfortable for me to dance with, and he was my idea of "the boy next door," with his boyish features and blond crew cut. He had smiling, gray eyes with dark eyelashes and a face so open and trusting that people probably took advantage of his good nature.

Like my U.S. Navy friend, Lieutenant Oates, he was from Iowa, with the same Midwestern drawl. "There sure 'nuff isn't much to tell ya about myself, Bunty," he said as we sat out a dance one evening. "Ah was born and raised on a farm in 'Ioway', God's country, ya know, and ah enlisted in the Army after ah graduated hah skewl. Never went any fu'thur from home than over to the naybrin' town, once't in awhile to the movies fer a change of pace. It's shure 'nuff different here in London."

Arnie was unsophisticated, with decent, old-fashioned values that were refreshing after the brash worldliness of some of the G.Is I had met; his only vices appeared to be ice cream, cake and Coca-Cola! Assigned to the large A.P.O. in London, he seemed unperturbed by the V-1 and V-2 menace, viewing himself simply as just another Londoner, accepting life as it happened, and in the meantime "keeping calm and carrying on" with his everyday job like the rest of us. In him I felt I had found a safe, unexciting, but dependable dance partner and friend. I thought to myself: "Thank heavens, he's just like Peter, Paul and William, a good pal." But was he? Time would tell.

I told Mom about Arnie. "He's a typical 'home town boy,' Mom, like the ones in those family stories in the movies. He's a very good dancer and taught me how to do the Jitterbug without getting maimed for life. Think I'll keep him for awhile."

Mom laughed: "I can feel another reverse Lend-Lease coming to Bishop's Hill, Bunty, but he sounds interesting."

"SATURDAY, FEBRUARY 10TH: LETTER FROM FRANK'S BROTHER, BOB, MAILED IN GERMANY. TOOK NINETEEN DAYS TO GET HERE. HEAVILY CENSORED. ALSO LETTER FROM MAGGIE IN WREXHAM. SHE'S ORGANIZING A 'WELCOME BACK'TEA PARTY FOR ME WHEN I VISIT IN MARCH."

Bob must have been on the move in the midst of the fighting in Germany; his letters obviously had trouble getting to an A.P.O. He wrote about himself and his life in America, his well-phrased writing style showed a strong, witty personality.

Maggie was still the staunch friend I remembered from my two years in Wales, but our lives had drifted apart since our days at Wrexham Park. I pondered: "She's making sure I'll see as many of the old Wrexham Park gang as possible; I wonder how they've changed since our school days? What will they think of my lifestyle here in London? I bet Wrexham is still as dull as ditch water!"

I heaved a huge sigh of relief that I hadn't stayed in Wales, after all. At present my world was my oyster, and I loved it.

"TUESDAY, FEBRUARY 13TH: DRESDEN DESTROYED BY ALLIED BOMBING ATTACKS."
My diary doesn't mention the rationale for these controversial air raids, but their postwar defenders cited the city's importance as a hub of road and rail traffic, while detractors deplored the destruction of an exquisite, undefended city, resulting in enormous civilian casualties. Such are the ravages of war, and its utter senselessness.

"FRIDAY, FEBRUARY 16TH: A HAPPY NINETEENTH BIRTHDAY. THE GIRLS AT B.O.A.C. TOOK ME OUT TO LUNCH. WENT TO RAINBOW CORNER AFTER WORK. DANCED WITH ARNIE. HE GAVE ME A BIG BOX OF 'EVENING IN PARIS' FOR MY BIRTHDAY--NO, NOT CHOCOLATES!"
"So begins my last year as a teenager," I must have thought to myself as I wrote my diary entry, "and so completely different from all those other wartime birthdays!"

Restaurants had special ration allowances; eating lunch out was a gala event, making us all forget about the short rations at home. Freddy didn't even bat an eyelid when I came back to the office an hour late.

After the dance that evening, Arnie insisted upon coming with me to the train station, carrying a large package wrapped in brown paper. Just before I stepped on the train, he put the package in my hands, and told me not to open it until I got home. Mom was as excited as me as

I ripped off the brown paper wrapping. Out popped a large, flat, dark blue box, with "Evening in Paris" in silver lettering. Inside, each item nestled in its own white satin niche: perfume, lotion, powder, creams. Mom only had one word to say: "Wow!"

I thought I would burst with so many surprises in one day, but I was really unprepared for the surprises that were yet to come!

Bunty in Show *Biz*

"SATURDAY, FEBRUARY 17TH: WENT UP TO RAINBOW CORNER THIS AFTERNOON FOR FIRST MEETING OF THE SHOW CAST. TOTAL CHAOS. DATE OF THE SHOW HAS BEEN SET FOR MARCH 11TH! REHEARSALS BEGIN NEXT WEEK. SPENT TIME VOLUNTEERING AT THE RECEPTION DESK."

My show-biz experience so far had been limited to several informative skits put on at school assemblies in Wrexham by fellow members of the Geographic and Scientific Society, and performed for a captive and uncritical schoolgirl audience. Just for fun, I volunteered to audition for the show at Rainbow Corner. I was stunned when I was one of sixteen girls who were chosen.

After much wrangling at the chaotic first meeting, a format for a variety show finally emerged, the acts joined by what my diary called "a thin plot." But as yet, the show had no name.

Exhausted, I went downstairs, picked up a sandwich, and checked to see if anyone was needed to sit at the Reception Desk, to calm my nerves before going home. The more I had become involved at Rainbow Corner, the more comfortable I felt there. Sometimes I stayed for an hour or two after work and on weekends, attending monthly volunteer meetings and on occasion sitting out the dances all evening to talk with one of the wounded G.I.s who could only watch from a wheelchair.

Taking a turn at the Information Desk was something I enjoyed, now that I had enough experience to answer questions and to recognize the difference between "wolves" and "non-wolves" so I could take evasive action when needed! I had just settled into the desk chair early that evening when a staff sergeant came along carrying a large bird cage containing a parrot. "Say, ma'm," he said, politely enough, "could I leave my parrot with you while I grab a bite to eat?"

I replied, "Of course, I'd be glad to take care of it for you. Just put the cage down on the floor behind the desk."

The burly G.I. tipped his hand to his cap in a mock salute, and disappeared in the direction of Dunker's Den for dinner. I dreaded the sound of the squawks and whistles I expected to hear from the parrot, which would bring an endless stream of wisecracks from passing G.I.s, but the parrot was silent. It was fairly dark and quiet where the cage had been deposited behind the desk, out of the mainstream of traffic, so I presumed the parrot had gone to sleep. Minutes stretched into hours, still with no sign of the parrot's owner. I began to worry about getting home.

Still hidden behind the desk, the parrot suddenly came to life and began to repeat loudly, over and over: "Polly wants a cracker." I started getting strange looks and grins from the G.I.s passing the desk, and an occasional: "Give that poor girl a cracker; she's hungry." Desperately, I fished around in the desk drawer and found a mangled package of crackers in a back corner. The parrot snatched them, demolished them with its beak and resumed its loud demands. My quiet evening was developing into a nightmare.

Where the parrot's owner went after dinner I don't know, but when he eventually wandered back to collect his bird cage with its cackling occupant, I literally ran out of the Club, boarding the ten o'clock last train back to Upper Woodside by the "skin of my teeth".

I knew Mom would be waiting up in her night clothes, having expected me home after a short meeting. On the train, I mentally rehearsed in various tones of voice how I would say: "Just couldn't get away from the club, Mom, I've been parrot-sitting!"

I giggled to myself, wondering how this explanation for being so late would go down with my nail-biting mother, who would undoubtedly have been worrying that this time I really had missed the last train home and was stranded in the blacked-out city. In fact, Mom laughed when she heard my tale, but I never did find out whether it was from sheer relief or whether she thought, as Dad would have, that it was "just a good yarn."

"SUNDAY, FEBRUARY 18TH: PACIFIC ISLANDS BEING RECLAIMED BY AMERICAN FORCES BUT AT HIGH COST. WROTE TO BRUCE; I OWE HIM TWO LETTERS. WENT UP TO LONDON FOR THE FIRST REHEARSAL OF OUR SHOW AT RAINBOW CORNER."

We had followed every detail of the advance of the Allies into Germany, but news from those distant battlefronts in the Pacific seemed disconnected from my life and those of my friends. Nevertheless, we were cheered by the news that American troops were succeeding in wrenching a chain of islands out of Japanese hands, one by one, but saddened by the high cost in casualties. Among the strange new names filtering through to us on the B.B.C. news were Luzon and Corregidor. Now the latest one, Iwo Jima, was at the top of the B.B.C. news headlines.

Where Bruce was he couldn't tell me, and I could only surmise that he was somewhere in the Pacific. He sounded despondent and anxious for mail. I tried to keep my letters light and humorous. My diary said, tongue in cheek: "I FEEL IT'S MY DUTY TO THE ROYAL NAVY TO TRY TO KEEP HIS SPIRITS UP!" I remember thinking: "I don't dare mention to him my life at Rainbow Corner because that would really send him into a tailspin of misery."

Bruce had met Frank and Bill, but they were probably the only Americans he ever tolerated, and his letters showed his general disapproval of the "Yanks" he had met through the Royal Navy. Mom was impatient with this intolerance. "I think it's just a lot of sour grapes," she huffed. Clearly she was becoming Americanized!

The initial rehearsal of the forthcoming show at Rainbow Corner was chaotic, to say the least. It had a large cast of about thirty, counting the individual performances by musicians, singers, dancers and comedians, also the sixteen of us who filled in with short acts of our own, between each one. And the show still didn't have a name.

"THURSDAY, FEBRUARY 22ND: THIS MORNING THREE OF US FROM THE OFFICE WENT TO TAKE A TOUR OF CROYDON AIRPORT. AFTER WORK I RUSHED OFF TO A REHEARSAL OF OUR SHOW, WITH MRS. BUD FLANAGAN DIRECTING."

They say variety is the spice of life, and I was getting plenty of variety! That morning, Brad, Buzz and I rode the shuttle bus from Airways House to Croydon Airport, where a uniformed B.O.A.C. staff member gave us a tour. Buildings bombed in error by the Luftwaffe in the Battle of Britain in 1940 had been patched up or replaced. Bomb craters in the runways had been filled in and repaved. The busy airport looked normal once more. After a trip to the control tower, we climbed into the cockpit of an empty passenger plane and were shown how the instruments worked. Buzz said: "I wish it would take off and go - anywhere - to get us away from this wartime life we're living!"

But at Rainbow Corner, fun was back in my life again. Red Cross staff member Blossom Brown had recruited Mrs. Bud Flanagan, the show-biz wife of one of Britain's most famous comedians, to direct the show. "Mrs. F." slowly established order out of the chaos of our first rehearsal, and we were on our way.

Blossom Brown's father was American-born Teddy Brown, billed in those days as the world's greatest xylophone player. He moved his family to live in England before World War Two. Blossom was raised among stage and screen stars, musicians and dancers, many of whom she persuaded to donate their time and talent at Rainbow Corner. Among them was twelve-year-old British singer Petula Clark. "Pet" became Rainbow Corner's mascot; she came on club outings and sang with the band at our dances. We felt like proud parents as she grew up to be an international radio, T.V., stage and movie star.

Another show business celebrity who worked regularly as a volunteer at the club was dancer Adele, Fred Astaire's sister and his first dancing partner, who had left the U.S. to marry a British lord and to live in England. Adele signed on with the American Red Cross and could be found sometimes seven days a week at Rainbow Corner helping the G.I.s: talking with them, listening to them, shopping for them. She also became adept at writing letters home for them, very often autographing them with her famous name, Adele Astaire, followed by her English aristocratic title, Lady Charles Cavendish.

In addition to countless other luminaries, America's First Lady, Eleanor Roosevelt, visited the Club on several occasions and officiated at its closing after the end of the war.

"SATURDAY, FEBRUARY 24TH: CANADIAN, BRITISH AND AMERICAN ARMIES HAVE ADVANCED TO THE RHINE RIVER. MOM AND I WENT CLOTHES SHOPPING IN LONDON."
We didn't know it, but Frank's brother, Bob, was at that moment on the front line in Germany, looking out across the River Rhine!

Again, Mom and I were again off on a hunt to replace our old clothes, and this time, Hooray! After two hours of vigilantly searching through London's Oxford Street department stores, and thirteen clothing coupons later, a beautifully soft, warm camel-hair coat (without a "Utility" logo), was mine,! Mom and I took in a movie before starting home, to rest our feet!

"SUNDAY, FEBRUARY 25TH: WENT UP TO LONDON FOR SHOW REHEARSAL AT 3 P.M. BY 6:30 P.M., WE HAD JUST ABOUT DRIVEN EACH OTHER NUTS! I'M WONDERING IF IT WILL EVER BE READY IN TIME!"
My diary described it as a "thin script" and the rehearsal as "without much progress." Every corner of the ballroom was occupied by people rehearsing their own little pieces of the show. Pandemonium reigned. Those of us who were to fill in the time between the acts each had a comic song to sing; a well-known tune with lyrics parodied to appeal to the typical G.I. Blossom taught us some simple dance routines, including the one I remember best: "Shuffle off to Buffalo"--a series of

sideways hopping steps with which we each had to conclude our act and get off-stage.

All the confusion that afternoon left me in despair. I muttered gloomily to myself: "It will be a miracle if this mess can ever straighten out into a decent show; right now it could be the biggest flop of all time!"

"TUESDAY, MARCH 6TH: WENT TO DOCTOR'S—FEEL LOUSY. DOCTOR SAYS I SHOW SIGNS OF MALNUTRITION. MISSED REHEARSAL AT RAINBOW CORNER."

Since my last bout in bed with a cough and cold, I hadn't been feeling one hundred per cent, and Mom now insisted that a trip to our family doctor was necessary. The gentle old man took my temperature, pulse and blood pressure, looked into my throat, eyes and ears, and pronounced his verdict: "Well, young lady, you're a healthy enough specimen, but all those colds and 'flu this winter have weakened your resistance and left you tired out. I think the culprit has been, and still is, malnutrition. I'll prescribe a tonic, and don't forget, plenty of rest."

A good quality diet was an impossibility with our skimpy food rations. My developing body had protested through bouts of illness as I grew up during the war years, but I was one of a whole generation who eventually became healthy adults under the National Health Service.

"FRIDAY, MARCH 9TH: FEELING O.K. AGAIN. ALLIES HAVE CROSSED THE RHINE! BRIDGE AT REMAGEN CAPTURED BY U.S. NINTH ARMY. HOPE BOB IS O.K. AT THE DANCE AT RAINBOW CORNER, U.S. CAMERAMEN MADE A MOVIE, PART OF A NEWS REPORT TO BE SHOWN IN THE U.S.A."

Whatever was in the doctor's "tonic" my diary doesn't say, but in a couple of days I felt fine, and all free of charge! The newsreels showed the Rhine crossing and we wondered if Bob had taken part in this milestone of World War Two. In obedience to Hitler's order to destroy the Rhine bridges, all of significance had been severed except one. The railroad bridge at Remagen was of supreme importance, both to the retreating Germans and to the advancing Allies for transporting troops, materiel and war supplies in large quantities. Until the last possible moment, the Germans battled desperately for more than a week to hold off U.S. forces in order to transport as many of their troops and as much war materiel as possible back into Germany across the bridge; then they wired it for demolition.

American heroes emerged as U.S. Army demolition squads risked their lives under German fire to find and dismantle the primed explosive charges along the bridge and its underpinnings before they could be detonated. When the Germans finally retreated, U.S. Army engineers worked feverishly to weld tons of new beams into the weakened bridge to make it safe and serviceable. Once reinforced, the bridge at Remagen proved invaluable in hastening the Allied advance across the Rhine into the heartland of Germany.

As movie cameras rolled at the Rainbow Corner dance that evening, I hoped that Bill and Frank wouldn't see me in the newsreel when it was shown in the U.S.A. If they saw me flinging myself around doing the Jitterbug, I could imagine them saying, "Hey, that *looks* like the Bunty we knew; but she's really gone to the dogs since we left!"

Life Gets Complicated

"SUNDAY, MARCH 11TH: THE GREAT DAY! THE SHOW NOW HAS A NAME: IT IS "T.S." THEY TELL ME THIS MEANS 'TOUGH SITUATION.' HAD TO BE AT THE CLUB BY 10 A.M. TWO REHEARSALS. HAD A HUGE LUNCH."

We assembled at the Club at ten o'clock and had a rehearsal. Then came lunch, and another rehearsal. "T.S." made its debut this evening.

The lump in my stomach that had been lunch felt as if it hadn't moved an inch as I waited my turn to come on the stage. Each individual act by a talented musician, actor, singer or dancer was followed by the stage curtains being drawn and the appearance in front of them of a girl dressed in a costume representing a country or place where G.I.s were stationed. Accompanied by Frank Rosato's band, she would sing a popular song whose lyrics had been cleverly parodied to fit, after which she would leave to make room for the next act that had assembled behind the curtains in the meantime.

Blossom had taught each of us how to slink seductively onto out the stage in front of the closed curtains. I was announced: "Here's Bunty, representing the coalfields of Wales, to sing "That Coal Black Magic."

Dressed in my one black suit, a black kerchief around my head, and a large piece of black coal from Dad's coal shed in my hand, I tried as best I could to look cool and calm as I "slinked" out in front of the audience. Straight-faced, I began what sounded like a serious lecture on Wales as the source of Britain's coal heat. I could feel the watching G.Is. getting restless. Then, as planned, the band blared a loud chord, stiffening them and me into silence and scaring me half to death as my adrenalin shot up several notches.

But this was the signal I was waiting for. I whipped off my black kerchief and shook my hair down around my shoulders, with a seductive little wiggle as I did so. Holding up the coal in one hand, I caressed it with the other, as I sang to it a soulful parody of Johnny Mercer's lyrics to "That Old Black Magic." The words went like this:

"A place called Wales is where we get our coal,
To keep us toasty is its only goal.
Those icy fingers up and down your spine,
You'd never feel them if they're warm like mine.
For you're the one that I have waited for,
The G.I. Joe I was created for,
And round and round I go,
Down and down I go,
In a spin, that nice toasty spin I'm in,
Loving that old black magic called COAL."

Then, with a grin (mostly relief), and waving my hand at the audience in what I hoped looked like a seductive farewell, I made my exit with the "Shuffle off to Buffalo" steps that Blossom had taught us. There followed what seemed to me, in my keyed-up state, to be a long silence from the audience. My heart sank, then, miracle of miracles, I heard wolf whistles and applause! I breathed a short prayer of relief: "Thank heavens, God, I wasn't a flop after all."

Dear old Arnie was full of praise, but I suspected that loyalty may have masked the truth! However, the show itself was a smash hit, and in the following weeks we gave several more performances, each time greeted with thunderous applause and wolf whistles. I never did find out what "T.S." really meant!

"FRIDAY, MARCH 16TH: U.S. FORCES RECAPTURE IWO JIMA IN PACIFIC WITH HEAVY LOSSES. LETTER FROM MAGGIE CONFIRMNG ARRIVAL TIME OF MY TRAIN AT WREXHAM WHEN I COME TO VISIT. FOUR AND A HALF TONS OF AIR FREIGHT FOR RED CROSS. ARNIE HAS THE 'FLU.'"

After a month of bloody fighting, Iwo Jima was reclaimed by U.S. forces. The battles lasted for a month, and cost twenty thousand American casualties. The now-famous iconic photo of the raising of the American flag on that island was translated into a statue that has become a national symbol.

Maggie was making sure of the smooth running of my schedule when I came to visit Wrexham and I was getting excited about my visit.

At the office, almost every day we were processing tons of air freight for the Red Cross, a reminder that there was still a hot war going on in Europe with thousands of casualties in hospitals urgently needing antibiotics and medications.

"SUNDAY, MARCH 18TH: WENT TO RAINBOW CORNER THIS MORNING TO HELP DECORATE THE BALLROOM. THIS AFTERNOON WE'RE GIVING A TEA DANCE FOR THE CAST OF THE SMASH

CANADIAN NAVY HIT, 'MEET THE NAVY,' RUNNING IN LONDON. EVEN BETTER THAN MEETING THE NAVY, I MET AL GREENE!"

London was short of good stage shows during the war, with most young talent away fighting. When the Royal Canadian Navy came up with an outstanding musical, "Meet the Navy," it ran with great success in London's West End, and Rainbow Corner's House Committee voted to invite the cast to a tea dance. I promptly volunteered to help decorate the ballroom.

Elsie Celli, the club director, stopped me as I signed in at the reception desk. "Wait up, Bunty," she said. "I'm coming up to the ballroom with you. There's someone there I want you to meet." She led me over to where volunteers were busily decorating the walls of the ballroom, getting it ready for the tea dance. A lanky G.I. was standing with his back to us on a ladder. Elsie tapped him on the leg. "Come down a minute, Al. I have someone I want you to meet."

A pair of army boots came down the ladder, followed by the rest of a tall, handsome soldier. Our eyes met, and for the first time in my life I had a strange feeling that my insides had turned to jelly. "Don't be silly, Bunty, I thought to myself." So what if he does remind you of James Stewart? He might be a wolf like all the rest of them. Forget it!"

"Bunty," said Elsie. "I want you to meet Al Greene."

He and I smiled at each other and politely shook hands. My diary added: "HE'S ON THE HOUSE COMMITTEE AND HE'S STATIONED IN LONDON. HOPE I'LL SEE HIM AGAIN!"

"SATURDAY, MARCH 24TH: BRITISH AND INDIAN TROOPS NOW IN CONTROL IN BURMA. ALLIES HAVE CROSSED RHINE IN GERMANY. HAD A WONDERFUL TIME AT RAINBOW CORNER. AL GREENE AND HIS GIRLFRIEND JOINED ARNIE AND ME AT THE DANCE."

The war was now on a landslide on both fronts in favor of the Allies, but their victories were won at a cost against German and Japanese troops, both determined enemies toughened by desperation. Tokyo was again bombed by the B-29s, but the Japanese emperor announced that Japan would never surrender.

Arnie had recovered from his bout with the 'flu. Al asked if he and his partner could join us at our little table, then asked me to dance with him. I was in seventh heaven but he obviously was with another girl. I gave a mental shrug of resignation. "So that's that," I thought, "he already has a girlfriend. I might have known it was too good to be true. Oh rats, how I'd have loved Mom and Dad to meet him."

But there was Arnie. It hadn't taken him long to find his way to Bishop's Hill unaided, and like Paul, Peter and William, he soon became a fixture, arriving on weekends on the train with his bike and staying a day or overnight.

In the next few weeks my diary mentions I had a "smashing time" every time Al appeared at the Club dances, and it was becoming obvious that Arnie and I were changing partners with increasing frequency. I melted every time I looked at Al, and he held me close when we danced without being suggestive or pushy. When we talked, he was unassuming, quiet and thoughtful, with an old-fashioned touch of chivalry about him that I found charming.

"TUESDAY, MARCH 27TH: LETTER FROM BRUCE. HE'S EITHER IN THE PACIFIC OR THE MEDITERRANEAN--HE CAN'T SAY, OF COURSE. TO OUR SURPRISE, MY COUSIN LEW SUDDENLY ARRIVED ON OUR DOORSTEP THIS EVENING!"

Mom and I had just finished the dinner dishes when the doorbell rang. "Whoever is this, at this time of night?" she exclaimed, on her way to the front door with her flashlight.

I heard a man's voice, then a shriek from Mom, and I froze in horror. "It must be someone she doesn't know," I thought, "and she sounds terrified. What should I do?" Before I could answer my own question,

I reached the front hall, and there stood my oldest cousin Lew, now a flight training instructor in his officer's uniform with its navigator/bombardier insignia. He took his arm from around Mom's shoulders and rushed to give me a bear hug. "Hello, Bunty. Gosh, it's wizard to see you again. Didn't mean to give poor Auntie Ida such a shock, though."

The unannounced arrival of the son of her older sister Hylda, threw Mom into a joyful tizzy. She produced a cup of tea for Lew, then clumped off upstairs to make up a bed in the guest room for him. We hadn't seen him for several years, so he and I sat in the dining room exchanging updates on our lives, while Mom added hers from the kitchen through the serving hatch, hurrying to make Lew some sandwiches.

My diary reports that she took the next day off from work, and brought Lew to Airways House to take me out to tea, after which Lew took a train from London back to his camp.

"WEDNESDAY, MARCH 28TH: I CAN'T BELIEVE IT--A LETTER FROM BILL WRITTEN ON FEBRUARY 15TH! I THOUGHT HE WAS OUT OF THE PICTURE! LIFE IS GETTING TOO COMPLICATED--BILL IS TALKING IN HIS LETTER ABOUT OUR GETTING ENGAGED! GLAD I'M GOING AWAY TO VISIT MAGGIE FOR AWHILE. I NEED SOMEWHERE TO GO, TO THINK!"

When I arrived home that evening, Mom said: "Guess what, Bunty?" and handed me a letter from Bill, postmarked six weeks ago! After arriving back in the U.S., he and Frank had been moved from camp to camp, and my mail forwarded from his home in Wisconsin didn't catch up with him. The boys had finally been sent to a training camp where they were now assigned as gunnery instructors. In his letter Bill sounded exactly as affectionate as before he left for the U.S., and he was talking very seriously about sending me an engagement ring. I wondered how I would tell him I didn't want one! Confused, I went upstairs and began to pack for my visit to Wales.

"THURSDAY, MARCH 29TH: UP AT 6:00 A.M. TO CATCH A TRAIN FROM LONDON TO WREXHAM. ARRIVED ON TIME AT 2:40 P.M. MAGGIE'S MOTHER MET AT THE STATION, AND WE PICKED UP MAGGIE AT HER OFFICE. BESSIE CAME FOR THE EVENING. HOW GREAT TO SEE THEM BOTH AGAIN!"

Entailing having to hunt for a seat, making a couple of train changes, and being delayed by an inordinate number of stops, I found the train journey hectic as well as long. I arrived at Wrexham very tired, but it was wonderful to see my two friends again. Maggie and Bessie looked different; the giggly schoolgirls in their awful baggy Wrexham Park uniforms were now two attractive, self-assured young women dressed as fashionably as Utility styles and clothing coupons would allow.

We talked, interrupting each other in our eagerness to exchange news. The years melted away and we were three schoolgirls again, laughing together and enjoying one another's company. Maggie didn't mention any men in her life, but was happy with her office job. Bessie admitted shyly, "Well, I'm dating a Polish airman who wants to stay behind in Wales after the war. He escaped from the Nazis when they occupied Poland, and served here with the R.A.F. in a special Polish squadron." Her face shone with enthusiasm as she told us about her beau, but I couldn't help thinking: "I wonder how this is going down with her strict Baptist father?" Bessie's Dad had softened and allowed Bessie to come with me to ballroom dancing classes, but to accept a Polish Catholic for a son-in-law-- well, that was another matter!

I was interrupted in my thoughts when Maggie, tactless as ever, grinned and blurted: "Hey, Bunty, did you hear about the girl who had a wooden baby?"

This was a new one on me, and I hadn't a clue. "No, Mag--go on, tell me!"

"She married a Pole!" Maggie hugged Bessie as if to ask her forgiveness. Bessie hugged her back, while I just groaned. The following year, Maggie wrote to me in the U.S. that Bessie had married her Pole!

That joke has haunted me ever since, but in the following years I lost track of Bessie, and I never did hear whether or not she had a wooden baby!

Victory in Europe Approaches

"SATURDAY, MARCH 31ST: TOOK THE BUS INTO CHESTER WITH MAGGIE AND BESSIE. BOUGHT A PIN AND EARRINGS FOR MOM, ALSO SOME POSTCARDS TO SEND. WALKED ALL DAY, INCLUDING ROMAN WALL!"

We celebrated our first outing together in three years with a day in the picturesque town of Chester, just across the English border from Wrexham. I remembered when Ken Knight had brought me here, an excited schoolgirl, to experience my first opera, starring that elderly substitute for a young Pagliacci. It felt like a lifetime ago. Browsing in the quaint bi-level shops in the ancient town center and walking on the Roman wall surrounding Chester stored up new memories for me to take home.

Nostalgia haunted me in the next few days. On Sunday morning Maggie and I walked across town to find Wrexham Park School for Girls, passing by the house where Mom and I had such a happy home during our exile in Wrexham. Impulsively, I knocked on the door, wondering if Mr. Evans and Bronwyn were still there. Bronwyn opened it, then stood for a moment, giving me a blank look that suddenly warmed. "Dad, come here quick," she cried. "It's Bunty!"

Mr. Evans came hurrying down the hall to see what all the commotion was about, followed by Davey on his little Welsh Corgi legs, who gave a bark of greeting and jumped up on me, licking my hands as I fondled his silky head and ears.

Nonstop conversation and cups of morning tea filled the next hour before Maggie and I left to walk by our old school, standing in all its red-brick dignity, almost out of sight behind tall trees. Maggie said: "I wonder if anyone is still growing veggies in that flower border?" But there was no time to investigate and we continued on our walk to revisit the local park.

Maggie laughed. "Remember that park attendant who threatened to have us arrested when he caught you up that lime tree, Bunty?" In my mind's eye, I was looking down on the furious face of the park attendant from the tree branch, where I was happily ripping off bunches of lime blossoms and dropping them into Maggie's herb-collecting sack below. "Oh yes," I joined in Maggie's laughter, "but remember, you didn't have the presence of mind to faint, Maggie. I think you were as scared stiff as I was."

We went on to Bessie's home for tea with her family; it was as if I had never left.

"MONDAY, APRIL 2ND: WENT BY BUS TO OVERTON BRIDGE WITH THE GIRLS. A LOVELY DAY. TOOK A PICNIC LUNCH AND LOTS OF PHOTOS."

Maggie's attempts to have a reunion tea party hadn't succeeded, but I was just as happy to spend my time with my two old pals. They took some days off from their work in honor of my visit. We picnicked at Overton Bridge by the canal, near the lovely town of Llangollen, chattering and laughing as we remembered that last picnic with our mothers in 1942, before Mom and I left Wrexham to return to London.

Bessie doubled up with laughter. "Bunty, remember when the canal barge horse almost ate your Mom's bouquet of wild flowers? What with her arthritis, I never thought she could fly through the air and land on that barge so expertly. She never even dropped her flowers!"

We all giggled at the memory of Mom's heroic, now historic leap onto the barge to escape the hungry horse.

"WEDNESDAY, APRIL 4TH: CAUGHT THE 9:44 A.M. TRAIN FOR LONDON. HAD A SEAT ALL THE WAY! LETTERS FROM BILL AND BOB

WERE WAITING AT HOME. WROTE A THANK-YOU TO MAGGIE'S MOM FOR LETTING ME STAY WITH THEM."

My diary reminded me that, during my stay in Wales, Bessie, Maggie and I took sixteen photos with each other's cameras and precious rolls of film. Years later, as I looked at their smiling faces on the fading prints, I wondered: "Where are they now? Too bad I lost touch with them when I got busy with babies after I was in the United States a few years. I hope they would always remember meeting me that first day at Wrexham Park School, a refugee from the London Blitz, in my Ravenhurst school uniform and with my South Country accent. They took me to their hearts and kept me there for two years. I hope their lives have brought them as much love and happiness as mine has."

But now I was back in London, faced with trying to sort out my romantic entanglements!

"TUESDAY, APRIL 10TH: 'U.S. 9TH ARMY TAKES HANOVER IN GERMANY. IN THE PACIFIC, THE JAPANESE HAVE LOST THE YAMATO'".

The announcement on the B.B.C. news enabled us to surmise that Bob Kopeck and his antitank unit might now be only seventy-five miles from Berlin. The Nazis were being squeezed into an ever-diminishing area, pushed back by the Russians from the north and the Allies from the south.

Bob was probably sure that he and his comrades would be among the first Allied troops to enter Berlin, and that the honor would go to the Americans. However, a political decision in favor of the Russians taking Berlin was made, and instead of continuing north to Berlin, the Ninth Army was ordered to turn south. The taste of this decision must have remained sour in many American mouths for years to come.

In the meantime, the Pacific war raged on, with the U.S. invasion of Okinawa and the sinking of Japan's most powerful battleship, Yamato.

History tells us that, when she sank, she took with her more than two thousand lives to add to the carnage of World War Two.

"THURSDAY, APRIL 12TH: PRESIDENT ROOSEVELT DIED. ALL FLAGS FLYING AT HALF MAST IN BRITAIN. ENTERTAINMENT FOR U.S. ARMED FORCES CANCELLED. IN GERMANY, NAZI CONCENTRATION CAMPS LIBERATED."

The British mourned the passing of one of the best allies this country had ever known. We knew that Roosevelt saw the "big picture" of the Nazi threat to the U.S., if Britain was overrun, and that he was perhaps the only American politician who fully recognized the consequences. On this day the Allies liberated the Buchenwald and Belsen death camps. Nothing is mentioned in my diaries about the Nazi atrocities and mass extermination at the camps. To our knowledge they had been forced labor camps housing not only Jews, but people from countries conquered by the Nazis who were made to work inhuman hours in Hitler's weapons factories. We had not yet heard of Hitler's diabolical "final solution" to exterminate the Jews. I obviously knew nothing of this, or my diaries would certainly have contained some record of it.

Now the truth was out. We were hearing the gruesome details of the plight of millions of Hitler's victims, targeted for extinction because he saw in them a barrier to his achieving a pure Aryan master race. Looking with horror at the newsreels showing the pitiful skeletal survivors, and the stacks of emaciated bodies waiting to be cremated in the ovens of Belsen and Buchenwald, audiences were shocked beyond imagination. What was even more horrifying was that there were many more such death camps, wherever the Nazis had chosen to build them.

"FRIDAY, APRIL 13TH: HAD A LETTER FROM BILL, ALSO FROM KATE AND FRANK, FROM TEXAS, AND FROM HELEN, BOB'S WIFE, FROM OHIO. THAT COMPLETES THE WHOLE KOPECK FAMILY. DANCES

AT RAINBOW CORNER CANCELLED UNTIL FURTHER NOTICE TO HONOR PRESIDENT ROOSEVELT'S MEMORY."

Kate's letter was ecstatic. She and Frank were reunited, living in Texas. Frank was at an Air Force training center as an air gunnery instructor until the end of the war. There was also a letter from Helen, Bob's wife, thanking us for contacting him. Their letters united us in our thoughts, prayers and hopes for a better world once the war came to an end.

Bill's letters were frequent, warm and caring as ever; I couldn't bear to hurt his feelings. What was I to do?

"SUNDAY, APRIL 15TH: ARNIE APPEARED ABOUT 9 A.M. AT OUR FRONT DOOR, WITH A BOX OF CANDY FOR MOM. WE TOOK THE TRAIN TO KEW GARDENS. MY, BUT IT'S THE LOVELIEST PLACE-- ALMOST LIKE HEAVEN!"

My hair was up in curlers, and I had just taken a bite out of my breakfast toast, when the doorbell rang. "Whoever could that be, at this hour on a Sunday?" asked Mom. "I'll bet it's your cousin Lew, back for another surprise visit." She dashed to the door in her bathrobe, and I heard her say: "Oh, my goodness, you're out early on a Sunday! Come in." Arnie appeared in the dining-room doorway, seeing the real "me," without any makeup, in my pajamas and with my hair looking like an advertisement for a bad hairdresser. He had a box of American chocolates tucked under his arm, which he gave to Mom. She still looked bewildered, but she thanked him, put them aside for a special occasion, then hastily fled upstairs to get dressed.

I was embarrassed. "You know, Arnie, it's customary in England for you to let people know before you come to visit," I said, trying not to sound cross, "but it's such a beautiful day. Let's take a picnic lunch and go to Kew--I've been wanting to show it to you." I thought I'd better get him out of the house to let Mom have a bit of peace and quiet on her Sunday away from her office. Arnie almost purred as he sat down next to me at the Morrison shelter with a cup of tea. I thought to myself: "Oh dear, I've got to do something about him; he's beginning to think he lives here! But he's so sweet, what can I say to him? I don't want to hurt his feelings!"

In the pale spring sunshine we took the train to Kew Gardens, England's foremost botanical paradise, to wander among spectacular beds of spring flowers, ornamental ponds and lush greenhouses. I put aside my dilemma about Bill, Al and Arnie; for now, this was the perfect escape!

"TUESDAY, APRIL 17TH: LAST OF NAZI TROOPS IN THE RUHR SURRENDERED. RUSSIANS ARE ADVANCING ON BERLIN. ALLIES CONTINUE SWEEP OF PO VALLEY IN ITALY. RECEIVED PHOTOS FROM MAGGIE OF REUNION IN WREXHAM. ARNIE CALLED ME AT THE OFFICE; HE HAS BOOKED RESERVED SEATS FOR US TO SEE SENSATIONAL MOVIE *HENRY V* ON FRIDAY!"

The war was winding down; the Nazis were in full flight. They would undoubtedly make a stand to defend Berlin, but it was now obvious that their defeat was inevitable. In the strategic Po Valley, Allied troops were "mopping up," effectively forcing the Nazis from their last positions in northern Italy.

Arnie called me at the office. He sounded breathless. "Hey, Bunty, guess what? I've got reserved seats for us to see Laurence Olivier's *Henry V*! How ja like that?"

I was stunned. "Terrific," I gasped. "I heard they were as scarce as hen's teeth! However did you do it, Arnie?"

There was a moment's silence. Sounding like the cat that swallowed the canary, he said: "Now wouldn't ya like to know?"

I dropped the subject.

This was the movie that everyone at the office had been talking about. Acclaimed as a masterpiece, Shakespeare's saga of British hero King Henry the Fifth was the first movie of its kind to be made in

Technicolor, and starred famous Shakespearean actor Laurence Olivier. Hailed by critics as "a triumph of color, music, spectacle and soaring heroic poetry," it was the most talked-about film in London.

There was a strain on London's theaters and cinemas; the city was bursting at the seams with visiting servicemen and women, and civilians returning to live again in city and suburbs. Good entertainment was at a premium; to be sure of seats for a really popular movie, reservations had to be made sometimes weeks in advance. Arnie knew his way around the city better than most of the natives. He knew every box office in the Theatre District, and how to get unclaimed reserved seats to good shows that were otherwise sold out.

Suddenly I was the envy of everyone at the office.

V-E Day, at Last!

"FRIDAY, APRIL 20th: ANOTHER LETTER FROM BILL. HE'S AS ARDENT AS EVER! ONE OF THESE DAYS I'LL HAVE TO GET UP THE COURAGE TO TELL HIM I'M NOT INTERESTED IN ENGAGEMENT OR WEDDING RINGS! ARNIE PICKED ME UP FROM THE OFFICE AND WE WENT OUT TO DINNER, THEN TO SEE *HENRY V.* IT WAS SUPERB! ARNIE CAME HOME WITH ME FOR THE WEEKEND."

The movie was all it was promoted to be. How could I thank Arnie for a treat like this? Well, the least I could do was to ask him home for the weekend! That warm, sunny Sunday we picnicked near Hampton Court, a few miles from the city, on the banks of the wide, prettily flowing stream that would become London's River Thames. My diary enthused: "IT'S EVEN MORE HEAVENLY THAN KEW GARDENS!"

My life was wobbling on an uneven keel. I realized how lucky I was to be basking in Arnie's overwhelming devotion, and in Bill's, too, but something was missing: overwhelming devotion to either one of them on *my* part!

"SUNDAY, APRIL 22ND: WENT TO A VOLUNTEERS' MEETING AT RAINBOW CORNER, FOLLOWED BY A DANCE. WONDERFUL TIME. AL GREENE AND KAY WERE THERE."

Enter Al Greene again! Dances at Rainbow Corner had resumed after being cancelled in honor the memory of President Roosevelt. From this day on, Al, his girl Kay, Arnie and I became a foursome. We changed dance partners frequently; I didn't even protest when Al taught me his version of the Jitterbug. I asked myself: "Did he really mean that look we exchanged when Elsie Celli introduced us? He hasn't followed up; what should I think?" I felt a stronger attraction between Al Greene and myself than I had ever experienced before; if he had it on his mind to change partners permanently, would he ever say what was on his mind? Meantime, there was Arnie!

"SATURDAY, APRIL 28TH: MUSSOLINI HAS BEEN EXECUTED BY ITALIAN ANTI-FASCISTS. WENT TO A VERY SPECIAL DANCE AT THE GROSVENOR HOUSE HOTEL WITH ARNIE. HAD A HEAVENLY TIME."

Mussolini and his mistress, Clara Petacci, were caught while trying to escape to Switzerland, and shot to death by anti-Fascists. The life of "Il Duce" was thought by many in Italy to have come to a fitting end. His body and Clara's were taken to Milan and hung upside down on meat hooks for public inspection, ridicule and abuse. The killing and exhibition were savage retribution for the brutality Mussolini's regime had inflicted on the Italian people. The gruesome pictures appeared on the front pages of our newspapers.

Happily unconcerned, my diary had been announcing "WE'RE EXPECTING V-E DAY ANY DAY NOW" for almost a week. Behind the scenes in London, preparations were already being made for the victory celebrations. The posh Grosvenor House Hotel on London's exclusive Park Lane was very hospitable to Americans in World War Two; Generals Dwight Eisenhower and George Patton were frequent visitors. When an invitation was extended to the G.I.s at Rainbow Corner for a dance to be held at the hotel, I think Arnie must have been at the head of the line for tickets!

My diary expended just a few words on this event, but I remember being dazzled by the opulence of the hotel and the excellence of the dance band. Arnie and I sat in upholstered swivel chairs at a small table on a balcony overlooking the dance floor, sipping our "cold Cokes"; periodically Arnie would suggest we go down and join the dancers. I wrote in my diary that the evening had been heavenly, that said it all.

"MONDAY, APRIL 30th: HITLER RUMORED TO BE DEAD. NO DETAILS YET. END OF BLACKOUT! WHOOPEE! IT'S BEGINNING TO LOOK LIKE I REMEMBERED BEFORE THE WAR!"
Rumors had leaked out of Germany that Hitler had committed suicide in his bunker in Berlin, but there was no confirmation by the Germans, who still held their capital city, although the Russians were almost on their doorstep.

On the home front, the ending of the blackout was celebrated that evening by the ceremonial lighting of London's signature clock tower, Big Ben, almost two thousand days after the blackout began. Children five years old and younger had never seen the street lights lit before. I had almost forgotten what our street lights looked like when dusk came that evening to Bishop's Hill. Early in 1939, before the war, new lights had been installed on top of our lamp-posts that gave off a ghastly, pale green glow. Mom and I looked at each other in dismay when we first viewed each other in this strange light; the two of us both resembled the Wicked Witch of the West, in *The Wizard of Oz.*

Back in those days Prince, my little fox terrier, looked forward every evening to his last walk in the dusk, before bedtime. I used to call to him: "Walks, Prince." He needed no second call. His tongue lolling out of one corner of his mouth gave him a lopsided grin as he jumped up and down on his short legs in anticipation. On the first night of the new street lights, I attached the leash to his collar, and as usual he made a dash for the front door. Once outside, he stopped in his tracks, then sat down and looked up at our nearest lamp-post. A ridge of hair raced along his spine in a panic-stricken ripple. He stood up, legs stiffly planted, looked intently at the offending light and began to bark at it, probably to scare it away and protect me from its evil intent. I bared my greenish teeth and howled with laughter.

Prince died before the war, but now that memory had Mom and me giggling as we joined our neighbors, all glowing green as they danced around, cheering and clapping to welcome back those long-lost street lights.

"THURSDAY, MAY 3RD: WE'RE EXPECTING V-E DAY ANY TIME NOW. IN LONDON THEY ARE TAKING THE BLAST NETTING OFF BUS WINDOWS, DEMOLISHING PUBLIC AIR-RAID SHELTERS, AND PREPARING FOR THE VICTORY PARADE."
While London prepared to celebrate victory in Europe, it was hard to remember that a full-scale war was still being waged on the other side of the world. But the U.S. forces in the city were off on a roll of parties.

"MONDAY, MAY 7TH: GERMANY HAS SURRENDERED UNCONDI-TIONALLY! HITLER OFFICIALLY REPORTED DEAD. V-E DAY WILL DEF-INITELY BE CELEBRATED THIS WEEK. NONE OF US COULD WORK AT THE OFFICE. JUST HAD ONE CUP OF TEA AFTER ANOTHER ALL MORNING, THEN WE CLOSED THE OFFICE AND ALL WENT OUT TO LUNCH WITH PHONES RINGING. I WENT TO RAINBOW CORNER AF-TER WORK. THE ATMOSPHERE THERE IS ELECTRIC!"
The truth was out: the story of Hitler's death was confirmed. Long since, he had fled to his bomb-proof underground bunker in Berlin, accompa-nied by his mistress, Eva Braun. They were married in the bunker. Less than forty hours later, Eva committed suicide by cynanide poisoning and Hitler fatally shot himself.

In London the excitement in anticipation of V-E Day was almost palpable. At Airways House we were unable (and unwilling) to concentrate on work; at Rainbow Corner the excitement was such that it was like walking into a powder keg ready to explode.

"TUESDAY, MAY 8TH: TODAY IS V-E DAY! ARNIE CAME TO PICK ME UP AT HOME AT 11 A.M. TOOK A BUS TO LONDON; PEOPLE JAMMING STREETS, CHEERING, SINGING, DANCING. IT TOOK FROM 3 P.M. TO 7 P.M. TO WALK TO VICTORIA STATION TO GET A TRAIN HOME. THE WHOLE NEIGHBORHOOD CELEBRATED IN BISHOP'S HILL UNTIL 2:30 A.M.!"

Arnie and I managed to get a front seat atop the double-decker bus to London. From this vantage point, we could watch V-E Day celebrations unrolling and augmenting as we rode from the suburbs into the city. Neighborhoods all along the route were filled with crowds of people singing, cheering, dancing and enjoying picnics at tables in the side streets which had been cleared of traffic. As we approached the heart of London, the roads became clogged with a wildly gyrating sea of humanity. Eventually the bus driver stopped the bus, and the conductor yelled to the passengers: "NAH LISTEN EVERYBODY, THE DRIVER CAN'T MOVE THIS BLEEDIN' BUS ANY FARTHER; FROM NOW ON YER'LL ALL HAVE TO WALK!"

We walked past Big Ben in Whitehall, our pace getting slower and slower. The moving mass of people seemed to be pushing the sidewalks toward Trafalgar Square in the distance. Hanging onto each other, Arnie and I flowed with the crowd until we finally came to a complete stop at Trafalgar Square. There we found ourselves in the middle of a scene we would never forget. In front of and around us it was as if the entire world was celebrating; civilians mingled with servicemen and women in uniforms from a multitude of different countries, welded into a single, delirious mass of humanity.

The statue of British hero Admiral Nelson presided as usual atop the tall column in the spacious square bearing the name of his naval battle that marked the defeat of the French a century before. Today, Nelson was looking down on an incredible sight: wall to wall people, some of them breaking away to hurl themselves into the spray of the two large fountains in joyful abandon. Trafalgar Square's resident pigeons had fled in terror to take refuge in the eaves of nearby old churches and galleries. People were sitting astride the bronze lions at the base of Nelson's Column, cheering and wildly waving red, white and blue Union Jack flags of all sizes, their cheers drowned out by hundreds of merrymakers who had linked arms to sing and dance London's favorites: "The Lambeth Walk" and "Knees Up, Mother Brown." We staggered through the throng to where hundreds more had formed a long, convoluted conga line that was jerking away from the Square towards the Haymarket, the bobbing heads of its leading dancers already almost out of sight. We joined onto the end of it, and it propelled us on our way for awhile; we dropped off when it began to go back again towards Trafalgar Square.

Realizing that it would be sheer disaster if we got separated, Arnie and I hung onto each other desperately. We had decided to try to work our way to Rainbow Corner, still several blocks away. Arnie proved to have strong elbow power, as he bulldozed a path through the crowds with me in tow. It was slow going, but at last we had left Trafalgar Square behind and made it into the Haymarket, one of the streets leading up to Piccadilly, from where we could hopefully get to our destination. Streets and sidewalks seethed with the mass of people surging around us singing familiar songs of the Allied nations, one after the other. As we fought our way toward Piccadilly, we joined in singing "Frère Jacques," "I'm a Yankee Doodle Dandy," and "There'll Always Be an England." By now the crowd was so dense that we couldn't move backwards, forwards or even sideways, so we had to stand still on our aching feet and hope someone would move an inch or two so we could follow.

After being immobilized by the crowd for almost half an hour, we gave up trying to reach Rainbow Corner; moving in that direction was impossible, so we decided to take the train back to Upper Woodside. Struggling to stay on course in the crush of bodies, it took Arnie and me four hours to reach Victoria Station and find a train that was still running. Normally, it would have taken forty minutes! London's buses had given up; they were parked at the sides of the roads like beached red whales, abandoned by their passengers and also by bus drivers and conductors. Arnie observed: "I shore hope they can remember where they parked their buses; they're prob'ly all out here dancin' and singin' with everyone else!"

As our train pulled out of the station, the roar of the crowds now settling in for a night of celebration receded slowly into the distance. Arnie and I finally reached Upper Woodside. While we were gone, Bishop's Hill had been hung with red, white and blue streamers. Our neighbors were sitting chatting on chairs they had brought out into the middle of the street, where tables were laden with sandwiches and candy, cookies, cakes and wine, some of which had been hoarded for years, waiting to be shared with each other on the day war ended. As darkness fell, the street lights went on again, their greenish glow dispelling, at last, the dark shadows of wartime. All over the street people were dancing to music playing on ten-inch black records rotating on a hand-cranked phonograph.

Arnie and I joined the dancers until, by 2:30 a.m., we couldn't dance another step, so we gave up and tottered home to our beds.

A Nation Rejoices

"WEDNESDAY, MAY 9TH: SLEPT VERY LATE, EXHAUSTED AFTER V-E DAY. NATIONAL HOLIDAY. BELLS RINGING, HOOTERS HOOTING! ST. JOHN'S CHURCH BELLS ARE PEALING WITH JOY. WE CAN HEAR THE HORNS OF BUSES IN THE DISTANCE, TOOTING JOYFULLY. ARNIE AND I TOOK THE BUS UP TO LONDON AGAIN

TODAY. PEOPLE ARE STILL IN THE STREETS, SHOUTING, SINGING, DANCING. JOINED AL GREENE AND KAY AT THE MAY DAY DANCE AT RAINBOW CORNER. PETULA CLARK WAS CROWNED MAY QUEEN. WONDERFUL DAY!"

An official national holiday was declared in Britain to celebrate the end of the war in Europe. Church bells were heard once again, this time not to announce an invasion but to join in with the other sounds of rejoicing already filling the air. The holiday was a fitting runner-up to V-E Day the day before. From the upper deck of the bus, Arnie and I could see that the crowds had thinned out, but I wondered how many of those people still in the streets had even slept!

In his victory speech to the nation, Churchill said: "We may allow ourselves a brief period of rejoicing but let us not forget for a moment the toil and efforts that lie ahead. Japan with all her treachery and greed remains unsubdued."

In his speech to Parliament, Churchill finished by saying they would adjourn to St. Margaret's Church "to give humble and reverent thanks to Almighty God for our deliverance from the threat of German domination."

The May Day dance at Rainbow Corner had been postponed until the date for V-E Day was announced. May Day, an ancient Roman festival, was observed in Britain on May first, culminating in the crowning of a May Queen to represent Flora, the Roman goddess of flowers and fruit, love and romance. Blossom Brown again produced a celebrity for the occasion, our own little singing mascot "Pet" Clark, who was solemnly crowned by Blossom with a sparkly cardboard coronet as Rainbow Corner's May Queen.

Al, Kay, Arnie and I changed partners at the May Day dance more often than ever. A strange new feeling came over me. I thought: "What's this? Butterflies in my stomach, every time Al puts his arm around me? I've got to find out if he feels he same way about me, but how can he, when he's still dating Kay?"

"THURSDAY, MAY 10TH: ALLIES HAVE LIBERATED CHANNEL ISLANDS. NAZI PROPAGANDA CHIEF GOEBBELS HAS KILLED HIS FAMILY AND HIMSELF IN HITLER'S BUNKER IN BERLIN."

Fifteen miles off the coast of Normandy, the British Channel Islands sit in the English Channel. After France fell to the Nazis in 1940, they were overrun; the swastika flew from their flagpoles to replace the Union Jack in the only British territories to be occupied by the Nazis in World War Two. The Germans set about erecting fortifications on the islands as part of the Atlantic Wall, and for five years the islanders who had chosen not to be evacuated before the occupation experienced Nazi brutality at close range. The islands were not liberated until after the German unconditional surrender, when, at long last, the Union Jack flew again from their flagpoles.

Goebbels and his family had moved into the bunker in Berlin with Hitler, Eva Braun and some of his top aides. Before committing suicide, Hitler made a will appointing Goebbels his successor as Chancellor of the Third Reich. The day after Hitler committed suicide, Goebbels and his wife had their six children sedated with morphine, then killed them, one by one, by inserting a crushed cyanide tablet into each of their mouths. Goebbels and his wife then committed suicide, but their partially burned bodies did not make it clear how they died, whether from cyanide poisoning or from gunshot wounds, or both.

"SUNDAY, MAY 13TH: A DOUBLE DATE! AL, KAY, ARNIE AND I MET AT RAINBOW CORNER, THEN TOOK THE TRAIN TO CHESSINGTON ZOO. WONDERFUL DAY, LOVED EVERY MINUTE. PICNICKED AMONG WALLABIES AND PEACOCKS."

On this cloudless, delightfully warm spring day we arrived after a short train ride at what was in those days a small zoo. It was lunchtime, so we followed a signpost that said "Wallaby Wood, Picnicking Allowed". Finding a deserted grassy clearing, we sat down and unpacked the sandwiches, little cakes and cookies provided by Kay's and my Moms, pouring ourselves tea from the two thermos flasks.

To our surprise, a large peacock came strutting along! It stopped, and looked inquiringly at us. Al said " Now I know *that's* a peacock, but I wonder why the sign says 'Walllaby Wood'? What's a wallaby?" As if on cue, a small kangaroo hopped boldly up to Kay, nosing her lap, where her sandwich was probably sending out irresistible smell signals. Kay screamed, sprang to her feet, and hid behind a tree. The sandwich flew into the air, landing at the feet of the wallaby, now frozen in terror from Kay's screams. Other wallabies must have heard the message; in minutes we were surrounded by the furry little fellows. I could almost hear them saying: "Come on, guys, eat up, free lunch!" The ensuing scramble took care of poor Kay's sandwich in seconds.

Arnie and Al rose to the occasion. Rolling up their zoo guidebooks, they swatted at the wallabies, who retreated to a respectable distance, standing on their hind legs watching for another opportunity to charge. A few more peacocks appeared, some spreading their tails in a beautiful display, as if to say: "Look, we're performing for you, a few crumbs would be welcome payment." We left bits of our sandwiches and cookies behind when we packed up, leaving the unexpected menagerie behind, to go and explore the rest of the zoo, where the resident animals were behind bars.

"SATURDAY, MAY 19TH: AUNTIE LIL DITCHFIELD ARRIVED FOR A WEEK'S VACATION. MET AL, KAY AND ARNIE'S TRAIN WITH PERCIVAL, STOWED HIM ABOARD, AND WE ALL WENT TO KINGSWOOD, SURREY. PICNICKED UNDER A WILD CHERRY TREE. LOVELY DAY."

Poor Mom, here she was in "visitor preparation mode" again! With all the comings and goings, the neighbors must have dubbed our house "Bishop's Hill Revolving Door"! Mom's oldest sister, Lily, lost no time in resuming her peacetime visits with us in Upper Woodside. This time I wasn't there to greet her arrival, but I took off a couple of days from the office later in the week for some London sightseeing and shopping with her.

Meantime, another double date! Al, Kay and Arnie had stowed their bicycles in the baggage car on the electric commuter train at Victoria Station in London. I met the train at our local station and Percival was safely stowed in the baggage car too. We unloaded the bikes at Kingswood in Surrey, a commuter town surrounded by picturesque countryside perfect for picnics, and found a spot near a little grove of wild cherry trees. We parked our bikes and unpacked our picnic. As we packed up to leave, Al grinned and commented: "You know, I actually *missed* the peacocks and wallabies!" He dodged a hail of empty paper bags.

On the way back to the railway station, I found myself cycling with Al, and once more I had the feeling that we "belonged."

"SUNDAY, MAY 27TH: MET AL AT NOON IN LONDON AND WE PROCEEDED TO PAT'S WEDDING NORTH OF THE CITY. LOVELY CEREMONY. I CRIED AS USUAL. NICE RECEPTION. ARNIE THINKS HE'S GOING TO BE SENT TO PARIS."

I was thrilled to receive an invitation to the wedding of B.O.A.C. and college friend Pat, who was marrying a G.I. she had met at Rainbow Corner. She knew Al from the House Committee and invited him, too. As soon as Al knew I was going to the wedding, he asked me if we could go together. What a delightful "first date" for just the two of us. At the end of the day, Al said: "Bunty, I want you to know I have told Kay that I'll no longer be dating her. I just want to be with you."

My head was reeling. Thoughts kept tumbling out: "Was it Pat's wedding that rubbed off on him? Or maybe seeing me cry? I always cry at weddings! But at last he's come out and said he cares about me and has done something about it, and now I can tell him I feel the same way about him! That takes care of Kay, but what about Bill, lonely and lovesick in Wisconsin; Arnie, faithful in London; and Bruce, out in the Pacific, where absence makes the heart grow fonder, and fonder? And now here's Al! What a mess I'm in; how am I ever going to unravel it all? Oh well, at least Arnie's transfer to Paris will solve part of the problem!"

"MONDAY, MAY 29TH: ARNIE CALLED ME TO SAY HE'S DEFINITELY
NOT GOING TO PARIS. HE'LL BE STAYING ON AT THE A.P.O. IN
LONDON. RATS! NEVER MIND, I'LL JUST HAVE TO MAKE THE BEST
OF IT."

How Arnie avoided being shipped out to Paris I'll never know. Somehow,
he managed to sidestep the transfer and stay behind in London. "Rats!"
was putting it mildly! Not a very charitable diary entry, but I was trying
to figure out how to give Arnie a painless "heave-ho," and Paris would
have provided the perfect solution. What I couldn't know was that in
another few days it would all come to a head.

"TUESDAY, JUNE 5TH: THE ALLIES ARE DIVIDING UP GERMANY, ALSO
BERLIN. WENT TO CLUB DANCE AFTER WORK. AL SAYS HE MAY BE
SHIPPED OUT TO GERMANY SOON. DOESN'T KNOW WHEN. TOUGH
LUCK. FRANK ROSATO'S BAND SHIPPING OUT TODAY. CLUB IS LIKE
A MORGUE."

The four Allies, Britain, France, the United States and Russia, were
agreed on splitting up the Third Reich into four divisions, each to be ad-
ministrated by one of the victors until the dust of the aftermath of World
War Two had settled. After the Yalta Conference in February, Churchill,
Roosevelt and Stalin had agreed to meet again after Germany had surrendered to hammer out the question of reparations and to establish
European borders. A meeting was scheduled for July 18th at Potsdam
in Germany with Churchill, Stalin and the U.S. successor to Roosevelt,
President Harry Truman. It would be called the Potsdam Conference.

With the bulk of American servicemen serving either in postwar
Europe or being shipped to the Pacific, where war was still raging,
London was no longer bursting at the seams with Yanks. Rainbow
Corner was a shadow of its former self; gone were the G.I.s milling
around in Dunker's Den and surging up the staircase into the ballroom. The dances now took place in a different atmosphere; the G.Is
had their minds set on getting home.

The latest blow was today, when Frank Rosato's band shipped out, but
not back to the U.S. They were given the honor of being slated to play at

the upcoming Potsdam Conference in July and August, also at flag-raising ceremonies in Europe's liberated capital cities. The same flag that was flying over the Capitol building in Washington on the date of Pearl Harbor and the declaration of war by President Roosevelt, was taken to Europe and ceremonially raised in each vanquished Axis capital in turn, on the day it held the celebration of its liberation. It was named the Flag of Freedom.

After the Potsdam Conference, Frank Rosato and his band followed President Truman to Berlin. When the Flag of Freedom was raised in Berlin, Frank Rosato is quoted, in part, as saying: "When I directed the 'Star-Spangled Banner' that day ... it was a strong feeling ... I was proud. I felt the heartbeat of everybody in the band. I don't think we ever played the 'Star-Spangled Banner' any better."

Al Greene's Beachhead

"SUNDAY, JUNE 10TH: INVITED AL TO COME TO UPPER WOODSIDE FOR LUNCH. IT POURED WITH RAIN. ARNIE ARRIVED (UNINVITED) BEFORE AL--DISASTER! TO MAKE IT WORSE, IT RAINED ALL AFTERNOON AND WE ALL HAD TO STAY INDOORS! WHATEVER WILL AL THINK OF ME? I JUST WANT TO DIE!"

I had decided to take the bull by the horns and invite Al to Bishop's Hill for lunch. The heavens had opened in a downpour; it was raining "cats and dogs," so hard that raindrops were dancing up and down on the sidewalk. My heart leaped as the doorbell rang. I ran to open it, expecting to see Al Greene's tall, lanky frame.

Horrors! There at the door stood "Little Arnie," grinning broadly and waiting to hear me say: "Oh, Arnie, what a nice surprise! Do come in." All he heard was: "Aaagh!"

What to do? I was devastated. Arnie could at least have phoned to ask if it was O.K. for him to visit! He must by now have sensed the chemistry between Al and me. I couldn't leave him standing in the rain, so in he came, dripping all over Mom's front-hall carpet. I said: "Oh, Arnie, we didn't expect you today. I'm sorry, but I've invited Al Greene to come for lunch. He should be arriving any minute."

Arnie smiled sweetly and said: "Now say, that's O.K., he's good company," and made himself comfortable in an armchair. Half an hour later the doorbell rang again. This time it was Al, all smiles … until he saw Arnie standing at my elbow!

Through gritted teeth, I explained that Arnie had come to Upper Woodside to surprise us. It must have been obvious to Al that Arnie was used to finding his way to Bishop's Hill; his bicycle stood drying off, next to Percival, in the front hall!

After coming to join us in the living room and exchanging the usual British comments about the weather, Mom shook hands with Al to welcome him, then retreated hurriedly back into the kitchen where she was preparing lunch. I made an excuse that I was going out to help her, leaving the two men alone.

"What do you think of Al?" I whispered to Mom.

"He looks like a nice boy, dear; but I think you've got yourself painted into a corner this time, Bunty!"

Lunch was strained, to say the least. Al kept his "cool," as Arnie stayed on and on, throughout the whole awful, soggy afternoon. It rained and rained; I couldn't even take them both out for a walk around Spring Glen Park to relieve the tension! Dismally, I thought: "This is the last I'll ever see of Al Greene!"

"TUESDAY, JUNE 12TH: SURPRISE! AL CALLED ME AT THE OFFICE TO ASK IF I WOULD GO WITH HIM TO A D'OYLY CARTE OPERA COMPANY PERFORMANCE OF *THE GONDOLIERS* TONIGHT!"

Al had managed to get last-minute cancellation tickets. I would never have turned down a chance to see the famous D'Oyly Carte Opera Company perform Gilbert and Sullivan, but when the invitation was from Al, it was the icing on the cake.

At the theater my hand crept into his; *The Gondoliers* had never seemed to be performed more brilliantly!

"THURSDAY, JUNE 14TH: AL GOT TICKETS FOR GILBERT AND SULLIVAN'S *IOLANTHE*, PERFORMED BY THE D'OYLY CARTE. WHAT

A TREAT--HE REALLY HAS GOOD TASTE! WONDERFUL SHOW, WONDERFUL EVENING. AL GAVE ME HIS PHOTO. HE MUST BE GETTING SERIOUS! DAD WILL BE HOME TOMORROW FOR HIS VACATION."

We had good seats for this performance, and I was thrilled that Al enjoyed Gilbert and Sullivan. I tingled when I felt his arm around my shoulder as we shared the British humor and the lilting songs in Iolanthe. I somehow felt secure with Al; he gave me a feeling of permanence I had never experienced before.

Al handed me a large envelope. It contained a framed portrait photo of himself uniform. In those days, a soldier's portrait photograph was usually reserved for mothers, wives and sweethearts. Al looked at me thoughtfully. "Bunty, I'm not much good at fancy words, but I want you to know I think you are very special. I want you to keep my photo near you always if I have to go away."

I thought to myself: "What's he trying to tell me? I'll bet he's going to be shipped out!" My spirits sank.

Now that V-E Day had come and gone, I took stock of my life. The greatest miracle was that the war was over for us in Britain, and I had survived! I was blessed with a wonderful home and parents, and a job I enjoyed with prospects of a fascinating future as B.O.A.C. expanded into a peacetime world. Arnie had turned down a chance to live in Paris in order to stay in London; Bill's latest letter from the U.S. talked about ordering a diamond ring; Bruce now ended his letters "With all my love," and now I had a framed photo of Al Greene! What to do? I felt so mixed up I could have died.

With tears in my eyes, I recalled the words of Winston Churchill when North Africa had been won from the Nazis in November, 1942: "This is not the end. It is not even the beginning of the end. But it is, perhaps, the end of the beginning." And here I was, at the "end of the beginning." But of what? With all of my life's uncertainties, I felt I was standing, as if on tiptoe, waiting with a feeling of breathless anticipation for the next chapter in my life to unfold. Dad was coming home for a week's vacation; I wanted him to meet Al Greene.

"SUNDAY, JUNE 17TH: DAD IS HOME FOR A WEEK'S VACATION. AL CAME OUT TO BISHOP'S HILL FOR THE DAY. WE WENT BY TRAIN TO HAMPTON COURT--NEVER WAS IT SO WONDERFUL! THE MOST PERFECT DAY I'VE EVER KNOWN! HEY, WHAT'S HAPPENING TO ME?" Dad's time at home lately had been fleeting, but now he had settled in for a week of leisure at Bishop's Hill. Mom took a few days off from her office so the two of them could enjoy each other's company without worrying about checking in at work. I wanted *so* badly for Dad to like Al. When he arrived, Mom made cups of morning tea for us as we sat and chatted in the living room.

"Come on, lad, tell us a bit about yourself. We're always glad to meet Bunty's friends, you know."

Al remained cool and collected, "Well, sir, I actually have relatives here in Britain, an aunt and uncle living in South Wales near Pontypridd. I've been to stay with them a couple of times since I was transferred to London. It's nice to have folks here that are family, and easy to get to their home town from London by train. My aunt is my mother's cousin, and they correspond regularly. She has joined the Voluntary Fire Service for the duration of the war. My uncle is a high school teacher."

He paused, reassuring himself that he still had my parents' attention, then went on: "My grandmother came from Wales, and when she and my grandfather married, they emigrated to America and settled in a coal-mining town in Pennsylvania, where an uncle in the family was Superintendent of a large coal-mining company and had offered my grandfather a well-paying job. Grandpop was born and raised in the southwest of England, Somersetshire. He had grown up working out of doors as a stonecutter; he was skilled in erecting stone walls without mortar to enclose farmers' fields. Grandmom used to tell us about her young bridegroom with his healthy outdoor looks and the ruddy complexion that disappeared after he began to work in the coal mines. He died in his fifties, of "black lung," a disease that was contracted by coal miners in those days from inhaling coal dust as they worked at the coal face."

"Aye, lad," Dad's face was solemn, "conditions down the mines in those days were scandalous, and there was nobody to protect the miners from the abuse they took from greedy mine owners. It was a good day when things changed, although now the miners' unions are getting too much of an upper hand, I'm afraid." He seemed to enjoy talking to Al, the first American I knew who could really spark his interest in a meaningful conversation.

Dad suddenly realized the conversation had gone on long enough and that Al and I should be on our way to spend the day together. He got to his feet. "Well, you two, be off with you, and enjoy yourselves. "Thank heavens," I thought, "he likes Al!"

We were soon on our way out the door, delighted with each other's company and alone at last to enjoy it, holding hands as we walked to the local suburban railway station.

About a twelve-mile train ride from Upper Woodside, Hampton Court had been the favorite royal palace of King Henry VIII and many kings and queens after him, stretching from the 1500s through the 1700s. I was thrilled to be able to show this historic treasure to Al, and flabbergasted when it turned out that Al knew all about King Henry and Hampton Court! I had shown so many of my favorite historic places to lukewarm G.I.s, including Bill and Arnie, both of whom were absolutely clueless about British history, that I had assumed that, since it probably wasn't included in their history books, all Americans were unaware of it.

I thought: "Wow, he's a history buff, too!" and mentally added this to my list of Al Greene's assets. Proud of his British ancestry, also an avid reader, Al had soaked up British history as absorbedly as the G.I.s at Rainbow Corner imbibed Coca-Cola through a straw. I began to wonder if I had at last found a soulmate! But wasn't it a bit too soon to know?

I reread the end of my gushing diary entry with amusement, but when I wrote it, I had been deadly serious! Little did I guess then what was just around the corner! Again, a strange feeling came over me, as if I stood on tiptoe, waiting for the next step in my life to begin. And begin it did!

My diaries went on to chronicle the incredible story of the ups and downs in the next challenging months. As I sampled each successive diary entry, I said to myself: There's enough here for another book, Bunty. I could call it *"Bunty's New World." And I did.*

References

Battle of South London, The (1944): Crystal Publications, U.K.

Eden Camp Museum, Malton, North Yorkshire, England (exhibit information)

Fleming, Peter: *Operation Sea Lion (1956):* Simon and Schuster

Grun, Bernard: *The Timetables of History (1946):* Simon and Schuster

Illustrated Guide to Britain (1977): Drive Publications, Ltd.

Croydon, Old and new (1975): Local publication, Croydon, Surrey, England

London Blitz, The: The Daily Mail and Evening Standard press

Mantale, Ivor: *World War II (1987):* Military Press

Manchester, William: *The Last Lion (1988):* Little, Brown

Mason, David : *Churchill (1972):* Ballentine Books

Nicolson, Harold: *The War Years Diaries and Letters 1939-1945 (1967).* Edited by Nigel Nicolson. Athenaeum Press

Victory Book, The: Odhams Press (no publication date)

World Book Encyclopedia: Field Enterprises Educational Corporation (1965)

CDs: *The Second World War.* (sound) B.B.C. Archives

Video Series: *Winston Churchill*

In addition: careful verification, where necessary, of information and historical data via countless articles and links on the Internet.